Advances in

QUANTUM FLUX PARAMETRON COMPUTER DESIGN

STUDIES IN JOSEPHSON SUPERCOMPUTERS

D C Flux Parametron — A New Approach to Josephson Junction Logic
by E Goto and K F Loe

Fluxoid Josephson Computer Technology — Proceedings of the
3rd, 4th and 5th RIKEN-ERATO Symposia
Eds. E Goto, T Soma and K F Loe

Issues in Josephson Supercomputer Design — Proceedings of the
6th and 7th RIKEN Symposia on Josephson Electronics
Eds. E Goto and K F Loe

Quantum Flux Parametron — A Single Quantum Flux Superconducting
Logic Device
by W Hioe and E Goto

Advances in Quantum Flux Parametron Computer Design
Eds. E Goto, Y Wada and K F Loe

Studies in
Josephson
Supercomputers

Advances in

QUANTUM FLUX PARAMETRON COMPUTER DESIGN

Editors

E Goto

Kanagawa University and
Research Development Corporation of Japan (JRDC)

Y Wada

Research Development Corporation of Japan (JRDC)

K F Loe

National University of Singapore

World Scientific

Singapore • New Jersey • London • Hong Kong

Published by

World Scientific Publishing Co. Pte. Ltd.

5 Toh Tuck Link, Singapore 596224

USA office: 27 Warren Street, Suite 401-402, Hackensack, NJ 07601

UK office: 57 Shelton Street, Covent Garden, London WC2H 9HE

British Library Cataloguing-in-Publication Data
A catalogue record for this book is available from the British Library.

ADVANCES IN QUANTUM FLUX PARAMETRON COMPUTER DESIGN

ISBN-13 978-981-02-0826-4
ISBN-10 981-02-0826-X

PREFACE

The Quantum Flux Parametron (QFP) is a circuit device consisting of a pair of Josephson junctions. The polarities of the flux in the device are used to represent binary information. The study of the Quantum Flux Parametron was initiated in 1983. It took about two years to complete the preliminary study of the device. In the preliminary study the characteristics of the device, such as the limit of the clocking speed and the junction current, noise problems and the device coupling problems which affect the operation of the device were analysed. Since QFPs couple to each other through inductance flux signals which can be inductively transferred, it is possible to have three dimensional packaging. Thus three dimensional packaging and the computation of three-dimensional inductance became new issues which needed to be studied. Three dimensional packaging and the use of the parametron to realise logic and memory design have set a new direction for computer architecture design. The cyclic pipeline computer was conceived to take advantage of this technology.

Theoretical studies and some experiments being done in Hitachi Central Research Lab have shown that QFP is a promising technology. The QFP project was supported by the Research Development Corporation of Japan (JRDC) as an Exploratory Research for Advanced Technology Project (ERATO) from October 1986 for a period of five years. Being an ERATO project, it is regarded as a technology which can go beyond the horizon of the current technology and it is expected to find practical solutions to the problems of the technology. Three research groups were formed for this purpose. They are the fundamental research group, the computer architecture group and the magnetic shielding group.

The fundamental research group studied the properties of the QFP as a logic element and a memory element. It also looked into the three dimensional integration of the QFP into the computer system. The computer architecture group studied a new architecture based on the QFP. The magnetic shielding group studied the proper shielding of magnetic interference, the technique of removing trapped flux, and the efficient helium liquefier which provides the proper environment in running the Josephson computer. In the last four years of the project, under the support of JRDC, the project has made much improvement on how to control the QFP to realise better performance in terms of speed, integration and reliability. The technological development of the project included the fabrication of logic components for high speed operation, the development of a prototype computer system for the new architecture and the exploring of feasible technology for three dimensional integration of the computer system, removal of trapped flux, shielding of magnetic interference and the building of a helium liquefier.

Much of the above work was reported in the previous four volumes of the series *Studies in Josephson Supercomputers*. The volumes are *DC Flux Parametron — A New Approach to Josephson Junction Logic* written by E. Goto and K. F. Loe, *Fluxoid Josephson Computer Technology* edited by E. Goto, T. Soma and K. F. Loe, *Quantum Flux Parametron — A Single Quantum Flux Superconducting Logic Device* written by W. Hioe and E. Goto, and *Issues in Josephson Supercomputer Design* edited by E. Goto and K. F. Loe.

By September 1991, the QFP project will conclude its work on the study of the QFP. The purpose of this volume is to capture the new developments which were not reported in the last four volumes, and some new improvements of the work reported earlier.

Computer technology is being stretched to its physical limit in this decade, and there does not seem to be much scope for new computer technology in the next decade. Further, it is even more difficult to find a new technology which has been advancing to the stage as what the QFP project has achieved so far. We hope that these five volumes of studies on the Josephson Supercomputer will serve as a precursor for the advancement of the QFP for future computer technology.

E. Goto, Y. Wada and K. F. Loe
August 1, 1991

CONTENTS

Highly Functional Logic Circuits and Logic Design

Willy Hioe, Mutsumi Hosoya, Eiichi Goto and N. Miyamoto

Abstract

The Quantum Flux Parametron is evaluated with respect to logic design. An important issue is the reduction of gain due to fabrication variations. Theoretical and experimental results are given for the booster, an auxiliary circuit that improves gain. Another issue is interaction between active gates. The D-Gate which was designed mainly to alleviate interaction problems is presented. Finally, logic design which exploits the self-latching property of QFP's is discussed.

1. Introduction

The central component of a computer at the device level is the family of logic gates that enables one to form all logic functions. In the extreme, there may be only one logic gate. Several evaluation criteria are common to all logic gates. One group of criteria which indicates how fast is a logic circuit built with the gates includes switching speed, fan-in and fan-out. The functionality, or the complexity of logic that is performed by a single gate, may also be included in this group. Another group of criteria which indicates how complex is the circuit that can be integrated in a single chip includes size, margin and power dissipation.

The QFP is capable of high speed and low power dissipation that are not easily matched. Its gain is ideally very large but may be significantly reduced owing to fabrication variations. Being a two-terminal device, interaction between active QFP's is a further cause of gain reduction. Hence, a critical issue in the design of QFP logic gates is how to reduce interaction.

In this paper, we will first discuss the factors affecting gain and what are the problems accompanying low gain. The theory underlying the operation of the booster, an auxiliary circuit to improve gain, and the results of experimental verification are presented. Next, a brief review is given of QFP logic gates including a wired-majority gate and the D-Gate, a highly functional gate which has been designed to reduce interaction and improve margin. Finally, logic design with the D-Gate, which exploits the self-latching property of QFP's, is discussed.

2. Gain

2.1 Factors affecting Gain

In general, the maximum gain of the QFP may be written as

$$\text{gain} = \frac{I_{OUT}}{I_{imbalance} + I_{coupling} + I_{noise} + margin} \qquad (1)$$

I_{OUT} is the total output of the QFP. $I_{imbalance}$ is the bias current due to imbalance between the two arms in the QFP, including variation in critical currents and other geometric variations. $I_{coupling}$ is the bias due to stray coupling, mainly from clock lines, and interaction between QFP's because of their two-terminal nature. I_{noise} is the maximum equivalent current due to noise mainly from the environment. It can be reduced by proper magnetic shielding and noise filtering. This section considers $I_{imbalance}$ while the next considers $I_{coupling}$.

We assume that the reader has some familiarity with QFP operation and the terminology we use, otherwise, the reader should refer to the first part in the earlier paper "Physics of QFP Operation".

Imbalances arise from fabrication variations of the JJ critical current and transformer inductances. Since they are alike, only critical current variations will be discussed, which will be referred to as δI noise. The normalized Hamiltonian which includes the effect of δI noise is

$$u = -\cos \alpha \cos \phi \pm \delta \sin \alpha \sin \phi + \frac{b}{2}\left(\phi - \beta\right)^2 \qquad (2)$$

where δ is the fractional variation of the QFP's JJ critical currents. The inequality of critical currents introduces the second term in (2) which has the effect of a variable input bias when $\sin \alpha \neq 0$. The effect may be visualized from **Fig 1**. For correct QFP operation the output state must be on the correct side of the potential barrier when it first appears. In the limit, this is given by the condition

$$\partial^3 u/\partial\phi^3 = \partial^2 u/\partial\phi^2 = \partial u/\partial\phi = 0 \qquad (3)$$

By eliminating ϕ and α, a relation between β, δ and b is found.

$$\left(b \sin \beta\right)^2/\delta^2 + \left(b \cos \beta\right)^2 = 1 \qquad (4)$$

Considering only δI noise, the variation of gain with respect to load factor may be found from Eq.4 and $\partial u/\partial\phi = 0$. This is plotted in **Fig 2** for various degrees of

δI noise.

2.2 Booster

When a booster [1], which is a pre-activated QFP, is attached to the output of a clock-activated QFP, **Fig 3**, the Hamiltonian becomes

$$u = -\cos \alpha \cos \phi \pm \delta \sin \alpha \sin \phi + b \left(\phi - \beta \right)^2$$

$$- \cos \alpha_B \cos \phi \pm \delta_B \sin \alpha_B \sin \phi \qquad (5)$$

α_B is the booster's activation flux angle and δ_B is the fractional variation of the booster's Josephson junction critical currents. A booster is fully activated when $\cos \alpha_B = -1$. Under this condition, the term with δ_B disappears. Hence, only the critical current imbalance of the QFP has an effect on correct operation. The output current, however, is doubled, assuming that the load inductance is halved. Hence, gain is doubled.

Actually, the minimum input will not be the same, in general, with and without a booster. The improvement in gain can be accurately obtained in the follow manner. The condition for correct operation is again given by (3). A relation similar to (4) can be obtained for a QFP with booster,

$$\left(2b \sin \beta - \delta_B \sin \alpha_B \right)^2 \Big/ \delta^2 + \left(- \cos \alpha_B - 2b \cos \beta \right)^2 = 1 \qquad (6)$$

Let us compare the maximum gains for the same δ and b, assuming the booster is fully activated, $\cos \alpha_B = -1$. For example, for the case when $\delta=0.2$ and $b=2/\pi$, the improvement in gain is about 1.6 times. **Fig 4** plots the gains for various load factors for the same critical current variation.

The experimental results verifying the operation of the booster have been reported in [2]. The fabricated test circuit is shown in the photograph in **Fig 5**. Improvement in gain was found to be about 1.88 as compared to the theoretical improvement of 2.31 for the same load factor, $b=0.26$. Why a lower improvement was observed is not clear. A possible cause may be less than full activation of the booster. Nevertheless, the experiment was able to show a significant improvement in gain.

2.3 Effect of Gain Reduction

A smaller gain means a smaller fan-out. It has been shown that as long as fan-out is greater than fan-in by one, all logic circuits can be built with the same number of logic stages [3]. Since the QFP is a two-terminal device, part of the output couples back through the input lines. Hence, a three-input gate will need at least a fan-out of 4 or a gain of 7. It may be seen from **Fig 2** that the variation of critical current cannot be worse than 20% if ambient noise and other biases are not considered.

A more serious problem is the smaller load inductance per output line that results from a smaller gain. The output flux angle is usually designed to maximize output current and hence may be considered as constant. The main contribution to the load per output line comes from the line inductance. Hence,

$$\frac{I_{OUT}}{gain} L_{line} = \frac{\mu\, l \left(g + 2\lambda\right)}{W \cdot gain} I_{OUT} = constant$$

$$(7)$$

where L_{line} is the line inductance, l, W and g are respectively the length, width and gap to ground plane of the line, and λ the penetration depth of its superconducting material. g cannot be easily reduced. Hence, a smaller gain implies a larger W or a smaller l. Since the per square inductance of a micro-stripline is relatively large, about 0.5pH, compared to the total load inductance, 10pH for a QFP using 25µA junctions, line lengths are short if gain is small. The constraints of line length on design of large logic circuits are considered in another paper [4].

A secondary problem that results from larger line currents due to smaller gain is stronger interaction between QFP's. The problem of interaction is considered in the next section.

3. QFP Logics

3.1 Wired-Majority Logic

Wired-majority logic [5] is the simplest form of logic circuits that may be built using only inductors, inverting transformers and QFPs. There is only one basic logic gate, a majority gate, shown in **Fig 6**, if we do not consider the inverting transformer which does a NOT operation to be a proper gate. Logic is performed by the junction of input lines which algebraically adds the input signals. Thus, if the absolute input levels are equal and if there are an odd number of inputs, the output has the majority signal polarity. A QFP is used to amplify, stabilize and hold the output signal.

Logical AND and OR can be obtained from a majority operation. Let x, y and z be the inputs of a 3-input majority function, $M(x,y,z) = xy + yz + zx$. Then,

$$AND(x,y) = M(x,y,F) = xy \tag{8a}$$

$$OR(x,y) = M(x,y,T) = x + y \tag{8b}$$

Hence, all logic functions can be obtained using only majority devices and invertors.

A network of QFPs is activated by an n-phase clock, where n is 3 or more. QFPs along the direction of signal flow are activated at successive phases and logic signals are "baton-passed" from active QFPs to those activated next. Quenched QFPs serve also to partly shunt away back-coupling signals.

Wired-majority logic suffers from a number of problems [6]. The back-coupling of signals is a source of *relay noise* affecting the correct activation of QFP's. Forward coupling through the junction of input lines in the next majority gate causes *homophase noise* which affects QFP's activated late in the same stage, and *reaction hazard* which affects the stability of active QFP's providing the minority input signals. The coupled noise level is a function of the signal level, fan-in, fan-out and dummy load. Furthermore, wired-majority logic is a linear input logic whose input margin is inversely proportional to the fan-in. Hence, the fan-in is usually small. Whereas the other problems may be improved by better process technology and circuit designs, this problem has no solution without fundamentally changing the way logic operations are physically implemented.

3.2 Variable Activation QFP

The wired-majority gate has a low input margin because of interaction between inputs. Hence, input margin can be improved significantly if inputs are isolated. A different means of performing logic operation instead of algebraically adding inputs is needed.

The QFP can be used as a logic element by itself instead of only as a signal amplifier as in wired-majority logic. It has two input lines: the line for the input signal to be amplified and the activation input line. If the activation clock signal is replaced by the output of one or more QFPs, then a QFP activated in this way has an output which is a function of two or more inputs. A QFP activated by the output of other QFP's works like a relay switch and will be known as a *Variable Activation QFP* or *VAQ*.

A QFP's output in terms of flux angle at maximum current output is $\pm 0.5\pi$ while the activation flux angle is $\pm \pi$. From this observation alone, it appears that activating a QFP by the sum of two QFP outputs of the same polarity should be possible. However, this had not been feasible before because the typical activation current is much larger than a QFP's total output current. A smaller activation current required large activation transformer inductances which caused activation delay because of flux loss. This problem is solved by attaching a puller [7], which is a dc-activated QFP, to the VAQ's activation line. Due to the effect of its puller, smaller activation currents can be used without causing activation delays. An additional refinement to the VAQ's scheme is to use an I/O transformer type QFP (or I/O-type QFP). The I/O-type QFP has the advantage of incorporating within a QFP an I/O transformer for inverting signals and impedance matching when connecting QFP's far apart, besides allowing a more streamlined layout. The scheme described above is shown in **Fig 7**.

A VAQ has three inputs: x, the I/O-type QFP's input, and s and t, the inputs to the QFP's providing the VAQ activation. The latter will be referred to as driving QFP's. The VAQ performs a 3-state logic operation

$$V(s,t;x) = x\left(st + \overline{st}\right) \tag{9}$$

When s and t have the same polarity, the VAQ is active and its output is x, but when s and t have opposite polarities, the VAQ is quenched and its output is indeterminate. It is a typical relay switch except that it has two control or select signals. The best application of VAQ's is probably the D-Gate which consists of two complementary VAQ's, and it will be in the context of D-Gates that we will discuss the VAQ's properties with respect to coupling noises.

3. 3 D-Gate

The D-Gate was designed with the aim of improving the input margin by reducing coupling noise and freeing QFP logic from the input margin problem of wired-majority logic. The basic scheme is shown in **Fig 8**. Two main parts may be identified: the activation group and the logic group. The activation group consists of two driving QFP's activated by a clock signal. The inputs to these driving QFP's are the select signals of the D-Gate, which are in general independent. The outputs go into a transformer which implements a 2x2 Hadamard matrix, that is, the outputs are sum and difference of the inputs. For convenience, we will refer to the transformer as a Hadamard (or H2) transformer. When these outputs are used to activate 2 VAQ's, only one, determined by the D-Gate select signals, will be activated. The logic group consists of two VAQ's and an output transformer which adds the VAQs' output fluxes to give the D-Gate's output. Since only one VAQ is active at any one time, the D-Gate's output is that of the active VAQ. In addition to the basic scheme, one booster is attached to each of the driving QFP's and the logic group output. These boosters serve to increase the output current of the QFP's and VAQ's without increasing the input bias due to imbalance within each QFP.

Decoupling of inputs and outputs is much better in the D-Gate compared to the wired-majority gate. The improvements, summarized in **Table 1**, come from the additional shunting effect of quenched boosters and I/O transformers. In addition, the fan-in no longer affects the input margin because inputs are much better isolated. Each of the driving QFP's and VAQ's within the D-Gate, in fact, has only one input. Interaction comes about through the output connections but is relatively much smaller. The margin of activation signals is the same as that for the basic QFP. Since activation currents are much larger than signal currents, a small margin is sufficient.

The fundamental operation of the D-Gate has been confirmed experimentally [7]. However, the margin has not been determined because of problems in designing transformers with close coupling. Leakage inductance in the I/O transformers causes delayed activation or, in more severe cases, non-activation, while that in the H2 transformer causes non-quenching. Cutting holes or slits in the groundplane below the transformers [8] has not been successful in sufficiently improving coupling. Moreover, adverse effects due to flux concentration and stray magnetic fields have been observed. The D-Gate's design remains an incompletely solved issue.

The size of the D-Gate is much larger than that of a wired-majority gate. The D-Gate has at least 9 QFP's and several transformers with large inductances whereas the wired-majority gate has one QFP or two if a booster is attached. Using 5μm technology and 25μA Josephson junctions, a D-Gate is about 400μm by 400μm, **Fig 9**. Although probably smaller after optimization, at this size, not only will the integration level be poor but also the circuit speed may be low because of propagation delay (see below). The D-Gate also has a longer switching delay because of two activation stages, the driving QFP's and the VAQ's.

4. High Performance QFP Logic Design

The D-Gate's output has the logic function

$$D(s,t; x,y) = x\left(st + \overline{s}\overline{t}\right) + y\left(\overline{s}t + s\overline{t}\right) \tag{10}$$

where x and y are the VAQs' inputs and s and t are the select signals. This is basically a multiplex operation but actually the D-Gate has much more logic-forming power than this suggests. We will demonstrate the D-Gate's functionality through several examples of common combinatorial circuits in the first subsection. The second subsection discusses some issues involved in pipelined applications. General methods of synthesizing D-Gate logic [cf. 9] will not be discussed.

4.1 D-Gate Logic

The use of multiplexors will be described first since the D-Gate basically implements a 2-input multiplexing operation. In a multiplexor one select signal is used to choose one of two inputs, so a D-Gate multiplexor can be implemented as follows:

$$MUX(x, y ; s) = D(s, "1"; x, y) \tag{11}$$

A multiplexor for 2^n inputs can be built with an n-level binary tree of D-Gates. Another application is a $(2^n -1)$-bit shifter for an m-bit string which can be implemented with $m(2^n -1)$ multiplexors organized into n stages. At stage i, a multiplexor is used to choose between the current bit value and one 2^i bit places away. The number of bits shifted, which is a number between 0 and 2^n-1 inclusive, is

$$\sum_{i=0}^{n-1} s_i 2^i \tag{12}$$

where s_i is either 1 or 0. **Fig 10** illustrates the scheme.

In conventional logic design, logic functions are typically built from AND/OR functions. A D-Gate can form 2-input AND and 2-input OR in the following way.

$$AND(x, y) = D(x, y; x, "0") \tag{13}$$

$$OR(x, y) = D(x, y; x, "1") \tag{14}$$

The small fan-in per gate is a disadvantage if D-Gates are used only as AND/OR gates since many more gate levels will be needed compared to gates with larger fan-in. An AND/OR function with a large number of inputs will need a binary tree of AND/OR gates and QFP's serving as latches where necessary. We note that in general Josephson logic gates have low fan-in. The D-Gate, on the other hand, can form other more complex functions with a single gate.

XOR and 1-bit EQUALITY operations require only a single D-Gate, hence, they have the same delay as 2-bit AND or OR in D-Gate logic. These operations are obtained as follows:

$$XOR(x, y) = D(x, y; "0", "1") \tag{15}$$

$$EQ(x, y) = D(x, y; "1", "0") \tag{16}$$

n-bit equality can be implemented with n XOR gates and an n-input OR binary tree or n 1-bit EQ gates and an n-input AND binary tree.

The most important operations that a single D-Gate can implement are the 3-input MAJORITY and the 3-input PARITY operations, given below,

$$M(x, y, z) = D(x, y; x, z) \tag{17}$$

$$P(x, y, z) = D(x, y; z, \bar{z}) \tag{18}$$

SUM is a parity operation and CARRY is a majority operation. Using D-Gates, a full adder is implemented with one gate delay. The majority operation can also be used for an XY-Symmetric Carry Lookahead Adder [10]. An 8-bit fixed point adder with carry lookahead is illustrated in **Fig 11**. With only D-Gates and latches, an n-bit adder can be built efficiently with $\log_2 n + 2$ gate levels. Fixed point multipliers may be built from a network of full adders. Since their design can be found in a number of textbooks, for example, the book by Kai Hwang [11] is an excellent introduction, further discussion will be omitted. Floating point arithmetic requires, in addition to circuits discussed so far, a priority encoder for renormalization of addition results. A recursively structured priority encoder can be built by noting that if the position of the first "1" bit is encoded in the binary number, $x_i \cdots x_0$, then

$$x_{i-1} \cdots x_0 = \left(x_{i-1}^1 \cdots x_0^1\right) y_{i-1}^1 + \left(x_{i-1}^2 \cdots x_0^2\right) \overline{y_{i-1}^1} \tag{19}$$

$$x_i = \overline{y_{i-1}^1 y_{i-1}^2} \tag{20}$$

$$y_i = y^1_{i\text{-}1} + y^2_{i\text{-}1} \qquad\qquad (21)$$

where y_i is a bit encoding whether the first "1" is found in the corresponding block of bits. The smaller superscript is for the lower bit-position block. Only MUX, AND and OR operations are used in this priority encoder.

The designs of several complex logic circuits have been presented without consideration of fan-out, propagation delay nor limitations to lengths of propagation lines. In practice, these considerations are extremely important and strongly affect designs for high performance logic circuits.

The maximum fan-out of the D-Gate depends on its gain. The main factors affecting gain have been discussed in the first section. QFP loads are normally designed for maximum output current and are therefore independent of fan-out. Consequently, QFP switching times are also independent of fan-out. However, input variations will affect switching times. Interaction between gates exists because QFP's are two-terminal devices, but it has been greatly reduced in the D-Gate. Interaction problems should still be considered when a large fan-out is used. If it is assumed that fabrication variations can be controlled within 10% and boosters are used, then a maximum fan-out of 5~6 may be expected for the D-Gate. Additional amplification stages will still be necessary in the above logic designs, in the case of long connection lines such as for the select signals in the shifter, for the carry lookahead outputs and for generating partial products in the multiplier.

The question of propagation delay is best discussed in the context of pipelined logic designs which will be the subject of the next subsection.

4.2 Pipelined Logic Design

The self-latching property of QFPs makes them suitable for pipelined logic designs used in supercomputers. A Cyclic Pipeline Computer (CPC) [12] architectural design has been investigated which can exploit QFP-like self-latching logic gates. The reader should also refer to the papers in this volume on super-pipelined architectures. Conventional transistor logic families such as ECL, TTL and CMOS require additional registers to implement pipelines, which increase fall-through delay and cost. Slower computation speeds than without pipelining may result if a computation has strong data dependencies when one computation has to wait for a previous one to finish. However, in QFP logics fall-through delay remains the same irrespective of the pipeline pitch and the advantages of pipelining can be fully enjoyed.

High performance circuits are usually pipelined to maximize throughput. A rough estimate of the performance improvement due to pipelining is to multiply the non-pipelined throughput by the number of pipeline stages. QFP circuits can be thought of as pipelines with gate-level pitch, that is,

$$pitch = n_\phi \cdot (\tau_s + \tau_p) \qquad (22)$$

where n_ϕ is the number of clock phases, τ_s is the switching delay of a gate (which is a constant) and τ_p is the longest signal propagation delay. The fall-through delay, that is, the time taken to pass through the pipeline, is the product of the number of gate levels, n_g , and $\tau_s + \tau_p$.

$$fall\text{-}through = n_g \cdot (\tau_s + \tau_p) \qquad (23)$$

In the design of arithmetic circuits above, we have mainly considered reducing n_g. In these designs long connection lines may be necessary such as in shift and carry lookahead operations. In both cases, there are operations between bits that are separated by half the input bit-string length. At the high speeds QFP circuits are expected to operate, the propagation delay becomes comparable to the switching delay or greater if device sizes are large. For example, in a 64-bit adder the longest line spans 32 bits giving a maximum propagation distance of about 1mm if the gate width is 30 microns including wiring space. Assuming a switching delay of about 25 psecs, a 4-phase clock and that signals travel at 1/3 light speed in micro-striplines, the maximum propagation delay is about 10 psecs, the fall-through delay for 8 gate levels is 280 psecs and the pipeline pitch is 4 x (25 + 10) = 140 psecs. Halving the longest line span increases the number of gate levels by one, *reduces* fall-through delay to 270 psecs and *reduces* pipeline pitch to 120 psecs.

It was noted earlier that amplification stages may be required to achieve fan-out. In some cases, such as the select signals in the shifter design, long connection lines are required at the same time. With extra amplification stages, shorter lines suffice. Hence, in such cases these two problems can be solved together.

5. Discussion

QFP logics have a high switching speed and low power dissipation. The self-latching property of QFP's also make them suitable for pipelined designs. The basic QFP, however, has a number of problems that affect the gate design and in turn the logic design. These are the loss of gain due to non-uniformity, the large contribution of line inductances to loads, and the poor input/output isolation. It may be noted that if signal currents can be reduced by improving uniformity, gain increases and the latter two problems are also alleviated at the same time. Improving input/output isolation also leads to alleviation of the other two problems. The problem of input margin in the wired-majority gate, however, may become more acute. On the other hand, increasing the output while keeping signal currents at the same level improves gain but does not alleviate the problem of line inductances. In fact, if the gate size increases such as when a booster is attached, the problem will be aggravated.

The D-Gate offers a solution to the isolation and input margin problems. However, it leads to a dramatic increase in gate size. The problem of line inductances is aggravated. Moreover, because the amount of logic performed in each clock phase is limited to one gate level, although the D-Gate has excellent functionality, the effect of propagation delay on clock speed and fall-through delay is relatively large.

Assuming that the D-Gate's remaining problems can be solved, it offers the possibility of very high throughput processor designs. The fine pipeline pitch is well-suited for digital signal processors where operations are highly repetitive and data dependencies are relatively low. In computer applications, its advantages can be fully exploited through architectural designs for super-pipelined processing.

Acknowledgements

The authors are grateful to the Central Research Laboratory, Hitachi, Ltd. for fabricating the test circuits.

References

[1] E. Goto & K.F. Loe, *DC Flux Parametron*: World Scientific, Singapore, 1986, pg 92.

[2] W. Hioe, et al., "Improving the Gain of the Quantum Flux Parametron", Presented at Int. Conf. on Solid State Materials and Mechanisms, 1991.

[3] Goto, E., "A Note on Logical Gain", *IEEE Trans on Electronic Computers*, Oct 1964, pp606-608.

[4] R. Suda, et al., "Signal Interconnection in Highly Integrated QFP Chips," this volume.

[5] Y. Harada, et al., "Basic Operations of the Quantum Flux Parametron", *IEEE Trans. Magn.*, vol MAG-23, No. 5, Sep 1987, pp3801-3807.

[6] W. Hioe, M. Hosoya & E. Goto, "A New Quantum Flux Parametron Logic Gate with Large Input Margin", *IEEE Trans. Magn.*, Vol MAG-27, No.2, Mar 1991, pp2765-2768.

[7] M. Hosoya, et al., "Experimental Study of a Dual-input-multiplexor gate," *IEEE Trans. Magn.*, Vol MAG-27, No.2, Mar 1991, pp2847-2850.

[8] M. Hosoya, et al., "Proto-type model of three-dimensional QFP circuits," Presented at Int. Superconductive Electronics Conf. '91, Scotland, 1991.

[9] W. Hioe & E. Goto, *Quantum Flux Parametron*, Series in Josephson Supercomputers, World Scientific, Singapore, 1991.

[10] H. Takahashi, (ed) *Parametron Computer*, Iwanami, Japan, 1969, (In Japanese).

[11] K. Hwang, *Computer Arithmetic: Principles, Architecture and Design*, John Wiley, 1979.

[12] K. Shimizu, E. Goto and S. Ichikawa, "CPC (Cyclic Pipeline Computer) - An Architecture Suited for Josephson and Pipelined-Memory Machines", *IEEE Trans. Computers*, Vol.38, No.6, June 1989.

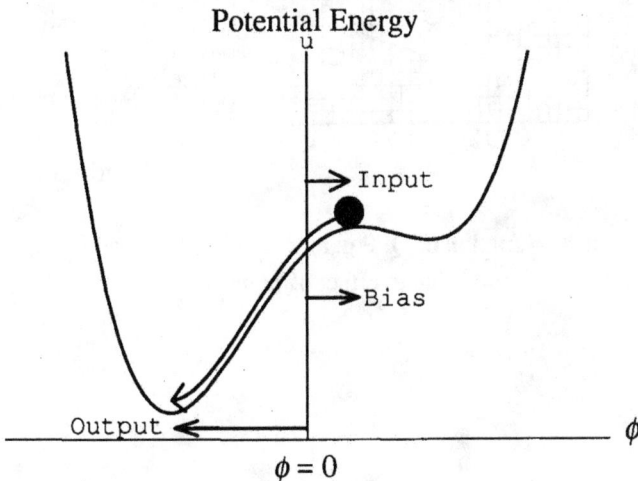

Fig 1 Illustration of Error due to δI noise

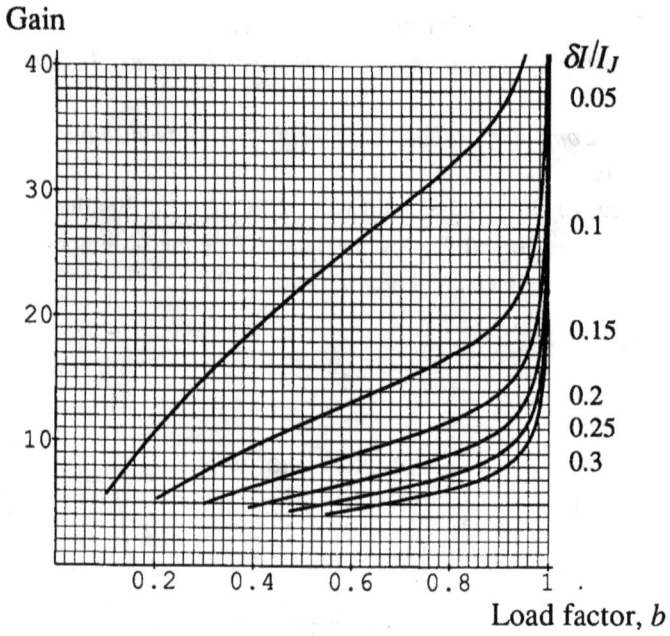

Fig 2 Variation of QFP gain with respect to load factor
due to effect of δI noise

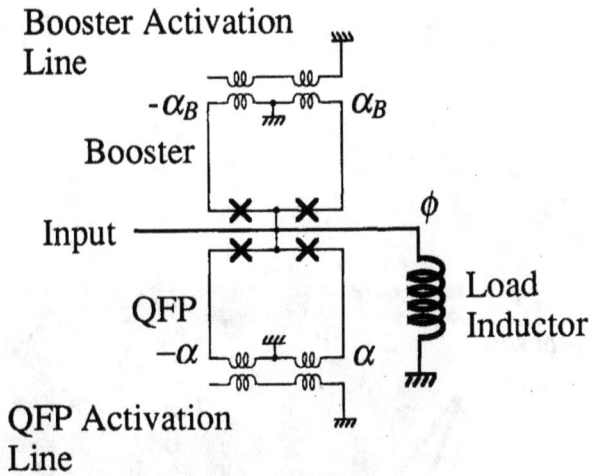

Fig 3 Illustration of QFP with attached booster

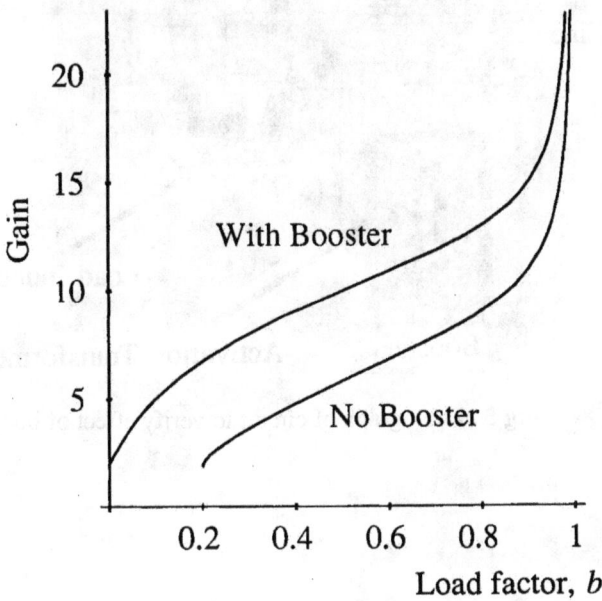

Fig 4 Comparison of gain between QFP only and
QFP with booster for various load factors when δ=0.2

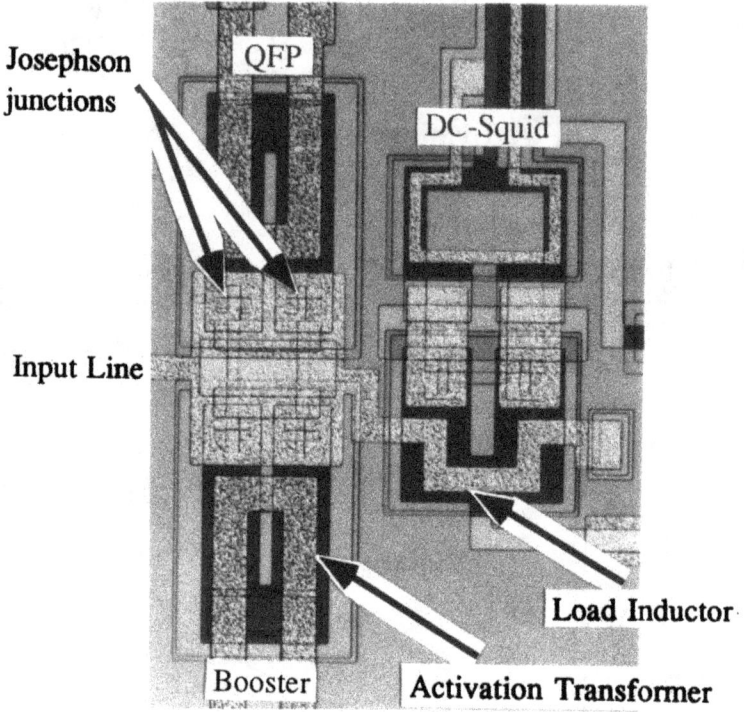

Fig 5   Photograph of circuit to verify effect of booster

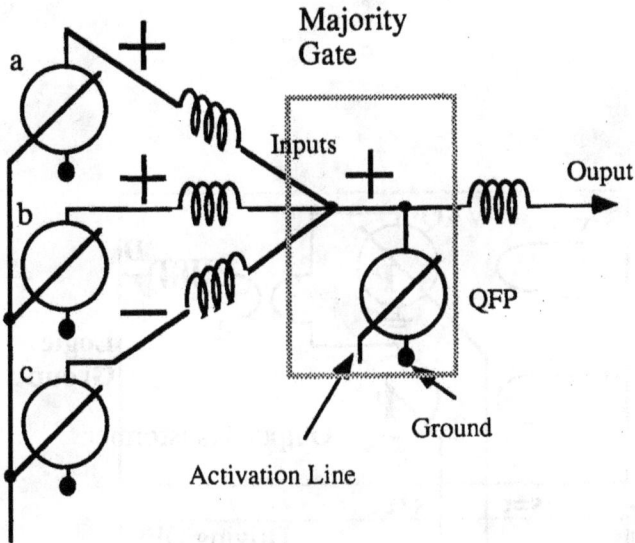

Fig 6 Wired-majority gate

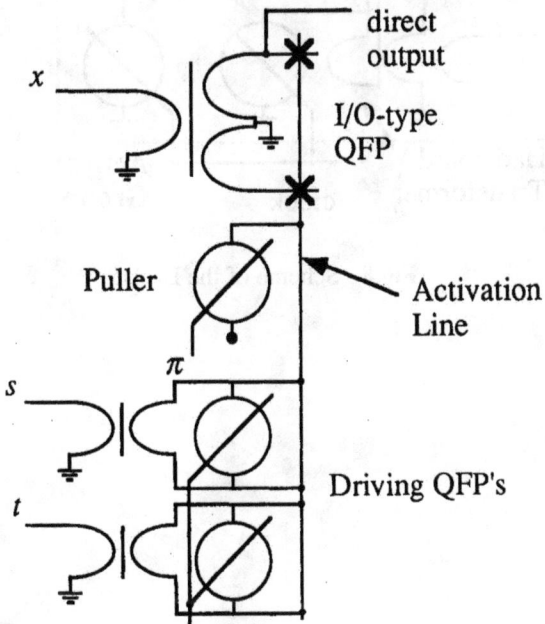

Fig 7 Scheme of Variable Activation QFP

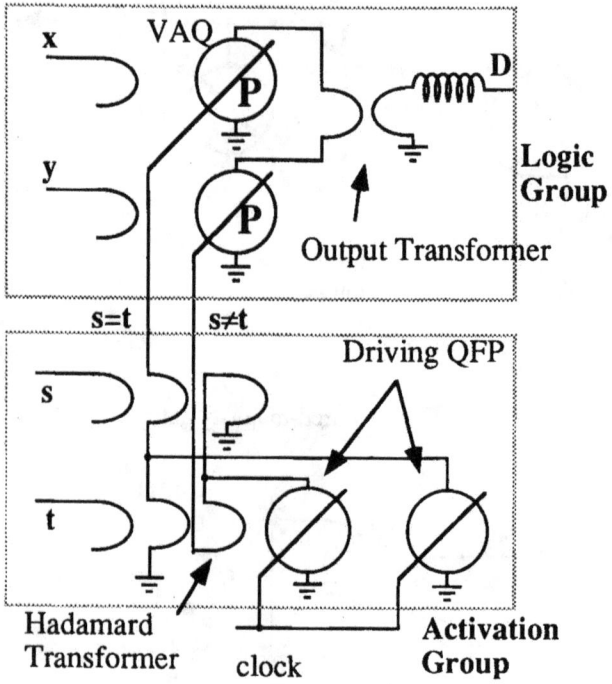

Fig 8 Scheme of the D-Gate

Noise/Problem	Wired-Majority (a)	D-Gate (b)	Improvement (c) = (a) / (b)
Relay Noise (Output to input coupling)			
	13.7%	d -> x/y = 4.68%	2.93
	13.7%	d -> s/t <1.17%	>11.71
Direct Homophase Noise			
	>100%	0%	>>100
Relayed Homophase Noise or Reaction Hazard			
	27.5%	x <-> y = 4.87%	5.65
	27.5%	x/y <-> s/t ≈ 0.%	>100
	27.5%	s <-> t ≈ 0.%	>100
Input Margin			
	<33.3%	<71.4%	>2

Table 1 Percentages show for noise: the ratio between noise and signal, for margin: the largest variation. Arrows show direction of coupling through a quenched gate.

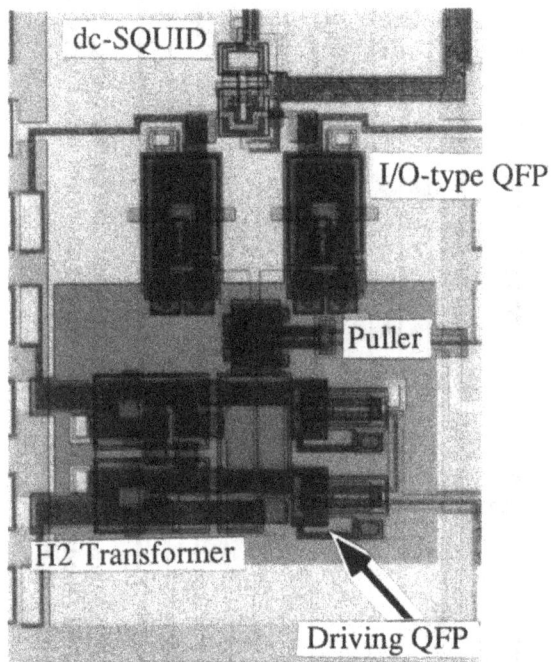

Fig 9 Photograph of a D-Gate test circuit

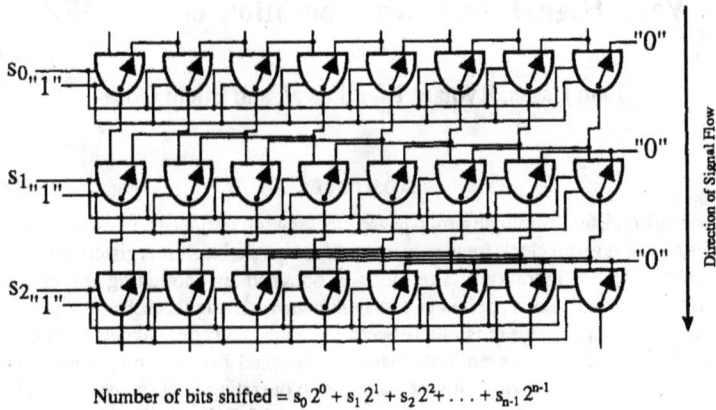

Number of bits shifted $= s_0 2^0 + s_1 2^1 + s_2 2^2 + \ldots + s_{n-1} 2^{n-1}$

Fig 10 Pipelined Left Shifter Design Example

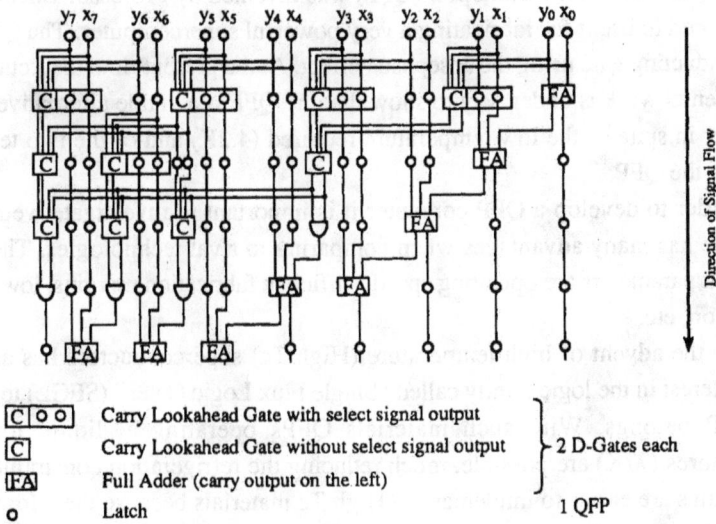

$\boxed{C\ \circ\ \circ}$	Carry Lookahead Gate with select signal output	
$\boxed{C}$	Carry Lookahead Gate without select signal output	2 D-Gates each
$\boxed{FA}$	Full Adder (carry output on the left)	
$\circ$	Latch	1 QFP

Fig 11 Pipelined 8-bit Adder Design Example

Very High Frequency Operation of the QFP

Juan Casas, Ryotaro Kamikawai, and Eiichi Goto

Abstract

QFP shift registers employing four-phase clocking are designed. In order to generate subharmonics of a given clock frequency, one to four single-bit shift registers are cascaded in a closed loop configuration. The clock is obtained by shortening the end of the microstrip clock lines, and is applied as a standing wave. Using this scheme it is observed that for some frequencies, the crosstalk between the output and clock signals is dramatically reduced. The clock current amplitude margin is deduced from the maximum operating frequency of some of the devices, it is at least 17% at operating frequencies beyond 5 GHz. The 1-bit device is observed to operate from dc up to 16.2 GHz and the 4-bit shift register structure functions at frequencies over 5 GHz.

1. Introduction

The Quantum Flux Parametron (QFP) was invented by Professor Eiichi Goto. He proposed to use it for fabricating a very powerful supercomputer. The QFP is a superconducting gate using the Josephson effect. At the present time theoretical and experimental work is under way to show that the QFP is a viable alternative to the transistor in spite of the low temperature required (4.2K) and of the two terminal nature of the QFP.

In order to develop a QFP computer it is important to investigate wether the QFP gate has many advantages when comparing to rival technologies. The most important parameters are operating speed, sufficient fabrication margins, low power dissipation, etc.

Also the advent of high temperature (High Tc) superconductors has aroused much interest in the logic family called "Single Flux Logic Gates" (SFGL) to which the QFP belongs. With such materials QFPs operating at liquid nitrogen temperatures (77K) are possible, much reducing the refrigeration constraints. The SFGL gates are easier to implement in High Tc materials because their Josephson Junctions are usually damped by a resistor, in contrast to the more conventional Josephson voltage logic that need hysteretic Josephson junctions.

The aim of this work is design and implement a Quantum Flux Parametron (QFP) gate which is able to operate at very high frequencies.

In order to prove that a QFP is able to operate at very high frequencies all pertinent problems have to be recognized in order to devise a successful design of a device as well as of the measuring apparatus. From the beginning [1] it was clear that because of the low power dissipation of the QFP, high frequency testing could be relatively difficult (especially if the output waveform is to be recorded in time domain). This is because for measuring a QFP, only a fraction of its operating power can be used for performing an external measurement. In order to prove the high frequency operation it was proposed to use ring-oscillators. These devices produce an output signal that is a subharmonic of the clock frequency. For detecting the subharmonic a microwave receiver was proposed because of it high sensitivity[1]. Recently the advent of microwave spectrum analyzers, of fairly low noise and wide-band microwave amplifiers and of high frequency coaxial transmission lines have much simplified the testing of the QFP.

The basic cell is a single-bit shift register, and one to four of them are cascaded serially around a closed loop. Some of the circuits include a bit inversion operation. For simplifying the QFP testing, all of the devices are designed to produce subharmonics of the clock frequency. The measurements are done in the frequency domain where the subharmonics can be easily recognized. Four devices are designed: 1, 2 and 3-bit shift registers used as frequency prescalers with the prescaling factors being two, four and six or two respectively; and a 4-bit shift register (it is shown to be able to operate as a 4-bit programmable pattern generator). These devices have already been reported [2-3].

Shift registers are very useful devices and are indispensable in many signal processing applications [4-5]. They can be used for example in A/D converters, in serial to parallel logic data converters (and vice-versa), in pattern generators, in pseudorandom data generators, in noise generators, in frequency prescalers, etc. Also, it has been proposed [6] that the maximum number of bits of a shift register is an indirect means of assessing how large a circuit can be built. This number of bits depends on the device margins as well as on the fabrication uniformity.

Previously, superconducting shift register circuits operating experimentally above 1 GHz have been reported: they are, to our knowledge, an 8-bit shift register [7] operating at 2.3 GHz and a pseudorandom bit-sequence generator [8] operating at 2.2 GHz both using MVTL (Modified Variable Threshold Logic) gates, and a 4-bit shift register [9] operating at 4 GHz using DCL (Direct-Coupled Logic) gates. In this paper, a 1-bit shift register using QFP gates is shown to be able to operate at a clock frequency of 16.2 GHz, to the best of our knowledge it is the fastest measured superconducting shift register circuit. It is also the fastest externally clocked superconducting device. The only superconducting digital families that rival the QFP in measured operating frequency are binary counters [10] developed for A/D conversion and a RSFQ (Rapid Single Flux Quantum) T-flip-flop [11].

Their maximum operating frequency is 100 GHz and 50 GHz respectively. Such high frequencies are possible to obtain because these logic elements are driven by an on chip SFQ (Single Flux Quantum) pulse generator.

Semiconductors (GaAs) shift registers [12-13] and frequency prescalers (some of which are analog) [13-17] have been developed for applications in fast frequency synthesizers, fiber optic communications, etc. Their operating frequency span between 1 GHz to 33 GHz and they exhibit power consumption levels between 1 mW and 700 mW. The latter power consumption could be compared with an estimated 2 nW consumed by the QFP based frequency divide by two prescaler when operating at a clock frequency of 16 GHz.

This paper first presents a rapid introduction to the operation of the QFP. This is followed by the design and test of our devices. Finally, the gain in maximum operating frequency when using a better Josephson junction fabrication process is briefly discussed.

2.QFP Fundamentals

The QFP is a bistable device that depending on the polarity of an input signal before activation will produce an output current with a reproducible direction. The direction of the output current represent the logic "0" and "1". With the QFP "AND" and "OR" logic gates have been proposed and demonstrated experimentally [18].

According to computer simulations it was found that the Josephson Junctions had to be shunted by an external resistor in order to avoid high frequency resonances of the QFP [18]. These resistors are responsible for the thermal power dissipated by the QFP. A rough approximation to the power dissipated by a QFP is:

$$W = \frac{(4 \pi v L_d I_o)^2}{R} \tag{1}$$

where v is the clock frequency, L_d is the QFP load inductance and R and I_o are respectively the shunting resistance and critical current of each Josephson junction.

When operating the QFP at a clock frequency of 10 GHz and taking into account the parameters chosen in the actual design, the power dissipation is found to be 250 pW per QFP. This is similar to the power dissipated by RSFQ logic family [19], about three orders of magnitude below the power dissipated by voltage Josephson logic and about six orders of magnitude below the power dissipated by semiconductor logic circuits. Also, it should be pointed out that the clock lines do not dissipate power because no drawing resistors are used for distributing the clock current.

A more complete description of the operation of a QFP including hazards can be found in these proceedings or elsewhere [1,20].

3.Circuit Design

Four different circuits have been fabricated: a 1, 2, 3 and 4-bit shift registers each connected in a closed loop (Figure 1). All the circuits are able to generate subharmonics of the clock frequency. The clock is a sine wave and, for good directionality, a four-phase clocking scheme is employed. A 1-bit shift register stage is made by cascading four QFPs (see Figure 1c-d). Depending on the number of bits of the shift register, the size of the circuits (excluding the dc Squids used as QFP current sensors) range between 200μm x 450μm (1-bit) and 600μm x 450μm (4-bits). The minimum linewidth size is 5μm. The circuits' size should scale down if a better linewidth resolution is used.

The available Josephson junctions were fabricated using a lead-alloy process. Four superconducting layers and one resistive layer is used for interconnects. This process was developed for the Josephson computer effort at Hitachi [21].

Assuming that all the QFPs are activated by the same clock current amplitude and that the Josephson junctions' self-capacitance is below 1.5 pF, a 1-bit shift register wired in a closed loop configuration is simulated to operate correctly at 20 GHz. Another assumption is that the Josephson junction's critical current and shunting resistance is 25μA and 4Ω respectively. The latter values fit well to the actual measurements. As it will be discussed later, it is possible that the Josephson junction's self-capacitance might exceed 1.5 pF.

4. Power Distribution and QFP Clock Current Margin

The QFPs are clocked using a standing wave. The clock lines dissipate no power, thus it is a suitable method for clocking a QFP based circuit. The standing wave is obtained by shorting the end of the microstrip clock lines, see Figures 1 and 2. Because a standing wave is used, the clock current amplitude I_{clk} is not constant along the clock lines (Figure 2b). It is at its maximum at the short and decreases with increasing distance from the short until vanishing when the length is $\lambda/4$, where λ is the wavelength in the microstrip line corresponding to the clock frequency. This means that the clock current amplitude received by each QFP varies according to its position along the clock line. Depending on the QFP

Table 1. N_{QFP} is the number of QFPs, d_{tot} clock lines length from the first powered QFP to the short, $\Delta I_{clk}/I_{clk}$ clock current amplitude margin deduced from the highest operating frequency, f_{max} observed maximum operating frequency. FD2, FD4 and FD6 refers to the frequency divide by two (1-bit shift register), four (2-bit shift register) and six (3-bit shift register) respectively. SR4 is the four bit shift register.

Circuit	N_{QFP}	d_{tot} [µm]	$\Delta I_{clk}/I_{clk}$ [%]	f_{max} [GHz]
FD2	4	480	7.5	16.2
FD4	8	1100	21.4	12.11
FD6	12	1710	22.1	7.93
SR4	16	2340	17.3	5.1

activation margin, the standing wave clock power distribution scheme can limit the maximum operating frequency of a QFP based circuit.

The clock power is distributed serially in all the circuits (see Figure 2a). Thus with increasing circuit size (i.e. increasing number of QFPs or increasing clock line length), the maximum operating frequency can be expected to decrease. In Table 1 the clock microstrip lines' length and maximum operating frequency are shown for each circuit. In Figure 2b the activation current margins deduced from the maximum operating frequency for each circuit are displayed. It can be seen that all the circuits can be powered within 8 to 22% margins in the clock current amplitude. The frequency divide by two circuit's (1-bit shift register) maximum operating frequency is limited either by the Josephson junctions' characteristics or the package and is not a representative measurement of the QFP margins. Therefore, the maximum operating frequency of the other circuits can be used to calculate the activation margin of the QFP. It is found that the QFP can be clocked at multi-gigahertz frequencies within an electrical current amplitude margin of 17% to 22%.

It is important to point out that the QFP activation margin is deduced under "real world" experimental conditions - they take into account the spread of the fabricated Josephson junctions' characteristics. Concerning the actual Josephson junctions, their critical current distribution is impossible to measure because there are no dc connections to the QFPs. The critical current is deduced from the measured characteristics of the dc Squids used as current sensors and which lie within immediate proximity of the shift registers. The Josephson junctions' experimental critical current is consistently lower than the the target (25µA) and it ranges between

18μA to 24μA. Devices exhibiting a lower critical current do not operate properly perhaps because the QFP output current decreases drastically when β_d decreases below 0.2 [3]. According to critical current measurements in a series of 100 Josephson junctions within an area of about 500μm x 500μm, the critical current variation is about 10%.

5. Experimental Considerations

Because the power consumption of a QFP gate is extremely low, it can be expected that the output power level extracted from a QFP for an external measurement will be even lower. Also, the QFP is very sensitive to external disturbances so a suitable means of measuring the output current of a QFP has to be employed.

The current circulating between a pair of QFPs is measured by using a damped dc Squid (Figure 1e-f). The dc Squid biased into the voltage state is a suitable current sensor because it causes negligible disturbances to the QFPs. This is because its a.c. screening current is of a much higher frequency than that of the clock and its average amplitude is a fraction of the Josephson junction critical current [22]. Its major drawback is that its output voltage amplitude is at most a few tens of microvolts. At microwave frequencies such a low level signal is masked by broadband white noise of the detecting dc Squid or of the microwave amplifiers (depending on which one is higher), and by crosstalk with the clock frequency. This is the reason why the measurements are done in the frequency domain (here the noise bandwidth can be reduced) and why all the circuits are subharmonic generators.

The chip containing the QFP circuits is wire bonded to a ceramic carrier. The inductance of the wire bonds is expected to be the order of 150 pH and the clock current amplitude circulating across the bonds can be as high as 830 μA. Therefore, voltage oscillations in the chip ground plane of the order of 10 mV are possible (to be compared with some tens of microvolts that can be obtained across the detecting dc Squid). It was then made a goal to reduce crosstalk with the sensing dc Squid ground plane. The chip layout contains three completely floating ground planes: one for the clock lines, one for the QFPs (without any d.c. connection with the external world) and one for the detecting dc Squid. The ceramic carrier also has separated ground planes for the high level signals (i.e. clocks and dc bias) and the low level signals (i.e. dc Squids output and their current bias). Both grounds are interconnected only at the room temperature side.

For certain frequencies the total clock microstrip lines length inside the chip is made to be $\lambda (n + 1/4)$, where n is an integer. At such a frequency the wire bond is at a distance of $\lambda (n + 1/4)$ from the short and the current amplitude across it is at its minimum. This implies a minimum in the amplitude of the voltage oscillations of the clock's ground plane. Experimentally, a tremendous reduction of the crosstalk between the clocks and the detecting dc Squid is observed when clocking the QFP at the frequency yielding a wire bond to short distance of $\lambda/4$ (see Figure 3a). An example of the detected power spectrum when the crosstalk with the clock frequency is near its minimum is shown in Figure 3b. Here it can be seen that the main subharmonics are of similar or higher amplitude as the peak at the clock frequency.

6. Experiments

All the superconducting devices are inside a liquid helium dewar (at 4.2 K) enclosed in a three layer μ-metal magnetic shield. The liquid helium dewar and low noise amplifiers are inside a radio-frequency shielded room that is used as the general ground for all our instrumentation.

The measurements are done by using a spectrum analyzer with a Rosenfell detector, a resolution bandwidth of 30 KHz and a video bandwidth of 3 KHz (Hewlett-Packard HP70000 series with a RF section HP 70908A, local oscillator HP 70900A, IF section HP 70902A and Precision frequency reference HP 70310A). The noise floor is limited by the microwave amplifiers (Figure 4). The microwave amplifier where either two MITEQ AFS4-00101000-50-8P-4 (BW 0.1 GHz to 10 GHz) or a OMEGA No 1-002904 BW 6 GHz to 18 GHz). The absolute peak amplitude error is ±3.1 dB due to the microwave amplifier's gain tolerance. Furthermore, the subharmonics' relative amplitudes are deformed by the settings of the sensing dc Squid that unexpectedly depends on the clock frequency.

The experimental set-up is shown in Figure 4. If both clock lines length are equalized by using the phase shifters (adjustable delay lines), usually the only parameter to adjust when varying the clock frequency is the microwave signal generator output power. Then all the circuits are able to accept the variations of phase and relative amplitude that occur between the outputs of our broadband 90° hybrid coupler (typically ± 5° and ± 1 dB = ± 12% of current variation, depending on the clock frequency the coupler is either an ANAREN 1A0310-3 or a MRD H626-90). The signal generator's output power adjustment is further complicated by the poor thickness and dielectric tolerances of the ceramic chip carrier.

Resonances in the ceramic carrier are speculated to be responsible for the observed structure of the crosstalk data of Figure 3a.

The simplest device is the 1-bit shift register. This device is able to operate at a frequency as high as 16.2 GHz, see Figure 5. The frequency is either limited by the experimental set-up or by the QFP itself (see next chapter) and not by the standing wave power distribution scheme.

The 2 and 3-bit shift registers' maximum operating frequency seem to be limited by the standing wave power distribution method. The frequencies are 12.11 GHz and 7.93 GHz respectively (see Figures 6 and 7). In order to increase their operating frequency all the experimental parameters should be readjusted. This is particularly difficult because the available continuously variable attenuators (Figure 4) vary the transmission line length when changing their attenuation value. The attenuators are 20 dB variable attenuators model 4798 made by NARDA.

Also, the 3-bit shift register should store two different 6-bit logic patterns: 111000 ($v/6$) and 110011 ($v/2$). At high frequencies it was found to be impossible to unlock this device from the 111000 state. It is still not clear why this happens.

The last device is the 4-bit shift register circuit and it is the largest reported device that employs the QFP, this circuit is capable of stable operation at a clock frequency of 5.1 GHz (see Figure 8). The standing wave scheme prevents a further increase in the operating frequency. This circuit can store four different 4-bit logic patterns: 1100, 1010, 1110 and 1111 (the complementary and period shifts are equivalent in the frequency domain). Because of crosstalk with the clock frequency, at microwave frequencies all logic patterns with the exception of 1111 can be easily recognized in the frequency domain (see Figure 8). Although it is masked, state 1111 is assumed to exist. The patterns are changed by disturbing the circuit or by using the "store pattern" line (see Figure 1f), the signal is provided by an unlocked synthesized generator operating at half or one fourth of the clock frequency. Then the error free operation of this circuit can be assessed at microwave frequencies by looking at the stability with time of any given pattern. For example, after memorizing the 1100 pattern its respective power spectrum should be observed. If one of the QFP gates produces an error, the most likely event is that only one of the bits will be inverted resulting in the 1110 pattern being stored by the device. This circuit was able to run without the observation of an error during time intervals of the order of one hour at a clock frequency of 3.1 GHz. A minimum number of 10^{14} error free operations per QFP is recorded [2]. In principle a commercial computer would require a much larger number of error free operations. Following an example from the literature [23]: if we presume that a single error per year is tolerable in a 32 Mword (word = 32 bits) DRAM array, with a refresh time of 100 ps, this corresponds to at least 3×10^{26} error free operations per gate. To demonstrate such a low error rate with the 4-bit shift register requires an unrealistically long experimental time ($\approx$ 30 thousand years). Nevertheless the error free operation of the 4-bit shift register gives us confidence in the good stability of the QFP.

7. Discussion

The 1-bit shift register is able to operate at frequencies as high as 16.2 GHz and it is not clear whether the frequency is limited by the Josephson junction's characteristics or by the package. According to computer simulations, the 1-bit shift register should work at 20 GHz if the Josephson junctions' self-capacitance is below 1.5 pF. The QFP is designed assuming a 1 pF Josephson junction's self-capacitance. Previously the Josephson junction specific capacitance had been investigated [24-26]. In Ref. [25] a very good fit between the oxide layer thickness (deduced from ellipsometric studies) and the Josephson junction critical current density is shown. In Ref. [26] two sets of junction current density versus specific capacitance pairs for Nb-Pb alloy (identical process as ours) are given. They are: $\{10^9 \text{ A/m}^2, 0.17 \text{ F/m}^2\}$ and $\{10^8 \text{ A/m}^2, 0.09 \text{ F/m}^2\}$. From these values, a Josephson junction critical current density of 10^6 A/m^2 corresponds to a junction self-capacitance of 1.08 pF when the junction area is 25 μm^2 [25]. A considerable error in the estimation of our Josephson junction capacitance is very possible because: (a) the capacitance is deduced from a statistically low number of points - only two; (b) the critical current densities reported in Ref. [26] are much larger than ours and (c) the capacitance versus critical current density data reported in Ref. [24] has a large spread. Thus a larger than expected capacitance and the combined effect of the natural spread of the Josephson junctions' characteristics can account for the limit of 16.2 GHz of the maximum operating frequency of the 1-bit shift register. In order to rule out that the maximum operating frequency is not limited by our package, a direct measurement of the Josephson junction self-capacitance is required. However, because we will switch to a new trilayer process such a measurement is impossible at this time. Also the clock frequency evolution of the phase noise of the signal at half the clock frequency of the 1-bit shift register can give some insight into the onset of misoperations of the QFP gates. Such errors will occur with greater frequency when the intrinsic limiting frequency of the device is approached. Unfortunately we do not have the adequate equipment for performing phase noise measurements. Also, the low level signal of the 1-bit shift register will certainly complicate the experiment.

If indeed the maximum operating frequency of the 1-bit shift register is limited by our process then when switching to a more up to date "fashionable" process, the operating frequency can be much increased. If the "experimental" frequency (for Pb alloy process it is 16.2 GHz) scales in the same way as the plasma frequency $v_p = 1/R\,C$ then operating frequencies in excess of 100 GHz can be expected when using, for example, a Nb-Al$_2$O$_3$-Nb process for fabricating Josephson junctions' with a linewidth resolution of 1 µm [26].

It is shown that by building a $\lambda/4$ resonance in the clock microstrip lines inside the chip, the crosstalk between the QFP output and the clock frequency can be dramatically reduced. Finally the QFP clock current amplitude margin is calculated for each device from its maximum operating frequency. Eventually, by improving the experimental set-up the maximum operating frequency can still be increased. The 2, 3 and 4-bit shift registers are able to operate at 5.1, 7.93 and 12.11 GHz respectively within a clock electrical current amplitude margin of 17% or larger.

References

[1] K. Loe and E. Goto, "DC-Flux Parametron - a new approach to Josephson logics", World Scientific, Singapore, 1986.

[2] J. Casas, R. Kamikawai, Y. Harada and E. Goto, "Subharmonic generators and error detection by using the Quantum Flux Parametron (QFP)", *IEEE Trans. Magn.*, MAG-27, pp. 2851-2854, March 1991.

[3] J. Casas, R. Kamikawai and E. Goto, "High frequency operation of Quantum Flux Parametron (QFP) based shift registers and frequency prescalers", Submitted to *IEEE Solid-State Circuits* (1991).

[4] J. X. Przybysz, "Josephson Shift Registers", *Proc. IEEE*, vol. 77, no. 8, pp. 1274-1279, 1989.

[5] P. Horowitz and W. Hill, "The art of electronics", Cambridge University Press, 1980, Sections 7.19 and Chap. 9.

[6] P.-F. Yuh, Ch.-T. Yao and P. Bradley, "Josephson 32-bit shift register", *IEEE Trans. Magn.*, MAG-27, pp. 2898-2901, March 1991.

[7] N. Fujimaki, S. Kotani, T. Imamura and S. Hasuo, "Josephson 8-bit shift register", *IEEE J. Solid-State Circuits*, vol. SC-22, no. 5, pp. 886-891, 1987.

[8]   N. Fujimaki, T. Imamura and S. Hasuo, "Josephson pseudorandom bit-sequence generator", *IEEE J. Solid-State Circuits*, vol. SC-23, no. 3, pp. 852-858, 1988.

[9]   J. X. Przybysz, D. L. Meier and J. Kang, "Shift register performance at 4 GHz", , *IEEE Trans. Magn.*, MAG-27, pp. 2773-2776, March 1991.

[10] C. A. Hamilton, "100 GHz binary counter using Squid flip flops", *IEEE Trans. Magn.*, MAG-19, pp. 1291-1292, May 1983.

[11] V. K. Kaplunenko, M. I. Khabipov, V. P. Koshelets, K. K. Likharev, O. A. Mukhanov, V. K. Semenov, I. L. Sepluchenko and A. N. Vystavkin, "Experimental Study of the RSFQ logic elements", *IEEE Trans. Magn.*, MAG-25, pp. 861-864, March 1989.

[12] K. C. Wang, P. M. Asbeck, M. F. Chang, D. L. Miller and G. J. Sullivan, "High-speed MSI current-mode logic circuits implemented with heterojunction bipolar transistors", *Tech. Dig. 1986 GaAs IC Symp.*, pp. 159-162, Oct. 1986.

[13] H. P. Singh, R. A. Sadler, A. E. Geissberger and D. G. Fischer, "A comparative study of GaAs logic families using universal shift registers and self-aligned gate technology", presented at the *IEEE GaAs IC Symp.*, pp. 11-14, 1986.

[14] H. Tsuji, H. I. Fujishiro, M. Shikata, K. Tanaka and S. Nishi, "Ultra-high speed DCFL dynamic frequency divider with 0.2μm gate BP-Mesfet", Fall Joint Conf. *IEICE* Japan, 1990 (in Japanese).

[15] H. P. Singh, R. A. Sadler, W. J. Tanis and A. N. Schenberg, "GaAs prescalers and counters for fast-settling frequency synthesizers", *IEEE J. Solid-State Circuits*, vol. SC-25, no. 1, pp. 239-245, Feb. 1990.

[16] R. A. Sadler, A. E. Geissberger and H. P. Singh, "A 5.1-GHz 1.9-mW GaAs binary frequency divider", *IEEE Electron Device Lett.*, vol. 10, pp. 440-442, Oct. 1989.

[17] Telemus Electronic Systems Inc., "Frequency product guide", June 1988.

[18] Y. Harada, H. Nakane, N. Miyamoto, U. Kawabe, E Goto and T. Soma, "Basic operations of the Quantum Flux Parametron", *IEEE Trans. Magn.*, vol. MAG-23, 3801-3807, 1987.

[19] O. A. Mukhanov, V. K. Semenov and K. K. Likharev, "Ultimate performance of the RSFQ logic circuits", *IEEE Trans. Magn.*, MAG-23, pp. 759-762, March 1989.

[20] M. Hosoya, W. Hioe, J. Casas, R. Kamikawai, Y. Harada, Y. Wada, H. Nakane, R. Suda and E. Goto, "Quantum Flux Parametron (A Single

Quantum Flux Device for Josephson Supercomputer)", accepted for publication in *IEEE Trans. Appl. Superconductivity*.

[21] S. Yano, Y. Tarutani, H. Mori, H. Yamada, M. Hirano and U. Kawabe, "Fabrication and characteristics of NbN-based Josephson junction for logic LSI circuits", *IEEE Trans. Magn.*, MAG-23, pp. 1472-1475, 1987.

[22] C. D. Tesche and J. Clarke, "dc Squid: noise and optimization", *J. Low Temp. Phys.*, Vol. 27, 303-331, 1977.

[23] P. A. Layman and S. G. Chamberlain, "A compact thermal noise model for the investigation of soft error rates in MOS VLSI digital circuits", *IEEE J. Solid-state Circuits*, Vol. 24, 79-89, 1989.

[24] J. H. Magerlein, "Specific capacitance of Josephson tunnel junctions", *IEEE Trans. Magn.*, MAG-17, pp. 286-289, 1981.

[25] S. Basavaiah, J. M. Eldridge and J. Matisoo, " Tunneling in lead-lead oxide-lead junctiond", *J. Appl. Phys.*, vol. 45, 457-464, Jan. 1974.

[26] Y. Tarutani, M. Hirano and U. Kawabe, "Niobium-based integrated circuit technologies", *Proc. IEEE*, vol. 77, no. 8, pp. 1164-1176, 1989.

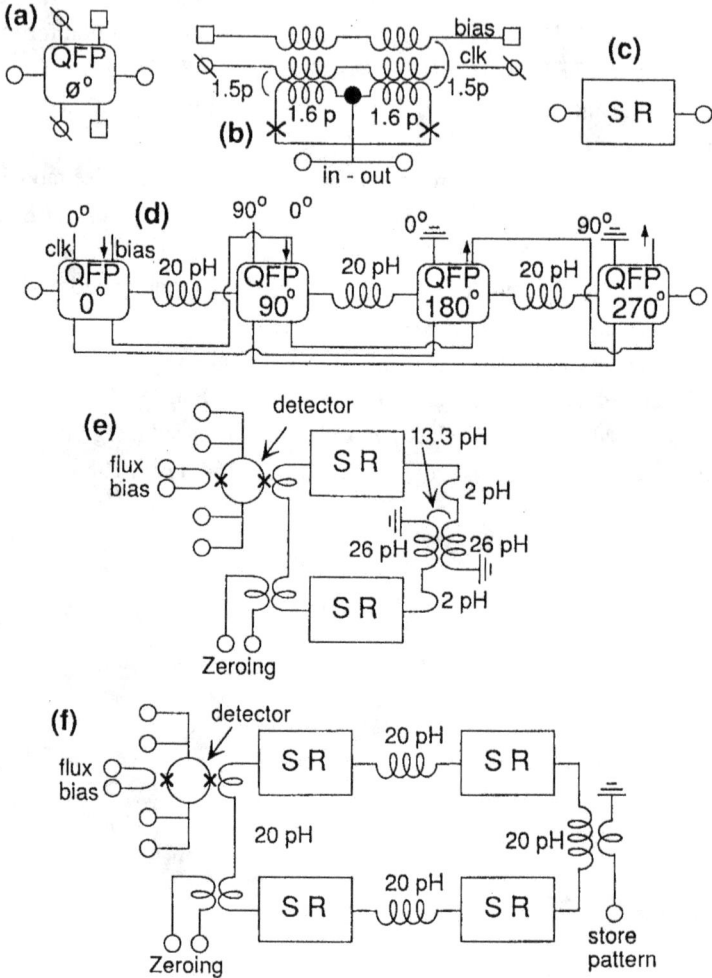

Figure 1: Hierarchical circuit description. (a) QFP symbol, (b) QFP cell (the Josephson junctions' shunting resistance of 4 Ω and self-capacitance of 1 pF are not represented), (c) 1-bit shift register symbol, (d) 1-bit shift register cell. Clock and dc bias lines are shown, (e) frequency divide by four circuit (2-bit shift register). The inductance between two shift registers is always 20 pH to maximize the output current; the "zeroing" line is used to cancel a seed that can eventually be introduced by the detecting dc Squid. (f) 4-bit shift register wired around a closed loop. NOTA: the inductance values indicated in this figure were design targets, experimentally the inductance values that were possible to measure were systematically about 15% below the design value.

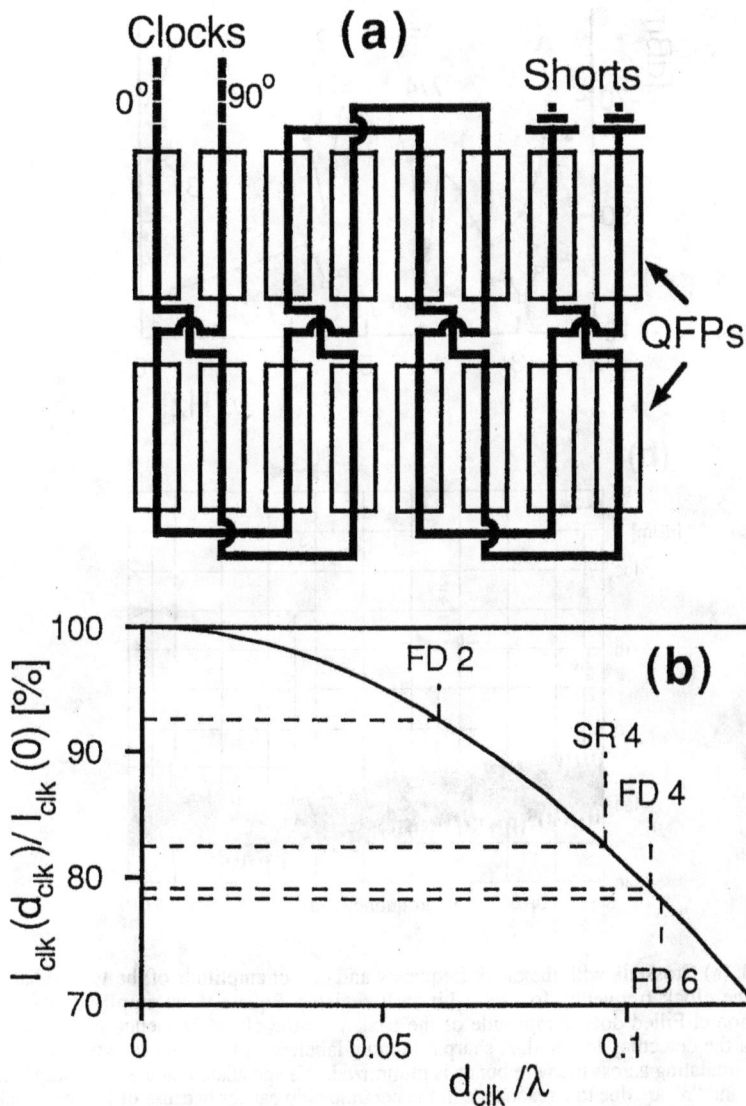

Figure 2 Limitation in frequency by using a standing wave. (a) Schematic layout of the 4-bit shift register. Each clock line meanders through eight QFPs before being shorted. The QFP size including shunting resistors was 180μm x 25μm and the typical separation between adjacent QFPs was 50μm. (b) Clock current amplitude I_{clk} as a function of the distance to the short d_{clk}. FD2, FD4, FD6 and SR4 show the clock's microstrip line length between the first QFP and the short for the 1, 2, 3 and 4-bit shift registers respectively. The length is normalized by λ, where λ is the wavelength in the microstrip medium corresponding to the maximum operating frequency f_{max} for each circuit (see Table 1).

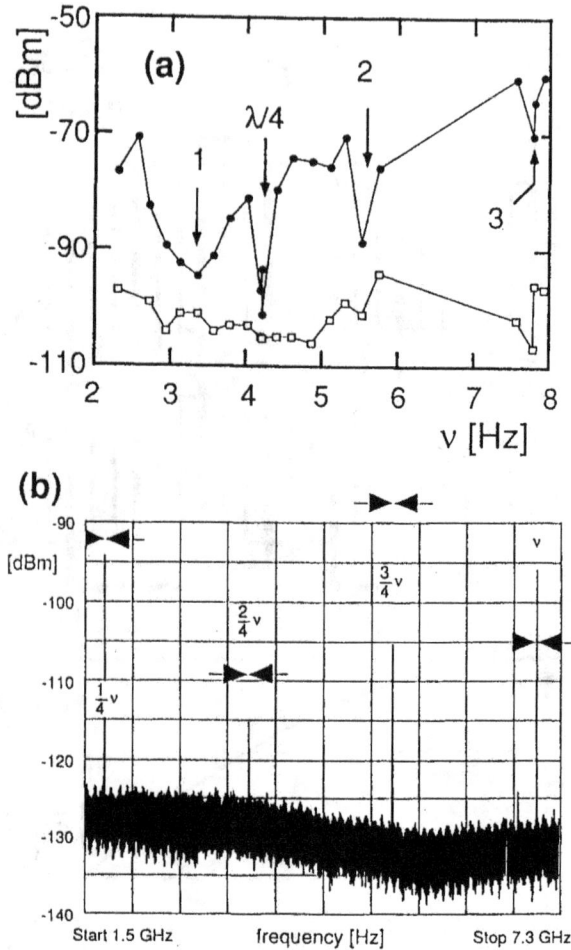

Figure 3: (a) Crosstalk with the clock frequency and output amplitude of the $\nu/6$ subharmonic versus the clock frequency for the 3-bit shift register. Square dots: amplitude of the $\nu/6$ subharmonic. Filled dots: Amplitude of the peak with the clock frequency measured at the output of the detecting dc Squid. A sharp minimum labeled "$\lambda/4$" occurs as expected when the current circulating across the wire bonds is minimized. We speculate that the minimums labeled "1", "2" and "3" are due to a resonance in the ceramic chip carrier because of its poor thickness and dielectric constant tolerances. The resonance occurs at frequencies where the ceramic carrier's microstrip length (about 22mm) is $(2n+1)\,\lambda/4$, where n is an integer. At such a frequency a standing wave is built in the chip carrier's microstrip: a minimum in the current amplitude at the coaxial (50Ω)-microstrip (46Ω) transition occurs (i.e. a minimum in the carrier's ground plane voltage oscillations) and the current amplitude is always large at the wire bond because of the low impedance (13Ω) of the microstrip line inside the chip. (b) Output spectra of the 2-bit shift register when operating at 7.003 GHz. Notice that the first subharmonic has a larger amplitude than the peak at the clock frequency ν. The marks indicate the peaks amplitude expected from low frequency measurements.

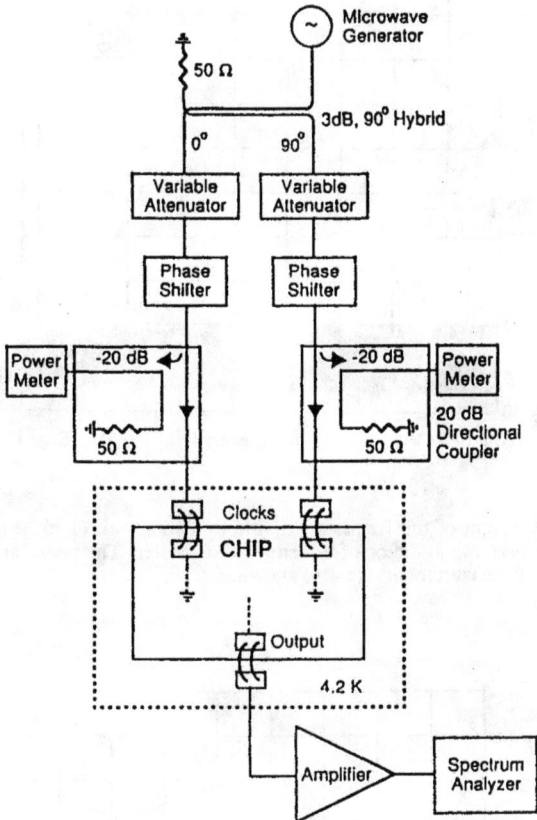

Figure 4: Experimental set-up. The operating bandwidth of the couplers, phase-shifters and attenuators is 2 to 18 GHz. The microwave amplifiers bandwidths were 0.1 to 10 GHz (NF = 5 dB) or 6 to 18 GHz (NF = 7 dB).

38

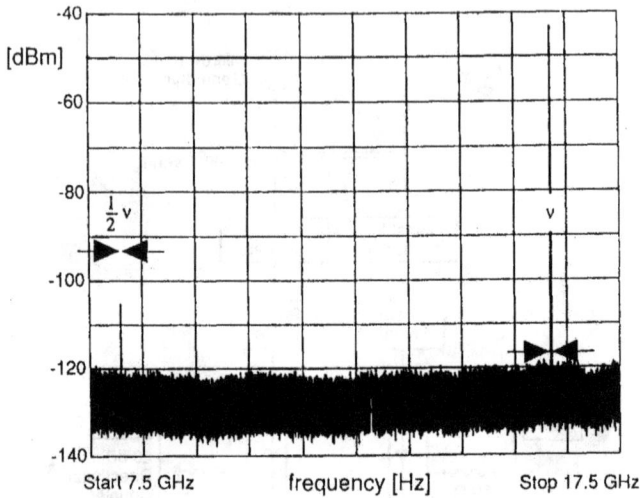

Figure 5: Output spectra of the frequency divide by two circuit (1-bit shift register with bit inversion) when operating at a clock frequency of 16.2 GHz. The peaks amplitudes expected from low frequency measurements are also shown.

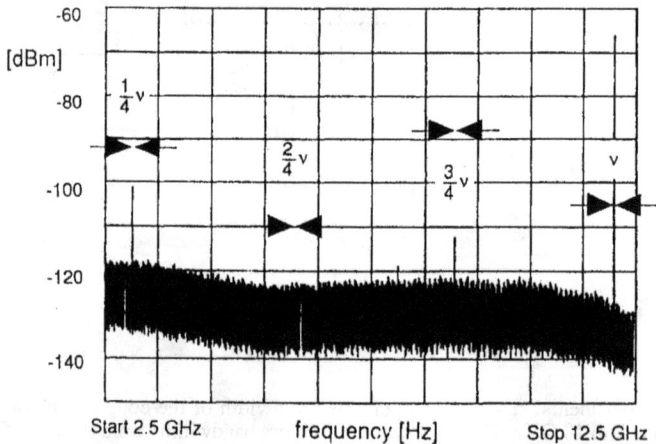

Figure 6: Output spectra of the frequency divide by four circuit (2-bits shift register with bit inversion) when operating at a clock frequency of 12.11 GHz. The peaks amplitudes expected from low frequency measurements are also shown.

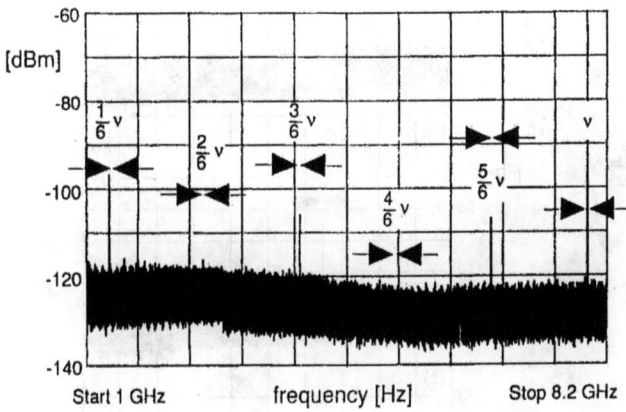

Figure 7: Output spectra of the frequency divide by six or two circuit (3-bits shift register with bit inversion) when operating at a clock frequency of 7.93 GHz. The peaks amplitudes expected from low frequency measurements are also shown.

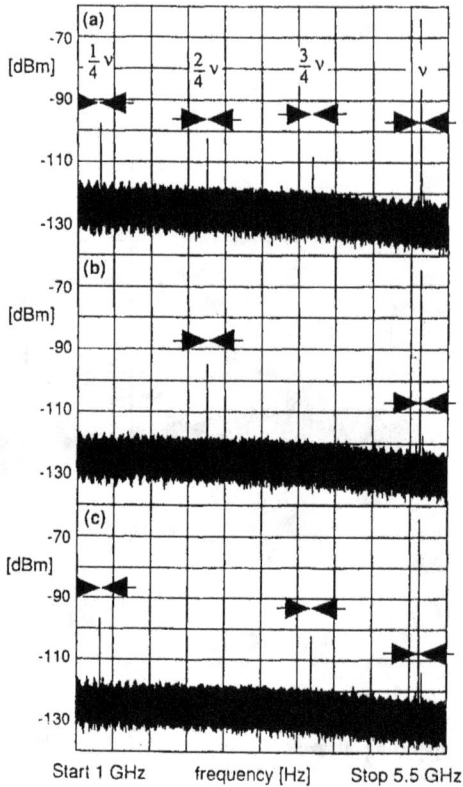

Figure 8: Output spectra for the 4-bit shift register when operating at a clock frequency of 5.1 GHz. The three power spectra are very easy to distinguish by looking at the $v/4$, $v/2$ and $3v/4$ subharmonics. (a) 1110 pattern, (b) 1010 pattern and (c) 1100 pattern. The peaks amplitudes expected from low frequency measurements are also shown.

Stability and Microwave Time Domain Testing of the QFP

Juan Casas, Ryotaro Kamikawai, and Eiichi Goto

Abstract

Until recently most of the high frequency measurements related to the QFP have been done in the frequency domain. In this work it is shown that it is possible to sample in time domain the output waveform of a QFP circuit. Crosstalk with the clock frequency and wideband white noise are the main problems to solve. Crosstalk is reduced by using an active cancellation technique. Against white noise a low noise amplifier and an averaging oscilloscope are used. Time domain measurements are done for a single-bit and a 12-bit shift registers working at 5 GHz and 2.4 GHz respectively. The 12-bit device is the largest ever reported device using the QFP (48 QFPs) and it employs an inductive tree for clock power distribution. The 12-bit shift register is also used for demonstrating that 10^{15} error free operations per QFP are possible.

1.Introduction

The QFP is a superconducting gate capable of very high frequency operation with a very low power consumption. Typically a single QFP operating at a frequency of 10 GHz dissipates about 1 nW. This is similar to the power dissipated by the RSFQ logic family [1], about three orders of magnitude below the power dissipated by voltage Josephson logic and about six orders of magnitude below the power dissipated by semiconductor logic circuits. The low QFP power consumption offsets the power lost for cooling down to 4.2 K: about 1 kW of cooling power is required for extracting 1 W at 4.2 K [2]. Such a low QFP power dissipation permits in principle a very high level of integration.

Towards the development of a QFP supercomputer key issues to show are a low intrinsic error rate, high operational margins and fast operation speed. This work aims toward the demonstration of the fast and stable operation of the QFP. Then a QFP based device capable of very fast and stable operation, as well as its related instrumentation have to be implemented.

Experimentally the QFP has been found to be able to operate at a clock frequency of 16.2 GHz [3] in spite of the technology used for fabricating its Josephson junctions (NbN-Pb alloy with 5μm minimum size). The output current of a QFP is typically detected by using a dc Squid. According to frequency domain measurements the dc Squid's output voltage amplitude is of the order of 10μV and is polluted by crosstalk with the clock frequency and by broadband white noise (typically the dominant noise is at the input stage of our microwave amplifiers). In order to overcome the previously mentioned problems the QFP circuits' output is most of the time analyzed by using a spectrum analyzer.

Nevertheless some means of measuring in time domain the output waveform of our devices has to be implemented. This is essential when testing complicated circuits because their output waveform will be a complex array of logic "1"s and "0"s that is very difficult to analyze with only frequency domain capabilities.

For performing time domain measurements the problems are crosstalk with the clock frequency and wideband white noise. The origin of crosstalk with the clock are voltage oscillations of the clock's ground plane. This ground plane is capacitively connected to the detecting dc Squid's ground plane [3]. For reducing crosstalk noise, the dc Squid's ground plane is made to oscillate with the clock frequency but with opposite phase [4]. On the other hand white noise can be reduced by using low noise microwave amplifiers (the lowest value is determined by market availability) and by averaging the output waveform with a sampling oscilloscope. For averaging and sampling the output waveform of any circuit it is essential that trigger and signal waveforms are phaselocked. Phaselocking can be lost for instance when a single QFP mis-operates. Then the ability of time-domain measurements is a further proof of the good stability of the QFP.

A multi-stable logic circuit is fabricated in order to test the stability of the QFP. The circuits that were fabricated are N-bit shift registers wired in a closed loop. In this case several logic N-bit patterns exist and by looking over the stability on time of any given pattern, the error free operation of the QFP can be demonstrated. In practice 10^{15} error free operations per QFP have been recorded. This experiment is performed by using a 12-bit shift register: this circuit operated at 2.4 GHz and during 2 1/2 hours no error was observed.

2.Circuit Description

The Josephson junctions were fabricated using a lead-alloy process. Four superconducting layers and one resistive layer are used for interconnects. The minimum feature size is 5μm. The process was developed for the Josephson computer effort at Hitachi [5].

The basic element of all the circuits designed for high frequency operation is a single-bit shift register. Figure 1a-d show how this element is made. Because the QFP is a two terminal device a multiphase clocking scheme is employed. A four-phase clock is used and then for fabricating a 1-bit shift register four QFPs are necessary. All the circuits are a series of 1-bit shift registers cascaded around a closed loop, also some of the devices have an inverting transformer (Figures 1e-f, 2).

The devices that have been tested in time domain are a 1-bit and a 12-bit shift registers. The 1-bit shift register has an inverting transformer. By performing frequency domain measurements this device is shown to work at frequencies as high as 16.2 GHz [3]. The 12-bit shift register work either as a programmable frequency prescaler or as a programmable 12-bit logic pattern generator. The frequency prescaling factor can be either 2, 4, 6 or 12. The 12-bit device is the largest ever reported circuit using the QFP; it is made by 48 QFPs.

The 12-bit shift register has a new detection wiring that permits to measure the output current of a single QFP, see Figure 2. Previously the detecting dc Squid was placed along the load line connecting a pair of QFPs (Figure 1e-f). For the 12-bit shift register one of the QFPs has three load inductors: two that are connected with the output and input terminals of two different QFPs and one that is connected to ground. Along the latter load line the detecting dc Squid is placed and the current circulating along this inductor is mainly the output current of a single QFP. With this wiring configuration it is much easier to recognize what bit pattern is memorized in the shift register loop. Also with this new detecting scheme a given logic pattern and its complementary can be easily differentiated. This is not the case for the detector used for instance with the 4-bit shift register [6].

According to computer simulations the single-bit shift register should work at frequencies as high as 20 GHz as long as the Josephson junction self-capacitance is below 1.5 pF (Figure 3). The simulation assumes that the Josephson junction's critical current and shunting resistance are 25μA (junction area is 5 x 5 μm^2) and 4Ω respectively. The latter values fit well the actual measurements. It is possible that the Josephson junction's self-capacitance might exceed 1.5 pF [3].

The 12-bit device is not able to work at 20 GHz because of the standing wave clocking scheme. The length of the clock lines limit its maximum operating frequency (Figure 4). In order to increase its maximum operating frequency the clock is distributed in parallel: each of the clock branches feeds 8 QFPs before being shorted; see Figure 2. This circuit should operate at similar maximum frequencies as a 4-bit shift register that was previously reported [3]: 5.1 GHz.

One of the main advantages of the QFP is an extremely low power consumption. This is lost if a resistive network is used for powering the QFPs [7]. In order to take full advantage of the low power consumption of the QFP, the clock is applied as a standing wave. The standing wave is obtained by shortening the clock microstrip lines. The clock current can be divided by using an inductive network (12-bit shift register, see Figure 2). With this powering scheme no power is dissipated at any point along the clock lines. The conventional power trees use resistors for dividing the clock current. Such resistor networks are the main dissipating factor of most of the superconducting logic circuits designed to date.

The total circuit area ranges between 200μm x 450μm (1-bit) to 1800μm x 450μm (12-bit, the actual layout is shown on Figure 5). It should be kept in mind that the minimum feature size is 5μm and so if a more sophisticated fabrication process (i.e. Nb-Al2O3-Nb with 2μm linewidth resolution) the circuits size can be much reduced.

3.Experimental Considerations

Because the power consumption of a QFP gate is extremely low, it can be expected that the output power level extracted from a QFP for an external measurement will be still lower. Also the QFP is very sensitive on external disturbances and then a suitable means of measuring its output current has to be employed. The current circulating between a pair of QFPs or at the output of a single dc Squid is measured by using a damped dc Squid (Figure 1e-f). The dc Squid biased into the voltage state is a suitable current sensor because it causes negligible disturbances to the QFPs: its a.c. screening current is of a much higher frequency than that of the clock and its average amplitude is a fraction of the Josephson junction critical current [8]. The major drawback is that the output voltage amplitude is at most a few tens of microvolts [6]. At microwave frequencies this low level signal is masked by broadband white noise of the detecting dc Squid or of the microwave amplifiers (depending on which one is higher) and by crosstalk with the clock lines. This is why the measurements are much simpler to make in the frequency domain than in the time domain. All the devices designed for microwave operation should be capable of generating subharmonics of the clock frequency. In the frequency domain the noise bandwidth can be reduced and the subharmonics can be easily recognized from crosstalk with the clock frequency.

In order to tackle broadband white noise a wideband and very low noise microwave preamplifier is necessary. The front end of our amplification stage (*MITEQ* AFS4-0100800-20-10-P4) has a noise figure NF $\leq$ 2 dB with a frequency band Δf of 0.1 GHz to 8 GHz. The peak to peak noise voltage V_n referred to the input is of the order of:

$$V_{amp} \cong 6 \sqrt{4 \, k_b \, T_n \, R_n \, \Delta f} \approx 360 \, \mu V \qquad (1)$$

where k_b is the Boltzmann constant, T_n is the noise temperature of the preamplifier (160 K) and R_n is 50 Ω. It can then be seen that the noise voltage is about an order of magnitude higher than the typical output voltage (Figure 6). The noise voltage produced by the dc Squid is roughly given by:

$$V_{sq} \sim 6\left[\sqrt{2\,k_b\,T\,R} + V_\phi\,L_s\,\sqrt{2\,k_b\,T/R}\,\right]\sqrt{\Delta f} \approx 60\,\mu V \tag{2}$$

where T is the helium bath temperature (4.2 K), R is the dc Squid's Josephson junction shunting resistance (3.5 Ω), V_ϕ is the voltage versus flux transfer coefficient (about 1720 $\mu V/\Phi_0$) and L_s is the dc Squid self-inductance (15 pH). According to Equations (1) and (2) the dominant noise source is the microwave amplifier (although Eq. 2 might underestimate the dc Squid's actual noise level). The dc Squid noise masks the output signal even if a noiseless microwave amplifier exists. Then, a sampling and averaging oscilloscope (*TEKTRONIX* CSA-803) is necessary for recording the output of our QFP circuits. Of course dc Squids are not the only means of detecting the QFP output and eventually better means of measuring the QFP will be proposed and implemented.

The chip containing the QFP circuits is wire bonded to a ceramic carrier. The inductance of the wire bonds is expected to be of the order of 150 pH and the clock current amplitude circulating across the bonds can be as high as 830 μA. Therefore voltage oscillations in the chip ground plane of the order of 10 mV are possible (to be compared with some tens of microvolts that can be obtained across the detecting dc Squid). It was then made a goal to reduce crosstalk with the sensing dc Squid ground plane. The chip layout contains three completely floating ground planes: one for the clock lines, one for the QFPs (without any d.c. connection with the external world) and one for the detecting dc Squid. The ceramic carrier has also separated ground planes for the high level signals (i.e. clocks and dc bias) and the low level signals (i.e. dc Squids output and their current bias), both grounds are interconnected only at the room temperature side.

For certain frequencies the total clock microstrip lines length inside the chip were made to be $\lambda\,(n + 1/4)$, where n is an integer. At such a frequency the wire bond is at a distance of $\lambda\,(n + 1/4)$ from the short and the current amplitude across it is at its minimum, meaning also a minimum in the amplitude of the voltage oscillations of the clock's ground plane. Experimentally a tremendous reduction of the crosstalk between the clocks and the detecting dc Squid was observed when clocking the QFP at the frequency yielding a wire bond to short distance of $\lambda/4$ (see Figure 7a). An example of the detected power spectrum when the crosstalk with the clock frequency was near its minimum is shown in Figure 7b, it can be seen that the main subharmonics are of similar or higher amplitude as the peak corresponding to the clock frequency.

For eliminating the peak at the clock frequency a notch filter, a $\lambda/4$ resonance or an active cancellation technique can be combined or used independently. The active cancellation technique produce voltage oscillations of the detecting dc Squid ground plane with same amplitude as the crosstalk but with opposite phase (Figure 8). This technique do not produce phase rotation versus frequency as is the case for a notch filter and can be used at any frequency.

4.Low Frequency Measurements

Low frequency measurements are relatively easy to perform. A dc Squid is used as QFP current detector. The dc Squid operates as a current (magnetic flux) to voltage transducer. The QFP circuits' output waveform is clipped by the dc Squid because its magnetic flux to voltage transfer coefficient is not constant. This explain the difference between the simulated and measured output waveform (Figure 3 and 6). About 50 μV is the maximum peak to peak voltage amplitude that can be obtained with the fabricated dc Squids.

The 1-bit shift register output waveform is shown in Figure 6; it can be seen that it fits well what is expected from computer simulations (Figure 3).

The 12-bit shift register can store any arbitrary 12-bit logic pattern. Figure 9 shows, non exhaustively, some of the patterns that can be memorized by the 12-bit shift register. With the new detection scheme, any logic pattern is easily recognized.

5.High Frequency Measurements

The simplest device to measure is the 1-bit shift register. This device is a frequency divide by two prescaler and its output waveform is determined mainly by two harmonics at 1/2 and 3/2 the clock frequency [4]. Also the harmonic with the clock frequency should have a very low amplitude [4]. For time domain measurements the harmonic at the clock frequency is suppressed. The two harmonics of interest should fall within the instrumentation bandwidth. Figure 10 shows the output waveform of the 1-bit shift register when operating at a clock frequency of 5 GHz.

The second device that has been tested in time domain is the 12-bit shift register. This shift register can produce a much more complex logic pattern than any QFP circuit previously designed. The crosstalk with the clock frequency was actively cancelled. In order to adjust the cancelling wave, a pattern with no harmonics at the clock frequency is stored in the 12-bit shift register loop. These patterns can be for example "101010101010", "110011001100", "111000111000" or "111111000000". Once any of the previous patterns is memorized, the harmonic at the clock frequency can be suppressed. After that the pattern stored in the 12-bit register loop is changed by using an external logic pattern generator (*ANRITSU* MP1650A). The 12-bit logic patterns stored by the 12-bit shift register and externally generated (seed) were not identical most of the time. Figure 11 shows some of the 12-bit logic patterns that are possible to store in the 12-bit shift register circuit when operating with a clock frequency of 2.4 GHz (the external logic pattern generator is off during the acquisition time).

A final consideration when making time domain measurements by using a sampling oscilloscope is phase locking. Typically the oscilloscope has to be triggered by a subharmonic of the clock frequency, it should be the lowest subharmonic of the circuit under investigation (1/2 and 1/12 of the clock frequency for the 1 and 12-bit shift registers respectively). The triggering waveform and QFP output waveform should be phase locked. Both waveforms can be unlocked for instance when a QFP gate mis-operates. Then the ability of making time-domain measurements is a further proof of the good stability of the QFP.

At high frequencies the QFP stability can be assessed. For this a 4 or 12-bit shift registers is used for storing an arbitrary logic pattern. The stored logic pattern is lost when an error occurs. The most likely error is the inversion of a single bit, resulting in a new logic pattern stored by the shift register loop. This event is easily recognized either by analyzing the output in the frequency or in the time domain. At first the 4-bit shift register was used for showing that about 10^{14} operations per QFP can be accomplished without the occurrence of an error [6]. For this the 4-bit shift register stored a 4-bit logic pattern during 1 hour when operating at 3.1 GHz. With the availability of the 12-bit shift register 10^{15} error free operations per QFP are recorded. The 12-bit shift register is capable of stable operation during 2 1/2 hours at a clock frequency of 2.4 GHz. In principle a commercial computer would require a much larger number of error free operations per logic gate. Following an example from the literature [9]: if we presume that a single error per year is tolerable in a 32 Mword (word = 32 bits) DRAM array, with a refresh time of 100 ps, this corresponds to at least 3×10^{26} error free operations per gate. Such a low error rate cannot be assessed in view of the extremely long measuring times. Nevertheless the fact that our shift register circuits are able to operate practically at full speed and without an error, gives us confidence that indeed the logic gates based on the QFP are very stable.

6.Conclusion

It is shown that microwave time domain measurements of a QFP based circuit are possible in spite of the large crosstalk with the clock frequency and of the low amplitude obtained across the detecting dc Squid. Time domain measurements were made by using a 1 and a 12-bit shift registers with a clock frequency of 5 and 2.4 GHz respectively. The 12-bit shift register stores the 12-bit logic pattern during the acquisition time, demonstrating the QFP stability. Typically shift registers are analyzed in series, in this case the input pattern is produced by an external pattern generator and the obtained waveform averages towards the expected logic pattern even if some of the gates produce an error from time to time.

The 12-bit shift register output was analyzed in frequency and time domain. The consistency between both types of measuring techniques is then demonstrated experimentally.

A 4 and a 12-bit shift registers are used to show the good stability of the QFP gate. 10^{15} error free operations per QFP are recorded. Typically a commercial computer operating at 10 GHz would require 10^{26} error free operations per gate. Such a low error rate cannot be demonstrated with the 4 or 12-bit shift registers because of the extremely long measuring times. Nevertheless the QFP seems to be a very stable gate.

References

[1] O. A. Mukhanov, V. K. Semenov and K. K. Likharev, "Ultimate performance of the RSFQ logic circuits", *IEEE Trans. Magn.*, MAG-23, pp. 759-762, March 1989.

[2] M. Nisenoff, "Superconducting electronics: current status and future prospects", *Cryogenics*, Vol. 28, pp. 47-56, January 1988.

[3] J. Casas, R. Kamikawai and E. Goto, "High frequency operation of Quantum Flux Parametron (QFP) based shift registers and frequency prescalers", accepted for publication in *IEEE J. Solid-State Circuits* (1991).

[4] J. Casas, R. Kamikawai, N. Miyamoto and E. Goto, "Multigigahertz Time-Domain Testing of theQuantum Flux Parametron (QFP)", extended abstracts of 3rd *International Superconductive Electronics Conf.*, pp. 179-182, Glasgow 1991.

[5]   S. Yano, Y. Tarutani, H. Mori, H. Yamada, M. Hirano and U. Kawabe, "Fabrication and characteristics of NbN-based Josephson junction for logic LSI circuits", *IEEE Trans. Magn.*, MAG-23, pp. 1472-1475, 1987.

[6]   J. Casas, R. Kamikawai, Y. Harada and E. Goto, "Subharmonic generators and error detection by using the Quantum Flux Parametron (QFP)", *IEEE Trans. Magn.*, MAG-27, pp. 2851-2854, March 1991.

[7]   J. Fleischman, D. Feld, P. Xiao and T. Van Duzer, "Evaluation of flux-based logic schemes for high-Tc applications", *IEEE Trans. Magn.*, MAG-27, pp. 2769-2770, March 1991.

[8]   C. D. Tesche and J. Clarke, "dc Squid: noise and optimization", *J. Low Temp. Phys.*, Vol. 27, 303-331, 1977.

[9]   P. A. Layman and S. G. Chamberlain, "A compact thermal noise model for the investigation of soft error rates in MOS VLSI digital circuits", *IEEE J. Solid-state Circuits*, Vol. 24, 79-89, 1989.

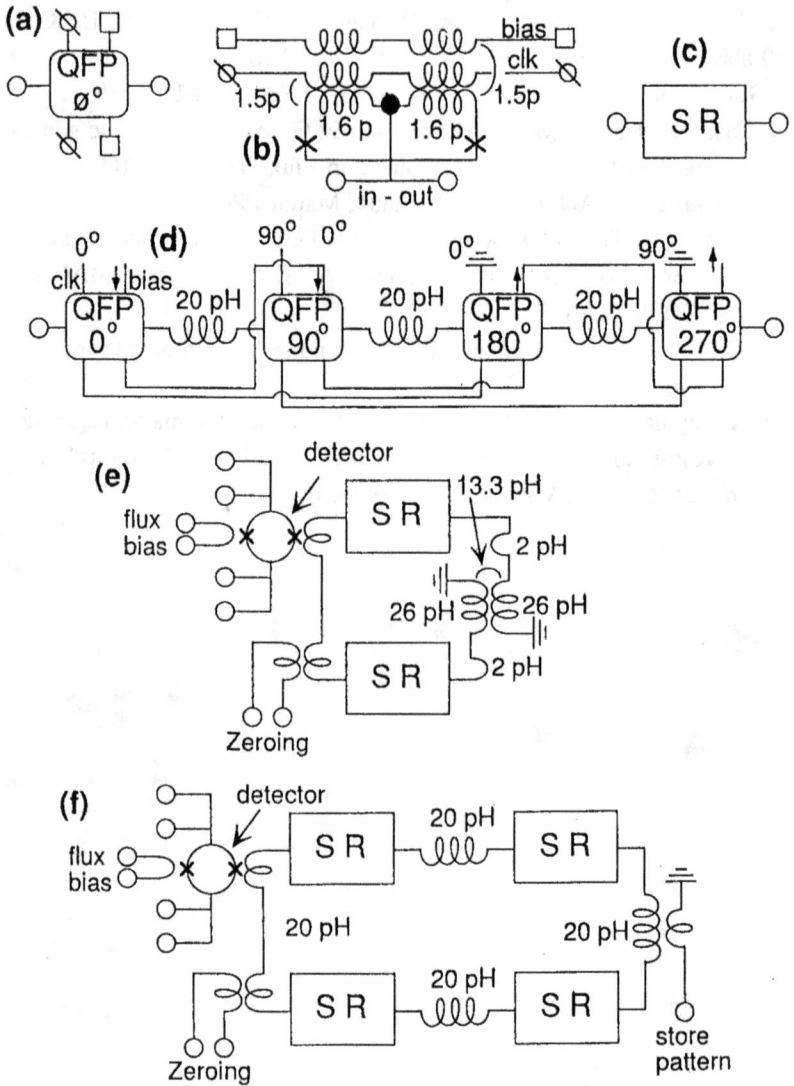

Figure 1: Hierarchical circuit description. (a) QFP symbol, (b) QFP cell (the Josephson junctions' shunting resistance of 4 Ω and self-capacitance of 1 pF are not represented), (c) 1-bit shift register symbol, (d) 1-bit shift register cell. Clock and dc bias lines are shown, (e) frequency divide by four circuit (2-bit shift register). The inductance between two shift registers is always 20 pH to maximize their output current; the "zeroing" line is used to cancel a seed that can eventually be introduced by the detecting dc Squid. (f) 4-bit shift register wired around a closed loop. NOTA: the inductance values indicated in this figure were design targets, experimentally the inductance values that were possible to measure were systematically about 15% below the design value.

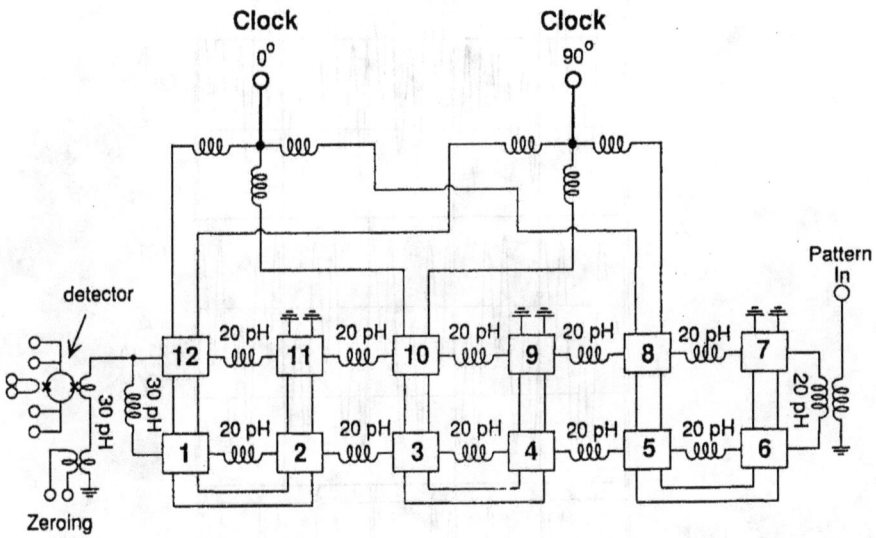

Figure 2: 12-bit shift register. The detecting scheme can be seen on the left. The 12-bit shift register is made by using 48 QFPs. The clock power is applied in parallel by using three inductive branches for each phase. Each clock branch applies the clock to 8 QFPs.

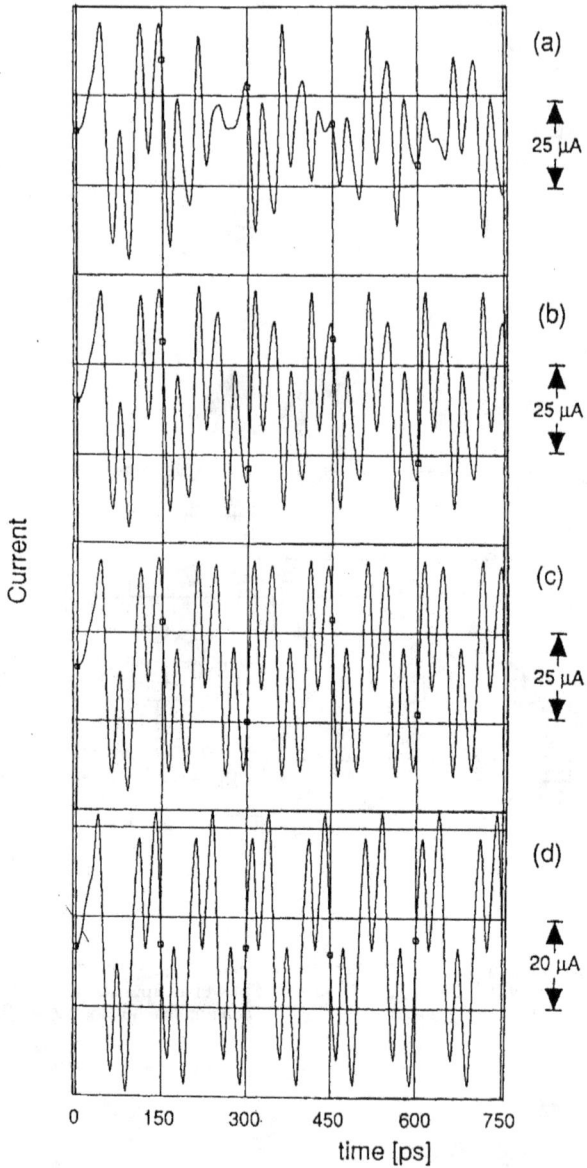

Figure 3: Simulations for the 1-bit shift register (frequency division by two) when operating at 20 GHz. It can be seen that when the Josephson junction self-capacitance is 1.7 or larger, the 1-bit shift register operation is wrong (periodicity with 100 ps period is completely lost). The parameters used for the simulations are: a Josephson junction critical current and shunting resistance of 25 μA and 4 Ω respectively. Josephson junction self-capacitances are: (a) 1.7 pF; (b) 1.6 pF; (c) 1.5 pF and (d) 1 pF.

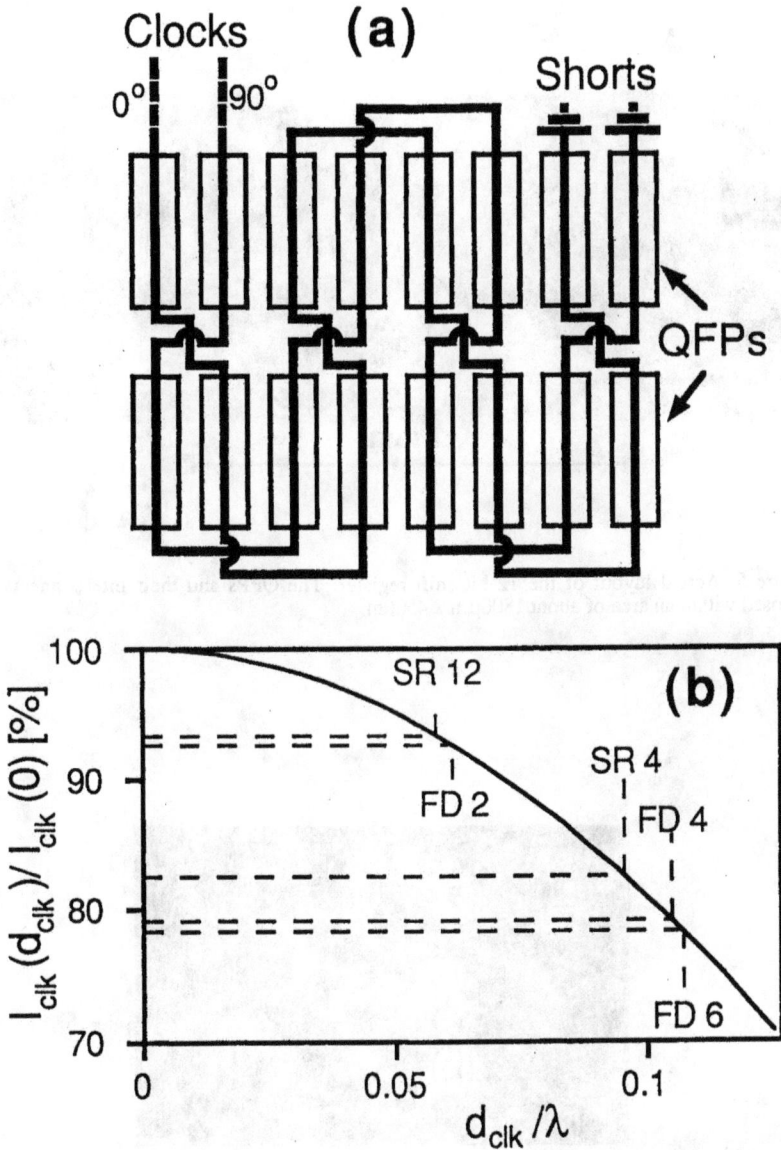

Figure 4: Limitation in frequency by using a standing wave. (a) Schematic layout of the 4-bit shift register. Each clock line meanders through eight QFPs before being shorted. The QFP size including shunting resistors was 180μm x 25μm and the typical separation between adjacent QFPs was 50μm. (b) Clock current amplitude I_{clk} as a function of the distance to the short d_{clk}. FD2, FD4, FD6, SR4 and SR12 show the clock's microstrip line length between the first QFP and the short for the 1, 2, 3, 4 and 12-bit shift registers respectively. The length is normalized by λ, where λ is the wavelength in the microstrip medium corresponding to the maximum operating frequency f_{max} for each circuit.

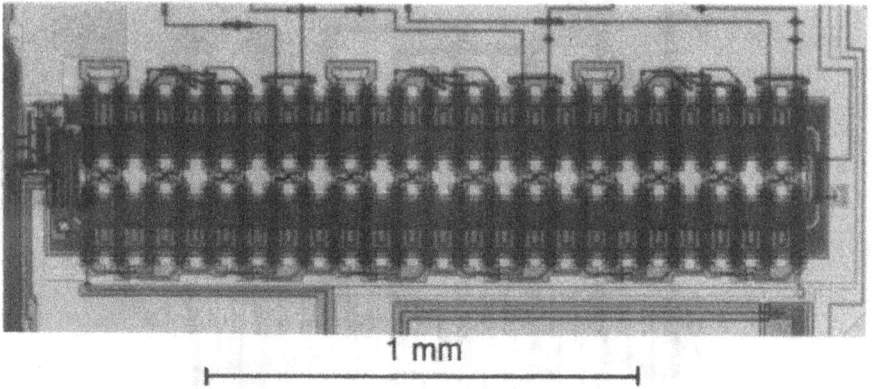

Figure 5: Actual layout of the 12-bit shift register. The QFPs and their interconnects are inclosed within an area of about 1800μm x 450μm.

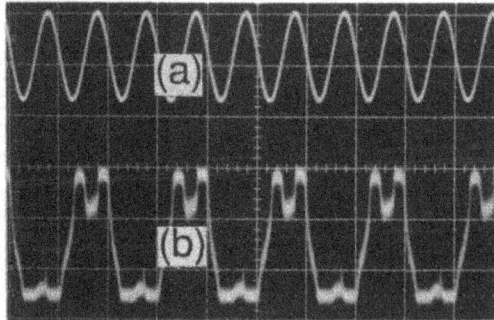

Figure 6: (a) Clock (amplitude is 830 μA peak to peak and frequency is 5 KHz) (b) Typical output waveform for the 1-bit shift register circuit (Vertical scale is 20 μV/Div).

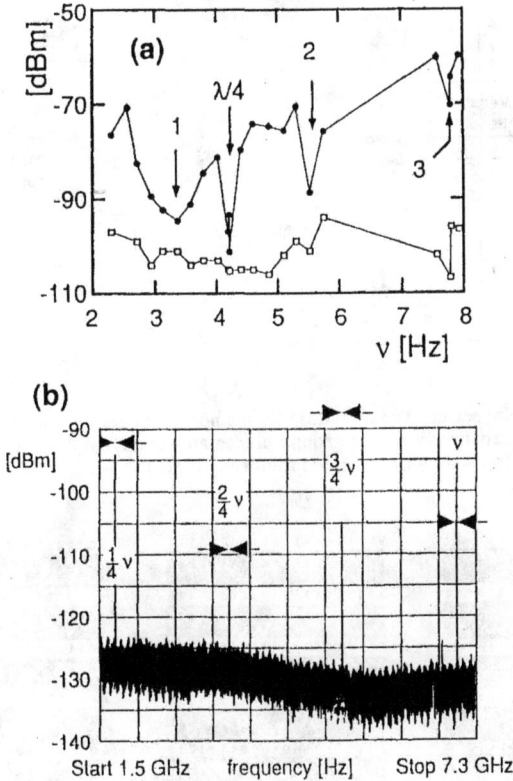

Figure 7: (a) Crosstalk with the clock frequency and output amplitude of the $v/6$ subharmonic versus the clock frequency for the 3-bit shift register. Square dots: amplitude of the $v/6$ subharmonic. Filled dots: Amplitude of the peak with the clock frequency measured at the output of the detecting dc Squid. A sharp minimum labeled "$\lambda/4$" occurs as expected when the current circulating across the wire bonds is minimized. We speculate that the minimums labeled "1", "2" and "3" are due to a resonance in the ceramic chip carrier because of its poor thickness and dielectric constant tolerances. The resonance occurs at frequencies where the ceramic carrier's microstrip length (about 22mm) is $(2\,n + 1)\,\lambda/4$, where n is an integer. At such a frequency a standing wave is built in the chip carrier's microstrip: a minimum in the current amplitude at the coaxial (50Ω)-microstrip (46Ω) transition occurs (i.e. a minimum in the carrier's ground plane voltage oscillations) and the current amplitude is always large at the wire bond because of the low impedance (13Ω) of the microstrip line inside the chip. (b) Output spectra of the 2-bit shift register when operating at 7.003 GHz. Notice that the first subharmonic has a larger amplitude than the peak at the clock frequency v. The marks indicate the peaks amplitude expected from low frequency measurements.

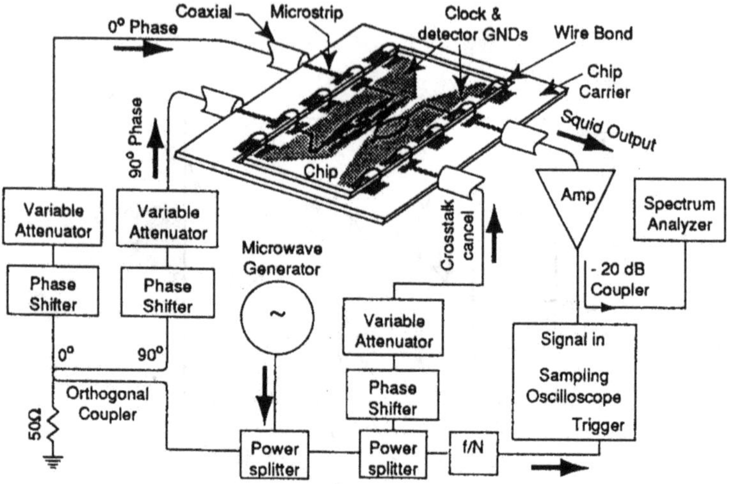

56

Figure 8: Experimental set-up. The chip lies inside a hole of a ceramic carrier. The chip and the ceramic carrier's microstrip lines and ground planes are connected by using wire bonds. The method of reducing crosstalk with the clock frequency is also shown.

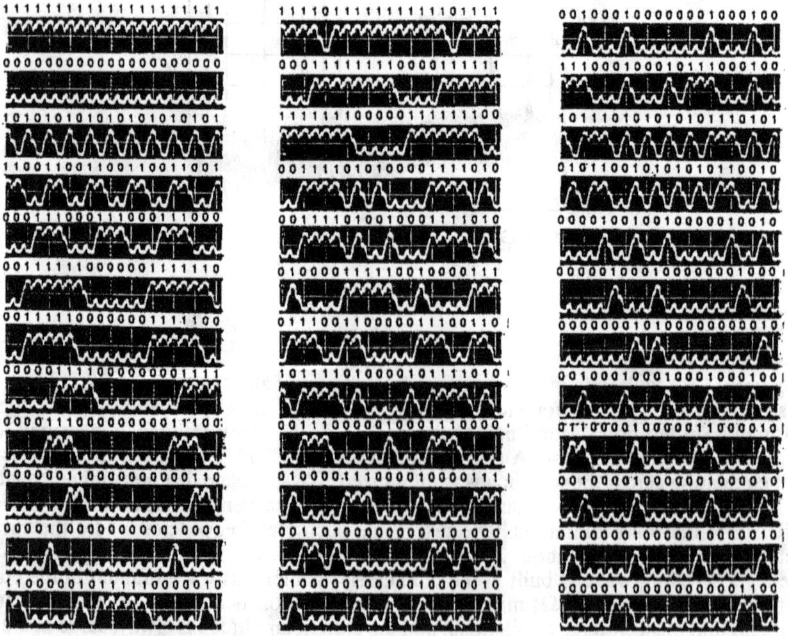

Figure 9: Low frequency testing of the 12-bit shift register. Some of the possible 12-bit logic patterns are shown. It can be seen that any pattern is easily recognized. Periodicity is 12 clock periods. Horizontal scale: 2 clock periods per division; vertical scale: arbitrary.

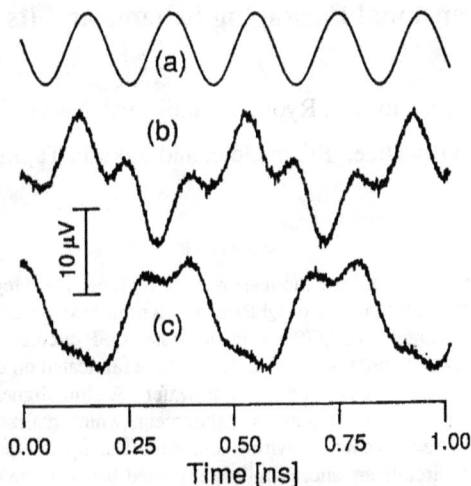

Figure 10: 1-bit shift register. (a) Clock waveform. Frequency is 5 GHz and vertical units are arbitrary.(b) and (c) Output waveform across the detecting dc Squids of two different samples. The periodicity at twice the clock period is clearly seen.

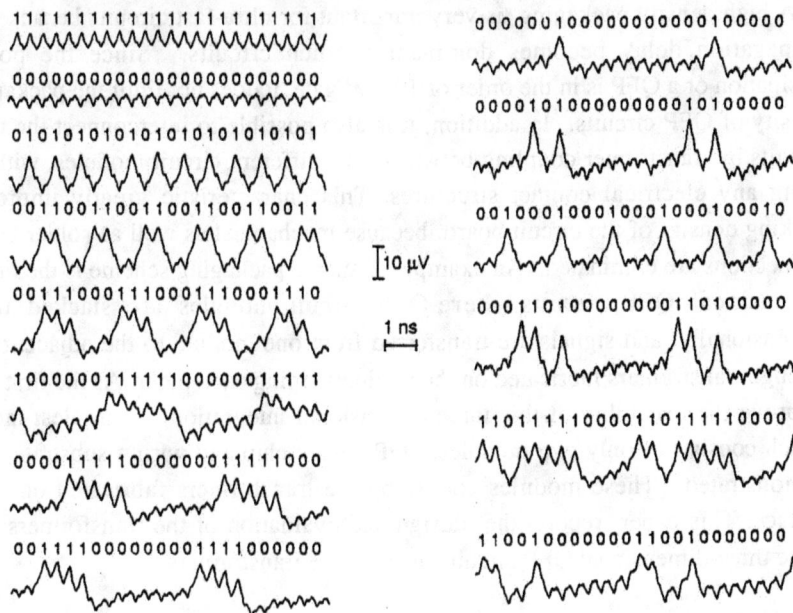

Figure 11: Some 12-bit logic patterns observed across the detecting dc Squid. The clock frequency is 2.4 GHz and the output signal amplitude is at most 20μV. Any of the 12-bit logic patterns is easily recognized. Also a given logic pattern and its complimentary are clearly distinguishable

Three Dimensional Packaging Scheme and its Realization

Mutsumi Hosoya, Ryotaro Kamikawai, Yasuo Wada,

Willy Hioe, Eiichi Goto, and Takeshi Tajima

abstract

As a first step to demonstrate the feasibility of high density integration by the three dimensional integration technology of QFP circuits, a prototype model is fabricated, which consists of a chip mounted on a QFP wiring substrate. QFP circuits are fabricated on the chip and wiring between QFP's and activation lines are fabricated on the wiring substrate, both by the same processing steps on a silicon wafer. A chip aligner is newly designed and constructed for the three dimensional alignment, which realizes less than a 3 μm alignment error between the chip and wiring substrate. The input/output and the activation signals of the QFP circuits are successfully transferred between the chip and the wiring substrate through the transformers.

1. Introduction

A high density packaging is very important for ultra-fast circuits because the propagation delay becomes dominant in such circuits. Since the power dissipation of a QFP is in the order of 10^{-9} W/gate, it does not limit the packaging density of QFP circuits. In addition, it is also possible to interconnect the QFP circuits by transformer coupling between two different circuit modules, without using any electrical contact structures. This characteristic greatly improves packing density of the circuit board, because mechanical as well as solder bump connections are eliminated. An example of such a packaging scheme is the three-dimensional QFP circuits where QFP circuit modules are stacked three dimensionally, and signals are transferred from one module to the adjacent one through transformers fabricated on the modules facing each other. As the first step to prove the feasibility of this three dimensional integration, a simplest model which consists of only two modules, QFP device chip and wiring substrate, was demonstrated. These modules couple by the transformers fabricated on each surface. This paper reports the design and evaluation of the transformers and basic three-dimensional QFP circuits using these transformers.

2. I/O Transformer

In order to transfer I/O signals between two stacked chips, an efficient transformer is necessary. Because the coupling tightness strongly depends on the gap between windings, a hole in a groundplane is required to increase the coupling in the case of a large gap such as three dimensional coupling. The following considers two kinds of closely coupled transformers to be used for the I/O transformers of QFPs.

2.1 U-type transformer

Figure 1 (a) shows the structure of a U-type transformer, which consists of two (or more) 'U'-shaped windings over a groundplane hole. An optional groundplane over these windings are sometimes used so as to reduce the leakage inductance. The numerical calculation shows [1] that if $r>3$, the self inductance of each winding is given by

$$L_s = 1.25\mu_0 d \,, \tag{1}$$

where, d is the size of the hole, r is the ratio shown in Fig. 1 (a), and μ_0 is the permeability. It is interesting to see the fact that $\mu_0 d$ is the inductance of a circular hole with diameter d in an infinitely large conductive plane, and the coefficient $1.25 = 4/\pi$ is the area ratio of a square hole and a circle hole. The leakage flux stored between the two windings weakens the coupling. Numerical analysis also shows that the leakage inductance between these two windings is well approximated by

$$L_l = 1.25 \frac{\mu_0 \pi g}{\log r}, \tag{2}$$

where g is the gap distance which includes London penetration depths of upper and lower windings. Again $L_l/1.25$ gives the leakage inductance in the case of circular windings. Eq. (1) and (2) give the coupling characteristics between two U-type windings.

The inductances of U-type closely coupled transformer composed of three windings were measureed by the dc-SQUID shown in Fig. 2 (a). This dc-SQUID has actually the same structure as a U-type QFP discussed later except for smaller damping resistances. L_1+M_{12}, L_2+M_{12}, and $M_{13}+M_{23}$ can be easily obtained by applying current to each winding selectively, and examining the flux modulation of the SQUID, where L_i is the self inductance of winding i and M_{ij} is the mutual inductance between winding i and j. L_1-M_{12} or L_2-M_{12} give the leakage inductance between windings 1 and 2, because it is given by the leakage flux when the unit current flows windings 1 and 2 in the opposite directions. If $M_{12} \approx M_{23} \approx M_{13}$ is assumed, coupling characteristics between windings 1 and 2 can be calculated. The winding 3 is sometimes fabricated on the wiring substrate (L_0 in Fig. 2 (b)). The flux modulation measured by the circuit shown in Fig. 2 (b) is $(M_{20}+M_{30})^2 / (2L_0 + L_{ref})$, where L_{ref} is the stripline inductance whose value is already known. Therefore, if the modulation is measured by changing L_{ref} (and $M_{10} \approx M_{20}$ is assumed), the coupling between the chip and the wiring substrate can be obtained. The results are summarized in Table 1.

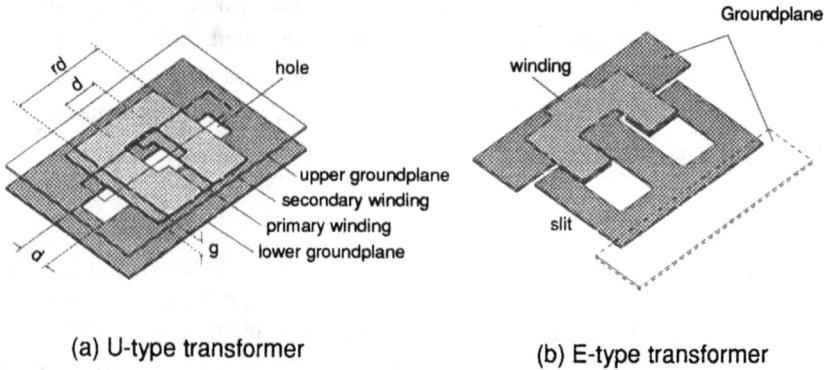

(a) U-type transformer   (b) E-type transformer

Fig. 1 Schematic structure of I/O transformer

2.2 E-type transformer

One of the biggest problem of a U-type transformer is a flux-trapping in the groundplane hole under a U-type transformer. To alleviate this problem, a groundplane slit may be used instead of a hole. However, if a slit is used, the transformer over the slit senses the ambient field through the slit. An E-type transformer shown in Fig. 1 (b) cancels the average ambient field through the slit. It is composed of two U-type windings which are connected to cancel the uniform field which passes through both holes. Because of its structure, the self and leakage inductances of E-windings are about one half of those of U-windings. The inductances of the E-type closely coupled transformer composed of three windings were measured by the same method discussed in 2.1. The results are summarized in Table 1.

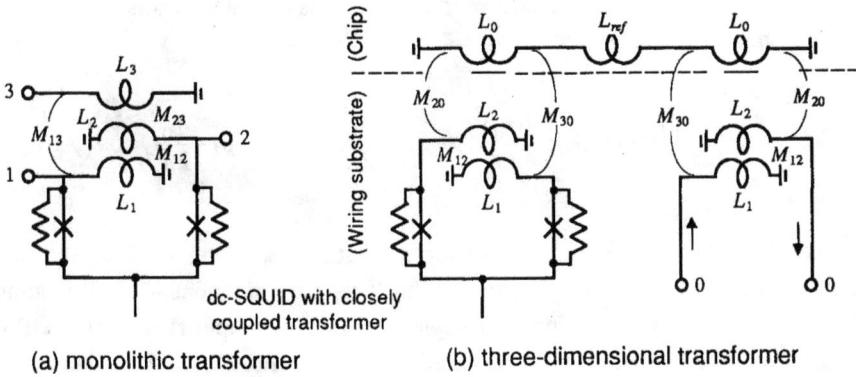

(a) monolithic transformer

(b) three-dimensional transformer

Fig. 2 Circuit to measure the coupling characteristics of the I/O transformer

	U-type	E-type
d	25 μm	35 μm
r	3	1.9
g_{12}	0.5μm	0.5μm
L_1	38.6pH	33.7pH
L_2	37.1pH	29.5pH
M_{12}	34.2pH	25.3pH
Eq.(1)	39.3pH	27.5pH
L_1-M	4.4pH	8.4pH
L_2-M	2.9pH	3.8pH
Eq.(2)	2.2pH	1.9pH
L_0	30.2pH	27.6pH
M_{10}/M_{20}	25.5pH	19.6pH

Table 1. Coupling characteristics of I/O transformer

3. I/O Type QFP

A circuit diagram of an I/O-type QFP is shown in Fig. 3, which contains a closely coupled transformer discussed above inside a QFP. A QFP of this type is mainly used to transfer signals between two stacked chips.

The normal behavior of the QFP may be analyzed from its quasi-static states, which are obtained from the equilibrium conditions of the Hamiltonian of the circuit. When the I/O transformer in Fig. 3 is an ideal transformer, the Hamiltonian is given by

$$U = \frac{1}{2L_a}\left(\frac{\Phi_0}{2\pi}\right)^2(\theta - \alpha)^2 + \frac{1}{2L_d}\left(\frac{\Phi_0}{2\pi}\right)^2(\phi - \beta)^2 - \frac{\Phi_0}{2\pi}I_J\cos(\phi - \theta) - \frac{\Phi_0}{2\pi}I_J\cos(\phi + \theta),$$

$$(3)$$

where L_a is the self inductance of the activation transformer, L_d is the load inductance, I_c is the critical current of the Josephson junctions, ϕ is the output flux angle, α is the activation flux angle, and β is the input flux angle. A flux angle is defined as the flux normalized by $\Phi_0/2\pi$. Eq. (3) is the same as the Hamiltonian of a conventional QFP [2,3]. Therefore, its behavior is the same as that of the conventional QFP.

An actual I/O transformer has a small leakage inductance and a finite shunt inductance. The shunt inductance can be considered as the inductance connected to the load in parallel. (The shunt inductance used now is four times of the standard load inductance.) The small leakage inductance does not affect the operation seriously as shown below. Actually, in Fig. 2, if $L_1 - M_{12} = L_J z(1 + \delta z)$, and $L_2 - M_{12} = L_J z(1 - \delta z)$, then the increase of the Hamiltonian (3) caused by these inductances are

$$\Delta U \approx -\frac{\Phi_0}{2\pi}I_J\frac{z}{2}(\cos 2\theta \cos 2\phi - \delta z \sin 2\theta \sin 2\phi), \qquad (4)$$

where $L_J = \Phi_0 / (2\pi I_J)$, and $z \ll 1$ is assumed. Therefore, the output current is given by

$$\frac{2\pi}{\Phi_0}\frac{\partial(U + \Delta U)}{\partial \phi} \approx I_J(2\cos\theta \sin\phi - z\cos 2\theta \sin 2\phi - z\delta z \sin 2\theta \cos 2\phi). \qquad (5)$$

When I_J is 25μA, L_J is 13.2pH, therefore, z / δz are 0.28 / 0.21 for U-type, and 0.48 / 0.33 for E-type, respectively. Therefore, the second and the third terms of Eq. (5) do not affect the output current seriously.

4. Three Dimensional Integration Technology

In order to demonstrate the feasibility of the three dimensional integration described in Introduction, three-dimensional QFP circuits shown in Fig. 3 were fabricated, and tested. Advanced technologies were applied, by which the chip was accurately aligned and glued on the wiring substrate, to actually construct the prototype model described above. This section briefly describes the outline of the three dimensional integration technologies and the three dimensional aligner utilized in the alignment .

4.1 Three dimensional integration procedure

The general approach of the prototype three dimensional integration is illustrated in Fig. 4. The chip and wiring substrate are bonded face-to-face, that is, with their

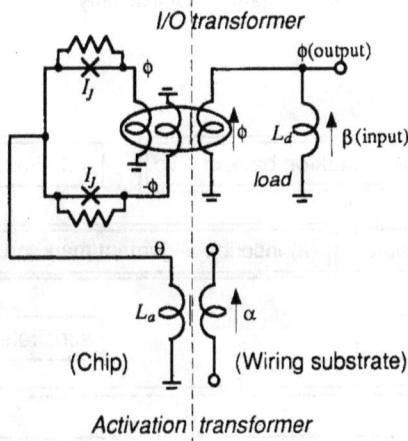

Fig. 3 Schematic diagram of I/O type QFP

fabricated circuitry facing each other. The chip is correctly positioned over the substrate with the aid of alignment marks formed on the backside of the chip, then glue is applied and the two modules are pressed to bond together [5]. To achieve this, process steps as also illustrated in Fig. 4 are employed in addition to conventional circuit fabrication processes. Those steps are summarized below.

(1) Form alignment marks on the front side of the wiring substrate
    During the QFP fabrication process, alignment marks are formed on the front surface of the wiring substrate with the same metal layer as the transformer layer to reduce the coupling loss arising from the alignment error between the chip and the wiring substrate.

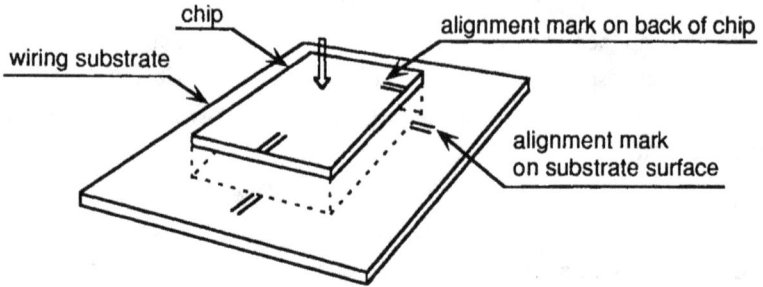

General approach of assembly

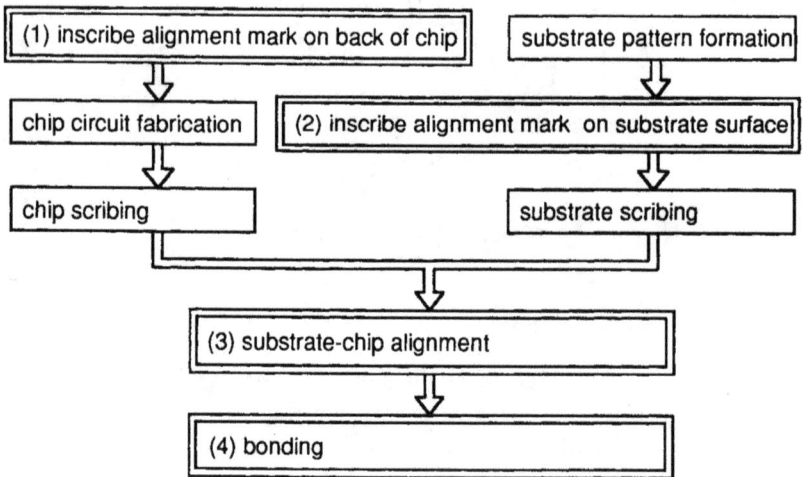

Basic model process steps

Fig. 4 Schematic figure of three dimensional integration and process

(2) Form alignment marks on the backside of the chip

With a commercially available double-sided mask aligner, alignment marks are formed on the backside of the chip by etching the silicon dioxide layer, with an alignment accuracy of about 3 μm.

(3) Substrate-chip alignment

With the use of the alignment marks on the chip and the wiring substrate, these QFP devices and wirings were bonded face to face, by bringing chip and wiring substrate into precise alignment. To realize the degree of precision needed, an assembly system, three dimensional aligner, was newly designed and fabricated. Advanced technologies, such as precise vertical movement and dual sight field microscope, were adapted for the machine [4].

(4) Bonding

Once the chip is in proper alignment with the wiring substrate, they were bonded together at an appropriate temperature and pressure. The adhesive to be used for the bonding must satisfy three fundamental criteria: it must provide good even coverage, it must withstand temperatures ranging from liquid helium to room temperature, and it must be free of dust particles and contaminants. Through preliminary testing, we determined that AZ-photo resist, cyanide-type adhesives and epoxy-type adhesives satisfy all these requirements.

Through the complete sequence of steps (1)-(4), we have sought to achieve an overall horizontal alignment accuracy on the order of ±5 μm. The alignment accuracy of the three dimensional aligner was designed to be ±3 μm, while the alignment accuracies of the device fabrication process and double-sided alignment were both ±3 μm.

4.2 Chip alignment system and alignment process

Since the three dimensional integration is a newly developed concept, no aligner was available to achieve the necessary processing. Therefore, an alignment system was newly designed and constructed to achieve the three dimensional alignment of the chip and the wiring substrate. The functional requirements of the aligner are summarized in the following specifications.

(1) Horizontal alignment accuracy   : ±3 μm

(2) Chip size	: 2 mm x 5 mm to 3 mm x 5 mm
(3) Wiring substrate size	: 5 mm x 7.5 mm to 10 mm x 20 mm
(4) Minimum space between chips	: 0.1 mm
(5) Thickness of chip and substrate	: 470 μm (±20 μm)
(6) Temperature control	: room temperature to 80°C
(7) Package assembly pressure	: 10-300 g

In order to achieve these functional specifications, the aligner was equipped with the mechanical functions such as individual x, y and θ movement of the both stages, very accurate z movement of the whole stage and dual sight field microscope [4]. The three dimensional integration process is made up of the following steps.

(a) Align the chip and the wiring substrate independently with the aligner by observing the alignment marks on those chips with the dual sight field microscope. Thus the chip and the wiring substrate are aligned with each other.

(b) Lift the chip and put it on the wiring substrate, then re-align the chip and wiring substrate by vertically moving those chips by getting the best focus.

(c) After good alignment is achieved, press the chip to the wiring substrate with some glue between them. Heat-up the chips, if necessary, to adhere firmly.

A photograph of the three dimensional aligner is shown in Fig. 5. The aligner is set in a clean bench during the actual use, in order to avoid possible dust contamination from the ambient air. The prototype three dimensional circuits consist of a silicon chip mounted on a silicon wiring substrate, where QFP circuits are fabricated on the chip, and wiring between QFPs and activation lines are fabricated on the wiring substrate. The chip is positioned within 3 μm lateral error over the wiring substrate, then pressure is applied to bond the two elements together , as shown in Fig. 6. The chip and the wiring substrate couple by the transformers fabricated on each surface. A U- or E-type transformer is used for the closely coupled I/O transformer of a QFP. Simple stripline transformers are used for the activation transformers, because the activation current is given from the outside, so the coupling of the activation transformer may be weak.

5. Results and Discussions

Shown in Fig. 7 is an example of the operations of these circuits, which are described by Eq. (3) and (4). The output flux is measured by a dc-SQUID [3]. The crosstalk between the activation line and the QFP is negligible.

Because the I/O-type QFP includes a closely coupled I/O transformer in it, signal inversion and the three-dimensional packaging scheme can be easily achieved. On the other hand, the I/O transformer occupies a large area, and some of the output flux is lost in the transformer shunt inductance.

If a flux quantum is trapped near the I/O transformer, the distribution of the magnet field along a groundplane slit has a gradient. In such a case, although an E-type transformer cancels the uniform field, the transformer senses the field gradient, which shifts the zero-point of the QFP, because the sensed field is equivalent to an input of the QFP. A flux-transfer device like a QFP requires a good magnetic shielding. The level of stray magnetic field permissible should satisfy the equation

$$S \cdot B < \Phi_0/2, \tag{6}$$

where B is the stray flux density and S is the surface area of a chip. For a 5mm by 5mm chip, B should be less than 0.4 μGauss.

The prototype model discussed earlier is the first step to three-dimensional QFP circuits. To achieve couplings between many chips, technologies to fabricate circuits on both sides, to connect them through a chip, and to align more than two chips should be developed.

5. Conclusion

1. U- and E-type transformers to be used for the I/O of QFPs are studied. The characteristics of these transformers are obtained analytically and confirmed experimentally.

2. QFPs with U- or E-type I/O transformer are fabricated, and tested successfully. Basic three-dimensional circuits by these QFPs are demonstrated.

3. In order to demonstrate the prototype three dimensional integrated circuit, an aligner was newly designed and fabricated, with an alignment accuracy of ±3 μm.

4. The three dimensional integration technology demonstrated here would lead to the future high density ultra-fast computer packaging technology.

References

[1] M. Hosoya, E. Goto, N. Shimizu and Y. Harada, "Inductance Calculation System for Superconducting Circuits," *IEEE Trans. Magnetics,* <u>MAG-25 (2)</u>, 1111-1114, (1989).

[2] Y. Harada, H. Nakane, N. Miyamoto, U. Kawabe, E. Goto and T. Soma, "Basic Operation of Quantum Flux Parametron," *IEEE Trans. Magnetics,* <u>MAG-23(2)</u>, 3801-3807, (1987).

[3] N. Shimizu, Y. Harada, N. Miyamoto and E. Goto, "Fundamental Characteristics of the QFP Measured by the dc-SQUID," *IEEE Trans. Electron Devices,* ED-36(6), 1175-1181 (1989).

[4] T.Tajima, Y. Wada and R. Kamikawai, "Design and evaluation of QFP Three Dimensional Packaging Aligner," *RIKEN Symposium on Josephson Electronics*, 129-136, (1991), (RIKEN, Saitama, Japan). (in Japanese)

[5] *Issues in Josephson Supercomputer Design*, E. Goto and K. F. Loe (Edts), World Scientific, Singapore (1990).

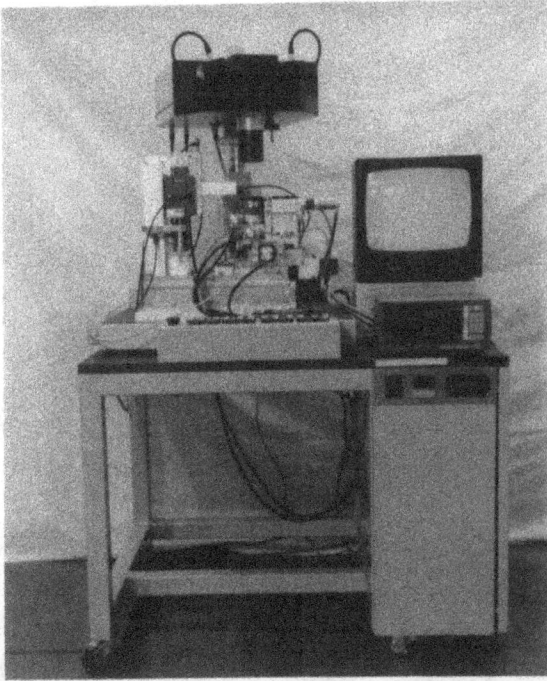

Fig. 5 Photograph of the three dimensional alignment system

Fig. 6 Photograph of the prototype three dimensional integration circuits

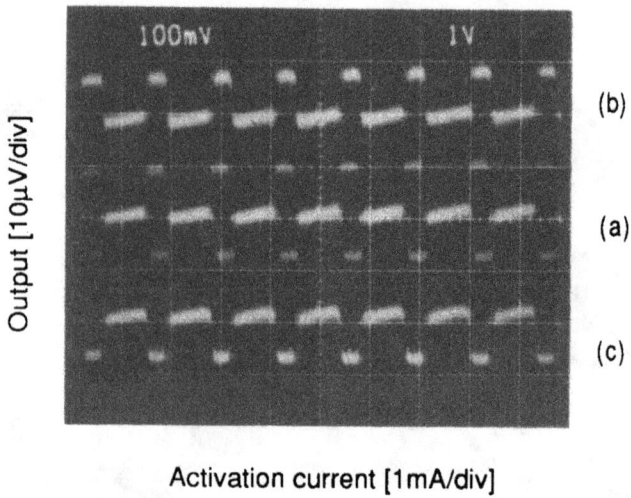

Fig. 7   Example of the operation of three-dimensional QFP

© 1992 IEEE. Reprinted, with permission, from
IEEE Trans. Appl. Superconductivity, 2(1) (1992).

High-speed Experiments on a QFP-based Comparator for ADCs with 18 GHz Sample Rate and 5 GHz Input Frequency

Yutaka Harada and Jonathan B. Green

Abstract

We report the high-speed operation of a superconducting comparator circuit, based on coupling the quantum flux parametron (QFP) to an rf SQUID, which can be used to build a flash-type analog-to-digital converter (ADC). Simulations of this circuit show that it is expected to achieve multigigaherts operation beyond that obtainable with either conventional semiconductor or voltage-state superconducting devices. A QFP-based comparator fabricated with a process using NbN/Pb-alloy Josephson junctions of 5 by 5 mm and a current density of 100 A/cm^2 has been examined to evaluate the properties of the QFP-ADC. Analog-to-digital conversion has been observed with a QFP activation frequency up to 18.2 GHz. Employing a sampling method, input signals with frequencies up to 5.4 GHz have also been digitized. These experimental results suggest that a multibit QFP-ADC would be capable of high-speed performance.

1. Introduction

The quantum flux parametron (QFP) is a novel switching device with excellent properties. Over the past several years many demonstrations of the QFP have been reported [1-8]. In one demonstration a 1/2 frequency divider circuit was built to evaluate the high-speed characteristics of the QFP. Operation of this circuit up to 16.2 GHz was observed [6,7]. In this paper we demonstrate that the QFP may also be used to construct a superconducting analog-to-digital converter (ADC) system.

Previously, low-speed operation of a 4-bit QFP-ADC has been demonstrated [2,5]. This 4-bit QFP-ADC consisted of a resistive ladder network coupled to four identical QFP comparators. In this device the input signal current was divided by two at every branch of the ladder network, with each branch current being passed to a QFP comparator. In this configuration the QFP comparator was the key device for the QFP-ADC. Functioning on the principles of single flux quantum devices, the QFP-ADC has a higher operating speed than do voltage-state superconductive devices [9-11]. Simulation results have shown that the QFP-ADC can achieve high-frequency sampling up to 20 GHz and a wide input bandwidth up to 5 GHz with a coarse 5-mm lithography technology and a low supercurrent density of 100 A/cm^2 [2].

2. Operating principles and circuit design

The 4-bit circuit reported previously was not optimized for operation or testing at high-speed. We have recently fabricated and tested the components of a 3-bit converter which was designed for high-speed operation and testing. Similar to before [2,5], in this circuit each QFP-based comparator is built with an rf SQUID, a QFP and a dc SQUID as shown in Fig. 1. As is well known, the rf SQUID is composed of a Josephson junction and an inductor in a superconducting closed loop. Magnetic flux passing through the superconducting loop results in a circulating current in the loop whose direction changes periodically with magnetic flux changes of one-half flux quantum. This operation corresponds to quantization of the analog input signal, converting the analog signal to digital signals in units of the flux quantum. The resulting current in the superconducting loop is sampled with an activation current applied to the QFP [2]. The output current of the QFP flows into a load inductor. The direction of the current in the QFP load inductor is determined by the direction of current flow in the rf SQUID at the moment of activation. The output current of the QFP is detected and transformed to a voltage signal at the output of the dc SQUID. In this comparator, the digitized signal current is sampled at the rising edge of the activation current and amplified at the QFP. The QFP output signal is latched as long as the activation current is applied.

The device parameters have been chosen for compatibility with a NbN/Pb-alloy Josephson-junction process with current density of $100 \, A/cm^2$ [1]. The critical current of the QFP Josephson junctions is designed to be 49 mA using a junction size of 7 by 7 mm. A fundamental property of the QFP is that its output current in the activated state is dependent on the input current present at the moment of activation. In order to minimize this effect the Josephson junction in the rf SQUID is chosen to be of the minimum-size (5 by 5 mm) with a critical current of 25 mA. The mutual inductance of the QFP activation transformer is 3 pH which results in an activation current of 0.7 mA. The QFP load inductance of 20 pH satisfies the QFP load condition described in [3].

In order to broaden the input bandwidth, the input inductor is designed to be as small as possible (0.8 pH). No damping resistor is connected to the Josephson junction of the rf SQUID, as the L-C resonance in the rf SQUID is adequately damped by the effect of the attached QFP. The output of the rf SQUID is predicted to be periodic for increases of analog input signal current of 2.5 mA. The complete integrated circuit for the QFP comparator is designed with separate grounds to isolate the current paths of the input signal, the activation signal and the output signal. This reduces crosstalk noise in the measured output signal.

3. Experiments

A photomicrograph of a single fabricated QFP-based comparator is shown in Fig. 2. As stated previously, this was part of a 3-bit ADC. Instrumentation limitations prevented us from evaluating all 3 bits simultaneously. Therefore, in evaluating a single QFP comparator, we focused on two characteristics necessary for high-speed operation: high sampling rate and wide input bandwidth. Because the output signal detected with the dc SQUID is very small (on the order of 10 mV), thermal noise in the room-temperature detection amplifiers makes the observation of high-speed operation difficult. Additionally, the high-frequency crosstalk noise arising from both the activation signal and the input signal also disturb the small-signal measurements. Hence, we examined the operating characteristics at 1-MHz bandwidth without observing the high-frequency phenomena directly.

The high-sampling-rate demonstration used a high-frequency activation signal. The sampling operation occurred during each activation period. The input signal was swept using a low frequency triangle wave of 50 Hz while a high-frequency sinusoidal signal up to 18.2 GHz was applied as the activation signal. The output signal was observed with a 1-MHz amplifier, which filtered the crosstalk from the high-frequency activation signal. Figure 3 shows the results of this measurement illustrating the relationship between the input signal and the QFP output signal demonstrating analog-to-digital conversion. Two cases are shown, for the activation frequency of 1 MHz in Fig. 3(a) and 18.2 GHz in Fig. 3(b). Three traces are displayed in Fig. 3(a), the upper trace representing the activation signal of 1 MHz, the middle trace representing the input signal of 50 Hz and the lower trace representing the output signal of the QFP comparator. The horizontal deflection of the oscilloscope is controlled by the input signal amplitude. The lower trace shows the "0" and "1" output signals varying periodically in accordance with the input signal for levels between -4.3 to 4.3 mA. This result illustrates successful analog-to-digital conversion.

Figure 3(b) shows two traces, the input signal from -5.7 to 5.7 mA and the output signal obtained with an activation frequency of 18.2 GHz. Both output signals in Fig. 3(a) and (b) are identical indicating the conversion period equal to 2.5 mA, our original design value. We did not detect any failures in conversion for this high-speed operation. The high-speed experiment was limited by the frequency range of the microwave synthesizer (with an upper frequency of 18 GHz) in addition to the limited bandwidth of the SMA connectors which were used. Judging from the experiment, we expect successful high-frequency operation at more than 18.2 GHz.

In order to examine the maximum allowable input bandwidth, we employed the sampling scheme illustrated in Fig. 4. In this scheme, the microwave signal is employed as the input analog signal and the pulse signal is used for QFP activation. Here, the microwave synthesizer and the synthesized pulse generator used a common 10-MHz reference oscillator in order to synchronize their output waveforms. The activation pulse waveform had a sharp leading edge with an 80-ps risetime. With the arrangement shown in Fig. 4 the position of this activation pulse edge could be set at a precise point with respect to the phase of the high-frequency analog input signal. This relative phasing could be adjusted by a variable delay line. The activation pulse repetition rate was set equal to 100 KHz so that the output signal could easily be observed with a 1-MHz amplifier. The amplitude of the microwave signal was modulated at a 1-KHz rate using a triangular sweep signal. This triangular waveform directly controlled the amplitude of the high-frequency input signal. The experimental results are therefore expressed as the relationship between the sweep signal for the input signal and the output signal.

Figure 5 shows the experimental results obtained using an input signal frequencies of 50 MHz and 5.4 GHz. Two traces are shown for the 50-MHz case in Fig. 5(a). The upper trace represents the input signal with 90% amplitude modulation from 11.2 to 1 mA, while the lower trace shows the output signal of the QFP comparator which indicates a sequence of "1, 0, 1, 0" showing successful analog-to-digital conversion. Figure 5(b) shows four traces of the output signal at 5.4 GHz with the input amplitude modulation of 0.3 to 3 mA. The leading edge of the activation pulse is delayed by 16 ps for every succeeding trace. The output signals show a combination of "0" and "1" signals indicating that analog-to-digital conversion is occurring. For the 5.4 GHz input signal measurement the 80-ps risetime of the activation waveform causes the output "0" and "1" values to sometimes be overlapping in the output waveform. The first and second traces show a sequence of "0, 1, 0", the third trace shows the sequence of "0/1, 1", and the fourth trace shows "1". Here, the designation "0/1" refers to the overlapped period of "1' and "0".

It may be noticed that the period of the analog-to-digital conversion is modified and that the output polarity is inverted as the relative phasing between the activation pulse and the input waveform is changed. This is exactly as one would expect when the position of the activation pulse edge is moved from the negative part of the input microwave signal through zero to the positive part. We have confirmed the periodicity of the output signal at approximately 190-ps delay intervals, which correspond to the period of the 5.4-GHz input signal.

In this experiment, it is also noticed that a crosstalk signal from the input waveform picked up by the dc SQUID disturbs the output observation. In particular, the crosstalk signal moves the operating point of the dc SQUID and destroys the ability to perform an accurate measurement. For this reason we did not apply a large input signal to observe a long alternating "1, 0, 1", sequence at the output. We therefore were not able to experimentally confirm our simulation results which predicted that converters based on this design should be able to digitize analog waveforms to at least 4-bit accuracy for 4-GHz input signals. Reduction of this crosstalk signal is important to building a fully functional multibit QFP-ADC.

4. Summary

As mentioned above, operation of the QFP-based analog-to-digital converter cannot be properly assessed using non-hysteretic dc SQUIDs at the output. The thermal noise of the necessary broadband room-temperature amplifiers would overwhelm the very small output of these non-hysteretic SQUIDs. A better design would be to use an output stage which provides higher voltage outputs, such as hysteretic dc SQUIDs as are found in conventional latching logic superconductive circuits. However, a disadvantage of these devices is associated with the necessity to reset such dc SQUIDs after each readout operation.

Nonetheless, we have examined a comparator based on the quantum flux parametron for a flash-type ADC for high-speed operation. The QFP-based comparator was fabricated with a NbN/Pb-alloy Josephson junction process with a minimum junction size of 5 by 5 mm and a current density of 100 A/cm^2. Analog-to-digital conversion operations at a high sampling rate have been observed with a QFP activation frequency of up to 18.2 GHz. By employing a sampling method, the input frequency bandwidth up to 5.4 GHz has also been examined. These experimental results illustrate that high-speed performance can be achieved by a QFP-based ADC.

Acknowledgements

The authors gratefully acknowledge the support by Prof. E. Goto, Dr. Y. Wada, and Dr. R. Kamikawai. The QFP integrated circuits were fabricated by the Hitachi Central Research Laboratory, Hitachi, Ltd.

References

[1] Y.Harada, N.Nakane, N.Miyamoto, U.Kawabe, E.Goto and T.Soma, "Basic operation of the Quantum Flux Parametron," *IEEE Trans. Magn.* **MAG-23**, 3801 (1987).

[2] N.Shimizu, Y.Harada, N.Miyamoto and E.Goto, "A New A/D Converter with Quantum Flux Parametron," *IEEE Trans. Magn.* **MAG-25**, 865 (1989).

[3] N.Shimizu, Y.Harada, N.Miyamoto, M.Hosoya and E.Goto, "Fundamental Characteristics of the QFP measured by the DC SQUID," *IEEE Trans. Electron Devices* **36**, 1175 (1989).

[4] Y.Harada, W.Hioe and E.Goto, "Flux Transfer Devices," *Proc. IEEE* **77**, 1280 (1989).

[5] Y.Harada, "Superconducting Analog to Digital Convertor," *US Patent* 4,956,642 September 11, 1990.

[6] J.Casas, R.Kamikawai, Y.Harada, N.Miyamoto, H.Nakane and E.Goto, "Subharmonic Generators and Error Detection by Using the Quantum Flux Parametron(QFP)," *IEEE Trans. Magn.* **MAG-27**, 2851 (1991).

[7] J.Casas, R.Kamikawai and E.Goto, "High Speed QFP Testing," *Proc. 8th RIKEN-ERATO Symposium*, pp.121-127, March 1991.

[8] Y.Harada, W.Hioe and E.Goto, "Quantum Flux Parametron with Magnetic Flux Regulator," *IEEE Trans. Appl. Superconduct.* **1**, 90 (1991).

[9] C.Hamilton, F.Lloyd, and R.Kautz, "Superconducting A/D converter using latching comparators," *IEEE Trans. Magn.* **MAG-21**, 197 (1985).

[10] E.Fang, D.Hebert, and T.VanDuzer, "A Multi-Gigahertz Josephson Flash A/D Converter with a pipelined Encoder Using Large-Dynamic-Range Current-Latch Comparators," *IEEE Trans. Magn.* **MAG-27**, 2891 (1991).

[11] P.Bradley, "Quasi-one junction SQUIDs as Comparators for Analog-to-Digital Conversion," *IEEE Trans. Magn.* **MAG-27**, 2895 (1991).

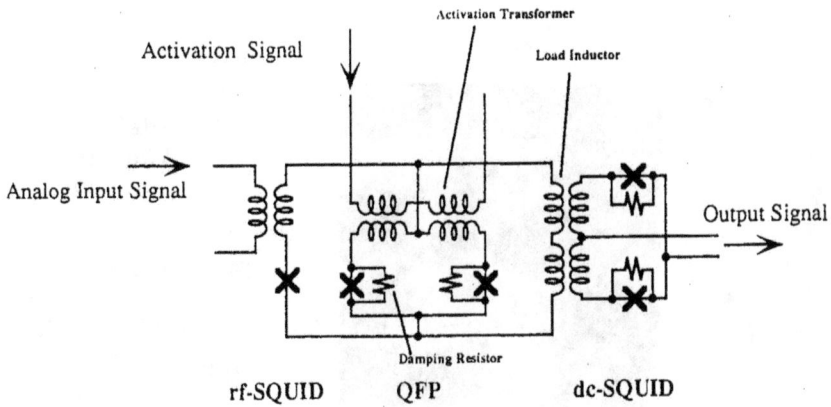

Fig. 1 Circuit diagram of the QFP comparator.

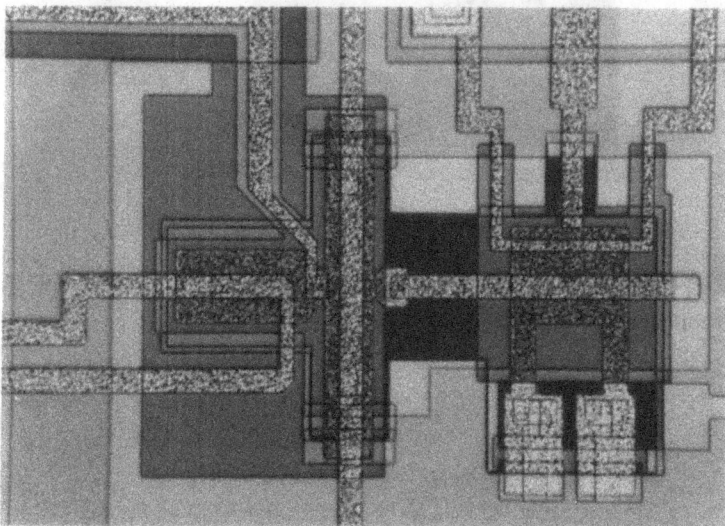

Fig.2 Fabricated QFP comparator with the NbN/Pb-alloy Josephson junction process.

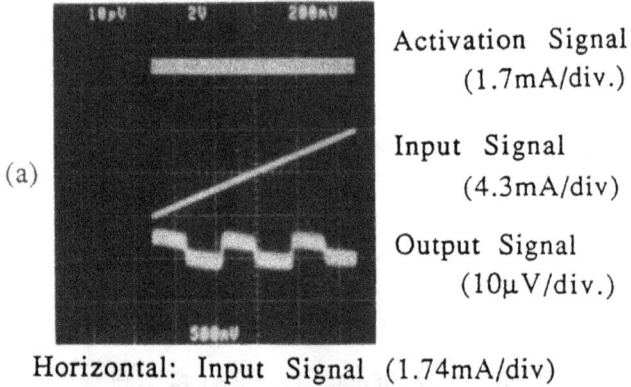

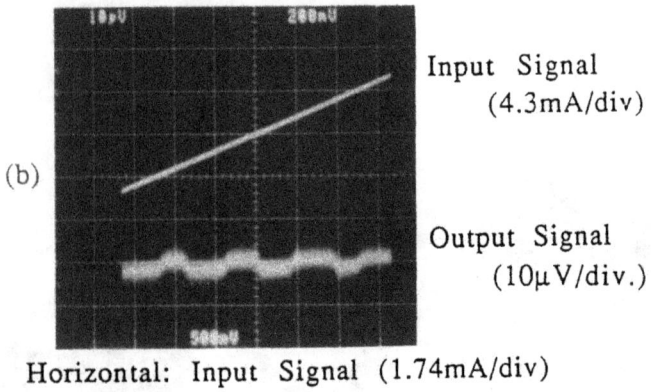

Fig.3 Experimental results on the high-speed sampling measurement for sampling frequencies of (a) 1 MHz and (b) 18.2 GHz.

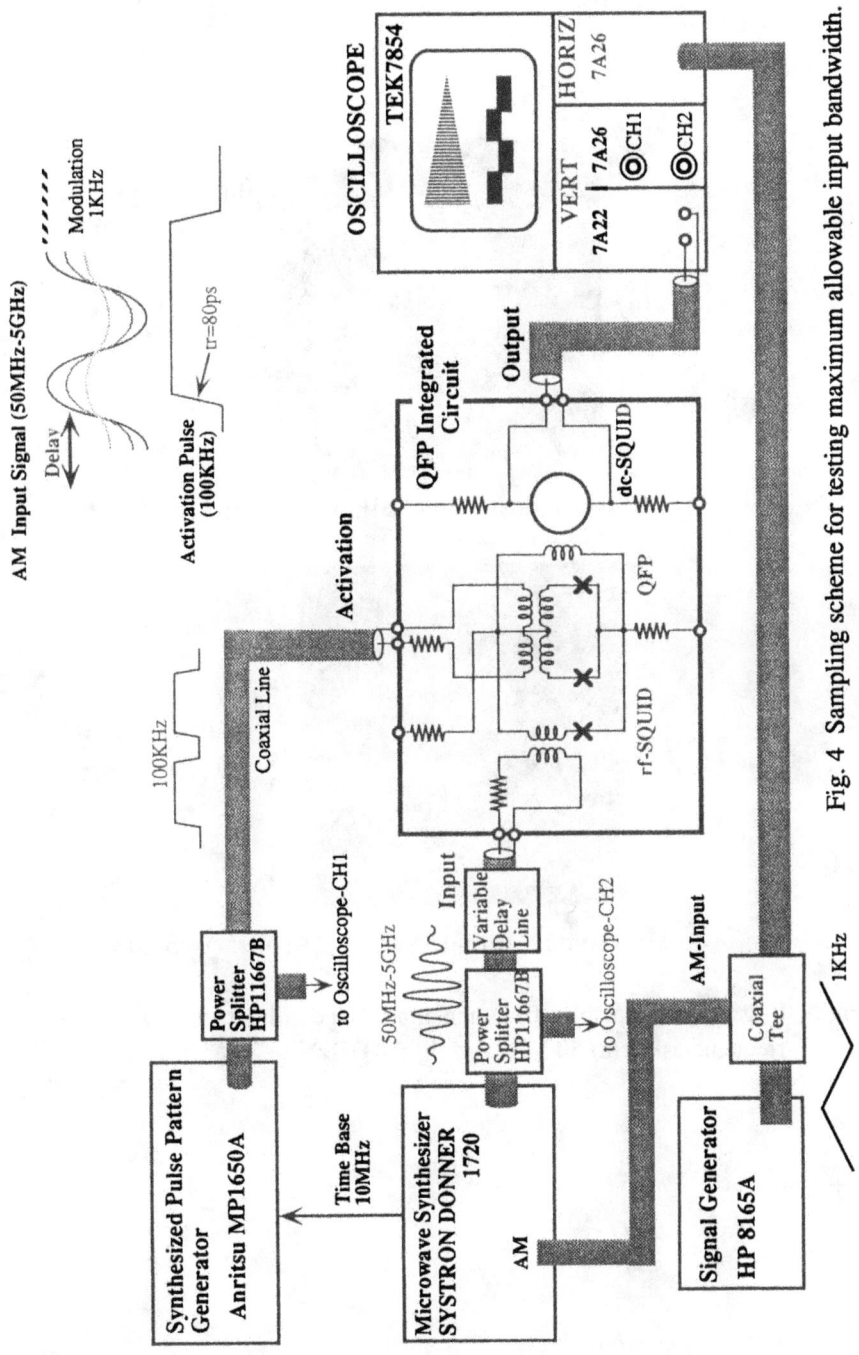

Fig. 4 Sampling scheme for testing maximum allowable input bandwidth.

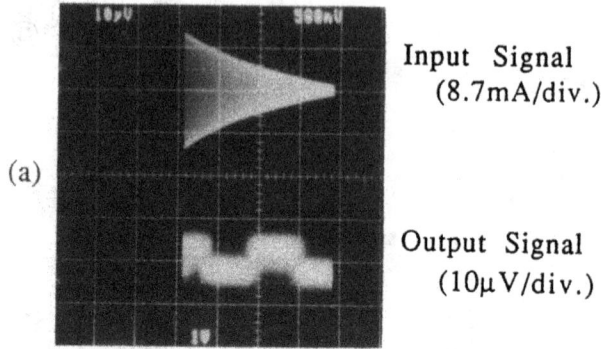

(a)

Input Signal
(8.7mA/div.)

Output Signal
(10μV/div.)

Horizontal: Input Signal (Arbitrary Scale)

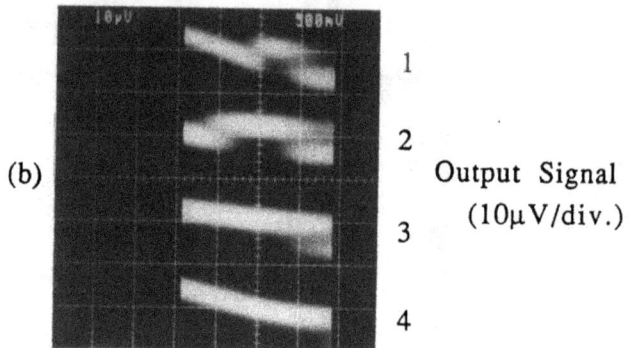

(b)

1

2

3

4

Output Signal
(10μV/div.)

Horizontal: Input Signal (Arbitrary Scale)

Fig.5 Experimental results from the input bandwidth experiments for input frequencies of (a) 50 MHz and (b) 5.4 GHz.

Scaling and Physical Limitations of Quantum Flux Parametron (QFP)

Yasuo Wada, Mutsumi Hosoya, Ryotaro Kamikawai, Willy Hioe,

and Eiichi Goto

Abstract

Quantum Flux Parametron (QFP) device uses single flux quantum trapped in a superconductor loop as a logic unit. Therefore, very fast and low power operation characteristics are expected. This paper describes the scaling principle as well as physical and fabrication limitations of QFP for 10^7 gate supercomputer on 1 cm^2 chip. The scaling principle is based on the constant product of critical current(I_j) and inductance(L), i.e., I_jL = Φ_0. Two types of scaling, three dimensional scaling and constant thickness scaling, reduce device delay by the scaling factor of k. Heat dissipation does not limit the scaling of QFPLSI's until 0.04 μm technology is reached, while conventional Josephson LSI's and semiconductor LSI's reach the heat limitations before they reach the device scaling limitations. London's penetration depth, thermal noise and quantum limitation should be seriously taken into consideration to determine the minimum device size. Variations arising from fabrication, such as pattern size and tunnel oxide thickness, do not limit the miniaturization if novel fabrication technology is applied. Therefore, QFPLSI's fabricated by a 0.35 μm technology would realize 10^7 gate QFP supercomputer on 1 cm^2 chip, operating at a speed of more than 100 GHz. In addition, QFP circuits, fabricated by high Tc superconductor technology will properly operate at 77 K by choosing appropriate power dissipation of QFP circuit. Therefore, pertinent materials and circuit design would realize high performance QFP supercomputer.

1. Introduction

The scaling principle of silicon devices [1] has created a new era of silicon LSI's, where reduction of device dimension leads to a reduction of device/circuit delay and power dissipation. Therefore, LSI's with the minimum dimension of sub-half micron have already been investigated and will appear in the market within a few years [2]. The progress of silicon LSI technology has made it possible to realize supercomputers with more than Giga FLOPS performances. It is necessary to shrink the processor size for further decrease of machine cycle time, and a processor size of less than 1 cm cubic should be realized within the next ten to twenty years for Tera (T) FLOPS supercomputing [3].

Therefore, beyond the silicon LSI age, there will be a superconductor LSI era, when power dissipation and circuit delay should be reduced by several orders of magnitude. Quantum Flux Parametron (QFP) device [3,4,5,6,7] is one of the most promising candidates for the supercomputers in the beginning of 21st century, when less than a 0.1 µm processing technology should become mature according to the scaling principle of silicon LSI's [1].

The speed-power diagram of QFP devices as compared with the conventional Josephson Junction devices and semiconductor devices are schematically depicted in Fig. 1 [4]. The quite notable advantage of QFP devices is the extremely low power consumption and fast switching speed, and a supercomputer, utilizing 10^7 gate QFP devices dissipates only 10 mW (1 nW/gate x 10^7), which is well within the capability of existing liquid helium cooling method. Conventional silicon LSI system should melt down due to the high power density of about 10 kW (1 mW/gate x 10^7). Therefore, QFP devices could be utilized to realize high performance supercomputer, because of its potential for higher operation speed and denser integration.

This paper describes the scaling principle and physical limitations of QFP devices to evaluate the possibility of realizing a supercomputer on 1 cm^2 chip, and compares the integration limitations with those of the conventional Josephson Junction devices and semiconductor devices.

2. QFP Operation Principle

In this section, the operation principle of QFP devices is briefly explained in order to formulate the basis of the following analyses [4,5,6,7]. The basic scheme of QFP is shown in Fig. 2, where, the current flows in or out of the I/O terminal with a synchronous excitation given through the excitation line to generate flux quantum in the superconductor loop. The one state, for example, current flowing out from I/O terminal, is referred to "1", and the other state is definedThe operation of a QFP device requires the preservation of flux quantum in the superconductor loop, and the optimum circuit parameter is expressed by the following equation [6].

$$8 \ I_j \cdot L = \Phi_0 \qquad\qquad (2\text{-}1),$$

where, I_j, L and Φ_0 denotes critical current of Josephson Junction, load inductance and flux quantum, respectively. Equation (2-1) is the only preserved quantity in scaling the QFP devices in the following discussions.

In addition, QFP devices operate by flux transfer mode, and non-hysteretic Josephson Junction can be employed. On the other hand, conventional voltate transfer type Josephson devices requires hysteretic Josephson Junction characteristics for proper operation. Therefore, QFP devices can employ non-hysteretic high Tc Josephson technologies, which is another notable advantage of QFP devices.

3. Switching Speed and Power Dissipation of QFP Devices

Intrinsic switching speed of QFP devices is determined by the switching speed of Josephson Junction, and is in the order of 0.1 ps [4]. The practical switching speed of QFP device is mainly dominated by the product of capacitance and inductance of the circuit,

$$\tau = \sqrt{LC} \qquad\qquad (3\text{-}1).$$

Experimental results show that half frequency divider successfully operated at 16.2 GHz, 4 phase, which was fabricated by a 5 mm lead alloy and niobium oxide technology. This result indicates that the switching speed of the present QFP device is around 15 ps [21], which coincides well with the circuit simulation. Further circuit simulation indicated that QFP devices operate at more than 100 GHz, 4 phase (2.5 ps switching speed), if 2.5 mm aluminum oxide technology is employed [3].

Heat dissipation of QFP devices (P) is mainly dominated by the current flowing through the damping resistance (R) during switching of Josephson Junction, and is estimated to be around the value expressed by the following equation,

$$P = (\frac{\Phi_0}{\tau})^2 / R \qquad\qquad (3\text{-}2),$$

Power dissipation of the current QFP device is around 10^{-9} W/gate based on the above derivation [6].

4. Scaling Principle of QFP Devices

Two scaling principles of QFP devices are discussed in this section. One is three dimensional scaling and the other is constant thickness scaling. The former scales down the lateral dimensions as well as thicknesses of the superconductor and insulator layers by a factor of k. The latter shrinks only the lateral dimensions, and was taken into consideration in case such physical limitations as London's penetration depth and mean free path of the superconductor limits the scaling.

4.1 Three dimensional scaling

Three dimensional scaling shrinks length (l) and width (w) of the superconductor pattern as well as thickness (t) of the insulator and superconductor by the factor of k. Assuming the constant product of critical current I_j and inductance L in eq. (2-1), the following scaling principles are derived.

Load inductance L of a QFP device is expressed by the following equation,

$$L' = L_0 \cdot l' \cdot \frac{t'}{w'} = L_0 \cdot \frac{l}{k} \cdot \frac{t}{k} \cdot \frac{k}{w} = \frac{L}{k} \tag{4-1}.$$

Then the critical current of a Josephson Junction I_j becomes,

$$I_j' = I_j \cdot k \tag{4-2}.$$

Therefore, the critical current density of a Josephson Junction (J_j) is denoted by the following equation, and is increased by a factor of k^3.

$$J_j' = \frac{I_j'}{l'w'} = I_j \cdot k \cdot \frac{k}{l} \cdot \frac{k}{w} = J_j \cdot k^3 \tag{4-3}.$$

In order to realize this critical current density increase, it should be necessary to decrease the tunnel insulator thickness, but not by a factor of k, which will be discussed in the latter section. However, the effect of Josephson Junction capacitance C_j over the total capacitance C becomes negligible with the increase of scaling factor k. Therefore, capacitance C is approximately expressed as,

$$C' = C_C \cdot \frac{l'w'}{t'} = C_0 \cdot \frac{l}{k} \cdot \frac{w}{k} \cdot \frac{k}{t} = \frac{C}{k} \tag{4-4}.$$

The switching speed of QFP devices is scaled by a factor of k, as expressed by the following equation,

$$\tau' = \sqrt{L'C'} = \sqrt{\frac{L}{k} \cdot \frac{C}{k}} = \frac{\tau}{k} \tag{4-5}.$$

Therefore, device delay is reduced by a factor of k in the case of three dimensional scaling. On the other hand, the current density of Josephson Junction and superconductor line are increased by a factor of k^3.

Heat dissipation of QFP devices are expressed by eq. (3-2), and R and P are scaled by the following equations by the critical damping equation [4],

$$R' = R \tag{4-6}$$

$$P' = \left(\frac{\Phi_0}{\tau'}\right)^2 / R' = P k^2 \qquad (4\text{-}7)$$

Therefore, power delay product increases by a factor of k in the case of three dimensional scaling.

4.2 Constant thickness scaling

Contrary to the three dimensional scaling, constant thickness scaling shrinks lateral dimensions, but not the film thicknesses. This scaling principle should be taken into consideration if physical limitations, such as London's penetration depth, dominates the scaling.

The load inductance and critical current of Josephson Junction are the same as the original values, following the preservation law expressed by eq.(2-1). Therefore, the current density becomes,

$$J' = J k^2 \qquad (4\text{-}8)$$

On the other hand, capacitance is also approximately scaled as,

$$C' = \frac{C}{k^2} \qquad (4\text{-}9)$$

Then, switching speed is expressed as,

$$\tau' = \sqrt{L'C'} = \frac{\tau}{k} \qquad (4\text{-}10)$$

Therefore, the switching speed of QFP devices is reduced by the factor of k, which is the same as the three dimensional scaling. Power dissipation of QFP devices is expressed as follows,

$$R' = R k \qquad (4\text{-}11)$$
$$P' = P k \qquad (4\text{-}12)$$

Therefore, power delay product is kept constant by the constant thickness scaling.

4.3 Power reduction / increase scaling

As will be discussed later, power dissipation of QFP devices should be increased if operated at 77 K, in order to avoid possible functional error due to thermal noise. On the other hand, it could be reduced if much lower power dissipation is required. In order to reduce or increase the power dissipation, it is necessary to increase or decrease the critical current density of Josephson Junction, respectively. If the critical current density of the Josephson Junction is increased by a factor of m, the device parameters are scaled by the following equations.

$$L' = \frac{L}{m} \tag{4-13}$$
$$C' = C \tag{4-14}$$

This scaling is accomplished by reducing both insulator thickness and superconductor line width by a factor of $\sqrt{m}$. Thus, dumping resistance, delay time and power dissipation are expressed by the following equations.

$$R' = \frac{R}{\sqrt{m}} \tag{4-15}$$

$$\tau' = \frac{\tau}{\sqrt{m}} \tag{4-16}$$

$$P' = P\, m^{3/2} \tag{4-17}$$

As indicated in eq. (2-1), the load inductance should be carefully redesigned in this power increase/decrease scaling.

5. Physical limitations of QFP Devices

In this section, various factors that limit the scaling of QFP devices are discussed.

5.1 Cooling limitation

The maximum heat dissipation from solid surface is in the order of 0.7 W/cm^2 in liquid helium [9]. Therefore, 7×10^8 gates/cm^2 can be integrated on one QFPLSI chip, taking 1 nW/gate power dissipation into account. Minimum pitch for one gate in such QFPLSI should be,

$$1/(7 \times 10^8)^{1/2} \approx 1/ (2.5 \times 10^4) = 0.4\ \mu m \tag{5-1}.$$

Assuming that one QFP device area requires about 20 to 30 times of the minimum dimension area (pixel) and one QFP gate consists of several QFP devices, the minimum dimension is almost equal to 1/10 of the minimum gate pitch. Thus the minimum dimension of a device is around 0.04 μm, and 7×10^{10}

devices can be integrated on a 1 cm^2 chip when the heat dissipation of QFP is 10^{-9} W/gate. The same derivation was conducted for cooling system of 10 W/cm^2 (liquid nitrogen) and 100 W/cm^2 (fluoro carbon) heat removal capability. Figure 3 summarizes the relationship between heat dissipation of one gate and the minimum dimension of the device, as well as the maximum number of devices integrated on a 1 cm^2 chip for these three cooling capabilities. The figure clearly indicates that a 10^7 gate supercomputer can be integrated on a 1 cm^2 chip by helium cooling if the heat dissipation is lower than 7×10^{-8} W/gate and minimum dimension of 0.35 μm can be employed. In the case of liquid nitrogen cooling, the heat dissipation can reach as high as 7×10^{-7} W/gate.

5.2 London's penetration depth

QFP operation requires the preservation of flux quantum within a superconductor loop. Therefore, it is necessary to eject the penetration of magnetic field from the superconductor loop. London's penetration depth [13] represents the penetration of magnetic field into the superconductors, which determines minimum achievable dimension of QFP's. London's penetration depth (l_L) is expressed by the following equation,

$$\lambda_L = (m/m_0 n_s e^2)^{1/2} \qquad (5\text{-}2).$$

Table 1 summarizes the typical λ_L values for some of the major materials, which spread out between 30 and 300 nm [9,12,14].

Temperature dependance of penetration depth is approximately expressed as [13],

$$\lambda(T) = \lambda(O)\,(1-(\tfrac{T}{T_c})^4)^{-1/2} \qquad (5\text{-}3).$$

Therefore, $\lambda(4.2\text{ k})$ values of the materials are almost equal to $\lambda(0)$, for those materials listed in Table 1. The magnetic field penetrates three dimensionally into the superconductor material, and the thickness as well as width of a superconductor line should be more than the penetration depth ($2\lambda_L$).

The most suitable material to fabricate QFP devices among those listed in Table 1 is Nb, which has the shortest penetration depth of $\lambda_L = 31.5$ nm. Therefore, the smallest dimension that QFP device can reach by the current technology and material is around 0.1 μm (>0.03x2). Materials with smaller penetration depth are necessary to fabricate QFPLSI's with smaller dimensions.

5.3 Mean free path

The dimension of the superconductor should be larger than the mean free path of superconducting electron to ascertain the device operation. Table 2 summarizes the mean free path of several materials [12]. Most of the conventional low Tc materials exhibit mean free path lengths of in the order of 10 nm. Therefore, it is quite possible that QFP devices fabricated on low Tc materials can be shrunk down to 0.1 μm level.

5.4 Thermal noise and quantum limit

QFP devices misoperate if thermal noise energy as well as quantum energy exceeds the device energy. Assuming that a 10^8 QFP device operates at 100 GHz, 4 phase, for one year without misoperation, the switching number becomes,

$$4 \times 100 \times 10^9 \times 10^8 \times 60 \times 60 \times 24 \times 365 = 1.26 \times 10^{27} \qquad (5\text{-}4).$$

Therefore, the error rate should be less than 10^{-27}, and can be drawn in the power-delay diagram.

The amount of energy stored in the QFP device, E_Q, should be large enough to prevent the thermal error, which is expressed by the following equation [6],

$$E_Q = \frac{\Phi_0}{\pi} I_l \qquad (5\text{-}5).$$

In the present experiment, the critical current density of the Josephson Junction was 100 A/cm^2 with the junction area of 25 μm^2, making the critical current of 25 μA [3].

The quantum limit should also be taken into consideration. The product of switching time and energy stored in the superconductor loop should exceed the Plank's constant, with the stability margin of more than 10^{27}, which will be explained in the later section.

6. Limitations Arising from Manufacturing Variations

The scaling limitations are assessed from the manufacturing technology point of view. In this section, the variations of structural parameters, such as barrier oxide thickness and pattern size are discussed and the necessary innovations are proposed.

6.1 Variation of tunnel current density

As described in the previous section, QFP operation requires the preservation of the product of junction critical current and inductance for optimum circuit operation,

$$8 \, I_j \cdot L = \Phi_0 \qquad (2\text{-}1).$$

Therefore, it is important to control the critical current of the Josephson Junction, I_j. The critical current density of a Josephson Junction is expressed by the following equation [11],

$$J_j = \frac{G_n}{A} \left(\frac{\pi \Delta(T)}{2e} \right) \tanh \frac{\Delta(T)}{2kT} \qquad (6\text{-}1),$$

where, A, G_n and $\Delta(T)$ represent junction area, tunnel conductance at high voltage regime (V>>2Δ/e) and gap energy of superconductor at a temperature of T, respectively. The values of $\Delta(T)$ and T are fixed if the superconductor material and operation temperature are determined. Therefore, the dependence of tunnel conductance, G_n, on the structural parameters, such as insulator thickness should be known to express the tunnel current density.

The tunnel current density (J_k) and tunnel conductance G_n is expressed by the following equation [10],

$$J_k = G_n/A = \frac{\alpha V^2}{A \cdot s^2} \exp(-\beta \frac{s}{V} (\frac{m^*}{m} \phi^3)^{1/2} (1 - \gamma \frac{\phi}{E_0}) \qquad (6\text{-}2),$$

where, A, s, and ϕ represents junction area, insulator thickness and potential barrier of the insulator, respectively. Factors α, β, and g are constants. Equation (6-2) indicates that tunnel current density depends exponentially on insulator thickness. Experimental results show that the relationship is approximately expressed by the following equation [9],

$$\log J_k = -2.5s + 8 \qquad (6\text{-}3),$$

where, s is measured by nm and J_k by A/cm^2. Therefore, the variation of s should be less than 0.7 % if the variation of J_k is controlled below ± 10 %.

The oxidation kinetics of the tunnel insulator indicates logarithmic behavior, and the control of oxide thickness should be accomplished by controlling the oxidation conditions. Experimental results show that the critical current is inversely dependent on oxygen partial pressure during oxidation [9]. Therefore, P_{O_2} should be controlled by less than a 1 % accuracy to achieve the J_j control within a necessary value. Conventional flow rate controllers should be able to achieve this accuracy, by diluting oxygen with inert gas.

Tighter control of J_j should enable higher circuit performance, and a novel insulator formation method, such as atomic layer deposition [14] if tunnel insulator deposition should be necessary in manufacturing advanced superconductor ULSI's. In addition, the gap energy Δ and critical temperature T_c of superconductor material are dependant on impurity concentration as well as the deposition conditions. Therefore, the purity of the raw material, deposition environment and treatment of the wafer should be very important and these processing conditions should be chosen by the most careful experiments.

6.2 Variation of pattern size

Variation of pattern size also affects the variation of critical current, as indicated by eq. (4-3). The variation of pattern size in advanced Si LSI processing is around 5 % of the minimum feature size [16]. Take, for example, the minimum feature size of 0.5 μm results in a pattern size variation of 0.025 μm. Taking the maximum allowable critical current variation of 10 %, the pattern size variation should be controlled to below 5 % level. Therefore, the advanced lithography technology can be applied to the sub-half micron QFPLSI fabrication.

6.3 Variation of the surface morphology

The amount of tunneling current is mainly determined by the thickness and morphology of tunneling oxide. It is well known in electrically erasable programmable read only memories (EEPROM's), the tunneling characteristics of thin oxide layers grown on polycrystalline silicon (poly-Si) varies with the poly-Si grain size [17]. This phenomenon is mainly due to the differences in surface morphology at the grain boundaries of poly-Si layers. Therefore, the grain size of superconductors, on which tunneling oxide of Josephson Junction is fabricated, should be smaller enough than the Josephson Junction area. Further materials processing technology development is necessary for the future QFPLSI's. Other innovation to yield highly reliable and uniform tunnel oxide layers is to form the oxide layer on single crystal niobium layers. These technologies should realize very uniform ands reliable tunnel oxide layers.

7.Discussions

7.1 Comparison of power dissipation

Semiconductor devices and conventional Josephson junction devices can be scaled until the thermal limitations is reached. In the case of semiconductor devices, the limitation is determined by the heat dissipation by fluorocarbon cooling system, measuring around 100 W/cm^2. Therefore, only 100/0.001= 1 x10^5 gates can be integrated on a 1 cm^2 chip, assuming 1 mW/gate power dissipation of ECL circuits. Even if the most efficient cooling scheme [19] is employed, the integration density would not exceed 10^6 gates/cm^2. Therefore, the integration density approximately becomes,

$$10^6 \text{ (gates)} \times 5 \text{ (devices)} \times 20 \text{ (pixels)} = 1 \times 10^8 \text{ (pixels/cm}^2)$$

$$1 / \sqrt{10^8} = 1 \times 10^{-4} = 1.0 \, \mu m \qquad (7\text{-}1)$$

Therefore, the minimum dimension in such LSI would be around 1.0 μm. The number represents the average integration density, and it does not necessarily mean that minimum dimension of silicon LSI's cannot reach sub-half micron. Almost the same discussion could be applied for the LSI's employing conventional Josephson Junction devices, in which the chip cooling is limited by the heat removal by liquid helium. Taking the 0.7 W/cm^2 heat dissipation into account, cooling by liquid helium enables an integration level of around 10^6 gates/cm^2, and the minimum feature size is also limited within around 1.0 μm. Therefore, the maximum integration of conventional semiconductor devices and Josephson devices is mainly determined by the heat dissipation. Again, the minimum feature size derived above represents the average device density, and does not necessarily mean that sub-half micron technology cannot be employed in these devices.

7.2 Speed power diagram of QFP device

The speed-power diagram of QFP gate is depicted in Fig. 4, where, various limitations discussed in the previous sections are listed. The broken lines show the thermal and quantum limitations of 10^{-100} error rate, which should be enough to guarantee the error free operation of future supercomputers, as indicated in eq. (5-4). The results clearly depicts that the present device should operate at high reliability of 10^{-100} at 4 K. They also indicate that reliable QFP operation with the present critical current will be limited by the quantum limitation if the minimum dimension reaches around 0.25 μm. However, the quantum limitation is overcome if the current density is increased by a factor of 3. They clearly show that quite reliable operation of 10^7 gate QFP supercomputer on 1 cm^2 chip is ascertained by employing QFP devices fabricated by a o.35 μm technology and dissipation energy of 2 x 10^{-8} W/gate.

7.3 Manufacturing technology innovation

Control of critical current, I_1 requires control of both critical current density J_1 and Josephson Junction area A. Variation of I_1 on pattern size is reported [20], as shown in Table 3. The following discussion assumes that these variations are due to the variations of junction area ΔA and tunnel oxide thickness Δs. It also assumes that the pattern size variation Δl is constant and that Δl is independent of the pattern size, l. It further assumes that the tunnel current density variation, ΔJ_1, is constant for all dimensions. Then, the total variation can be divided into these two variations, as listed in Table 3 [20]. Variation of the Josephson Junction critical current is mainly dominated by the pattern size variation of around 0.03 μm between 1 μm and 10 μm, and the variation of critical current density, or tunnel insulator thickness, does not practically affect the variation of critical current even in the smaller junctions. Advanced sub-half micron lithography technology, together with the advanced materials and processing technologies, should make it possible to realize well controlled Josephson Junction characteristics.

7.4 QFP devices by high Tc materials

High Tc application of QFP circuit is discussed here based on the results shown in Figs. 3 and 4. As described previously, QFP devices can operate with non-hysteretic Josephson Junctions, which could be the only junction characteristics that current high Tc technology can realize [22].

The minimum necessary energy for the reliable (10^{-100} error rate) QFP device operation at 77 K is indicated by a broken line in Fig. 4. The results clearly indicate that device operation is ascertained by increasing the critical current by a factor of 3 from the present device parameters. They also depict that constant thickness scaling of the QFP devices down to 0.2 μm is well within the thermal as well as quantum limitations if the critical current is increased by a factor of 3. Heat dissipation of up to 1 x 10^{-6} W/cm² at an integration density of

10^7 gates/cm^2 can be cooled at 77 K in liquid nitrogen. This is because of the higher cooling ability of liquid nitrogen measuring around 10 W/cm^2 as indicated in Fig. 3. These results clearly show that a supercomputer based on QFP technology on 1 cm^2 chip is achievable on high Tc technologies.

8. Summary

The scaling principle, physical and fabrication limitations of Quantum Flux Parametron (QFP) for a 10^7 gate supercomputer are discussed. The scaling principle is based on the constant product of critical current(I_j) and inductance(L), i.e., $I_jL = \Phi_0$. Two types of scaling, three dimensional scaling and constant thickness scaling, reduce device delay by the scaling factor of k.

Heat dissipation does not limit the scaling of QFPLSI's until 0.04 μm technology is reached, while conventional Josephson LSI's and semiconductor LSI's reach the heat limitations before they reach the device scaling limitations. London's penetration depth, thermal noise and quantum limitation should be seriously taken into consideration. Variations arising from fabrication, such as pattern size and tunnel oxide thickness, do not limit the scaling if novel fabrication technology is applied. QFP circuits properly operate at 77 K if enough energy is stored in the superconductor loop. This is accomplished by increasing the critical current of Josephson Junction. High Tc QFP circuits employing nonhysteretic junctions should be realized by choosing appropriate device parameters. QFPLSI's fabricated by a 0.35 μm technology would realize a 10^7 gate QFP supercomputer on a 1 cm^2 chip, operating at a speed of more than 100 GHz.

References

[1] R.H. Dennard, F.H. Gaensslen, H.-N. Nien, V.Leo Rideout, E. Bassous and A.R. LeBlanc, "Design of Ion-Implanted MOSFET's withVery Small Physical Dimensions," *IEEE J. Solid St. Circuits*, SC-9(5), 256 (1974).

[2] Y. Nakagome, Y. Kawamoto, H. Tanaka, K. Takeuchi, E. Kume, Y. Watanabe, T. Kaga, F. Murai, R. Nakazawa, D. Hisamoto, T. Kisu, T. Nishida, E. Takeda and K. Ito, "A 1.5 V Circuit Technology for 64 Mb DRAMs," Digest of Technical papers, 1990 Symp. VLSI Circuits P. 17, Honolulu, (1990).

[3] M. Hosoya, W. Hioe, J. Casas, R. Kamikawai, Y. Wada, Y. Harada, H. Nakane, R. Suda and E. Goto, "Quantum Flux Parametron," to be published

in *IEEE Trans. Applied Superconductivity* (1991).

[4] E. Goto and K. F. Loe, *DC Flux Parametron*, Singapore, World Scientific, (1986).

[5] E. Goto, T. Soma and K. F. Loe, *Fluxoid Josephson Computer Technology*, Singapore, World Scientific, (1988).

[6] W. Hioe and E. Goto, *Quantum Flux Parametron*, Singapore, World Scientific, (1991).

[7] Y. Harada, W. Hioe and E. Goto, "Flux Transfer Devices," *Proc. IEEE* 77(8), 1280 (1989).

[8] S. Basavaich, J. M. Eldridge and J. Matisoo, "Tunneling in Lead-Lead Oxide Lead Junctions," *J. Appl. Phys.* 45(1), 457 (1974).

[9] T. Van Duzer and C. W. Turner, *Principles of Superconductive Devices and Circuits*, New York, North Holland, (1981).

[10] H. A. Huggins and M. Gurvitch, "Preparation and Characteristics of Nb/Al-oxide-Nb Tunnel Junctions," *J. Appl. Phys* 57(6), 2103 (1985).

[11] V. Ambegaokar and A. Baratoff, "Tunneling Between Superconductors," *Phys. Rev. Lett.* 11(2), 104 (1963).

[12] H. Ihara and K. Togano, *Superconductor Materials*, Tokyo, Tokyo Univ. Press, (1987). (in Japanese)

[13] F. London , *Superfluids I*, New York, John Wiley, (1950).

[14] M. Tinkham, *Introduction to Superconductivity*, New York,McGreen Hill, (1975).

[15] J. Nishizawa, T. Kurubayashi, H. Abe and N. Sakurai, "Deposition Mechanism of   GaAs Epitaxy," *J. Electrochem. Soc.*, 134(4), 945 (1987).

[16] T. Tanaka, N. Hasagawa, H. Shiraishi and S. Okazaki, "A New Photolithography   Technique with Antireflective Coating on Resist: ARCOR," *J. Electrochem. Soc.*,   137(12), 3900 (1990).

[17] K. Ohyu, Y. Wada, S. Iijima and N. Natsuaki, "Highly Reliable Thin Oxide Layers   Grown on Heavily Phosphorus Doped Polycrystalline Silicon by Rapid Thermal   Oxidation," *J. Electrochem. Soc.*, 137(7), 2261(1990).

[18] W. H. Chang, "The Inductance of a Superconducting Transmission Line," *J. Appl.   Phys.*, 50(12), 8129 (1979).

[19] D.B. Tuckerman and RFW Pease, "High Performance Heat Sinking for VLSI," *IEEE Electron Device Letters*, EDL-2(5), 126 (1981).

[20] H. Nakagawa, I. Kurosawa, M. Aoyagi and S. Tanaka, "Fabrication Process for a   Josephson Computer ETL JC-1 Using Nb Tunnel Junction," *IEEE Trans. Magnetics*, 27(2), 3109 (1991).

[21] J. Casas, R. Kamikawai and E. Goto, "High Speed Operation of QFP Based Shiftregistors and Frequency Prescalers," submitted to *IEEE J. Solid St. Circuits*.

[22] D.K. Chin and T. Van Duzer, "Novel all-High Tc Epitaxial Josephson Junction," *Appl. Phys. Lett.*, 58(7), 18 (1991).

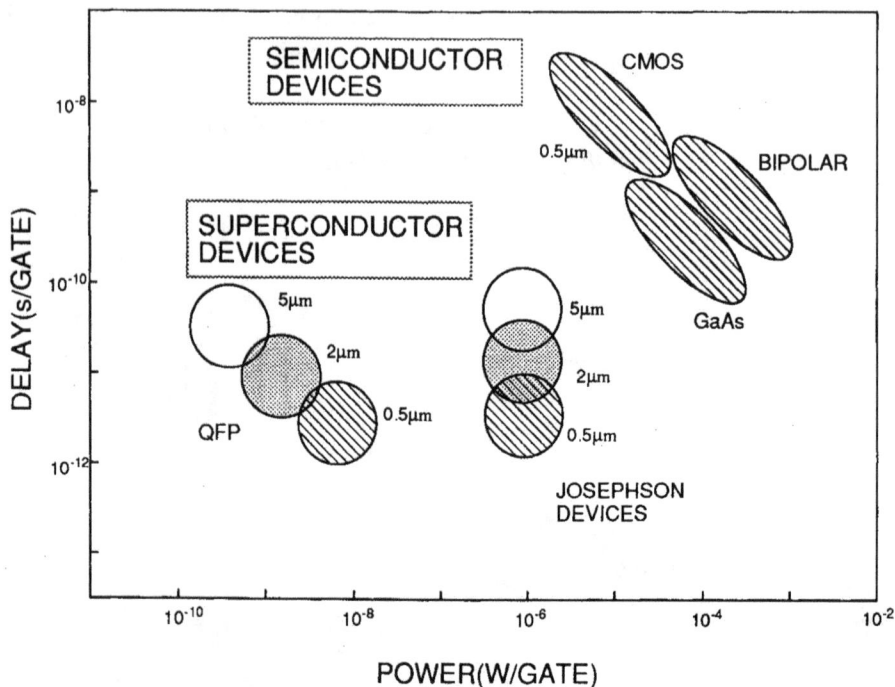

Figure 1 Comparison of switching speed and power consumption of semiconductor devices and superconductor devices for shiftresistor circuits. QFP device consumes only 10^{-6} of the power of conventional ECL based semiconductor device.

Table 1 London's penetration depth of some of the most widely utilized superconducting materials.

Material	Nb	V	Pb	Al	Sn	In	Nb3Ge	NbTi
London's penetration depth	31.5	37.5	39	50	61	64	130	300

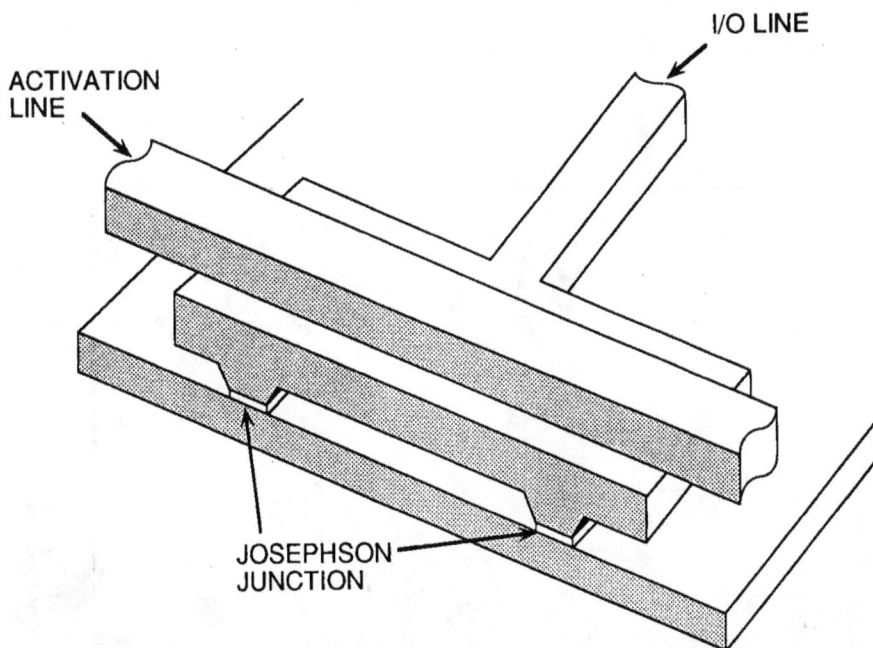

Figure 2   Schematic figure and cross section of a QFP device

Table 2   Mean free paths of some of the commonly utilized superconductor
materials

Material	Nb	V	Pb	Nb_3Ge	NbTi
mean free path (nm)	39	44	100	3	4

Table 3   Dependence of critical current variation on pattern size

minimum pattern size (mm)	variation of critical current (%)	variation of pattern size (mm)
10.0	0.5	0.025
2.0	2.0	0.02
1.0	7.0	0.035

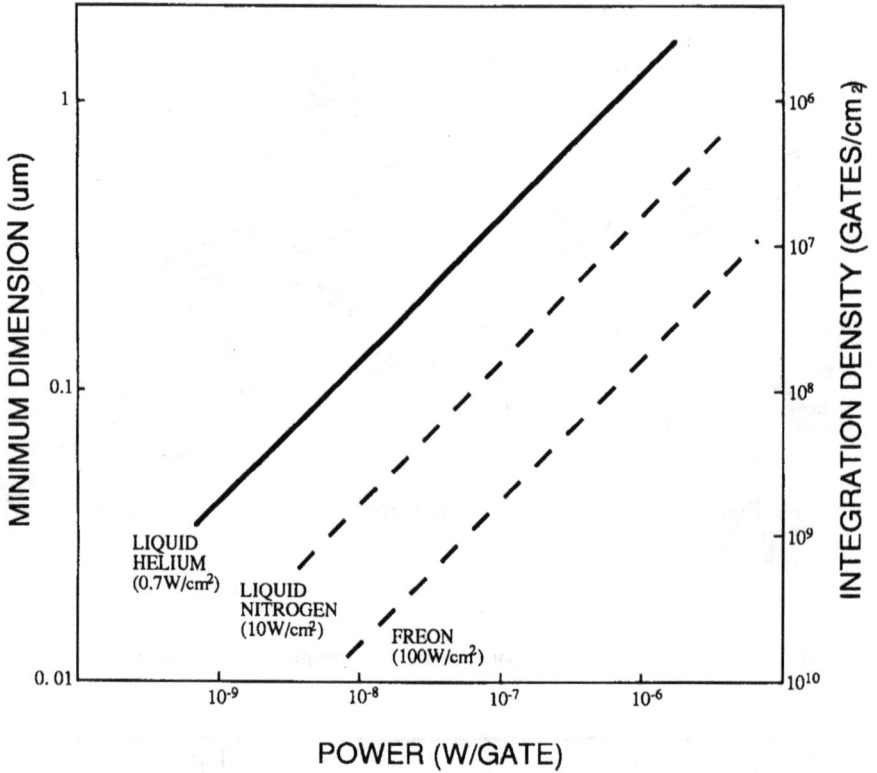

Figure 3   Relationship between heat dissipation of one gate and the minimum
achievable dimension of the device as well as the limitation of number
of devices integrated on a 1 cm^2 chip

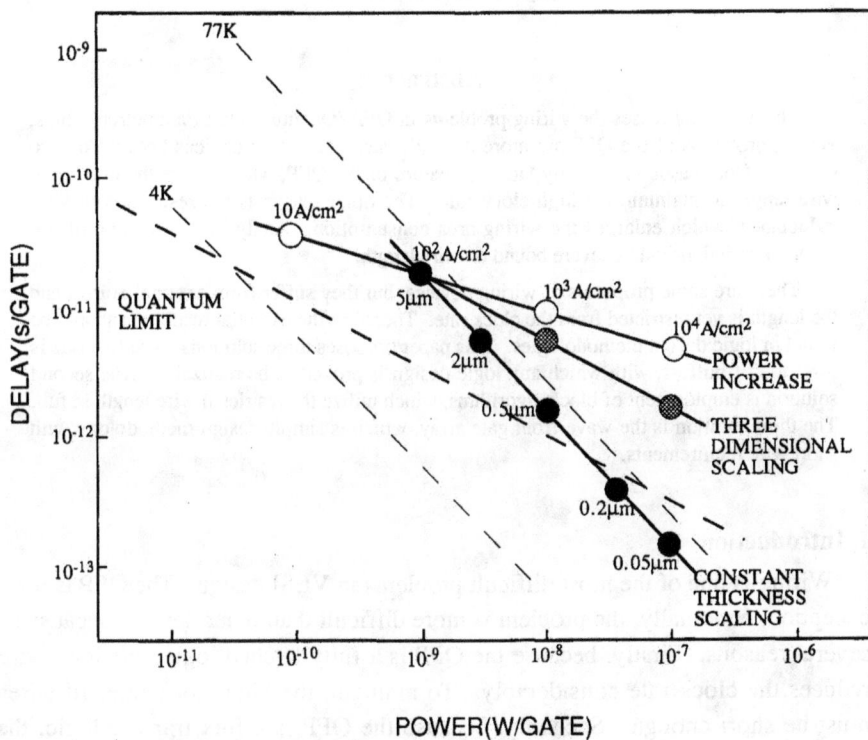

Figure 4   Speed power diagram of QFP device scaling principle, with quantum, thermal and physical limitations.

Signal Interconnection in Highly Integrated QFP Chips

Reiji Suda, Ryotaro Kamikawai, Mutsumi Hosoya,

Willy Hioe, and Eiichi Goto

Abstract

This paper discusses the wiring problems in QFP (Quantum Flux Parametron) chips. Wiring problems of the QFP are more difficult than other logic devices because of two reasons. One reason is the fully latching feature of the QFP, which limits the maximum wire length to maintain the high clock rate. The other reason is the restriction of wire inductance, which enlarges the wiring area consumption. Analytical estimation of the second restriction finds a severe bound on wire length.

There are some proposals of wiring devices, but they suffer from external noises, and the length is yet restricted from the clock rate. Therefore the essential resolution should be found in logic design methodologies. This paper proposes three solutions. The first one is insertion of buffers, with which any logic design is proved to be realizable. The second solution is employment of block algorithms, which utilize the restricted wire length in full. The third solution is the wave-front gate array, which is simple design methodology with short wire requirements.

1. Introduction

Wiring is one of the most difficult problems in VLSI design. The QFP is not a exception, or actually, the problem is more difficult than other devices because of several reasons. Firstly, because the QFP is a fully latched logic, one long wire reduces the clock rate considerably. To maintain the high clock rate, all wires must be short enough. Secondly, because the QFP is a flux transfer logic, the inductance of wires must be carefully designed. Long wires with small inductance tend to be very area-consuming. Thirdly, parallel signal lines must keep an appropriate distance to avoid the cross-talk noise. The area-efficiency is reduced, and multiple layer wiring is not usable. These facts make the problem considerably difficult. How do we tackle the problem?

Some clues to the solution will be found in the properties of the QFP. Since the QFP is a fully latched logic, the high throughput is not affected by increase of the number of the logic stages. D-gate is quite powerful in logic functionality, and circuits can be constructed using a small number of gates. The low power dissipation and the inter-chip connector allow highly dense three dimensional implementation. These properties will help us reduce the tight restrictions and design high performance QFP computers.

This paper is intended to clarify the limitation of wiring in QFP circuits and present the main ideas of solutions. The rest of Sec. 1 introduces the fundamentals of the QFP. Sec. 2 discusses the area-optimal design of wires. In Sec. 3, the area consumption is analyzed on some wiring models. Sec. 4 presents some ideas for long wires and their problems. Sec. 5 discusses logic design methodologies with short wire requirements as the essential solutions. Sec. 6 addresses some comments as a conclusion.

1.1 The QFP and the inductance of wires

This subsection presents the fundamental properties of the QFP and the inductance of wires. Details on the subjects will be presented somewhere else in this book.

The QFP (Quantum Flux Parametron)[1] is a flux-transfer type Josephson junction logic device. There has been proposed two QFP circuits as logic gates. One is the QFP itself as a buffer. The other is the D-gate[2], and its function is $D(s, t; x, y) = x(s \equiv t) + y(s \neq t)$. Its inputs and outputs are distinguished not by their configuration, but by the order in which the QFP's are activated; the signal is relayed from an earlier activated QFP to the nextly activated QFP. Therefore fan-out and fan-in should not be distinguished in QFP circuits. However, virtual fan-in and fan-out can be defined as in conventional logic devices. The word "fan-out" in this paper represents the virtual fan-out.

The output level of a QFP is determined by the inductance of the output line. Typically, the output inductance is chosen as $2 L I_m = \Phi_0 / 4$, where L is the total inductance of input and output lines, I_m is the critical current of the Josephson junctions, and Φ_0 is a flux quantum unit. In this case, the total output current is $2 I_m$ and the output flux is $\Phi_0 / 4$. If $I_m = 25$ μA, then $L = 10$ pH since $\Phi_0 = 2$ fWeb.

The inductance of a superconductive strip line is proportional to the ratio of its length and width, or equivalently, the number of squares of the line. The inductance of a line with the length l and the width w is $\frac{l}{w} L_0$, where L_0 is the square inductance of the superconductor. The inductance per square is a function of, mainly, the distance from the ground plane to the strip line and the penetration depth of the material. It is approximately $L_0 = L_{0h} h + L_{00}$, where h is the height of the strip line.

Since the theoretical gain of a QFP is infinite, the fan-out of a QFP is theoretically unbounded. However, the current level of an output is reduced as the fan-out grows, and low level input will lead to malfunction of QFP's because of physical incompleteness. To ensure the expected function of QFP's, the input current must be maintained at some level. If the minimum allowed input current is I_{min}, then the fan-out is bounded by $F \leq 2\,I_m\,/\,I_{min} - 1$. Here the decremental 1 is for the fan-in. The bound of F now is 3–6.

1.2 The restrictions on output wires

This subsection introduces the restrictions on signal lines. There are two restrictions; one is on the length, and the other is on the inductance.

The first restriction is on the length of wires. A long wire is not preferable in QFP circuits because it reduces the clock rate. To maintain the clock rate, all the wires must be shorter than a limit length. With the clock rate of 100 GHz, all the wire should be shorter than 250 μm. Even if a D-gate could be constructed in 25×25 μm including wiring area, the longest wire cannot pass through ten gates. This is a severe restriction, considering current designs of logic circuits. Although the restriction is reduced by a slower clock, the throughput becomes low, and in the worst case, the latency might be larger. A good design with short wire requirements will be better in both the throughput and the latency.

The second restriction is on the inductance of wires. As mentioned in the previous subsection, the inductance of the input and output lines is determined from the critical current of the Josephson junctions. Because the inductance of a line is proportional to the number of squares of the line, a long wire will have very large area if the allocated inductance is small.

The restriction on the inductance is loosened by the fact that the total inductance of parallel lines is the harmonic mean of that of each line. However, the fan-out is not infinite, and the assignable inductance to a line is bounded. Sec. 2 and Sec. 3 are dedicated to analyze the problem of the wiring area. Sec. 2 discusses the area-optimum design of wires, and Sec. 3 analyzes the area consumption of the wires on a chip.

2. Area-Optimum Design of Signal Wires

This section presents the basic consideration of QFP wiring. Subsecs. 2.1 and 2.2 discuss the area-optimum design of a wire and wires. Wires with the same inductance, uniform width, and parallel output strategy are found to be optimum. Subsec. 2.3 analyzes the multiple layer wiring. The area consumption is calculated as if the square inductance be the harmonic mean of those of the layers.

2.1 A signal line and its area

This subsection discusses the area-optimum design of a single line. The most natural strategy, uniform width, is found to be optimum.

Consider a signal line with length l and area S squares. If its width is uniformly $w = l / S$, then the occupied area is $l w = l^2 / S$. This natural design can be proved as optimum in terms of area consumption.

Divide the line into two parts, one having length $l_1 = p\, l$ and area $S_1 = P\, S$ squares, and the other having length $l_2 = (1 - p) l$ and area $S_2 = (1 - P) S$ squares. The area consumption is:

$$A \qquad = \left(\frac{p^2}{P} + \frac{(1 - p)^2}{1 - P} \right) \frac{l}{S} \tag{1}$$

To minimize the area:

$$\frac{dA}{dP} \qquad = 0 \tag{2}$$

$$P \qquad = p, \quad \frac{p}{2p - 1} \tag{3}$$

Since $P = p /(2 p - 1)$ is not appropriate, $P = p$ is the result. The widths of the parts are the same l / S, that means uniform width is optimum in terms of area consumption.

2.2 Parallel output lines

This subsection discusses the design of fan-out lines. The inductance of each wire should be the maximum allowed value to obtain the minimum area. This is a very natural result. However surprisingly, the serial fan-out will be found not to be preferable in terms of area consumption.

Consider a QFP and its k output lines. Let the available inductance for output lines be L and the limit of fan-out be F ($k \le F$). Because a larger inductance leads to a smaller area, the largest allowed inductance should be assigned to each output line. The inductance for an output line is bounded by $F L$ because of input margins. Therefore the area-optimum assignment of inductance is $F L$ for each output line.

Most conventional logic devices allow the "serial fan-out" scheme (Fig. 1), in which several inputs are connected serially. Although this is possible in the QFP, it is not recommended because of larger area consumption. Consider the branched output line depicted in Fig. 2-1, which has a trunk W_t and two branches

W_1 and W_2. Let their inductance be L_t, L_1, and L_2, and their length be l_t, l_1, and l_2. When the total current is I, the current flowing into W_i is:

$$I_i = \frac{I}{L_i\left(\frac{1}{L_1} + \frac{1}{L_2}\right)} \qquad (i = 1, 2) \quad (4)$$

Split the trunk into two parallel lines W_{t1} and W_{t2} with the inductances of $L_{t1} = L_t(L_1 + L_2)/L_2$ and $L_{t2} = L_t(L_1 + L_2)/L_1$, respectively (Fig. 2-2). Then the total inductance is again L_t, and the current flowing through W_{ti} is equal to I_i. Therefore when W_{ti} is connected to W_i, the two circuits are equivalent. Let the inductance per square be L_0. Since the lengths of W_{t1} and W_{t2} are l_t, the total area of W_{t1} and W_{t2} is:

$$l_t^2 \frac{L_0}{L_{t1}} + l_t^2 \frac{L_0}{L_{t2}} = l_t^2 \frac{L_0}{L_t} \qquad (5)$$

This shows that the area of the trunk is the same in both circuits, so the wiring area is not reduced by the serial fan-out scheme. Since the area consumption is minimized by uniform width, the minimum area condition requires:

$$l_t \frac{L_0}{L_{t1}} = l_1 \frac{L_0}{L_1} \qquad \text{and}$$

$$l_t \frac{L_0}{L_{t2}} = l_2 \frac{L_0}{L_2} \qquad (6)$$

This results in:

$$l_1 = l_2 \qquad (7)$$

$$L_t = \frac{l_t}{l_1} \frac{L_1 L_2}{L_1 + L_2} \qquad (8)$$

Therefore if $l_1 \neq l_2$, the serial fan-out consumes more area than the parallel fan-out.

2.3 Multiple layer wiring

In practice, two or more layers are available for strip lines. Utilizing multiple layer wiring, the area consumption will be reduced. This subsection discusses this subject.

Consider a wire with length l and inductance L. It is divided into n parts, and each of the parts is realized by different layers $L_1 \ldots L_n$. Let the length and the inductance of the i-th part be $p_i l$ and $P_i L$, respectively, and the square inductance of i-th layer be L_{0i}. The area consumption of the i-th part is $A_i = \dfrac{l^2 p_i^2 L_{0i}}{L P_i}$. Since the effective area consumption of this line is $\max\{A_i\}$, the minimum area condition requires all A_i's to be equal. This results in equations:

$$K = \frac{p_i^2 L_{0i}}{P_i} \qquad (1 \leq i \leq n) \quad (9)$$

This is:

$$P_i = \frac{p_i^2 L_{0i}}{K} \qquad (1 \leq i \leq n) \quad (10)$$

Noting that $\sum P_i = 1$,

$$K = \sum p_i^2 L_{0i} \qquad (11)$$

The area consumption is $K\, l^2 / L$, and is minimized by letting:

$$\frac{dK}{dp_i} = 0 \qquad (12)$$

Noting that $\sum p_i = 1$,

$$\frac{dK}{dp_i} = 2\, p_i L_{0i} - 2 \sum_{j \neq i} p_j L_{0j}$$

$$= 4\, p_i L_{0i} - 2 \sum_{j} p_j L_{0j} \qquad (13)$$

$$p_i L_{0i} = \frac{1}{2} \sum_{j} p_j L_{0j}$$

$$= H \qquad \text{(a constant)} \quad (14)$$

$$p_i = \frac{1}{L_{0i}} H \qquad (15)$$

$$H = \widehat{L_{0i}} \qquad (16)$$

where $\widehat{L_{0i}}$ is the harmonic mean of L_{0i}'s. The area consumption is now

$$\frac{l^2}{L} \sum p_i^2 L_{0i} = \frac{l^2}{L} \sum \left(\frac{H}{L_{0i}} \right)^2 L_{0i}$$

$$= \frac{l^2\, \widehat{L_{0i}}}{L} \qquad (17)$$

Therefore, the area consumption of a single wire in multiple layer wiring is estimated as if the square-inductance is equal to the harmonic mean of those of the layers. From Eqs. (10) and (15), the optimum area is attained by $p_i = P_i = \widehat{L_{0i}} / L_{0i}$.

The above discussion treats only a single line. Intuitively, when a group of lines is optimized at once, then better results might come about. However, the discussion below shows that the global optimization offers no more reduction on the area consumption.

Consider N lines implemented by n layers. Let the length of j-th line be l_j, the square inductance of i-th layer be L_{0i}, and the inductance of all wires be L. Each line is divided into n parts, and the i-th part of the j-th line has length $l_j p_{ji}$ and inductance $L P_{ji}$, and is implemented in the i-th layer. Then the total wiring area in the i-th layer is:

$$A_i = \sum_j \frac{l_j^2 p_{ji}^2 L_{0i}}{L P_{ji}} \qquad (1 \le i \le n) \quad (18)$$

Since the effective area consumption is $\max\{A_i\}$, we have restriction equations:

$$A_1 = A_i \qquad (2 \le i \le n) \quad (19)$$

The problem is equivalent to minimizing

$$\Phi = A_1 - \sum_i \lambda_i (A_1 - A_i) \qquad (23)$$

where λ_i's are Lagrange's multipliers. The derivatives are:

$$\frac{\partial \Phi}{\partial p_{ji}} = -(1 - \lambda_i)\frac{2 L_{01} l_i^2 p_{j1}}{L P_{j1}} - \lambda_i \frac{2 L_{0i} l_i^2 p_{ji}}{L P_{ji}} \quad (2 \le i \le n) \quad (24)$$

$$\frac{\partial \Phi}{\partial P_{ji}} = (1 - \lambda_i)\frac{L_{01} l_i^2 p_{j1}^2}{L P_{j1}^2} + \lambda_i \frac{L_{0i} l_i^2 p_{ji}^2}{L P_{ji}^2} \quad (2 \le i \le n) \quad (25)$$

$$\frac{\partial \Phi}{\partial \lambda_i} = \sum_j \left(\frac{L_{01} l_i^2 p_{j1}^2}{L P_{j1}} - \frac{L_{0i} l_i^2 p_{ji}^2}{L P_{ji}} \right) \quad (2 \le i \le n) \quad (26)$$

The first two equations require:

$$(1 - \lambda_i) L_{01} = \lambda_i L_{0i} \qquad (2 \le i \le n) \quad (27)$$

$$p_{ji} = P_{ji} \qquad (1 \le i \le n, \, 1 \le j \le N) \quad (28)$$

The third equation requires:

$$\sum_j l_j^2 \left(\frac{\lambda_i}{1 - \lambda_i} p_{j1} - p_{ji} \right) = 0 \qquad (2 \le i \le n) \quad (29)$$

Summing up for all i:

$$\sum_j l_j^2 \left(\sum_i \frac{\lambda_i}{1 - \lambda_i} p_{j1} - 1 \right) = 0 \qquad (30)$$

Therefore

$$\sum_j l_j^2 = \sum_i \frac{\lambda_i}{1 - \lambda_i} \sum_j p_{j1} \, l_j^2$$

$$= \sum_i \frac{L_{01}}{L_{0i}} \sum_j p_{j1} \, l_j^2 \qquad (31)$$

Here the area consumption becomes:

$$A_1 = \frac{L_{01}}{L} \sum_j p_{j1} \, l_j^2$$

$$= \frac{\widehat{L_{0i}}}{L} \sum_j l_j^2 \qquad (32)$$

where $\widehat{L_{0i}}$ is the harmonic mean of L_{0i}'s. This area consumption is the same result obtained when individual lines are independently optimized. Therefore, without any loss of efficiency, each wire can be optimized independently.

As a conclusion, the effect of the multiple layer wiring is as if the square-inductance becomes the harmonic mean of those of the layers. However in reality, to avoid cross-talk noise, two overlapping wire must cross vertically. For this reason, no more than two layers can be utilized.

This section has discussed the area-optimum design of wires. The next section develops the analysis on wiring area requirement being based on the facts derived in this section.

3. Wiring Models and their Analysis

This section introduces two models of QFP gate array and discusses the wiring limitation in these models. The first model is the square-grid gate array, in which the gates are placed at the grid points of a two dimensional chip. Subsec. 3.1 analyzes this model and finds that the wiring is difficult in this model. Subsec. 3.2 discusses three dimensional implementation, and shows that the wiring restriction is reduced. It is pitiful that the model is not very realistic, because the technologies of three dimensional implementation are not fully established. Subsec. 3.3 introduces the second model, the lock-step gate array, and discusses the wiring problems in it. Wiring limitation seems to be reduced in this model.

3.1 Square-grid gate array model

This subsection introduces and discusses the square-grid gate array model, in which the gates are assumed to be placed in a square grid array, but no specific configuration of wires is assumed. This is the simplest assumption, and some gate arrays of conventional logic devices are categorized in this model. The analysis on wiring area consumption derives a severe limitation in this model.

Let the area of a gate be G, and the ratio of the total area for gates and wires be R. The area for a gate and its wires is $(1 + R)G$, so the gate pitch D is $\sqrt{(1 + R)G}$.

Let the load inductance for output be L, the fan-out be F, and the inductance per square be L_0. Then the number of squares of an output signal line is $S = FL/L_0$.

Consider an output line. Let its length $l = pD$. Its width w must be l/S, so the area occupied by it is $A = lw = \dfrac{l^2}{S} = \dfrac{p^2 D^2}{S}$.

The total wiring area cannot exceed the allocated wiring area $R\,G\,M\,E$, where M is the number of gates and E is the area-efficiency. Therefore,

$$\sum A = \frac{G(1+R)L_0}{FL}\sum p^2$$
$$= \overline{p^2}\frac{L_0}{L}(1+R)G\,M$$
$$\leq R\,G\,M\,E \tag{33}$$

Here, $\overline{p^2}$ is the square-mean of p's. This results in:

$$\overline{p^2} \leq \frac{LRE}{L_0(1+R)} \tag{34}$$

Replacing the values by 10 pH for L, 1 pH for L_0 (two-layer wiring is assumed), 1 for R, and 0.5 for E, $\overline{p^2} \leq 10$ is obtained. Roughly speaking, p should be near $\sqrt{\overline{p^2}} \approx 3.2$. This means the wiring must be highly local. The above discussion is applicable to any uniformly distributed gates configuration, with the exception that D is not the gate pitch but its "mean."

There are reports on required wire length in this model[3]. That reports the distribution of wire length is:

$$P(p = x) = \frac{4}{\mu^2} x\, e^{-\frac{2}{\mu} x} \tag{35}$$

Integrating $x^2 P(x)$ from 0 to ∞, we have the square-mean $\overline{p^2} = \frac{3}{2}\mu^2$. Although that paper reports that $\bar{p} = \mu$ as 2, it treats the serial fan-out as short wires. Consider F fan-out is serially connected by F wires of the length l. Then the serial mean length is l, but the parallel mean length is $\dfrac{F(F+1)}{2F}l = \dfrac{(F+1)}{2}l$.

Assuming that F is uniformly 3, we have $\bar{p} = 4$ and $\overline{p^2} = 28$. This large $\overline{p^2}$ is not provided by the QFP. The rest of Sec. 3 is dedicated to search solutions of this problem. The next subsection will discuss three dimensional implementation, and analyze the effects on the wiring limitation.

3.2 Three dimensional implementation

Using a three dimensional implementation, more gates will be nearer, and the wiring limitation will hopefully be reduced. This subsection considers this subject.

There will many ideas for three dimensional wiring, but this subsection assumes a very simple model (Fig. 3). There are several QFP chips accumulated as layers, and we have an inter-layer connector which consumes inductance L_t and area $T = t\,G$. Consider a line which goes vertically through k layers and moves horizontally a length l. Then the inductance for the horizontal move is $F\,L - k\,L_t$ and the available number of squares is $S = \left(F\,L - k\,L_t\right)/L_0$. The occupied area is $A = k\,T + l^2/S$.

$$\sum A \quad = \sum \left(k\,t\,G + \frac{p^2 D^2 L_0}{F\,L - k\,L_t}\right)$$

$$= \frac{G\,(1+R)\,L_0}{F\,L} \sum \left(\frac{k\,t\,F\,L}{(1+R)\,L_0} + \frac{p^2}{1 - k\dfrac{L_t}{F\,L}}\right) \qquad (36)$$

Comparing with Eq. (33), we have $\dfrac{k\,t\,F\,L}{(1+R)\,L_0} + \dfrac{p^2}{1 - k\dfrac{L_t}{F\,L}}$ in place of p^2.

For an estimation of the effects of three dimensional implementation, the number of accessible gates is compared with that of two dimensional model. In the two dimensional case, a wire with the length $l = p\,D$ is accessible to $n_2 = \pi p^2$ gates. In the three dimensional case, the number of accessible gates is $n_3 = \sum \pi p(k)^2$, where $\pi p(k)^2$ is the number of accessible gates in the k-th layer. Assuming that $F = 4$, $L = 10$ pH, $L_0 = 1$ pH, $R = 1$, $t = 0.1$, $L_t = 10$ pH, and $p(0)^2 = 10$, we have $n_3 = 94$. Since the same assumption results in $n_2 = 31$, the number of accessible gates is increased by three times.

Although the effects of three dimensional implementation is considerable, the above discussion is not very realistic. The model of inter-layer connecter has not any reality. The discussion does not reflect the proposed connectless signal transfer device[4]. The method to connect two sides of a chip is not established. We do not know whether a signal can go through more than two layers at once.

For more precise analysis, more research on three dimensional implementation is required.

3.3 Lock-step gate array model

This subsection introduces the second model of QFP gate array. The main idea here is that if the gates are narrow, then the same length of wire will reach more gates. Actually we will see that the wiring limitation is considerably reduced. However, it is interesting that the aspect ratio of gates does not affect the wiring limitation. What is important is optimizing the aspect ratio of the lattice of gates.

The second model is the "lock-step gate array," which is illustrated in Fig. 4. The gates are placed in an array. Each of them has the same shape: it is rectangular, occupies area G, and the aspect ratio is $1 : z$. The width and the height of a gate are $D = \sqrt{z\,G}$ and $H = \sqrt{G/z}$.

Each wire has horizontal part(s) and vertical parts. Here, the vertical parts and the horizontal parts are assumed to have inductance of $C : (1 - C)$. Assuming that the horizontal and the vertical parts are realized by two different layers, the occupied area is separately estimated.

Consider a vertical line, and let l_i be the length of horizontal wires which cut the vertical line. Each of them should have the inductance $F L (1 - C)$ and $S_h = F L (1 - C) / L_0$ squares. Since their widths are $w_i = l_i / S_h$, their total width is:

$$\sum w_i = \frac{L_0 \sqrt{z\,G} \sum p_i}{F L (1 - C)}$$

$$\leq R H \tag{37}$$

$$\sum p_i \leq \frac{R F L (1 - C)}{z L_0} \tag{38}$$

Next the vertical wires are considered. The length of a vertical wire is the constant $l = R H$, and it should have $S_v = F L C / L_0$ squares. Therefore the area is $A = \dfrac{l^2}{S_v} = \dfrac{R^2 G}{z S_v}$. Let the area-efficiency be E_v. The total area is:

$$\sum A = \frac{F R^2 G}{z S_v}$$

$$= \frac{R^2 G L_0}{z L C}$$

$$\leq R\,G\,E_v \tag{39}$$

$$C \quad \geq \frac{R\,L_0}{z\,L\,E_v} \tag{40}$$

This leads to:

$$\sum p_i \quad \leq \frac{R\,F\left(z\,L\,E_v - R\,L_0\right)}{z^2\,L_0\,E_v} = 0 \tag{41}$$

To maximize $\sum p_i$,

$$\frac{\partial \sum p_i}{\partial R} \quad = \frac{F\left(z\,L\,E_v - 2\,R\,L_0\right)}{z^2\,L_0\,E_v} \tag{42}$$

$$R \quad = \frac{z\,L\,E_v}{2\,L_0} \tag{43}$$

$$C \quad = \frac{1}{2} \tag{44}$$

The result is:

$$\sum p_i \quad \leq \frac{F\,E_v\,L^2}{4\,L_0^2} \tag{45}$$

Letting L be 10 pH, L_0 be 0.5 pH, and E_v be 0.5, we have $\sum p_i \leq 50\,F$. Assuming that $F = 4$, we have $\sum p_i \leq 200$. This looks far better than the result of the square grid gate array, and this is analytically confirmed as follows:

Assume that the number of gates in one row is M, and consider a vertical line at the edge of each gate. There are $M - 1$ such vertical lines. Summing up $\sum p_i$ for all such lines, we have

$$\sum\sum p_i \quad = \sum p_i^2$$

$$= M\,F\,\overline{p^2}$$

$$< \frac{E_v\,L^2\,F}{4\,L_0^2}\left(M - 1\right)E_h \tag{46}$$

Here E_h is the area efficiency of horizontal wires.

$$\overline{p^2} \quad < \frac{E_v\,E_h\,L^2}{4\,L_0^2}\frac{M-1}{M}$$

$$\approx 25 \tag{47}$$

Therefore $\overline{p^2}$ is two and a half times larger than that of the two-layer square-grid gate array model. As previously mentioned, this loose bound of $\overline{p^2}$ is mainly due to the optimization of the aspect ratio of the lattice of gates. However, this is not the true optimum, since the width of wires is not uniform. The uniform width wiring is not modeled or analyzed here, because it requires that the total width of output wires may be wider than the width of gates, which is not realistic.

3.5 Conclusion

This section has discussed two wiring models and the restrictions on wire length. The square-grid gate array is a model in which conventional logic devices are implemented, but the wiring limitation has been found as severe in this model. In the lock-step gate array, the arrangement of gates is restricted, but the wiring has been found as somewhat easier. However, they are not able to provide enough wiring capacity to implement conventional logic design directly. The rest of this paper discusses resolution of the wiring problems. Sec. 4 presents some ideas for long wires, and Sec. 5 discusses logic design methodologies with short wires.

4. Long Wires

This section presents some wiring devices in which larger inductance is tolerated. These devices are useful if the restriction on the area consumption is much severer than that on the wiring delay. However, to avoid reduction of the clock rate, very long wires cannot be used. Another problem of these devices is that these tend to suffer from external noises.

4.1 Dummy outputs

The simplest method for longer wires is enlarging the fan-out. In the lock-step gate array model, this is obvious; since the sum of wire length is bounded by $50\,F$, the larger fan-out allows longer wires.

Similar result comes from the square-grid gate array model. Let the new fan-out $F' = f\,F$. Then,

$$
\begin{aligned}
\overline{p_{new}^2} &= \frac{\sum p^2}{F'\,M} \\
&= \frac{F}{F'}\frac{\sum p^2}{F\,M} \\
&= \frac{\overline{p_{old}^2}}{f}
\end{aligned}
\tag{48}
$$

$\overline{p^2}$ can be reduced as much as required. This is because the unused outputs have the length 0 and reduce $\overline{p^2}$.

However, the fan-out is restricted by the noise margin, and its limit now is 3–6.

4.2 One-to-n transformer

Consider the circuit shown in Fig. 5. Some calculation results in $I_3 = \dfrac{I_1}{1 + \dfrac{1}{n}}$

$\Phi_1 = \dfrac{I_1}{\dfrac{n}{L_w} + \dfrac{1}{L_1}}$. Therefore a larger n allows a larger transfer inductance L_w.

However, there are problems in this circuit. Firstly, the signal is weak in L_w and the noise margin is reduced. Secondly, good $1 : n$ transformers are not easy to implement on VLSI chips. This method is not acceptable with the current technology.

4.3 Matched termination wiring device

Kamikawai[5] has proposed a wiring device with arbitrary length (Fig. 6). It deforms the signal by a transformer, transfers it through a strip line with matched termination, and reforms the signal by an rf-SQUID. However, the signal level in the transferring strip line is very low. The main problem of this is again the noise margin.

This device has a good property which the other two do not have. The signal can be transferred in a pipeline fashion. Therefore the clock rate is not necessarily reduced by this device. However, much the same effect will be obtained by inserting buffers without the problems of external noises.

This section has introduced three methods for long wires with small area requirements. These devices may be useful if the problem of area is dominant.

There are two problems in these devices. One is that they are weak against external noises. The other is that a long wire reduces the clock rate considerably. Therefore the essential resolution should be found in logic designs with short wires. The next section discusses such methodologies.

5. Short Wire Design Methodologies

This section presents three solutions of the wiring problems. The first one is the buffering, in which any logic design is transformed into a circuit with short wires. The second one is block algorithms, which utilize the allowed wire length in full. The third solution is the wave-front gate array, which is a simple design methodology with the shortest wire requirements.

5.1 Buffering

Since all the QFP's are driven by activation clock, insertion of buffer gates incurs no reduction of the throughput. This subsection will show that the wiring of any logic design is possible by introduction of sufficient buffers.

Firstly the two dimensional square-grid gate array model is discussed. Assume that the value $\overline{p^2}$ is obtained from a logic design with M gates. The $\overline{p^2}$ is found as unacceptable, so v buffers are inserted for the output lines of N_v gates. The number of gates $M = \sum N_v$, and the number of inserted buffers $N = F \sum v N_v$. Let the area of a QFP be $B = b\,G$, then the mean distance between the original gates becomes $\sqrt{\frac{M+N\,b}{M}}D$, and including buffers, it is $D_{new} = \sqrt{\frac{M+N\,b}{M+N}}D$.

Consider an output line which had originally the length $l = p\,D$. The length becomes longer into $l_{new} = \sqrt{\frac{M+N\,b}{M}}\,l$, and from $l_{new} = p_{new}\,D_{new}$, $p_{new} = \sqrt{\frac{M+N}{M}}\,p$. Let the constant $m = \sqrt{\frac{M+N}{M}}$. If this line is buffered by v QFP's, there are $(v+1)$ lines with the length $p_{buf} = p_{new}/(v+1)$. The square-sum is:

$$p_{buf}{}^2 (v+1) = \frac{m^2\,p^2}{v+1} \tag{49}$$

Summing up for all the lines which have v buffer stages,

$$\sum p_v{}^2 = \frac{m^2}{v+1} F N_v \overline{p_v{}^2} \tag{50}$$

The total square-mean is:

$$\overline{p_{buf}{}^2} = \frac{m^2 \sum \frac{\overline{p_v{}^2}\,N_v}{v+1}}{M+N} \tag{51}$$

Assuming that $\overline{p_v{}^2} = \overline{p^2}$,

$$\overline{p_{buf}{}^2} = \frac{\overline{p^2} \sum \frac{N_v}{v+1}}{M} \tag{52}$$

It holds $\overline{p_{buf}{}^2} \le \overline{p^2}$ since $\sum N_v = M$ and $1/(v+1) \le 1$. In a special case in which all the outputs are buffered by v QFP's, $\overline{p_{buf}{}^2} = \overline{p^2}/(v+1)$. Therefore $\overline{p^2}$

can be reduced as much as needed by inserting sufficient buffers. The length of wires is also reduced. If all the outputs are buffered by v QFP's, then the wire length becomes:

$$l_{new} = \frac{\sqrt{\frac{M+Nb}{M}}}{v+1} l$$
$$= \frac{\sqrt{1+Fbv}}{v+1} l \qquad (53)$$

Since naturally $Fb \leq 1$,

$$l_{new} \leq \frac{l}{\sqrt{v+1}} \qquad (54)$$

Therefore the length itself is reduced by the factor of $\sqrt{v+1}$. This agrees intuitively with the fact that $\overline{p_{buf}^2} = p^2/(v+1)$.

Secondly the lock-step gate array model is considered, and a wiring algorithm is presented.

Let F be the fan-out and B be the width of a buffer gate. The width of a gate D is assumed to be FB without loss of generality; make wider the gates or buffers if necessary. Consider the gates in a stage and those in the next stage. Without loss of generality, we assume the number of gates in either stage is N. Assuming that the fan-in of a gate is not more than F, the problem is simplified into the wiring from FN output ports to FN input ports.

This problem is reformed into a sorting problem. Number the ports in the second stage sequentially and assign to each port in the first stage the number its destiny has. Sort the numbers in the first stage into the second stage by an in-situ sorting algorithm. Wires are connected as the exchanges of the sort occurs. Parallel sorting algorithms suited to linear array processors are preferable here. The simplest of such algorithms is the "parallel bubble sort," which is assumed to be employed here.

To implement the parallel bubble sort as wiring, a pair of exchange circuits is needed. The first circuit corresponds to the not-exchanged case, and the second one corresponds to the exchanged case. Fig. 7 shows such an example. Each of them has the inductance of three squares. When S is the available squares of a wire, up to $S/3$ exchange stages can be wired with this exchange circuits. If the sorting stages are more than $S/3$, arrays of buffers are inserted every $S/3$ stages. Since the sorting finishes after at most FN stages, the wiring finishes with at most $3FN/S$ stages of buffers.

116

Fig. 8 shows an example circuit which is equivalent to the circuit in Fig. 4. Here, dotted lines represent dummy signals. Clearly this algorithm is not the best one. Better algorithms which realize clever utilization of the dummy signals are required.

This subsection has shown that the buffering enables implementation of any logic design by QFP's. Although buffering does not incur any reduction of the throughput, it does not look very smart. Logic design which needs no more buffering is preferable. The next two subsections will discuss such examples.

5.2 Block algorithms

Suppose that the size of data is n bit. Although $O(\log n)$ or less complex algorithms for many arithmetic/logic functions are known, they are unusable in the QFP because of the wiring limitations. We are obliged to use at least $O(n)$ algorithms. To minimize the drawbacks from the limitation, block algorithms are preferable. Here, the word "block algorithms" represents a class of algorithms in which the bits are bundled into some groups, and fast algorithms are employed for calculations within the groups and serial algorithms are employed for calculations between the groups. Therefore, a block algorithm is a combination of two algorithms, rather than one novel algorithm.

The main decisions on block algorithms are (1) what algorithms should be employed for intra- and inter-block calculation, (2) how large is the blocks, and (3) how is the timing the bits to appear. The algorithms should be carefully selected to minimize the delay and to satisfy the wiring restrictions. The size of blocks will be determined so as to minimize the total delay, so the best choice of the size of blocks may be different in each algorithm. Therefore the size of blocks may be different in each logic component, but there is an alternative in which all the blocks are the same (carefully determined) size for the total system. The bits may be appear in parallel at once, or in serial from the firstly needed one to the lastly needed one. The most preferable situation is that the order of bits matches for an output unit and the input unit. However, this is not always true.

The block algorithms may be the most effective algorithms for QFP arithmetic /logic circuits. However, since the wiring limitation is changed according to the fabrication technology, the logic must be re-designed for every process technology. To avoid such re-designing of the logic, the extreme case, bit-serial algorithms can be employed. The configuration is named as the "wave-front gate array" in this paper.

5.3 Wave-front gate array

This subsection proposes bit-serial algorithms to be employed. Since the QFP is a latching device, a bit-serial circuit of QFP is a kind of systolic array. This paper proposes the name "wave-front gate array," associating the following vision with the waves at the seaside; The circuit will be a two dimensional array of gates and be rectangular in shape. The bits to be processed will appear at the left edge of the rectangle, one for each clock phase, from top to bottom. The process will proceed from the left upper corner to the right lower corner, again and again.

The wave-front gate array is a kind of systolic array, and the systolic array concept is proposed by Kung[6] to circumvent the wiring problems in VLSI. A systolic array consists of an iterative array of cells, and the wiring connection is allowed only between the nearest neighbors (In this paper, diagonal wiring is assumed to be allowed). In QFP chips, the wiring capacity is fairly weak, so the cells must be very small. This subject is analyzed as follows:

Suppose that each cell has n gates in it and its size is $b \times b$. Then the distance between the furthest gates in two adjacent cells is $l_{max} = 2\sqrt{2}\, b$. Since b is estimated as $b = \sqrt{n}\, D$, $l_{max} = 2\sqrt{2\, n}\, D$. No wire can be longer than this, so $p^2 < 8\, n$. Since the square-grid gate array model has resulted in $p^2 < 10$, an awful result $n < 1.2$ is reached.

The situation will be hopefully better in the lock-step gate array model. The transformation of the wave-front gate array into the lock-step gate array is depicted in Fig. 9. In this model, the cell has n gates, n_1 of them are in the first clock phase and n_2 of them are in the second. Then the longest wire has the length $p = n$. If the wiring is the same for all the cells, then no more than $F\, n$ wires cuts a vertical (now major diagonal) line. Therefore $\sum p < F\, n^2$. Since the result $\sum p < 50\, F$ has been reached in Subsec. 3.3, we have $n < 7.1$. Since this estimation is rather pessimistic, perhaps $n = 10$ will be safe.

Components such as arithmetic units, multiplexors, decoders, memories, and PLA's, which are usually highly regular in their configuration, are easily designed as wave-front gate arraies within the above restriction $n \leq 10$. Fig. 10 shows an example of PLA. However, the configuration of control units is usually random, so they are not suitable to block algorithms and the wave-front gate array configuration. Therefore we feel that the components which are suitable should be implemented either in block algorithms or in the wave-front gate array, and the other components should use buffering techniques.

5.4 Conclusion

This section has presented three proposals of resolution of the wiring problems; buffering, block algorithms and the wave-front gate array. Although buffering enables any logic design, designs with long wire requirements may fail to enjoy its advantages in full. The block algorithms will attain the maximum utilization of wiring capacity and the wave-front gate array requires short wires. However, these strategies do not look suitable to conventional control logics. More research on control logic design is required. Very new concepts in computer architecture may be needed.

6. Concluding Remarks

This section concludes this paper by overlooking the remaining problems and summarizing the discussion.

6.1 Remaining problems

Although solutions of the wiring problem have been presented, there remains some problems. This section briefly discusses such problems, to show the direction of future research.

Noise reduction technology

When the problems of noises are resolved, more fan-out will be available. Then the area restriction is reduced as mentioned in Subsec. 4.1. The main reasons of the noise problems are process incompleteness and external flux. They will be hopefully reduced when they are researched with more intensity. The problem of cross-talk noise must be also solved.

The wiring techniques

Although the buffering technique is found to enable any logic design in QFP, a large number of buffers may kill the essence of architectural ideas. Good algorithms for placement of gates, wires, and buffers are required. Experimental estimation is also needed.

The block algorithms may be the most effective in QFP circuits. The wave-front gate array is simple and requires short wires. They are suitable to components with highly regular configurations, but the main problem of these techniques is that implementing control circuits in these models looks hard.

Architecture

For QFP computers architecture, the Cyclic Pipeline Computer (CPC) has been proposed [7]. However, the CPC does not consider the wiring limitation. Control signal wires tend to be much longer than arithmetic/logic signal wires. Design methodologies for highly local control are required.

Memory

Memories for QFP computers are required to have a high-pitched pipeline. Since the clock rate of QFP computer is very high, the size of memory plane must be very small, say, up to 200×200 μm. This fact requires a very new type of memory.

When the number of virtual processors of CPC is N and the clock rate is K, a memory with access time of $K N$ will be usable for an unshared memory. However, CPC with unshared memory has not been studied.

Three dimensional implementation

Although a method of transferring a signal between chips is proposed and verified by experiment, the problems of three dimensional implementation are not fully resolved. Firstly, the method of connecting the two sides of a chip is not established. Without a concrete model for inter-layer connection, analysis on the three dimensional implementation can not progress. When a decisive model is established, design methodologies which fit to three dimensional implementation should be discussed. The situation is not a simple extension of the dimension, because of the severe restriction of wiring of QFP's.

6.2 Conclusion

The wiring problems of the QFP has been analyzed. The difficulties arise from two reasons: Firstly, the fully latching property of the QFP requires short wires. Secondly, the area consumption of signal wires is large because of the fixed inductance. Although there are methods for long wires, there are problems of noise and latency. This paper has proposed buffering, block algorithms, and the wave-front gate array as essential solutions. Buffering enables any logic design to be implemented by QFP's. The block algorithms are the most efficient for regular patterned components. The wave-front gate array offers simple and smart design of logic circuits without requiring long wires. More research on noise reduction, architecture, memory, and three dimensional implementation is needed.

References

[1] M. Hosoya, W. Hioe, J. Casas, R. Kamikawai, Y. Harada, Y. Wada, H. Nakane, R. Suda, and E. Goto, "Quantum Flux Parametron," IEEE Trans. Appl. Superconductivity, Vol. 1, No. 2, pp. 75–89, June, 1991.

[2] W. Hioe, M. Hosoya, and E. Goto, "A New Quantum Flux Parametron Logic Gate with Large Input Margin," IEEE Trans. Mag, Vol. 27, No. 2, pp. 2765–2768, Mar. 1991.

[3] M. Yamada, T. Chiba, and A. Masaki, "Considerations on the Factors of Wiring," IEICE Conference Proceedings, p. 2D-1, 1972 (in Japanese).

[4] M. Hosoya, W. Hioe, E. Goto, Y. Wada, R. Suda, R. Kamikawai, and N. Miyamoto, "Proto-Type Model of Three-dimensional QFP Circuits," ISEC '91 Extended Abstract, Glasgow, Scotland, pp. 188–191, 1991.

[5] R. Kamikawai, US patent, pending.

[6] H. T. Kung and C. E. Leiserson, "Algorithms for VLSI processor arrays," Symposium on Sparse Matrix Computations, Knoxville, Tenn, 1978.

[7] K. Shimizu, E. Goto, and S. Ichikawa, "CPC (Cyclic Pipeline Computer) — An Architecture for Josephson and Pipelined-Memory Machines," IEEE Trans. Comp, Vol. 38, No. 6, June 1989.

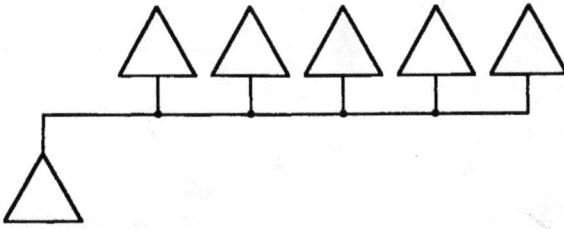

Fig. 1. Serial fan-out

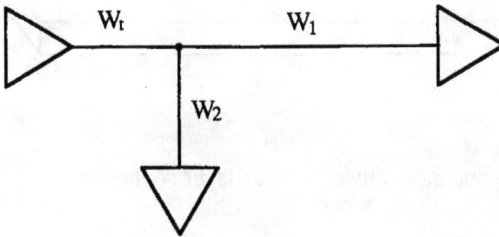

1. Serial fan-out wiring

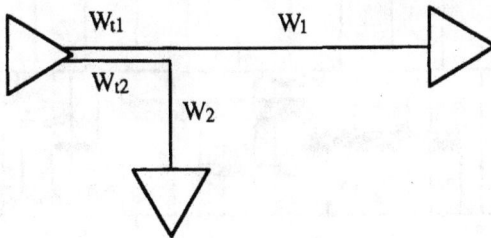

2. Equivalent parallel fan-out wiring

Fig. 2. Serial-parallel transformation

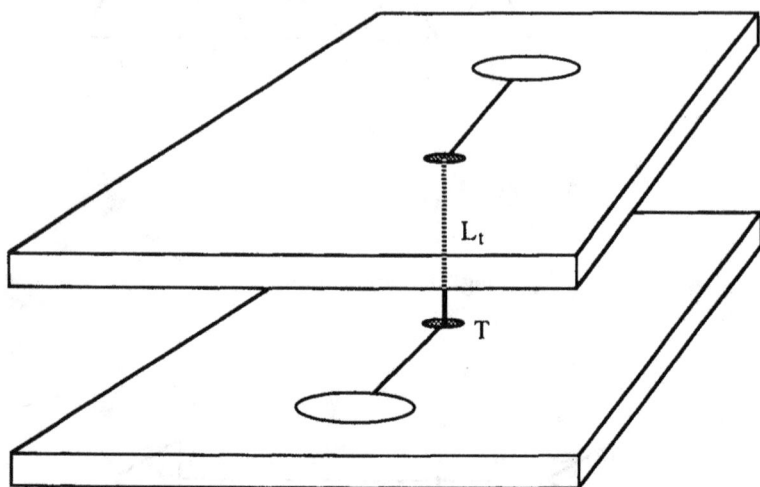

Fig. 3. A model of inter-layer connecter

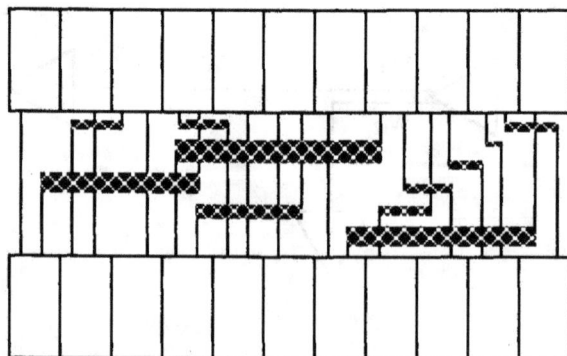

Fig. 4. The lock-step gate array model

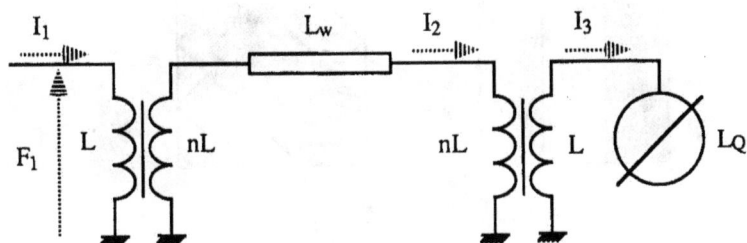

Fig. 5. A 1 : n transformer

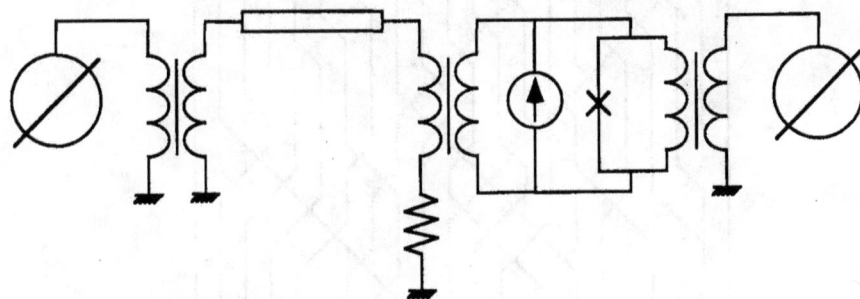

Fig. 6. Matched termination wiring device

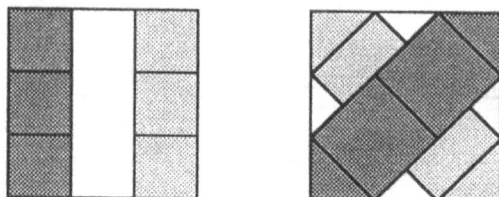

Fig. 7. A pair of exchange circuits

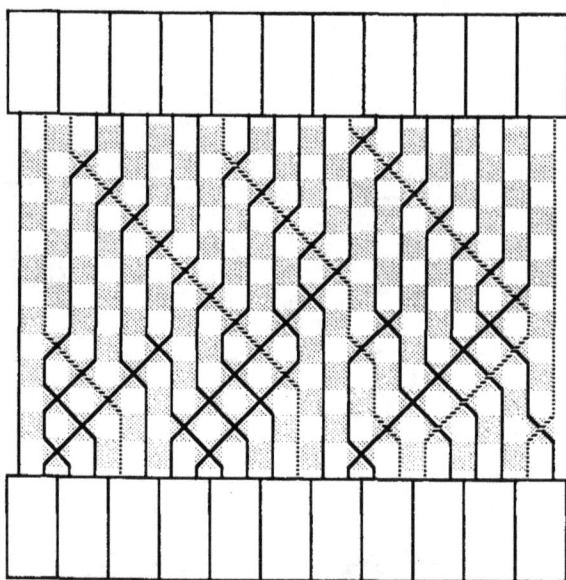

Fig. 8. Wiring example by parallel bubble sort

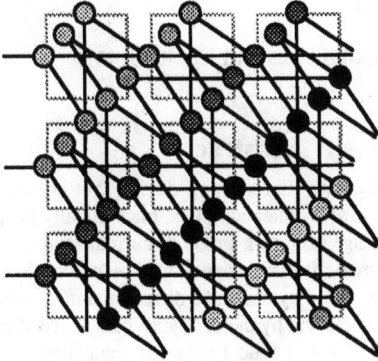

Fig. 9. The wave-front gate array model

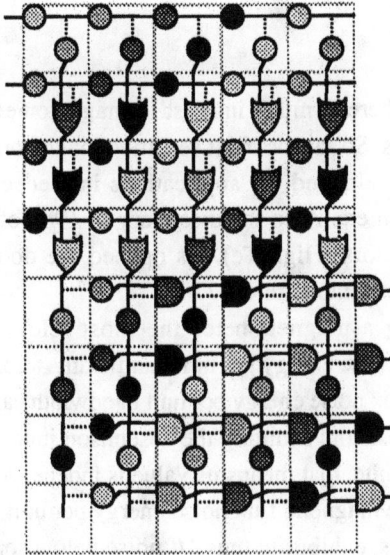

Fig. 10. An example of wave-front gate array circuit

Highly Sensitive Magnetometer

Juan Casas and Eiichi Goto

Abstract

This paper presents a magnetic flux sensing device that is made by using two dc Squids. The dc Squids are of similar characteristics, magnetically coupled by a common coil and are turned into the voltage state by a single dc current source. As the dc Squids are magnetically coupled, the magnetic flux noise generated by one of the dc Squids is sensed by the other one and vice versa. Then by making a differential measurement across both dc Squids, the magnetic flux noise detected by the dc Squids can be added either constructively or destructively. This means that magnetic flux noise cancellation is possible as it is demonstrated experimentally. The double dc Squid configuration can also be used in the add flux noise mode, case in which there is no loss of performance when comparing with what is possible to obtain with a single dc Squid. Another non-negligible advantage of the two dc Squids configuration is that the output impedance is twice as large that of the a dc Squid with Josephson junctions of same critical current and shunting resistance. Then in the former configuration the matching to room temperature electronics is simplified.

1. Introduction

At the present time there is much interest in magnetometers because of their wide array of applications. So far the most sensitive magnetometers are dc Squids. Dc Squids have been developped for applications in medecine, non-destructive evaluation, geomagnetism etc. Also the discovery in 1986 of a new kind of high temperature superconductors (High Tc) has opened the door toward dc Squids operating at liquid nitrogen temperatures (77 K).

When characterizing a magnetometer the most relevant parameter is the equivalent magnetic flux noise energy per unit bandwidth stored in the sensing area. The dc Squid magnetic flux noise energy per unit bandwidth can be easily estimated if it is produced by the resistors shunting the Josephson junctions. In this case the noise is supposed to be white, that means its value is independent on the frequency. From previous reports the magnetic flux noise energy per unit bandwidth increases when frequency decreases, exhibiting thus 1/f noise below some given frequency. For reducing the 1/f noise component, magnetic flux modulation techniques (Flux Locked Loop techniques) are usually employed. With flux modulation techniques 1/f fluctuations in the critical current of the Josephson junctions are effectively reduced. However there seems to be 1/f noise due to the motion of flux lines trapped inside the body of the Squid and at the present time no modulation technique exists capable of reducing this noise.

The motivation of this work is to realize a magnetic flux sensing device using a reactive element for matching an input coil with the multi-turn input coil of a dc Squid. Depending on the structure a magnetic flux noise cancellation technique can be implemented. In such a case a trade-off in magnetic coupling between the dc Squid input coil and its washer coil has to be made.

So far single and double dc Squids have been succesfully tested and fabricated. The process used for fabricating our devices is the same as the one employed for the QFP. Fortunately the QFP and the dc Squid Josephson junctions are both optimized with relatively low values for the critical current (about 20μA).

In this work it is also shown that two dc Squids can operate together. With the double dc Squid configuration magnetic flux noise cancellation is possible. The dc Squids are magnetically coupled by a common coil, thus magnetic flux noise present inside the washer coil of one of the dc Squids is sensed by the second dc Squid. Magnetic flux noise is converted into voltage noise by the dc Squids, then by making a differential measurement across both dc Squids magnetic flux noise cancellation occurs. To our knowledge it is the first time that a magnetic flux sensing device capable of reducing its intrinsic magnetic flux noise has been implemented. Also the double dc Squid configuration can be used in the same way as a single dc Squid. In this case the overall energy sensitivity is the same for both devices but the output impedance is higher for the double dc Squid configuration. Then for the latter device the matching to the room temperature electronics is simplified.

2.The dc Squid

The dc Squid is a superconducting loop interrupted by two Josephson junctions. The Josephson junctions are biased to the normal state by a dc current I flowing across the dc Squid. When a magnetic field is applied, the magnetic flux threading the dc Squid loop produces a screening current around the dc Squid loop and a voltage difference across the dc Squid. The dc Squid is then a magnetic flux to voltage transducer with a resolution much better than the quantum of flux Φ_o (Φ_o = $h/2e$, where h is the Planck's constant and e the electronic charge).

Nyquist noise across each resistor R shunting a Josephson junction limits the minimum magnetic flux noise energy ε stored in a dc Squid. These resistors generate noise via two uncorrelated mechanisms: voltage noise across the dc Squid and flux noise due to current noise circulating around the dc Squid loop. The voltage noise power spectral density is given by:

$$V_n(f)^2 = 2\,k_b\,T\,R \tag{1}$$

where f is the frequency, k_b the Boltzmann constant and T the shunting resistors temperature.

The magnetic flux noise power spectral density is:

$$\left[\Phi_n\,(f)\right]^2 = L_s^2\,[J\,_n(f)]^2 = \frac{2\,k_b\,T\,L_s^2}{R} \tag{2}$$

where $J_n[f]^2$ is the circulating noise current power spectral density and L_s is the dc Squid loop self-inductance.

The magnetic flux noise is converted into voltage by the dc Squid. When the dc Squid is biased with a magnetic flux of $\Phi_0/4$, the magnetic flux to voltage transfer coefficient V_Φ can be given approximately by:

$$V_\Phi = \frac{2}{(1+\beta)}\,\frac{R\,I_0}{\Phi_0} \tag{3}$$

where $\beta = 2\,L_s\,I_0/\Phi_0$ and I_0 is the Josephson junction critical current. Figure 1 compares V_Φ given by Equation 3 and calculated numerically.

The equivalent magnetic flux noise energy per unit bandwidth ε stored in L_s is proportional to the addition of magnetic flux noise and voltage noise converted to magnetic flux:

$$\varepsilon = \frac{\left[\Phi_n\,(f)\right]^2 + \left(V_n(f)/V_\Phi\right)^2}{2\,L_s} = \frac{k_b\,T}{\omega_c}\left[1 + \left(\frac{1+\beta}{\beta}\right)^2\right] \tag{4}$$

where $\omega_c = R\,/L_s$ is the characteristic angular frequency of the dc Squid.

The dc Squid output voltage versus bias current should be non hysteretic (single valued). Non hysteretic behavior is obtained when $\beta_c = 2\,\pi R^2\,I_0\,C/\Phi_0 \leq 1$, where C is the Josephson junction shunting capacitance. The best magnetic flux energy sensitivity is obtained when $\beta_c = 1$. Finally the magnetic flux noise energy can be minimized as a function of β in which case one finds:

$$\varepsilon \approx 8.13\,k_b\,T\,\sqrt{L_s\,C} = 3.4\,\frac{k_b\,T}{\omega_c}\quad\text{when}\quad\beta \approx 1.82 \tag{5}$$

Equation 5 is to be compared with $\varepsilon = 18\,k_b\,T\,\sqrt{L_s\,C}$ when $\beta \approx 1$ given by numerical simulations aiming at calculating the optimized magnetic flux energy sensitivity of a dc Squid[2]. Given the simplicity of the calculations that are presented in this section it can be concluded that the model presented is in relatively good agreement with much more accurate numerical calculations.

3. Coupled dc Squid

An autonomous dc Squid can have a very low magnetic flux noise energy approaching the quantum limit by simply reducing the dc Squid loop self inductance (the Josephson junctions capacitance are limited by technological constraints). However an autonomous dc Squid is only of academic interest because a dc Squid can have a wide array of applications only if it is magnetically coupled to an external circuit. In the case of modern planar technologies, the dc Squid loop is a square washer on top of which a multiturn spiral input coil is evaporated[3] (see Figure 2a). When the dc Squid self inductance is reduced below a certain limit, the magnetic flux coupling efficiency with the input coil decreases dramatically and the overall magnetic flux energy resolution of a coupled Squid decreases as well. Then it is of interest to calculate the relevant equations for a coupled dc Squid taking into account technological constraints.

Figure 2 presents a planar dc Squid with a multiturn input coil[3]. The minimum dimensions have to respect the fabrication layout constraints: all striplines widths and separations have to be greater than Δ, the minimum line resolution.

Taking into account coupling via the slit; the dc Squid self inductance L_s, the mutual inductance M between the Squid loop and the multiturn input coil and the multiturn input coil self inductance L_i are:

$$L_s = L_H + L_{para} + (2 N + 3) \Delta L_\delta \qquad (6)$$

$$M = N\left[L_H + \left(N + \frac{3}{2}\right) \Delta L_\delta\right] \qquad (7)$$

$$L_i = N^2 L_H + \left[\frac{2 N^3}{3} + \frac{3 N^2}{2} + \frac{7 N}{3} + 3\right]\Delta L_\delta + \left[(4 N - 1) w - (8 N^2 + 2 N - 1) \Delta\right] L_{strip} \qquad (8)$$

where L_H is the dc Squid central hole inductance, L_{para} the parasitic inductance of the connection to the Josephson junctions[4], L_δ the open or covered slit inductance per unit length[5], N the number of turns of the input coil, L_{strip} the stripline inductance per unit length of the input coil[5,6] and w the Squid washer width.

The central hole self inductance is well approximated by[3]:

$$L_H \cong 1.25 \, \mu_o \, d \quad \text{when } w \geq 3 \, d \qquad (9)$$

where μ_o is $4 \, \pi \, 10^{-7}$ H/m and d the Squid washer central hole width.

The magnetic flux coupling coefficient k can now be calculated:

$$k = M / \sqrt{(L_s - L_{para}) L_i} \qquad (10)$$

To conclude this chapter, the most important calculation is the coupled magnetic flux noise energy ε^c per unit bandwidth[3]. The coupled magnetic flux noise energy is related to the amount of magnetic flux noise to be applied across the dc Squid input coil to generate an amount of magnetic flux noise energy inside the dc Squid loop identical to its intrinsic magnetic flux noise energy ε.

$$\varepsilon^c = \varepsilon / k^2 \% \sqrt{L_s} / k^2 \qquad (11)$$

Figure 3 shows ε^c versus the dc Squid self inductance for a given number of turns of the input coil as well as for a given dc Squid self inductance with a varying number of turns. Table 1 shows the optimum dc Squid parameters along with the expected ε^c for minimum line resolutions of 2.5 and 5 μm.

A final point concerning the design of a dc Squid is that the parasitic capacitance between its square washer coil and its input coil can degrade the overall performance. It is usually recommended that the total parasitic capacitance do not exceed the Josephson junctions shunting capacitance. Table 1 shows that the best magnetic flux energy sensitivities are obtained for an input coil with moderate number of turns in which case parasitic capacitances should not make any troubles.

Table 1: Optimum coupled magnetic flux noise energy per unit bandwidth (Formulas 5 and 11) taking into account technological constraints. Calculations are done for a washer coil with the slit covered (lower L_δ) or not (higher L_δ).Shunting resistors temperature is 4.2K. L_s is calculated for N integer by using Formula 6. L_{para}, L_{strip}, L_δ and C values are somewhat arbitrarily chosen but their order of magnitude represent typical values.

$\varepsilon^c/_h$	Δ [μm]	L_{para}[pH]	L_s [pH]	N	k	L_{strip} [pH/μm]	L_δ [pH/μm]	C [pF]
13.7	2.5	7.5	18.3	8.6	0.84	0.167	0.02	0.25
19.7	2.5	7.5	33.1	3.3	0.81	0.167	0.39	0.25
34.9	5	14	31.4	6.8	0.85	0.12	0.02	1
54.9	5	14	64.4	2.9	0.81	0.12	0.48	1

4.Multiple dc Squids coupled by a common coil

A single dc Squid has an output inpedance that is difficult to match to room temperature electronics because of its low value. In order to increase its output impedance several dc Squids can be cascaded serially as shown in Figure 4. The analysis that is given below can be generalized to the case of N dc Squids cascaded serially.

The most relevant parameter is the energy sensitivity ε_p referred to the search coil of self-inductance L_p. In order to compare the performance of the devices shown in Figure 4, the energy sensitivity referred to the search coil is estimated. As can be seen in Figure 4, the equivalent inductance in parallel with the search coil is always L_i.

Single dc Squid (Figure 4a). In the case of a single dc Squid the magnetic flux noise energy ε_p^{sgl} referred to its search coil is:

$$\varepsilon_p^{sgl} \approx \frac{1}{k^2\, S_f(1 - S_f)}\, \frac{k_b\, T}{\omega_c}\left[(1 - k^2\, S_f)^2 + \left(\frac{1 + \beta}{\beta}\right)^2\right]$$ (12)

where S_f is a screening factor given by:

$$S_f = \frac{L_i}{L_i + L_p}$$ (13)

where L_i is the self inductance of the dc Squid multiturn input coil.

Double dc Squid with input coil in series (Figure 4b). In this configuration the dc Squid multiturn input coil self-inductance is $L_i/2$. Each dc Squid effective self-inductance L_{eff} is:

$$L_{eff} = \left(1 - \frac{k^2}{2} S_f\right) L_s \qquad (14)$$

The noise voltage produced across each dc Squid is:

$$\begin{cases} \Gamma_A = V_n^a + \left[L_{eff} \, i_n^a - \frac{k^2}{2} S_f L_s \, i_n^b\right] V_\Phi \\ \Gamma_B = V_n^b + \left[L_{eff} \, i_n^b - \frac{k^2}{2} S_f L_s \, i_n^a\right] V_\Phi \end{cases} \qquad (15)$$

It can be seen that each dc Squid senses part of the flux noise produced by the second dc Squid. The magnetic flux noise energy referred to the search coil is:

$$\varepsilon_p^{2s} \approx \frac{1}{k^2 \, S_f (1 - S_f)} \frac{k_b \, T}{\omega_c} \left[\left(1 - k^2 \, S_f\right)^2 + \left(\frac{1 + \beta}{\beta}\right)^2\right] \qquad (16)$$

Double dc Squid with input coils in parallel (Figure 4c). In this configuration the dc Squid multiturn input coil self-inductance is $2 L_i$. Each dc Squid effective self-inductance L_{eff} is:

$$L_{eff} = \left(1 - \frac{k^2}{2} S_f \frac{2 L_i + L_p}{L_i}\right) L_s \qquad (17)$$

The noise voltage produced across each dc Squid is now:

$$\begin{cases} \Gamma_A = V_n^a + \left[L_{eff} \, i_n^a + \frac{k^2}{2} \frac{L_p \, L_s}{L_i + L_p} \, i_n^b\right] V_\Phi \\ \Gamma_B = V_n^b + \left[L_{eff} \, i_n^b + \frac{k^2}{2} \frac{L_p \, L_s}{L_i + L_p} \, i_n^a\right] V_\Phi \end{cases} \qquad (18)$$

Again the magnetic flux noise energy referred to the search coil is:

$$\varepsilon_p^{2p} \approx \frac{1}{k^2 \, S_f(1 - S_f)} \frac{k_b \, T}{\omega_c} \left[\left(1 - k^2 \, S_f\right)^2 + \left(\frac{1 + \beta}{\beta}\right)^2 \right] \tag{19}$$

Then from the noise energy point of view no gain in performance is obtained when using the above multiple dc Squid structures when comparing with the single dc Squid case. However if several dc Squids are connected serially the output impedance will become larger simplifying the coupling of the magnetometer with the room temperature electronics.

5. Magnetically coupled dc Squids and magnetic flux noise cancellation

Fig. 5 shows a device made by using two dc Squids magnetically coupled together. The magnetic flux noises sensed by by the left Φ_n^l and right Φ_n^r dc Squids are given by Eq. 20 and depending on the parameters settings, it is possible either to cancel or add the dc Squids intrinsic magnetic flux noises.

$$\begin{cases} \Phi_n^l(\omega) = \left(1 - \dfrac{k_n^2}{2}\right) \Psi_n^l(\omega) + \dfrac{k_n^2}{2} \, \Psi_n^r(\omega) \\[2mm] \Phi_n^r(\omega) = \left(1 - \dfrac{k_n^2}{2}\right) \Psi_n^r(\omega) + \dfrac{k_n^2}{2} \, \Psi_n^l(\omega) \end{cases} \tag{20}$$

The equivalent magnetic flux noise power spectral density of the double dc Squid system when the magnetic flux noises of both dc Squids are added constructively S_Φ^+ (*conventional* mode) and destructively S_Φ^- (*cancelling* mode) are:

$$S_\Phi^+(\omega) = \frac{V_n^{l2} + V_n^{r2}}{V_\Phi^{c\,2}} + \left(\frac{V_\Phi}{V_\Phi^c}\right)^2 \left(\Psi_n^r(\omega)^2 + \Psi_n^l(\omega)^2\right) \tag{21}$$

$$S_\Phi^-(\omega) = \frac{V_n^{l2} + V_n^{r2}}{V_\Phi^{c\,2}} + \left(\frac{V_\Phi}{V_\Phi^c}\right)^2 \left(1 - k_n^2\right)^2 \left(\Psi_n^r(\omega)^2 + \Psi_n^l(\omega)^2\right) \tag{22}$$

If both dc Squids are identical, S_Φ^+ can be approximated by:

$$S_\Phi^+(\omega) \approx \frac{1}{2}\left(\frac{V_n^{l\,2}}{V_\Phi^{\,2}} + L_s^2\, j_n^l(\omega)^2\right)$$

(23)

where j_n^l and j_n^r are the noise current generators responsible for the dc Squids magnetic flux noise. From the last formula it can be seen that a double dc Squid configuration operated in the conventional mode has about $\sqrt{2}$ the magnetic flux noise sensitivity of a single dc Squid with self inductance L_s. However from the energy sensitivity point of view no gain is obtained when using this structure as it was explained in the precedent chapter.

6. Reactive Magnetometers

A reactive magnetometer can be for instance a dc Squid with a multiturn input coil matched to a search coil by using a negative inductance (Figure 6). The negative inductance can be for instance a Josephson junction or a dc Squid biased by a suitable magnetic flux.

The negative inductance value is adjusted in order that this inductance in parallel with the search coil are equilent to a very large value. In such a case the energy sensitivity referred to the search coil is given by:

$$\varepsilon_o = \frac{L_o}{L_i}\,\varepsilon_i$$

(24)

where ε_S is the energy sensitivity of the bare dc Squid. In Eq. 24 the ratio L_o/L_i can be made arbitrarily low. Then in the absence of noise the energy sensitivity of such a system can be made arbitrarily high.

A second approach is a the Quad magnetometer. The Quad magnetometer is shown in Fig. 7. Its principal elements are an input coil, a negative inductance and two coupled dc Squids. The negative inductance can be a dc Squid in the superconducting state biased by a suitable magnetic flux, its equivalent inductance value can be considered constant only for small input signals. Ideally the negative inductance in parallel with the input coil should present an infinite inductance to the dc Squids coupling coils, in order that current noise created by magnetic flux noise present in one of the dc Squids circulates only in the coupling coil.

The magnetic flux noise sensed by the left Φ_n^l and right Φ_n^r dc Squids (see Fig. 1) are respectively,

$$\begin{cases} \Phi_n^l(\omega) = \left(1 - \dfrac{k_n^2}{2}\right) \Psi_n^l(\omega) + \dfrac{k_n^2}{2} \Psi_n^r(\omega) \\[2mm] \Phi_n^r(\omega) = \left(1 - \dfrac{k_n^2}{2}\right) \Psi_n^r(\omega) + \dfrac{k_n^2}{2} \Psi_n^l(\omega) \end{cases} \qquad (25)$$

where k_n is the coupling efficiency between each dc Squid washer coil and its coupling coil of self inductance L_n and Ψ_n^l and Ψ_n^r are respectively the intrinsic magnetic flux noises of the left and right dc Squids. From herein superscripts l and r refer respectively to the left and right dc Squids.

By measuring differentially across both dc Squids, the equivalent magnetic flux noise power spectral density is:

$$S_\Phi(\omega) = \frac{V_n^r(\omega)^2 + V_n^l(\omega)^2}{V_\Phi^{c\,2}} + \left(\frac{V_\Phi}{V_\Phi^c}\right)^2 \left(1 - k_n^2\right)^2 \left(\Psi_n^r(\omega)^2 + \Psi_n^l(\omega)^2\right)$$

$$(26)$$

where V_Φ^c is the magnetic flux to voltage transfer coefficient across both dc Squids (typically twice V_Φ).

The magnetic flux Φ_i forwarded to both dc Squids when a magnetic flux Ψ_o is applied to the input coil L_o is:

$$\Phi_i = 2 \left(1 - \frac{k_n k'}{k_i}\right) k_i \sqrt{\frac{L_i}{L_o}} \, \Psi_o$$

$$(27)$$

where k' is the coupling constant between each dc Squid input coil L_i and coupling coil L_n and k_i is the coupling constant between each dc Squid washer and its input coil L_i.

The signal to noise ratio is obtained by calculating Φ_i/S_Φ and the Quad magnetometer is optimized when this quantity is maximized. It can be seen then that in the limit of perfect coupling (i.e. all coupling constants equal to unity) the dc Squids intrinsic magnetic flux noises are completely cancelled but on the other hand the input signal is completely screened by the coupling coil. Then a trade-off exists in choosing the magnetic flux coupling efficiencies.

Because the negative inductance, L^*, is always in the superconducting state, there is no need to shunt the JJs by external resistors. The equivalent shunting resistance of a JJ is then its subgap resistance that can have values much in excess that of the usual resistance shunting a JJ of a non-hysteretic dc Squid. Thermal noise current generated by the subgap resistance of the JJs limits the precision with which the value of L^* can be adjusted, thus limiting the minimum possible magnetic flux resolution. A more detailed description of the above devices will be presented elsewhere.

A final word of caution when using a reactive element to match an input coil with the multiturn coil of a dc Squid is that the dc Squid magnetic flux noise is amplified and fed to the input coil. Then if the sample under test is sensitive on reactive fields the above devices might not be used. For instance in the case of biological samples reactive fields are not of concern and then reactive elements can be used to increase the sensitivity of present magnetometers.

7. Experimental Results

The performance of the double dc Squid magnetometer is investigated by measuring its overall magnetic flux sensitivity, that of each dc Squid separately and the cross correlation S_{Φ}^{xy} of the magnetic flux noises sensed by each dc Squid. S_{Φ}^{xy} is obtained by multiplying Φ_n^l and Φ_n^r of Eq. 20:

$$S_{\Phi}^{xy} = \frac{k_n^2}{2}\left(1 - \frac{k_n^2}{2}\right)\left(\Psi_n^l(\omega)\,\Psi_n^l(\omega)^* + \Psi_n^r(\omega)\,\Psi_n^r(\omega)^*\right) \tag{28}$$

The magnetic flux noise power spectral densities of each dc Squid are:

$$\left| \begin{array}{l} S_{\Phi}^l(\omega) = \dfrac{V_n^l(\omega)^2}{V_{\Phi}^2} + \left(1 - \dfrac{k_n^2}{2}\right)^2 \Psi_n^l(\omega)^2 + \dfrac{k_n^4}{4}\,\Psi_n^r(\omega)^2 \\[4mm] S_{\Phi}^r(\omega) = \dfrac{V_n^r(\omega)^2}{V_{\Phi}^2} + \left(1 - \dfrac{k_n^2}{2}\right)^2 \Psi_n^r(\omega)^2 + \dfrac{k_n^4}{4}\,\Psi_n^l(\omega)^2 \end{array} \right. \tag{29}$$

S_{Φ}^{xy} is a complex quantity and has phase information. As the dc Squids are biased serially by the same dc current source, when magnetic flux noise is cancelled or added the phase between the dc Squids cross correlated magnetic flux noises should be 0° and 180° respectively.

On Fig. 5 the input labeled "synchro" was used to "synchronize" the voltage versus flux characteristics of both dc Squids in order to maximize their differential voltage swing. Inputs "a" and "b" were used respectively to operate the double dc Squid system in the conventional and cancelling mode. The double dc Squid parameters are shown in Tab. 2.

Fig. 8 shows the voltage versus flux characteristics of the double dc Squid magnetometer and that of each of its dc Squids. The effective magnetic flux noise sensed by each dc Squid can be equivalently produced by a noise current generator connected at input "a". Figs. 8b and 9 are of help in understanding how magnetic flux noise cancellation occurs when operating the double dc Squid in the cancelling mode. Fig. 8b shows that when $\Phi_0/4$ is applied by using input "b" (i.e. double dc Squid system biased into the cancelling mode), almost no voltage variation is detected across the double dc Squid magnetometer when applying magnetic flux by using the coupling coil, then a current noise generator at input "a" produce almost no voltage noise across the double dc Squid system. Fig. 8b can be understood by using Fig. 9: the output voltage across each dc Squid in the same conditions of those of Fig. 8b are shown, the difference between the two traces is almost constant.

Fig. 10 shows the magnetic flux noise power spectral density for each dc Squid when the double dc Squid system was operated in the conventional or in the cancelling mode. The preamplifier stage has a bandwidth up to 2 kHz, the noise level referred to its input is 250 pV $s^{1/2}$ and the FFT window function is *Minimum*. The amplification stage is made by a NF-LI 772L transformer, followed by a battery powered NF-LI 75A low noise preamplifier. The Squid and amplification stage were inside a shielded room.

The magnetic flux noise cross correlation spectrums when the double dc Squid system was operated in the conventional or cancelling mode are shown respectively in Fig. 11 and 12. As expected the phases between the cross correlated signals are either 180° or 0°. For obtaining Figs. 11 and 12 each dc Squid was biased to the voltage state by different dc current sources in order to prevent the introduction of extra correlated noise.

Table 2. Double dc Squid characteristics. Experimental and calculated values for the different parameters are indicated when both exist. The experimental and expected "optimum"[1] magnetic flux noise spectral density is also shown in the case of a single dc Squid. Refer to Fig. 1 for the meaning of the different symbols.

parameter	experimental	calculated
JJ critical current I_c	16 μA	
JJ capacitance	1 pF	
JJ shunting resistance R	4 Ω	
$\beta_c = 2\,\pi R^2 I_c\,C/\Phi_o$	0.778	
$\beta = 2\,L_s\,I_c/\Phi_o$	3.1	2.37
Squid inductance L_s	200 pH	153 pH
Input coil self inductance L_i		279 pH
Coupling coil self inductance L_n		3220 pH
Input mutual inductance M_i	112 pH	138 pH
Coupling mutual inductance M_n	588 pH	508 pH
input-coupling mutual inductance M'		588 pH
Coupling efficiency $k_i = M_i/\sqrt{L_s\,L_i}$		0.67
" " $k_n = M_n/\sqrt{L_s\,L_n}$		0.84
" " $k' = M'/\sqrt{L_n\,L_i}$		0.62
$\sqrt{S_\Phi} = (36\,k_b\,T\,\sqrt{L_s\,C}\,L_s)^{1/2}$	$7.9\ \mu\Phi_o/\sqrt{Hz}$	$\approx 1\ \mu\Phi_o/\sqrt{Hz}$

The overall performance of the double dc Squid system is shown in Fig. 13. Its equivalent magnetic flux noise in the cancelling mode is about half what was obtained for each of its dc Squids. For reference a single dc Squid identical to those

Table 3. Magnetic flux to voltage transfer coefficient for the double dc Squid system and for each dc Squid when operated in both the conventional and cancelling modes respectively. The values are deduced from the voltage versus magnetic flux oscillographs.

Magnetic flux to voltage transfer coeff.	add	cancel
V_Φ^c [μV/Φ_0]	1230	205
V_Φ^l or V_Φ^r [μV/Φ_0]	486	100

Table 4. Comparison between the calculated and measured magnetic flux noise power spectral densities of the dual dc Squid system in the white noise limit when it was operated in the conventional and cancelling mode. The calculated intrinsic magnetic flux and voltage noises for each dc Squid are also shown. For symbols explanation refer to the text.

Parameter	add		cancel	
	calc.	meas.	calc.	meas.
$\Psi_n^l \approx \Psi_n^r \; [\mu\Phi_0 \, s^{1/2}]$	5.8	-	7.7	-
$\left(V_n^r \approx V_n^l\right) \times V_\Phi \; [\mu\Phi_0 \, s^{1/2}]$	0.58	-	4.0	-
$(S_\Phi)^{1/2} \; [\mu\Phi_0 \, s^{1/2}]$	4.1	4	3.2	3

used in the double dc Squid magnetometer was investigated: its white magnetic flux noise level was found to be 7.9 $\mu\Phi_0 \, s^{1/2}$.

By measuring S_Φ^{xy}, then by using the data of Tab. 2 and 3 and Eq. 28, the intrinsic magnetic flux noises stored in each dc Squid can be calculated if both are supposed to have the same amplitude. Finally by measuring the magnetic flux noise power spectral densities of each dc Squid and by using Eq. 29, the contribution of the intrinsic voltage noise to the overall magnetic flux noise can be calculated. The results are summarized in Tab. 4. It can be seen that the calculated and measured overall performance of the double dc Squid system are in good quantitative agreement, meaning that the experimental results are self consistent.

8. Conclusion

In this paper an analysis of a single dc Squid as well as a multiple dc Squid structure has been made. The conclusion is that the overall magnetic flux noise energy referred to a search coil is similar in all the considered configurations. The main advantage of a multiple dc Squid structure is that the output impedance of such a system will be much larger than the one that is expected for a single dc Squid. Most of the dc Squids developed to date must use a more or less complicated impedance matching network between the Squid and the room temperature electronics. Then a higher output impedance will result in a simplified matching of the magnetic sensing elements with the room temperature electronics.

Also the use of reactive elements has been considered. When using a reactive element for matching a search coil with the input coil of a magnetometer, the overall magnetic flux noise sensitivity can be much improved.

Experimentally it has been shown that a double dc Squid configuration can be used in a very similar way as a single dc Squid. The resistance shunting each JJ is chosen in order that $\beta_c \leq 1$ and then a double dc Squid configuration is expected to a have an output impedance twice as large that of a single dc Squid. The matching of the double dc Squid system to the room temperature electronics is then simplified.

The overall magnetic flux sensitivity of the double dc Squid as well as that of each dc Squid was investigated. Their measurement permitted us to quantitatively know the intrinsic voltage noise and magnetic flux noise of each dc Squid. Also it is shown that by using the data obtained for each dc Squid, the overall performance of the double dc Squid system can be predicted and when comparing with the experimental data the agreement is very good.

In the case of the double dc Squid system magnetic flux noise was added either constructively or destructively. Then if excess magnetic flux noise is of concern a double dc Squid configuration can be used in order to reduce its negative influence.

References

[1] For a recent review see J. Clarke in *Superconducting Electronics*, Eds. H. Weinstock and M. Nisenoff, p. 87, NATO ASI Series, Springler-Verlag (1989)

[2] C. D. Tesche and J. Clarke, *J. Low Temp. Phys.*, 29, p. 301 (1977) and J. J. P. Bruines, V. J. de Waal and J. E. Moiij, J. Low Temp. Phys., 46, p. 383 (1982)

[3] J. M. Jaycox and M. B. Ketchen, *IEEE Trans. Mag.*, MAG-17, p. 400 (1981)

[4] W. H. Chang, *J. Appl. Phys.*, 51, p. 3801 (1980)

[5] M. Hosoya, *"Three Dimensional Inductance Calculation"*, Ph.D. Thesis, University of Tokyo (1988)

[6] W. H. Chang, *J. Appl. Phys.*, 50, p. 8129 (1979)

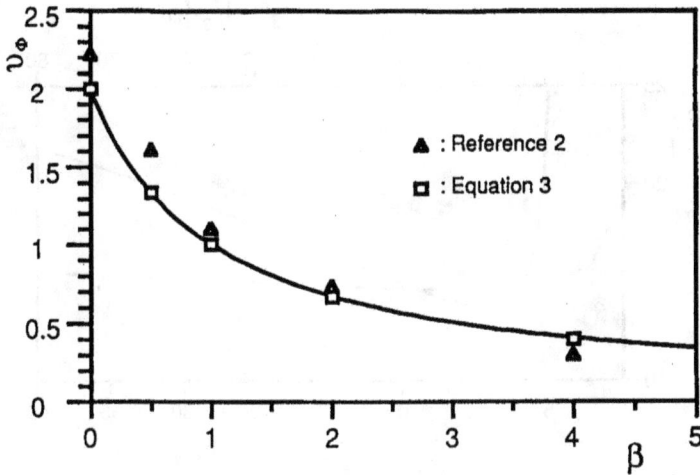

Figure 1 : Magnetic flux to voltage transfer coefficient V_Φ versus β. v_Φ units are $[R \, I_o/\Phi_o]$.

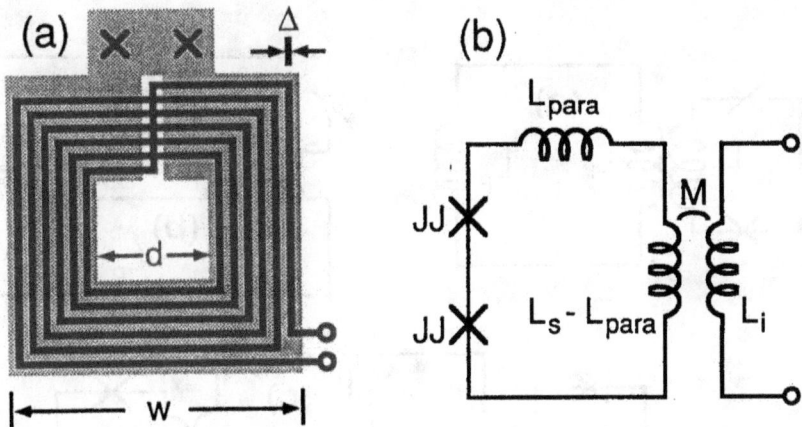

Figure 2 : (a) Layout of a planar dc Squid with a multiturn input coil. (b) dc Squid electrical scheme taking into account the parasitic inductance associated with the connection to the Josephson junctions.. Refer to the text for symbols definition.

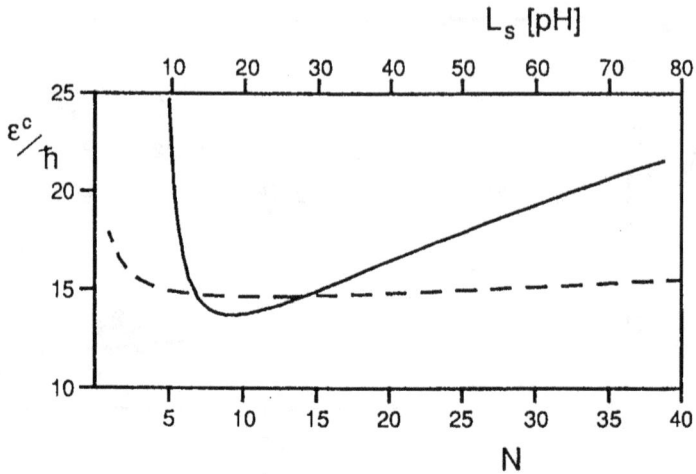

Figure 3 : Coupled magnetic noise energy per unit bandwidth ε^c over $\hbar$ versus dc Squid self inductance L_s with $N = 10$ (continuous line) and N with $L_H \approx 20$ pH (dashed line). Calculation parameters are shown in Table 1 for a covered slit and 2.5 µm linewidth resolution.

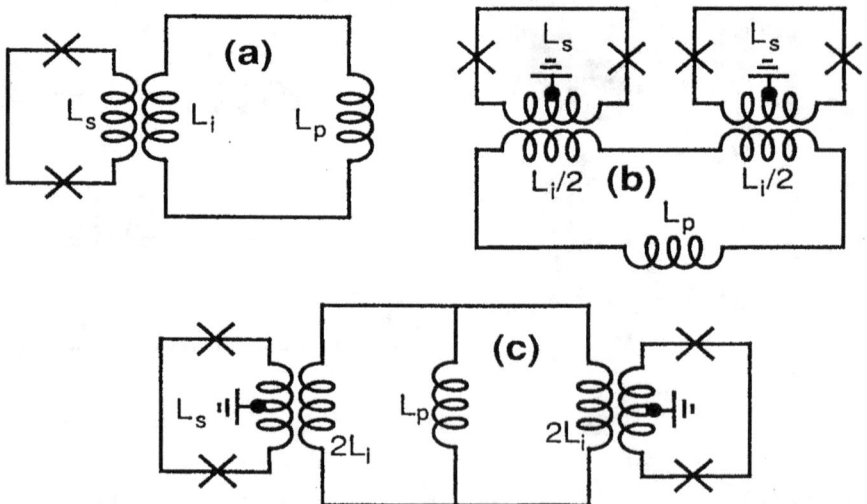

Figure 4 : dc Squid systems. (a) Single dc Squid with a coupling transformer; (b) double dc Squid with coupling transformer and dc Squids' input coils in series and (c) double dc Squid with coupling transformer and dc Squids' input coils in parallel. The double dc Squid system should be connected in series and share the same current bias source.

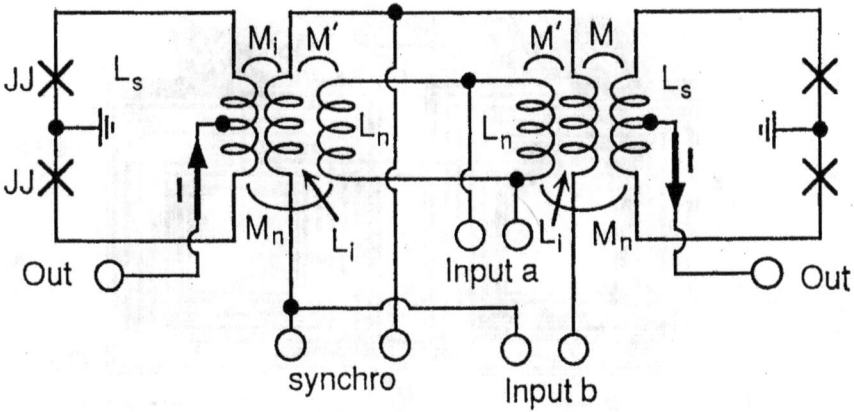

Figure 5 : Double dc Squid magnetometer diagram. A magnetic flux can be applied to the dc Squids by using either input "a" or "b". "Synchro" terminal is used to maximize the voltage swing across both dc Squids when a current is applied to input a or b. The characteristics of the experimental device can be seen in Tab. 1 and 2.

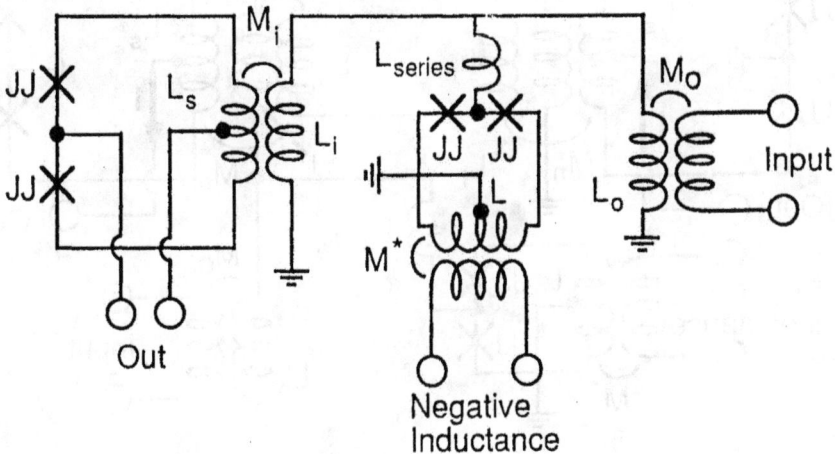

Figure 6 : Reactive magnetometer made by two dc Squid and a search coil. One of the dc Squids is used as a variable inductance in order to match the search coil with the multiturn input coil of the sensing dc Squid.

144

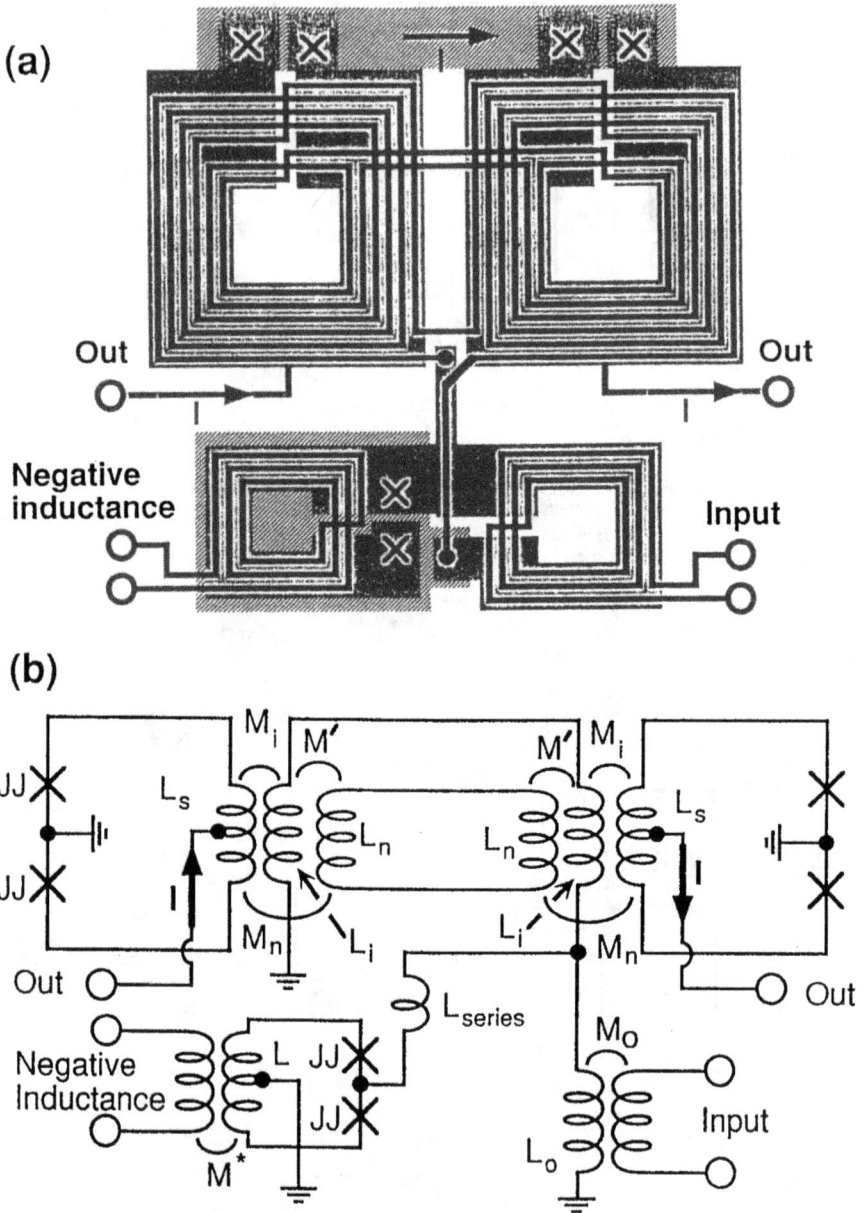

Figure 7 : Quad magnetometer. (a) Possible Quad magnetometer layout. The sensing dc Squids are at the top. The negative inductance is at the bottom left and the input coil at the bottom right. (b) Equivalent schematic diagram of the Quad magnetometer.

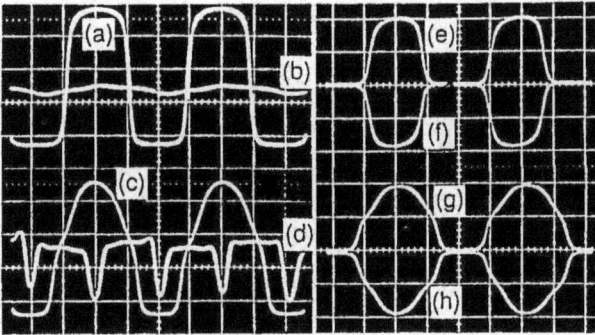

Figure 8 : Output voltage across the double dc Squid system versus input flux . (a): Voltage swing when the double dc Squid system was operated in the conventional mode. Magnetic flux noise measurements were done at about ± one div. from the center of the oscillograph. (b): Voltage swing when applying a current to "input a" and with the dc Squids biased into the cancelling mode. (c): Voltage swing when the double dc Squid system was operated in the cancelling mode. Flux noise measurements were done at about ± one div. from the center of the oscillograph. (d): Voltage swing when applying a current to "input b" with the double dc Squid system biased into the conventional mode. (e-h): Voltage swing across each dc Squid of the double dc Squid system for obtaining (a) and (c). (a) and (c) are respectively the difference between traces (e)-(f) and (g)-(h). Scales are vertical: 20 μV/div and horizontal: 2 μA/div for (a)-(b) and (e)-(f) and 20 μA/div for (c)-(d) and (g)-(h)

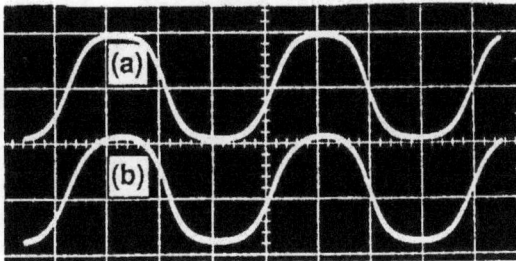

Figure 9 : Voltage swing across each dc Squid in the same conditions for obtaining Fig. 8b. Fig.8b is the differential output of the two traces. Scales are vertical: 20 μV/div and horizontal: 2 μA/div. Ground level (i.e. 0 Volts) is at the center of the oscillograph.

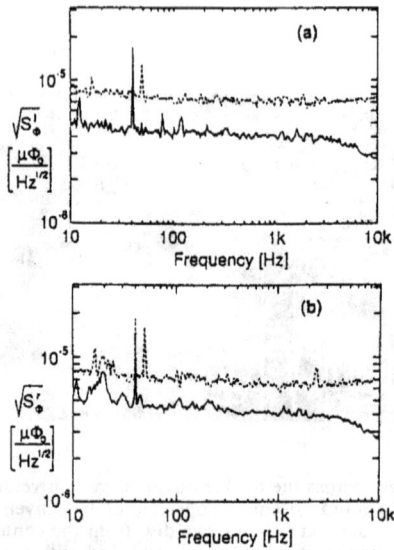

Figure 10 : Measured magnetic flux noise power spectral densities of each dc Squid of the double dc Squid system. (a) and (b) are respectively the magnetic flux noise power spectral density of the left and right dc Squids. Dashed trace: double dc Squid system operated in the cancelling mode. Solid trace: double dc Squid system operated in the conventional mode.

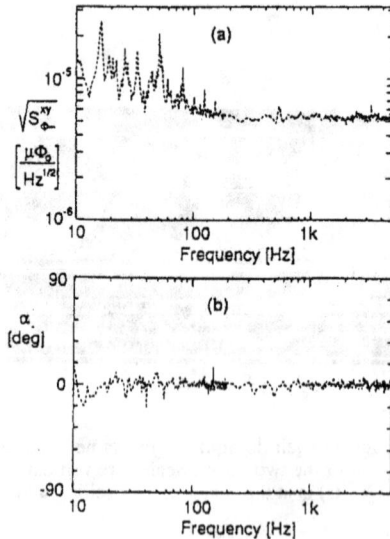

Figure 11 : Measured magnetic flux noise power spectral densities of each dc Squid of the double dc Squid system. (a) and (b) are respectively the magnetic flux noise power spectral density of the left and right dc Squids. Dashed trace: double dc Squid system operated in the cancelling mode. Solid trace: double dc Squid system operated in the conventional mode.

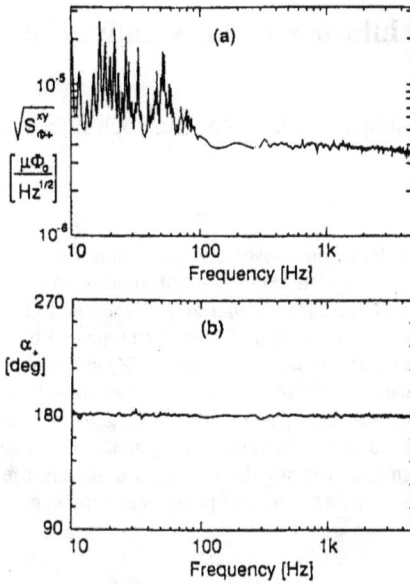

Figure 12 : Magnetic flux noise cross correlation between the right and left dc Squids of the double dc Squid system when it was operated in the cancelling mode. (a) Magnetic flux noise cross correlation power spectral density, (b) phase between the correlated signals.

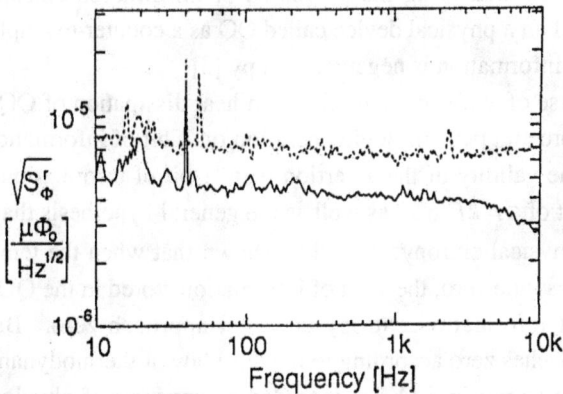

Figure 13 : Magnetic flux noise power spectral density of the double dc Squid system. Dashed trace: double dc Squid system operated in the cancelling mode. Solid trace: double dc Squid system operated in the conventional mode.

Must Information be Negative Entropy?

Nobuaki Yoshida, Eiichi Goto, Kia Fock Loe, and Willy Hioe

Abstract

A counter-example based on a Josephson junction device to be called QQ is used to show the hypothesis given by Brillouin that "information is negative entropy" and the related assertion given by Keyes, Landauer and Bennett that "1 bit of information loss inevitably generating heat of $\varepsilon = kT \ln 2$" are not in general true. Since applying their hypothesis and assertion to the information stored in QQ will lead to contradiction with the third law of thermodynamics. Furthermore, ε is shown to be heat production, instead of heat transfer. So ε should not equal to $kT \ln 2$ in general and, in the case of QQ, diminishes to zero and satisfies the nullheat requirement. Based on this counter-example we conclude that information entropy does not bear a universal relationship to physical entropy and information is not a negative of physical entropy in general.

1. Introduction

When the term 'information entropy' was introduced by Shannon in his well-known paper of information theory, there was no connotation at all that there is a profound universal connection of information entropy to physical entropy. In fact, the nomenclature was taken from the mathematical similarity in the functional form of the two quantities [1,2]. Unfortunately such a nomenclature has henceforth led to much confusion in the use of information entropy and its relation to physical entropy. The main theme of this letter is to report on physical arguments (PA's) clarifying the confusion of information entropy and physical entropy, based on a physical device called QQ as a counter-example to the general assertion that information is negative entropy [3].

In the course of analyzing the minimum heat dissipation of QQ [4], which can be used to store and perform logic operation on 1 bit of information, we were led to question the validity of the assertion that "1 bit of information loss inevitably generates heat of $\varepsilon = kT \ln 2$" as well as the general hypothesis that information is negative of physical entropy. It will be shown that when the temperature of QQ approaches absolute zero, the 1 bit of information stored in the QQ should persist, implying that information entropy does not approach zero. But the physical entropy approaches zero according to the third law of thermodynamics. Therefore if information stored in a QQ is regarded as negative of physical entropy then contradiction is inevitably. The only way to resolve the contradiction is to assume that information entropy and physical entropy are unrelated in general though we could not rule out the possibility of using physical entropy to represent information for some logic devices with certain parameter settings so that a negative of physical entropy is indeed a measure of information in those devices. In fact in this paper we only emphasize that since there exists a counter-example such as QQ against the hypothesis then information is negative of physical entropy is no more universally true.

2. Assertions by Keyes, Landauer and Bennett

To put the issue on the right perspective, we shall begin with the assertions given by Keyes, Landauer and Bennett for their proposal of "reversible computing scheme" [5]. They (KLB) asserted the following:

KLB1: It is possible to compute in "nullheat", i.e., ε, the heat produced per clock per device, can be made arbitrarily small by sufficiently slowing down the clock frequency $\omega/2$, ($\varepsilon \to 0$ on $\omega \to 0$).

KLB2: For nullheat, information loss is not permissible, since $\varepsilon = kT \ln 2$ of heat is produced per 1 bit of loss.

KLB3: "Reversible computing scheme" is the only way to realize information-losslessness and thus nullheat computing.

While some of the researchers in the field of semiconductor devices had questioned the validity of KLB1 and even considered it as Maxwell's demon [7], we expressed our doubts on KLB2 and KLB3 [5] but not KLB1. It should be noted that in logic devices energy is required to represent 1 bit of information. Under the nullheat computing scheme, information loss can be associated with heat generation through KLB1 alone.

Though there are some reversible computing devices being proposed, there is no proper physical argument to support the general validity of KLB2 and KLB3. For instance, Feynman had proposed a system which uses the orientation of an atom to represent 1 bit of information to realize a reversible computing machine [9]. But if we can find an irreversible logic device which violates KLB2 then 'the only way' for realizing nullheat computing as stated in KLB3 is no more true. In the following we shall briefly describe our analysis and simulation results on a fluxoid type of Josephson computing device to be called QQ, which is the collective name of Quantron [8] and QFP [4] to show the problem with KLB2 when QQ is used as a logic device. Details of the analysis was given in a paper in ISQM'89 [6].

This problem with KLB2 leads to a question of whether information must be negative entropy or not? We shall provide physical arguments (PA's) to answer this question.

3. Theoretical Argument

A QQ is a Josephson junction device which is flux driven by Φ_a on a shared terminal of input and output carrying flux of (Φ) as shown in **Fig. 1** (where $T_{I/O}$ is the shared terminal and G is the ground). Let I_C be the critical current of a JJ (Josephson Junction), $\Phi_0 = h/2e$, Φ_J be the flux across the JJ and $V_J = -(\Phi_0 I_C/2\pi)$ cos $(2\pi\Phi/\Phi_0)$ be the magnetic energy of the JJ, so that the super-current of the JJ is $I_S = \partial V_J/\partial \Phi_J$. By summing up the magnetic energies of the two JJ's and the external circuit, the magnetic energy V of a QQ is

$$V = -\frac{I_c\Phi_0}{2\pi} \cos\left(\frac{2\pi\Phi}{\Phi_0}\right)\cos\left(\frac{2\pi\Phi_a}{\Phi_0}\right) + \frac{(\Phi - \Phi_S)^2}{2L_L}$$

(1)

with $\partial V/\partial \Phi$ giving the total current flowing into the magnetic components. Since capacitive and resistive currents are $2C\dot{\Phi}$ and $2\dot{\Phi}/R$ respectively, the equation of motion for the flux Φ is

$$2C\ddot{\Phi} + \frac{2\dot{\Phi}}{R} + \frac{\partial V}{\partial \Phi} = 0$$

(2)

For sufficiently slow ω, (2) implies $\partial V/\partial \Phi = 0$ which gives the static equilibrium points of the QQ and $\partial^2 V/\partial \Phi^2 > 0$ (minimal energy) is the stability condition.

Fig. 2 gives V for two cases. In the fully activated case denoted by A, the potential V has two minima and 1 bit of information is stored according to the polarity $p = \pm 1$ of the flux Φ, whereas in the quenched case denoted by Q, no information is stored. QQ's are coupled to each other via superconducting inductors so as to transfer fluxes among one another. In Fig. 1, L_L represents the total inductance of such coupling and Φ_S is the effective flux transferred from other QQ's.

KLB1 was stated as a result of some gedanken experiments without showing any actual physical devices. However we have shown experimentally that QQ operates with good agreement with simulations based on eq. (2). And ε_R, heat generated at the damping resistors per clock cycle, is given by,

$$\varepsilon_R = \int dt \frac{V_1^2 + V_2^2}{R} = \int 2dt \frac{\dot{\Phi}^2 + \dot{\Phi}_a^2}{R}$$

Provided that $\omega << \omega_{MAX} \approx 10^{10}$ rad s^{-1} and that negative quenching is avoided, ε_R takes a nullheat form [6] $\varepsilon_R = H\omega$ with $H < 10^{-29}$ J.s so that

$$\varepsilon = \varepsilon_R + E = H\omega + E \tag{3}$$

where E is the term pertinent to the device entropy S. Denoting the information (bits) stored in the device by I and the device temperature by T, KLB postulated

$$E = ST = -kT \ln 2 \tag{4}$$

which may be traced back to Brillouin's negentropy hypothesis [3] (i.e., information is negative entropy):

$$\Delta S = S_{I=1} - S_{I=0} = -k \tag{5}$$

KLB2 is the consequence of (4) since one bit of information loss would generate heat of $kT \ln 2$. However, the following physical arguments namely PA1 and PA2 show that (5) and (4) respectively are questionable hypotheses in the context of QQ because,

PA1: whereas the third law of thermodynamics requires that $S \rightarrow 0$ on $T \rightarrow 0$, a QQ is supposed to store one bit of information ($I = 1$) even at arbitrary low temperature, so that (5) may have to be modified as,

$$\Delta S = -k'(T) \ln 2 \tag{5'}$$

where $k'(T)$ is a function of T such that $k'(T) \rightarrow 0$ on $T \rightarrow 0$.

PA2: Irreversible heat production should be given in terms of the entropy production rate $\dot{\sigma}$ with $E_P = \int dt\ T\ \dot{\sigma}$ which is a non-zero quantity because the second law of thermodynamics requires $\dot{\sigma} \geq 0$.

However S is the entropy transfer between the QQ and the heatbath under isothermal conditions. Its variation rate $\dot{S}$ satisfies $\int dt\ \dot{S} = 0$ so $\dot{S}$ should take alternatively positive and negative values in a clock cycle. It is obvious that (4) is the result of confusing entropy production σ for entropy transfer S, therefore it should be replaced by the following expression which contains a factor of ω, thus it also satisfies nullheat requirement,

$$E = E_P = \int dt\, T\dot{\sigma} \approx \int dt\, \frac{T_B S^2}{G} = H_2 \quad \omega > 0 \tag{6}$$

where $T_B \approx 4.2\ K$ is the heatbath temperature and $G = \kappa A/D$ is heat conductance, κ is the thermal conductivity and $A \approx (10\ \mu m)^2$ is the area of a ≈ 10 nW QQ and $D \approx 1$ mm is the distance between the QQ and the heatbath. For $\sigma \approx \dot{S}^2/G$ we assumed $1/T_B - 1/(T_B+\delta T) \approx \delta T/T_B^2$, $\delta T = T - T_B$ and $\omega\tau \ll 1$, where τ is the thermal relaxation time of a QQ and $\tau = 2\pi c D^2/\kappa \approx 10^{-8}$ s with c being the specific heat of the device material. When substituting eq.(6) into (3) we get, $\varepsilon = \varepsilon_R + E_P = (H + H_2)\, \omega$, showing that the device satisfies the nullheat definition as given by KLB1. But the device can be used as a majority logic device [4] which is not a reversible logic device and it contradicts KLB3. Also it contradicts KLB2 since information can be lost or discarded in nullheat. For an actual QQ, $H \approx 10^{-29}$ J.s and $H_2 \approx 10^{-40}$ J.s so that the effect of E_P is negligibly small.

In [6] we calculated the entropy of a QQ based on the statistical mechanics formalism as,

$$q = \frac{\sum E_n\, e^{-E_n/kT}}{\sum e^{-E_n/kT}}\ , \quad S = \int_0^T \frac{\partial q}{\partial T} \frac{dT}{T} \tag{7}$$

where E_n is the energy of the n-th quantum state relative to the ground state(s) and E_n was given through modelling the interaction between damping resistors and the QQ potential with harmonic oscillators. The result satisfies the third law of thermodynamics and Fig. 3 shows the QQ entropy calculated at $T = 4.2$ K. The difference of entropy $\Delta = S_A - S_Q$ between the 1 bit memory of active state A and the no memory of quenched state Q is chosen to be positive (in quenched state $\Phi_a = 0$) for technological reasons (i.e. for stability, speed, etc.). In fact Φ_a could be chosen otherwise as Φ_1, Φ_2 in Fig. 3 making ΔS positive, zero or negative so that $k'(T)$ in (5') is not necessarily positive definite, it depends on the device design parameters. This implies that there is no universal relation between information entropy and physical entropy. This leads us to the following statement,

PA3: "Information in not Negative Entropy in general."

It should be noted that entropy is sometimes defined as

$$S = k \ln \Omega \tag{8}$$

with the interpretation that "Ω" is the number of permissible quantum states at the given temperature". Since a QQ in the active state memorizing 1 bit of information (cf. Fig. 2) has two ground states, it seems as if $\Omega = 2$ and $\Delta S = +k \ln 2$ which is obviously opposite to (5) in sign. But it also violates the third law quantitatively. As we know that definition (8) is always used in the statistical sense for which a large number of states are being considered. It remains as an open question whether it is applicable for a system as QQ when very few number of states are being considered.

4. Conclusion

It may be worthwhile to note that in his work of information theory, Shannon introduced a function for information measure which is the same function appears in statistical mechanics, and on the advice of John von Neumann, Shannon called it "entropy". And once Shannon was asked why he had called his function by a name that was already in use in another field because it was bound to cause some confusion between the theory of information and the thermodynamics. He said that Von Neumann had told him: "No one really understands entropy. Therefore, if you know what you mean by it and when you are in an argument, you will win every time" [1]. Unfortunately Shannon's acceptance on the misnomer had caused the confusion dating back to Brillouin [3]. Had he named it differently, most of the confusions might have been avoided. We hope this letter would help to clarify the confusions.

Acknowledgement
Thanks are due to physicists R. Kubo, Y. Wada, M. Suzuki, S. Kobayashi and K. Hida of the University of Tokyo for enlightening discussions.

References
[1]   M. Tribus, *Maximum-Entropy and Bayesian Methods in Science and Engineering*, Vol. 1 edited by Gary J. Erickson and C. Ray Smith (Kluwer Academic Pub. 1988), pp. 31-52.

[2]   C. E. Shannon, *The Bell Sys. Tech. J.*, Vol. 27 (1948) 379.

[3]   L. Brillouin, *Science and information Theory* (Academic Press, New York, 1956).

[4]   E. Goto and K. F. Loe: *DC Flux Parametron* (World Scientific Publisher,

1986); Y. Harada, W. Hioe and E. Goto, *Proc. IEEE*, 77, 1280 (1989).

[5]   R. W. Keyes and R. Landauer, *IBM J. Res. Dev.* 14, 152 (1970); C. H. Bennett, *IBM J. Res. Dev.* 17, 525 (1973).

[6]   E. Goto, N. Yoshida, K. F. Loe and W. Hioe, in *Proc. of 3rd Int. Symposium on Foundation of Quantum Mechanics*, edited by S. Kobayashi et al. (Physical Society of Japan, Tokyo, 1990), pp. 412-418; R. Landauer, ibid. pp. 407-411.

[7]   C. Mead and L. Conway, *Introduction to VLSI Design Systems* (Addison-Wesley, Reading, Mass., 1981).

[8]   K. K. Likharev, *IEEE Trans. Magn.* MAG-13, 242 (1977); K. K. Likharev, S. V. Rylov and V. K. Semenov, *IEEE Trans. Magn.* MAG-21, 947 (1985); K. K. Likharev, *Int. J. Theor. Phys.* 21, 311 (1982).

[9] R. P. Feynman, *Optics News*, 11, 11 (1985).

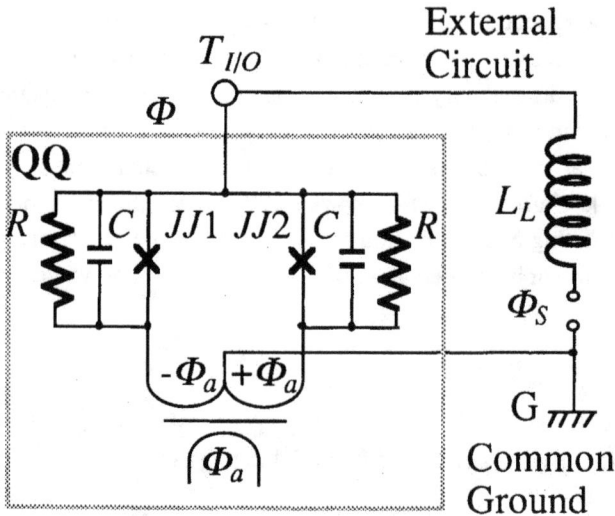

Fig. 1. Circuit of a QQ. (Typical values: $C = 1$ pF, $R = 10 \, \Omega$, $I_C = 50 \, \mu$A, $L_L = 5$ pH)

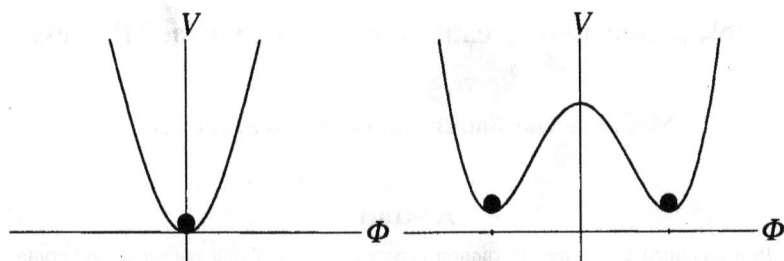

Fig. 2. Magnetic energy V of a QQ.

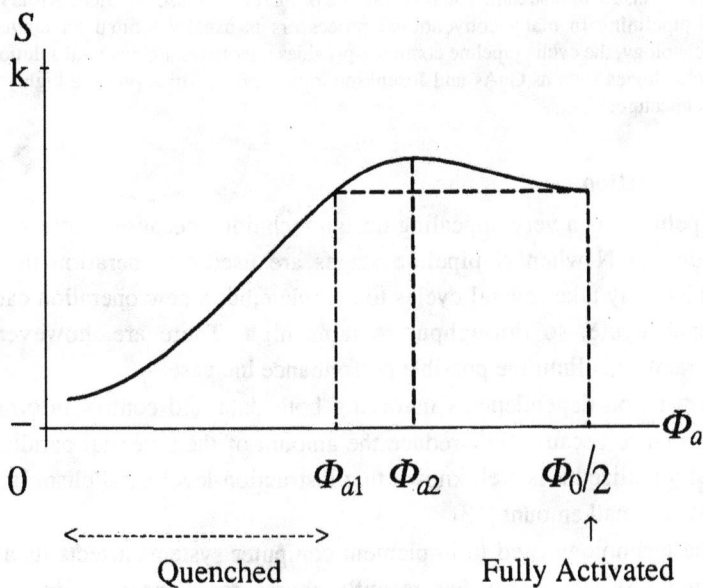

Fig. 3. Entropy S of a QQ.

Multiple Instruction Streams in a Highly Pipelined Processor

Mitsuhisa Sato, Shuichi Ichikawa, and Eiichi Goto

Abstract

In a pipelined computer, instruction dependencies involving both data and control information often limit its potential performance. A cyclic pipeline computer allows multiple instruction streams to share these pipeline stages in time to remove the data and control dependencies. These multiple instruction streams in the cyclic pipeline computer exploit more parallelism in the parallel program of scientific applications. In this paper, we define the basic model of a cyclic pipeline machine to examine the performance improvement of various configurations of cyclic pipeline machines compared to the same degree of pipelining of conventional architectures with single instruction stream. The simulation results indicate that pipelining within each instruction stream of a cyclic pipeline machine increases the performance to maximize the utilization of resources in a highly pipelined machine. FLATS2 is an experimental cyclic pipeline computer with two instruction streams. The BL addressing of FLATS2, which integrates memory addressing and range checking, exploits the microarchitectural parallelism to improve the performance of each instruction stream. The performance of FLATS2 is also reported. While the degree of pipelining in many conventional processors is usually limited on mature silicon technology, the cyclic pipeline computer provides alternative architectural solution for new technologies such as GaAs and Josephson logic device, which prefer a highly pipelined architecture.

1. Introduction

Pipelining is a very appealing design technique because it offers a theoretical speedup of N when N pipeline stages are used.An operation in a pipelined machine may take several cycles to complete,but a new operation can be started on each cycle, so throughput remains high. There are, however, practical constraints that limit the possible performance increase.

Instruction dependencies involving both data and control information limit performance because they reduce the amount of the potential parallelism that is actually realized.It is well known that instruction-level parallelism is limited to a relatively small amount [13].

The technology used to implement computer systems affects its architectural design.GaAs technology has recently shown rapid increases in maturity, and GaAs computer system design has already generated considerable interest.A highly pipelined architecture is extremely promising for this technology [11]. A new Josephson devices, QFP(Quantum Flux Parametron)[5] forces the entire system to be heavily pipelined.On mature silicon technology,the degree of pipelining in many conventional processors is usually limited. Traditional computer designs use resources inefficiently, resulting in machines whose performance is disappointing when compared to the raw speed of their components.

Even in silicon VLSI technology, asynchronous system designs such as micropipelines [16] and self-timed systems offer a highly pipelined system.

The pipelined memory is an attractive component for a highly pipelined system. A conventional memory chip consists of the address decoder, the memory cell array, the sense amplifier, and multiplexer. By positioning latches between them, the memory access is easily pipelined so that the cycle time rather than the access time is minimized. For data fetch, a processor can issue several memory requests concurrently as a pipelined functional unit.

The disadvantage of a pipelined memory system for a highly pipelined computer is that the increased pipeline depth places strict requirements on the optimizing compiler. For example, branch delays are longer, and early compiler efforts to replace the NOP instruction in the fill-in slots are most successful for short branch delay [12].

One way to remove the data and control dependencies in a highly pipelined system is to share these pipeline stages between different instruction streams. A *cyclic pipeline machine*[15] issues instructions periodically from a fixed number of instruction streams. The cyclic pipeline machine provides identical functionality as a true multiprocessor with shared memory. In a true multiprocessors system, contention for synchronization locks and delay waiting for synchronization events can substantially increase the running time of a parallel program. Among the multiple instruction streams in a pipelined processor, however, the synchronization cost can be reduced because its pipelined memory access causes no memory access conflict.

FLATS2[7] is an experimental cyclic pipeline machine implemented using silicon ECL technology. Ten pipeline stages are time-shared by two instruction streams. To get high performance per instruction stream, the instruction set is designed to allow rather complicated operations in the instruction as well as overlapped execution of instructions. For example, an instruction can take up to two memory operands, and perform operations of both the integer arithmetic function unit and the floating point function unit in one instruction.

The cyclic pipeline computer provides the identical functionality as the true multiprocessor with shared memory. We use the Force[8] as the parallel programming model. In the Force, many processes executes a single program.

The number of processes is arbitrary, but fixed at run-time. Each processes can be synchronized by *barriers* and *critical sections*. The synchronization is specified by the parallel directives. The parallel directives are placed in a source program to make use of multiple processes provided by the cyclic pipeline computer.

We are interested in the performance improvement obtained by general cyclic pipeline computers and a real cyclic pipeline computer, FLATS2, compared to conventional architectures. The cyclic pipeline architecture is a single processor architecture, while it allows the multiple instruction streams. In this paper, the cyclic pipeline computer is compared to other single processor architecture such as superpipelined architecture.

In Section 2, we define the model of the cyclic pipeline machine used as a basis for our simulations. In Section 3, the parallel programming model is described. Section 4 describes the simulation environment we used to measure the performance, and presents the detail of benchmarks and the result of our simulations. Section 5 reports and analyzes our experiments results on FLATS2 and the simulator. In Section 6, discussion on a cyclic pipeline machine is presented. Finally, Section 7 presents our summary and conclusions.

2. Highly pipelined Model

In this section, we introduce the machine models for a highly pipelined processor. A cyclic pipeline machine is defined as one of the models.

2.1 The base machine

We start with a typical pipeline composed of four stages: the instruction fetch (IF), the instruction decode (ID), the instruction execution (EX), and the write back (WB). For simplicity, we assume a register-register machine; this simplifies the pipeline and also makes it easier to quantify execution time. In this type of machine, instructions are classified into a small set of simple operations such as integer add/sub, logical ops, load, store, branch and floating-point ops.

An operation latency is the time (in cycle time) until the result of an instruction is available for use as an operand in a subsequent instruction. If the operation latency is one, the next instruction can use the result immediately.

To examine increases in performance due to highly pipelined structure, we define a base machine which has a non-pipelined execution pipe stage. In the base machine, instructions are issued at each machine cycle, and the latency of all operations are exactly one. Since the result of an instruction is always available for the successive instruction without delay, there are never any operation-latency interlocks in a base machine. Figure 1 shows a pipeline diagram for the base machine.

Because of the non-pipelined stage, only one instruction is in the execution stage at any one time. If the write-back stage can bypass the result to other pipe stages, it does not affect the operation latency. And perfect branch slot filling and/or branch prediction can save the control latency of branch instructions.

Actually, the time required for different classes of operations is not the same. For example, the time for register-register move is less than the time for floating-point ops. Although one could build machines whose cycle time was much longer than the time required for operation, it would be a waste of execution time and resources.

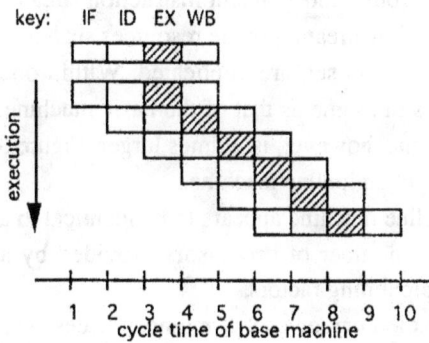

Fig. 1. Pipeline of base machine

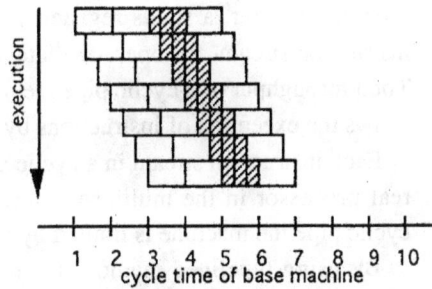

Fig. 2. Pipeline of superpipelined machine (degree 3)

2.2 Superpipelined machine

Superpipelined machines exploit instruction-level parallelism by pipelining instruction execution stages[13]. Each stage is divided into smaller pipeline segments. A superpipelined machine of degree m is a machine whose execution stages have parallelism of m. An existing example which has pipelined functional unit is CDC 7600.

Instructions are issued at every machine cycle, but the cycle time is $1/m$ of the base machine. The operation latency is m in its cycle time. When an operation takes a whole cycle in the base machine, given the same implementation technology it must take m cycles in the superpipelined machine. Figure 2 shows the execution of instructions by a superpipelined machine.

In a superpipelined machine, the cycle time granularity affects machine performance. The operation latency varies with complexity of the operation and cycle time granularity. The actual latency of the functional unit are rounded up to the nearest multiple of the machine cycle time. For example, the CRAY-1 has a floating point adder latency of 7 cycles. If the clock period is twice as long, it would takes 4 clock periods, which results in 8 cycles of CRAY-1 cycle time.

2.3 Cyclic pipeline machine

Cyclic pipeline machines exploit parallelism by multiple instruction streams time-sharing pipeline stages. A cyclic pipeline machine shares the same pipeline structure as a superpipelined machine. The difference is that a cyclic pipeline machine of degree n issues an instruction from n independent instruction streams at every n machine cycles. For each instruction stream, private resources such as a program counter, a status register, and registers set, are duplicated. Within one instruction stream, the operation latency is the same as that of the basic machine. Total throughput of a cyclic pipeline machine, however, is n times larger. Figure 3 shows the execution of instructions by a cyclic pipeline machine.

Each instruction stream in a cyclic pipeline machine appears to be identical to a real processor in the multiprocessor. The number of processors provided by a cyclic pipeline machine is limited by the pipelining factors.

By using pipelined memory for main memory or cache, memory access can also be pipelined so that several memory requests can be outstanding at the same time. It should be noted that pipelined memory access enables each processor to share the main memory without memory access conflict. Furthermore, no extra switching network is necessary between the processors and the main memory. Unlike true multiprocessors, multiple instruction streams of a cyclic pipelined machine can execute parallel programs without overhead for memory access to shared data.

FLATS2 is an experimental cyclic pipeline machine with two instruction streams. HEP is a resource-shared pipelined machine[9]. It issues an instruction in queues dynamically from the arbitrary instruction streams. It has several process execution modules (PEM) and complicated memory access mechanisms.

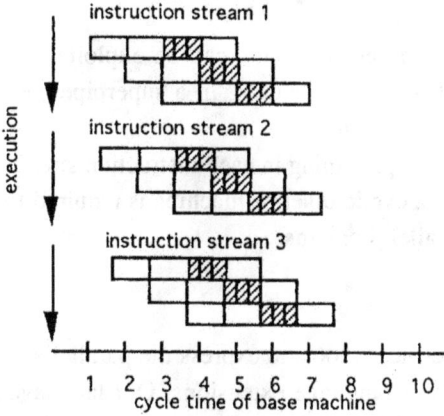

Fig. 3. Pipeline of cyclic pipeline machine (degree 3)

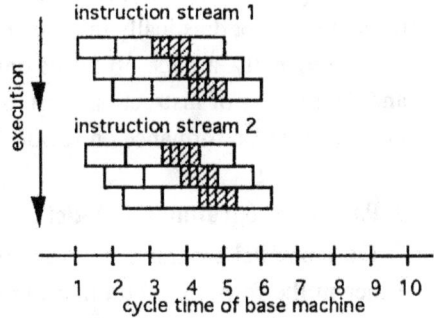

Fig.4. Pipeline of superpipelined cyclic pipeline machine (degree (2,2))

2.4 Superpipelined cyclic pipeline machine

Since two independent instructions in a instruction stream of a cyclic pipeline machine can be overlapped in the execution pipe stages, we can have a superpipelined cyclic pipeline machine. A superpipelined cyclic pipeline machine of degree (m,n) has a cycle time $1/mn$ that of the base machine, and issues instructions periodically from n instruction streams. There are m operations of each instruction stream in progress at the same time. Figure 4 shows the execution of instructions by a superpipelined cyclic pipeline machine.

A cyclic pipeline machine can achieve high throughput for highly parallel code. If the applications are dominated by highly parallel code, they can be divided into several processes executed in parallel. To perform a single task with multiple processes, some parts must be executed sequentially and process synchronization is inevitable. Even if there is no overhead to access the shared resources, such as lock and shared data, delays to wait for synchronization of events can substantially increase the running time of a parallel program, and seriously degrade processor utilization. For example, if other processes await an event set by one process, the execution time of the process to reach the event point dominates the total execution time. Even in highly parallel codes, the performance for one instruction stream affects the total performance as well as high throughput. Pipelining within the individual instruction stream can improve the performance of instruction stream.

On the other hand, instruction-level parallelism, which can be exploited by pipelining, is limited to a small amount. Highly pipelining in a superpipelined machine can not drastically improve the performance.

Consequently, a trade-off of the degree of pipelining in each instruction stream and the number of instruction streams for a cyclic pipeline machine is required to maximize the performance on various parallel programs.

3. Parallel Programming Model

For a parallel program, the programmer needs tools to express the parallelism, either in the form of subroutine libraries or language extensions. Our language extension of FORTRAN is from the Force[8]. The Force is based on the shared memory multiprocessor model of computation. The cyclic pipeline machine provides the identical functionality as the true multiprocessor with shared memory.

3.1 FORTRAN parallel directives

In the Force, multiple processes execute a single program. The number of processes is arbitrary, but fixed at run-time. The parallel constructs of our FORTRAN are:

Data allocation - All data in COMMON block are allocated globally, and can be referenced from any process. The local data is allocated in registers or stack area private for each process.

critical, end_critical - Specify the critical section which contains codes that are executed by all processes one at a time. It is often used for reduction operations such as summing into a global variable.

barrier, end_barrier - Specify the code which is executed by only one process and synchronize all process at the end of the code. The Force uses the generalized concept of a barrier. All processes stop at a barrier point until the last one has arrived. The last process then executes the code up to the **end_barrier**. Once the process has reached this point, all processes continue executing at the line following the **end_barrier**.

parallel DO - Two types of parallel DO loops are used to distribute the work of the loop whose iterations can be executed in parallel. A *self-scheduled* parallel DO specifies each iteration is dynamically assigned to the process. A *pre-scheduled* parallel DO specifies to partition iterations ahead of time so that each process will do a certain set of loop indices, no matter how long each one takes.«

SYNC function - The function SYNC forces the process to wait until the synchronization data of the specified location is non-zero. This function is used to synchronize on the data between processes. Writing non-zero value to the synchronization data by other processes releases the waiting process on the data. Although this function can be implemented by the loop reading the synchronization data, this function prevents the optimization such as loop invariant code motion.

These directives are placed in the source program as comments starting with "*$". In compilation, these are ignored as comments when parallel directives are disabled.

The choice between the two types of parallel loops depends on both the characteristics of applications and the cost of synchronization. If the work is naturally load-balanced, then pre-scheduling is preferred. In a cyclic pipelined machine, self-scheduling is also efficient because of its low synchronization cost.

3.2 Implementation of Parallel Directives

No special hardware is assumed for synchronization. As an atomic operation, the *load-and-store* instruction, which swaps the value between the private register and a global lock variable, is provided. Waiting for a synchronization event is implemented by "spinning" in a software loop, repeatedly reading a synchronization variable until it become available. Since there is no memory access conflict in a cyclic pipeline computer, the *hot spot problem* does not arise.

4. Simulation

4.1 Simulation Environment

The simulation system, originally designed for FLATS2, consists of an optimizing FORTRAN compiler (including assembler, linker and debugger) and a FLATS2 instruction-level simulator. In the simulation, a subset of FLATS2 instruction set is used, including loads, stores and arithmetic instruction between register operands. To specify the pipeline structure and functional unit, we classified the instructions so that instructions in the same class are likely to have identical behavior in any machine.

To investigate the effect of operation latency, we specify an operation latency for each instruction class at compile-time. The compiler includes a pipeline instruction scheduler using the algorithm in [6]. The scheduler reorganizes the instructions in a basic block to minimize the execution time. If an instruction requires the result of a previous instruction, the scheduler inserts NOP's or schedules the other independent instructions to avoid data dependency interlock until the result is available. Since the machine never stalls by data dependency interlock, the number of executed instructions gives the execution time in machine cycle.

Since scheduling is limited in a basic block, the instruction-level parallelism measured is limited within a basic block. Although particular compilation techniques such as trace scheduling and software pipelining can exploit the interblock instruction-level parallelism, the evaluation of these elaborate compilation techniques is beyond the scope of this paper .

We assume that control instructions such as branch take one cycle for any pipeline structure in the simulation. The cost of control instructions depends on the instruction fetch logic. A clever instruction issue logic and good branch prediction can reduce the branch performance penalty to flush the incorrect instructions in pipeline stages. Note that if we took these costs into account, the performance would decrease in a higher degree of superpipelined machines.

4.2 Workloads

To investigate the performance of various superpipelined and cyclic pipeline machines on scientific workload, we chose the following programs as workloads:

Linpack benchmark - This benchmark program solves a linear equation system, which is one of the most typical scientific computations. The benchmark program consists of two subroutines: **dgefa** and **dgesl** (double precision). **Dgefa** factors a dense matrix by gaussian elimination into its LU components. Dgesl solves the equation system by factored matrix. The time needed to factor a matrix of order N is proportional to N^3, while the time for the forward elimination and back substitution only increases as N^2. It is known that for matrices with N > 100, LU decomposition accounts for over 90% of the execution time. In our simulation, the order of matrix is 100. Transforming the matrix into diagonal form is accomplished by making N transformation passes over the matrix. A pass, K pass is divided into two parts: the first finds the Kth pivot element and performs a row exchange if necessary, and divides the element below the diagonal by the pivot to produce a set of *multipliers*. Then the second multiplies the part of the pivot row to the right of the diagonal times each multiplier and subtracts the product from the corresponding part of each row to make the Kth column consist of all zeros, except for the diagonal element. In the parallel version, each processor can perform the second part for different rows independently. The pre-schedule parallel DO loop construct is used to distribute to iteration on each row to each processor. The parallelism of this part contributes the significant performance improvement in the parallel version. At the end of this part, all processors are synchronized by a barrier. Since the cost of synchronization is very low in a cyclic pipeline machine, finding the pivot element and computing the multipliers in the first part are also distributed to each processor. For solving the diagonalized system, each step on row for the forward elimination and back substitution must be serialized. Only computations on columns in each step are distributed. At the end of each step, all processors are synchronized by a barrier.

FEM_BAND - The finite element method using the band matrix, taken directly from Mori[17]. The band matrix is solved by the modified Cholesky decomposition. The program solves the following Poisson's equation in a square region. The program consists of two subroutines: MATGEN and SOLV. The MATGEN computes an element matrix for each element to arrange the global matrix in band form, which is solved by SOLV.

In the parallel version of MATGEN, each element matrix is computed in parallel independently. When the element matrix is added to the global matrix, the addition is done in the critical section to make sure that the other processes do not modify the matrix simultaneously. In SOLV, the modified Cholesky decomposition decomposes the positive definite matrix faster than the LU decomposition. Like the LU decomposition, transforming the matrix into diagonal form is accomplished by making N transformation passes over the matrix. In a pass of transformation, the pre-schedule parallel DO loop construct is used to distribute to iteration on column to each processor. Since the transformation on column uses the result on the previous column, we introduce the additional vector to synchronize the data on each column.

For solving the decomposed matrix, the synchronization vector is also used to distribute iterations on row to processors. Because the width of the band matrix is relatively small, the synchronization on the data is effective to get more parallelism.

FEM_ICCG - The finite element method using the matrix in list vector form, also taken from Mori[17]. The matrix is solved by the ICCG (Incomplete Cholesky decomposition and Conjugate Gradient) method. The problem to be solved is the same as FEM_BAND. Like FEM_BAND, the program consists of MATGEN and SOLV. MATGEN of FEM_ICCG is similar to that of FEM_BAND except that the matrix is stored in list vector form.

In the CG method, finding the solutions and updating of the matrix are repeated until the expected precision is obtained. In the parallel version, the part to update of the matrix is parallelized because it consists many simple vector operations such as inner product. As the SOLV in FEM_BAND, the decomposing and solving of the matrix use the synchronization vector on row. Note that we can not exploit parallelism on column because the number of elements on row is at most 3.

4.4 Simulation Results

We ran the workloads to measure the execution time on different configuration and degree of pipelining. The operation latencies were estimated based on CRAY-1 instruction timing. It is assumed that the memory system can accept a new request at each clock cycle. The effects of cache misses and page faults are ignored.

We show the simulation results in Figure 5,6,7,8. The line (N,1) indicates the superpipelined processors. Note that loops in these programs are not unrolled. Loop unrolling will increase the instruction-level parallelism.

In Figure 5, the speedups of a superpipelined machine are limited to about two times by the instruction-level parallelisms of these subroutine. These results match the results reported in [13].

For **dgefa**, nearly linear speedup can be achieved in the cyclic pipeline machine. The reason is that the amount of codes executed in parallel is very large and delay times for waiting at a barrier is relatively small. The number of row operations required in each iteration decreases steadily, since only the columns that have not yet been diagonalized need to be manipulated. For each pass, the number of row operations done per processors is nearly balanced.

For **dgesl**, only vector operation on columns in each step can be executed in parallel by processors. The vector machine can execute **dgesl** very well. Since processors reach a barrier in a smaller number of instructions than in **dgefa**, the performance is dominated by the execution time of codes executed by one processor and the synchronization overhead. Therefore the cyclic pipeline

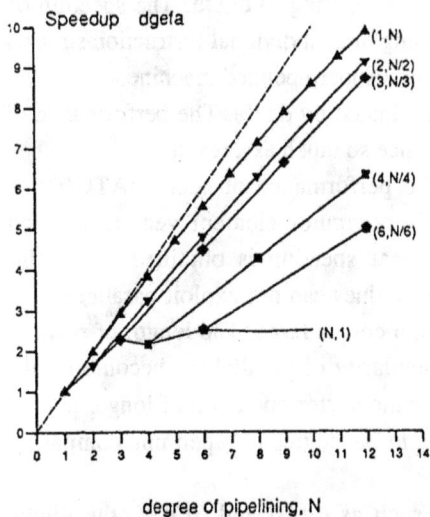

Fig. 5. Speedup of **dgefa** (Linpack)

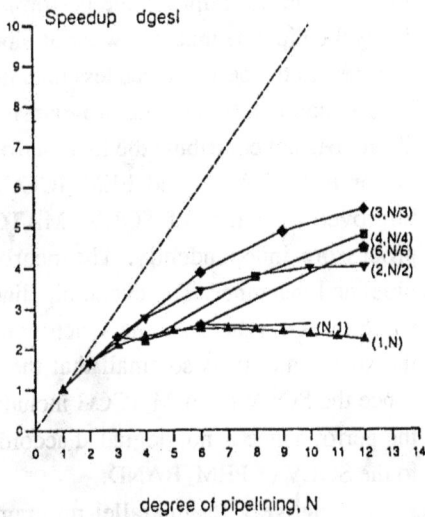

Fig.6. Speedup of **dgesl** (Linpack)

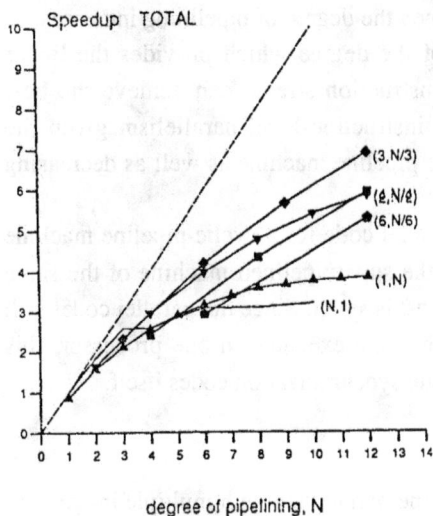

Fig. 7. Speedup of FEM_BAND
(size = 16*16)

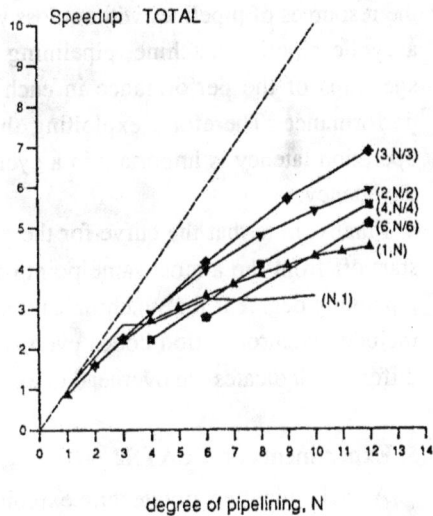

Fig. 8. Speedup of FEM_ICCG
(size = 16*16)

machine can not improve the performance comparing to **dgefa**. The speedup of the cyclic pipeline machine without pipelining in an individual instruction streams is increases the performance less than that of a superpipelined machine.

The computation of the program is dominated by dgefa. The performance of dgesl does not contribute the total performance so much as a result.

For FEM_BAND and FEM_ICCG, the performance of each MATGEN is improved than that of SOLV. MATGEN computes element vectors in each processors independently. The nearly linear speedup is obtained for cyclic pipelined machines. The cyclic pipeline machines can not exploit parallelism so much in SOLV because the synchronization cost is large. The length of rows in the sparse matrix is so small that the granularity of parallelism become small. Since the SOLV of FEM_ICCG includes some vector operation of longer length, the performance is not degraded according to the degree of pipelining comparing to the SOLV of FEM_BAND.

For relatively less parallel programs such as **dgesl** and SOLV, the cyclic pipeline machine with the pipelining degree of 2--3 in instruction streams provides the best performance. The reason is that this configuration can utilize the resources of a highly pipelined machine the most efficiently. In a superpipelined machine, the performance increases linearly up to the degree of 2--3 in all programs. The linear speedups in performance imply that the machine can utilize the resources of pipelines without loss when the degree of pipelining increases. In a cyclic pipeline machine, pipelining of the degree which provides the linear speedups of the performance in each instruction stream can achieve the best performance. Therefore, exploiting the instruction-level parallelism given the operation latency is important in a cyclic pipeline machine as well as decreasing the latency.

Finally, note that the curve for the parallel code for a cyclic pipeline machine start off from the almost same point of the superpipelined machine of the same pipelining degree if the synchronization cost is small. Since the parallel codes still include synchronization codes even if they are executed in one processor, this difference indicates the overhead to execute synchronization codes itself.

5. Experiments on FLATS2

A cyclic pipeline architecture exploits the parallelism with multiple instruction streams which share the same pipeline in time. In FLATS2, the degree of pipeline in execution stages is limited to a relatively small number. No pipelined memory access is allowed in FLATS2. The performance of an individual stream is improved with microarchitectural parallelism as well as overlapped execution in an individual instruction stream. In this section, we compare the FLATS2 with the conventional pipeline using the same pipeline structure.

5.1 The performance of FLATS2

We chose the Linpack benchmarks as our benchmarks. The cycle time of FLATS2 is 65 ns. The instruction is issued at every 2 cycles.

We have measured the speedup by two instruction streams for the Linpack benchmark to parallelize the program. The speedup of the benchmark is shown in Table 1.

FLATS2 provides the *BL addressing* and the *address tag* to support faster execution in each instruction stream. The BL addressing is a memory addressing mechanism which integrates memory addressing and range checking. The effective address is checked against the specified pair of base and limit addresses in registers during memory access. An address tag is a bit in a word, which indicates the capability for memory access. Combining them together, the test for terminating the loop of an array computation can be overlapped with its computational operation to reduce the execution time. We can also make use of these facilities to reduce the cost of run-time type checking in Lisp. The BL addressing also increases the performance in the parallel version.

Compile option	One instruction stream (MFLOPS)	Two instruction streams (MFLOPS)	Speedup
-O	1.96	3.70	1.89
-OB	2.66	5.00	1.87

Key: -O --- optimized without BL addressing.

-OB --- optimized with BL addressing.

Table. 1. Speedup of Linpack by Two instruction streams

5.2 The FLATS2 Pipeline

Figure 9 shows the FLATS2 pipeline. Each stage is executed in one cycle. The instruction is issued every 2 cycles from two instruction streams. As a result, the instruction of an individual instruction stream is issued every 4 cycles. The SP instruction uses the SP unit to execute the floating points operations and some integer operations such as MUL. The floating point registers are placed in the SP unit. The integer and address values are stored in the register memory. The GV instructions which perform the simple integer operation are executed in the GVEX stage. The GV instructions perform the computational operation only on register operands.

The pipeline of FLATS2 consists of ten stages as follows:

IF--- Instruction Fetch. Fetches the next instruction to execute from the instruction memory.

ID--- Instruction Decode. Decodes the instruction and fetch the long immediate word from the instruction memory.

GVR --- GV memory Read. Reads registers from the register memory.

GVEX --- GV unit EXecution. For the GV instructions; Executes the instruction. For the load and store; Calculates the memory address.

DMR --- Data Memory Read. For memory operand, reads the operands in the data memory.

GVW/EX1 --- GV memory Write and EXecute 1 in SP unit. Writes the result for the register memory. For the SP instruction; starts the execution.

EX2, EX3, EX4--- EXecute in SP unit. For the SP instruction; executes the instruction.

DMW --- Data Memory Write. Writes the result in data memory.

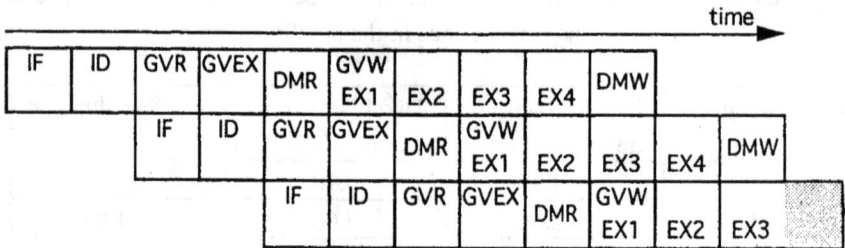

										time →
IF	ID	GVR	GVEX	DMR	GVW EX1	EX2	EX3	EX4	DMW	
	IF	ID	GVR	GVEX	DMR	GVW EX1	EX2	EX3	EX4	DMW
		IF	ID	GVR	GVEX	DMR	GVW EX1	EX2	EX3	

Fig. 9. FLATS2 pipeline

In each instruction stream, two computational instructions interlock when the instruction reaches the DMR stages and one of its source operands is not ready because it is the destination of a previous instruction that has not reached the DMW stage yet. If the instruction is about to enter DMR then the previous instruction is already done with EX4 and the result to be stored in DMW can be used as soon as it becomes available. The output of the EX stages can be written into *bypass registers*, which can be read in DMR. They allows the destination operand of a computational instruction to be used as the source of the next instruction. Physically, special hardware is used to detect that this memory operand is to be from the bypass registers not from the memory. The bypass registers eliminate the interlock due to data dependency.

Resource conflict never occurs because each stages is executed by only one instruction at any time. Some integer computational instructions are executed in the SP unit. For example, the integer MUL instruction is executed in the SP unit, and the result must be written into the register memory, Since the next cycle is taken to write the result, these instructions always take two cycles.

In the FLATS2 pipeline, the compare-and-branch instruction can be executed without delay. Since the comparison is performed in the GVEX stages, the IF stage can select the next-PC according to the result of the comparison. The BL addressing is thought as a variant of the compare-and-branch instruction because the GVEX stage calculates the effective address and compare with the BL pair to branch at the next cycle.

5.3 Single Instruction Stream Pipeline

Changing the instruction issue logic allows the instruction issued from a single instruction stream. We call this machine the single stream FLATS2 machine.

In the pipeline, there are two types of interlocks: an interlock between two SP instructions (interlock delay) and an interlock between a load instruction and a computational instruction (load delay). The two SP instructions interlock when the source operand of the instruction is not ready because it is the destination of the next instruction which has not finished its execution stages yet. The other interlock occurs when a load instruction loads a register from memory and the next instruction read this register. When the next instruction use this register for address calculation, this interlock is known as an AG (Address Generation) interlock. For both interlocks, the pipe is stalled for one cycle. We assume that the operand written by the GV instruction except the load instruction is bypassed to the source operand of the next instruction because the operand is ready after the GVEX stage.

The compare-and-branch instruction is not provided for the single stream machine. The separate compare instruction sets the conditional flags and the next conditional branch instruction computes the branch-target and selects the next PC according to the flags. Since the compare instruction evaluate the condition at the GVEX stage, the branch instruction can use the flags at the ID stages. The branch instruction is executed without delay.

5.4 Simulation Result

Since we assume that there is no hardware interlocking mechanism, the code generation phase of the compiler handles interlock due to the data dependencies. The code generator inserts NOP codes to handle all the interlocks. We define the path-length as the instruction count without NOP codes. The instruction count includes the executed NOP codes to give the execution time. For multiple instruction stream machines by a cyclic pipeline architecture, the instruction count is the total number of instruction executed in all instruction streams.

In the simulation, we used the same workloads in Section 4. The results are shown in Table 2. The values in these table are the instruction counts. The path-length is computed from the single stream version. Note that the code reordering is not done in this simulation.

Program	path length	FLATS2 single stream	FLATS2 without BL	FLATS2 with BL
Linpack				
dgefa	1308232	2051575(1.57)	1351441(1.03)	1009172(0.77)
dgesl	44165	66659(1.51)	85750(1.94)	57536(1.30)
TOTAL	1352397	2118234(1.56)	1437191(1.06)	1066708(0.79)
FEM_BAND (16*16)	684205	980353(1.43)	1048690(1.53)	1020879(1.49)
FEM_ICCG (32*32)	8774986	11086676(1.26)	13189680(1.50)	12796357(1.46)
FEM_BAND (16*16, BL)	684205	980353(1.43)	----	849308(1.44)

(Ratio): a ratio to the path length.

Table. 2. Instruction counts in FLATS2 and single stream FLATS2

For the single instruction stream execution, the interlocks degrades the performance by 20%-60% from the path length; the path length indicate the ideal execution time without interlock delay. Since there is no interlock in cyclic pipeline machines, the performance degradation is caused by the synchronization overhead and the time waiting the other processes.

The two instruction stream machines can execute the program of Linpack better than the single instruction stream machines because the routine **dgefa** involves large parallel codes. For **dgesl,** the average of vector length is less than 100 and then its performance is not improved.

Unfortunately, the performance of SOLV in both FEM_BAND and FEM_ICCG can not be improved by the two instruction stream machines. Since the size of the loops in the computation is small, the iterations over rows are distributed to each stream. These streams synchronize each other with the synchronization vector of rows. Because the synchronization cost is large compared to the performance improvement obtained by two instruction streams, its performance can not exceed the performance of single instruction stream machine even if the size is large. More instruction streams would increase the performance as shown in Section 4.

For the Linpack, the BL addressing eliminates the overhead to iterate the loop. The BL addressing can reduce the execution time in parallel execution as same as in sequential execution. In FEM_BAND and FEM_ICCG, the BL addressing can not be used because the synchronization code is the first instruction in the most loops to synchronize the data. Although the BL addressing mode is used for some loop, its contribution is small. In another version shown as FEM_BAND(BL) in Table 2, the program is modified to make use of the BL addressing. FEM_BAND(BL) can improve the performance over that of the single stream machines. Thanks to the two instruction stream, FLATS2 can implement the BL addressing without delay. As a result, BL addressing exploit microarchitectural parallelism in the cyclic pipeline architecture effectively.

6. Discussion

6.1 Latch overhead of pipelining

To increase the degree of pipelining, the pipeline latch registers must be inserted to keep the information for each pipestage. Latch overhead limits the performance of pipelining. Kunkel and Smith[10] studied the effect of latch overhead in various degrees of pipelining via simulation of CRAY-1S.

Latch propagation delay occurs in gate used to construct latches. A latch typically has a propagation delay from clock to output of at least two gate delays. It involves significant delay in pipelining system when the clock period becomes very short. To reduce the delay, we can use the latch which performs useful logic functions. The so-called Earle latch and the polarity hold latch can perform any combinational logic function as well as the latching function. One of the authors proposed a new latch design, G-series[3] gates base on ECL, which can perform any three-input logic function efficiently in gate level. If logic functions are performed with this latch, the propagation delay can be essentially eliminated.

The clock frequency is also limited by physical characteristics of signal propagation. Data skew is the difference between the maximum and minimum signal propagation times through combinational logic between pipeline stages, and in the latches that separate the stages. The clock period must be long enough to ensure reliable latching data.

In a synchronous system, global clock signal must be controlled to reach all latches at the same time. When designing real processors, however, there is always some uncertainty in the clock signal. For example, differences between maximum and minimum delays in clock fun-out logic and differences of propagation time in different length of wire for clock signals cause an unintentional variation in the arrival time of the clock at succeeding latches in a pipeline. This clock signal skew also increases the clock period.

Micropipelines[16] using self-timed logic are very attractive for a highly pipelined system. Since no global clock is needed in self-timed logic, there is no problem with clock skew. Each pipestage is connected with the two-phase bundled data convention, and communicates with each other. Micropipelines can achieve the speed of control event signal propagation, and provide very high throughput.

6.2 Memory system design of cyclic pipeline machine

The pipelined memory system is a key design in a cyclic pipeline machine. Pipelining is a technique that can be employed for both instructions and data. Given sufficient jobs which can be executed independently, pipelined memory allows a cyclic pipeline machine to achieve maximum throughput even without any cache because the pipelines are fully utilized. But for parallel programs executed by many processes, the performance of individual instruction stream reduces the delay time to await a synchronization event. Since caches are used to reduce the impact of memory latency on the performance of instruction stream, they are also effective in a cyclic pipeline machine.

When a processor is highly pipelined and the clock period becomes very short, it is necessary to issue instructions as fast as possible to achieve high throughput, so a highly pipelined machine requires high memory bandwidth. When the instruction fetch can be pipelined, the cycle time of memory is more essential than the access time. While the interleaved memory and the bank parallel memory achieve maximum throughput when there is no access conflict, pipelining is a very effective method for achieving performance increases with relatively small costs. If the memory access can not be pipelined to fetch instructions, independent instruction caches for each instruction stream could provide the same function as the pipelined instruction memory. For instruction cache, even if the memory is pipelined, multiple pipelined caches for different instruction streams help the increase of throughput in a cyclic pipeline machine when the cycle time of the pipelined cache is larger than the clock period.

For data memory, a pipelined memory enables the processor to give the cache several memory requests concurrently before getting any data back. In the pipelined system, the entire system operates at maximum throughput rate of its slowest pipestages. If the cycle time of the pipelined memory was larger than the clock period, the pipestages of data fetch limit the throughput of pipelining, because the successive memory requests were blocked. One way to reduce the performance degradation due to the difference of throughput is to place queues between processor and memory. If data from cache does not arrive in the expected time due to extra memory latency such as cache miss, the entire processor must block to await the data.

Note that the disadvantage of a cyclic pipeline machine is that random memory access pattern of different instruction streams decreases locality of memory reference. More instruction streams in a cyclic pipeline machine would need a larger cache. To balance the number of instruction streams and the cache size, a trade-off is required between them.

6.3 New technology for a highly pipelined computer

The cyclic pipeline machine was originally proposed as an architecture suited for a new Josephson logic device DCFP. One of the distinct characteristics of Josephson logic is that each basic logic device acts as a latch. Therefore, in this technology, high pitch, shallow-logic pipelining can be used without the delay time and cost of pipeline latch registers. By using the Josephson devices for the processor and the main memory (or cache), the over all system can be naturally pipelined with the same clock time.

A highly pipelined architecture is also extremely promising for GaAs technology. The high electron mobility of GaAs transistors results in very fast electron transit times across their active regions and hence generates the potential for extremely short gate propagation delay. This characteristic of GaAs devices offers high system clock rates compared to silicon devices. A signal processor implemented with GaAs technology can often be deeply pipelined and thus can exploit high system clock rate [2].

One of the most critical differences between silicon technology and GaAs technology is that the GaAs wafers have a higher density of defects. This results in a very low chip yield, indirectly limits individual chip area and transistor counts. The limitation needs the system to be divided into small components such as cache and co-processor. In GaAs technology, the ratio of off-chip memory access speed to on-chip memory access speed is larger than in silicon technology. The penalty for accessing off-chip memory forces the architects to minimize the number of off-chip access, or, alternatively, to minimize the penalties for going off-chip. The longer GaAs memory system delay does not result from the lower raw speed of the memory itself, but from longer relative propagation delays between the processor and the memory. Breaking the instruction fetch stage into multiple stages, pipelined instruction fetch can reduce these penalties.

Another major difference between silicon and GaAs is the more limited fan-in/fan-out capability of GaAs. This characteristic of GaAs prefers the simple and regular arithmetic functional unit design such as the ripple-carry adder. Pipelining of arithmetic functional units can not improve the latency, but can improve the bandwidth [4].

7. Summary and Conclusions

In this paper, we have presented an evaluation of cyclic pipeline machines for a highly pipelined processor. Although the performance of a highly pipelined processor is limited by instruction-level parallelism in application programs in a conventional approach of single instruction stream, a cyclic pipeline machine enables multiple instruction streams to exploit more parallelism in the parallel program of scientific workload even in a single highly pipelined processor. The simulation results indicate that effective pipelining in the individual instruction stream of the cyclic pipeline machine increases the performance to maximize the utilization of resources in a highly pipelined processor.

New technologies such as GaAs and QFP prefer a highly pipelined architecture to make use of the raw speed of components efficiently. A cyclic pipeline machine provides an alternative architectural solution of a highly pipelined system. Even in silicon VLSI technology, it may be an interesting architecture, especially for asynchronous self-timed systems.

We have examined the FLATS2 pipeline compared to the single instruction stream pipeline with the same structure by the simulator. For highly parallel programs such as Linpack, FLATS2 can obtain the performance improvement over the single instruction stream pipeline. But for less parallel program, the synchronization overhead between instruction streams is larger than the overhead due to interlocks in single instruction stream.

Recently, several techniques have been developed to exploit the parallelism of programs for multiprocessors [1] [14]. Scientific applications are often dominated by highly parallel codes, and a parallel computer would improve these application performances. The cyclic pipeline machine provides identical functionality as the true multiprocessor with shared memory. By using pipelined memory, there is no memory access conflict in a cyclic pipeline machine. As a result, the synchronization operation is very cheap. The cyclic pipeline machine can exploit such parallelism in a highly pipelined processor. Although the parallelism of programs may be expressed explicitly in the form of language extension as in our simulations, automatic parallelization compilers, including automatic program restructuring, is expected to exploit parallelism for a cyclic pipeline machine with minimum programming efforts.

References

[1] R. Allen, D. Callahan, and K. Kennedy, "Automatic Decomposition of Scientific Programs for Parallel Execution", Proc. 14th ACM Symp. Principles Programming Languages, ACM, 1987, pp 63-76.

[2] B.K Gilbert, B.A. Naused, D.J. Schwab, and R.L. Thompposon, "Signal Processors Based Upon GaAs ICs: The Need for a Wholistic Design Approach", IEEE Computer, Vol. 19, No. 10, Oct. 1986, pp. 29-43.

[3] E. Goto, W. Hioe, N. Homma and R. Kamikawai, "G-Series Gate - 1 GHz clock Silicon CML/ECL", to be prepared.

[4] T.G. Hallin and M.J. Flynn, "Pipelining of Arithmetic Functions", IEEE Trans. Computers, Vol. C-21, No.8, pp. 880-886, Aug. 1972. pp. 1901-1909.

[5] Y. Harada, H. Nakane, N. Miyamoto, U. Kawabe, E. Goto, and T. soma, "Basic operations of the quantum flux parametron," IEEE Trans. Magn., vol. MAG-23, pp. 3801-3807, Sept. 1987.

[6] J.L. Hennessy and T.R. Cross, "Postpass Code Optimization of Pipeline Constraints", ACM Trans. on Prog. Lang. and Sys., Vol.5, No. 3, July 1983, pp. 422-448.

[7] Ichikawa, S., A study on the Cyclic Pipeline Computer: FLATS2, Ph.d Thesis , 1991, the University of Tokyo.

[8] H.F. Jordan, "The Force", in The Characteristics of Parallel Algorithms , L.H. Jamieson, D.B. Gannon and R.J. Douglass Ed., MIT press, 1987.

[9] J.S. Kowalik, Ed., Parallel MIMD Computation: HEP Supercomputer and Its Application. Cambridge, MA: MIT Press, 1985.

[10] Kunkel, R.S., Smith, E.. "Optimal pipelining in supercomputers", Proceedings of the 13th Annual International Symposium on Computer Architecture, IEEE, June, 1986.

[11] V. Milutinovic, D. Fura, and W. Helbig, "An Introduction to GaAs Microprocessor Architecture for VLSI", Computer, Vol. 19, No. 3, March 1986, pp. 30-42.

[12] V. Milutinovic, D. Fura, W. Helbig and J. Linn, "Architecture/Compiler Synergism in GaAs Computer System", Computer, Vol. 20, No. 5, May 1987, pp. 72-93.

[13] Norman P. Jouppi, "The Nonuniform Distribution of Instruction-level and Machine Parallelism and Its Effect on Performance", IEEE Transactions on Computers, Dec. 1989, Vol. 38, No. 12.

[14] C. D. Polychronopoulos, "Compiler Optimizations for Enhancing Parallelism and Their Impact on Architecture Design", IEEE Transactions on Computers, Aug. 1989, Vol. 37, No. 8, pp 991-1004.

[15] Shimizu, K., Goto, E. and Ichikawa, S., "CPC(Cyclic Pipeline Computer) - An Architecture Suited for Josephson Pipelined-Memory Machines," IEEE Transactions on Computers, June 1989, Vol. 38, No. 6.

[16] Ivan E. Sutherland, "MICROPIPELINE", the lecture of Truing Award, CACM, June 1989, Vol. 32, No. 6, pp. 720-738.

[17] Mori Masatake, "Numerical Computation Programming", Iwanami-shoten, 1986, (in Japanese).

Evaluation of the Continuation Bit in the Cyclic Pipeline Computer

Paul Spee, Wong Weng Fai, Mitsuhisa Sato and Eiichi Goto

Abstract

The Cyclic Pipeline Computer (CPC) is a shared resource computer which shares its pipeline among multiple instruction streams to create distinct virtual processors. This effectively removes data dependencies which reduce the performance of highly pipelined computers. However, when executing unbalanced parallel programs, the CPC suffers from performance degradation due to synchronization overhead. In this paper we introduce a hardware extension called the continuation bit. The continuation bit indicates that no dependencies between the current and next instruction exist. If the continuation bit is set, the next instruction of the same stream is executed. Simulations of various programs indicate that the continuation bit is able to balance the execution of parallel programs by exploiting instruction level parallelism.

1. Introduction

Data and control dependencies often limit the performance of highly pipelined computers. Previous studies [7] have shown that *instruction level parallelism* (the number of instructions which can be executed in parallel), which can be exploited by a highly pipelined computer, is limited to a factor of three to four.

By timesharing the pipeline among multiple instruction streams, data and control dependencies are removed. The CPC [10] issues instructions from different instruction streams in a cyclic manner. If we assume that there are m instruction streams and the maximum operation latency is n cycles, then within each stream the latency between the issuing of consecutive instructions is n/m. The pipeline degree for each stream is in effect reduced to n/m.

For well balanced parallelized programs with little synchronization, it should be possible to get near linear speedup of up to n times. If n is larger than the instruction level parallelism, the CPC outperforms a superpipelined machine with the same degree of pipelining. Because of the low synchronization overhead, the CPC would perform well even if the parallelized program includes synchronization among the instruction streams. However, most parallelized programs are not well balanced, that is, some instruction streams execute less instructions before reaching a synchronization point than other instruction streams. Upon reaching the synchronization point, the instruction streams execute the synchronization code, which does not contribute to the computation at hand, until the synchronization condition becomes true. To improve the performance of unbalanced programs, we introduce a continuation bit as part of the instruction to specify whether data dependencies between the current and next instruction within an instruction stream exist.

In this paper we evaluate the effects of the continuation bit on the performance of several parallel programs. In Section 2 we describe the machine model of the CPC and the continuation bit. In Section 3 we describe the simulation environment which was used to obtain the results. In Section 4 we discuss the results of the simulation. Finally, in Section 5 we give our conclusions.

2. Cyclic Pipeline Computer

2.1 CPC pipeline structure

The CPC is a shared resource MIMD computer [4, 11, 1] in which both the functional units and the memory are pipelined and shared among multiple instruction streams. Only the hardware which can be considered part of the *context* of the particular instruction stream is duplicated.

Figure 1 shows the pipeline diagrams of a pipelined, superpipelined, cyclic pipelined, and cyclic superpipelined computer, respectively. We say that a processor whose execution stage is not pipelined, has a pipeline degree of one and we use this processor as our base machine in all our comparisons (Figure 1a). If the execution stage has n pipeline stages, then the processor has a pipeline degree of n. We call such a processor a superpipelined processor (see Figure 1b). In Figure 1c the number of instruction streams m of the CPC is equal to the operation latency n. For a CPC with a maximum operation latency of n and m instruction streams, each stream has a superpipeline degree of n/m if n/m is larger than one (see Figure 1d). The pipeline degree for the CPC is n in either case.

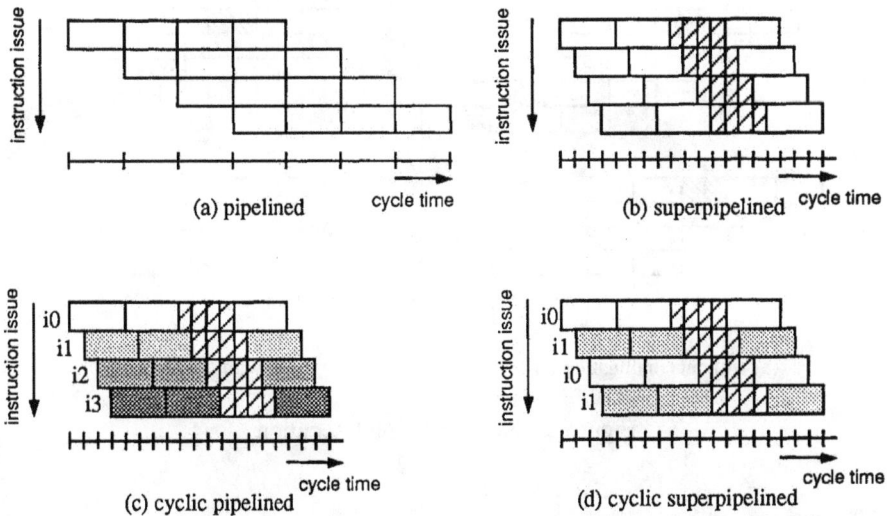

Figure 1. Pipeline diagrams

Although the ideal speedup (the ratio of the execution time against the base machine) would be n times, several factors limit the obtainable performance increase. On the assumption that the machine level parallelism n of a superpipelined processor is larger than the instruction level parallelism, which is limited by data dependencies, the maximum obtainable performance increase is limited by the instruction level parallelism. Studies have shown that the instruction level parallelism is often limited to between three and four for typical applications [7].

When two processors access the same memory location, a memory access conflict occurs and one of the processors has to be delayed. When several processors are spinning on a common lock (*busy-wait*), such memory access conflicts occur rather frequently. Not only are spinning processors delayed, as the busy-wait takes up valuable memory bandwidth, other processors are delayed as well [2]. Because both the processor and memory of the CPC is pipelined, the memory accesses are serialized. Therefore, a memory access conflict can never occur, neither are non-spinning processors delayed. While the CPC can efficiently synchronize among its instruction streams, the performance is drastically reduced when parallelized programs are not well balanced [9].

182

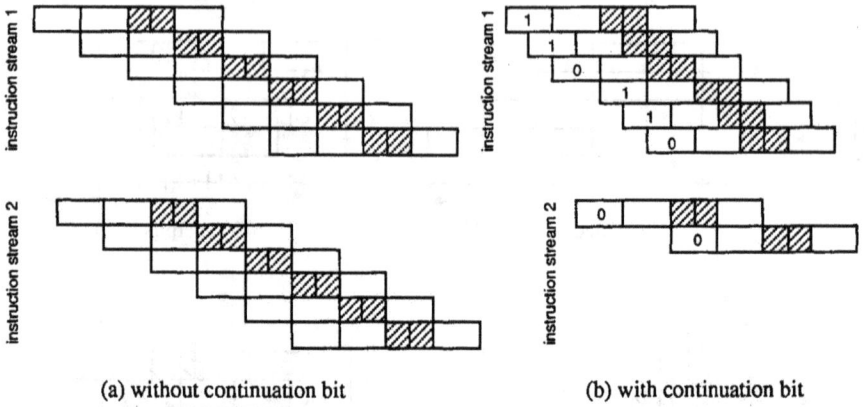

(a) without continuation bit

(b) with continuation bit

Figure 2. Cyclic Pipeline Execution

2.2 Continuation bit

If a parallelized program is well balanced, that is, the execution times of the instruction streams between synchronization points are nearly equivalent, the CPC obtains a good performance. However, if instruction streams are required to wait at synchronization points, performance may decrease. To improve the performance of ill-balanced parallel programs, we introduce a *continuation bit* as part of the instruction to specify whether data dependencies between the current and next instruction within an instruction stream exists. If no dependencies exist, instead of issuing an instruction from another instruction stream, the next instruction from the same instruction stream is issued (see Figure 2). The idea is that an instruction stream tries to do its own job as fast as possible. Only when it cannot execute an instruction because of data dependencies, will it 'pass' control to the next instruction stream. Figure 3 depicts the execution order of the instruction streams. As long as the continuation bit is set, instructions are executed from the same stream.

The value of the continuation bit is determined at compile time. Based on the operation latency and the number of instruction streams (m), the compiler can determine whether it is safe to set the continuation bit. If the continuation bit is set, the time until the issue of the next instruction is one cycle. If the continuation bit is not set, the time until the issue of the next instruction is at least m cycles. The continuation bit exposes the full pipeline depth to the instruction stream.

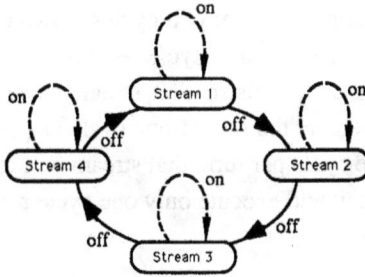

Figure 3. Instruction stream execution order

To illustrate the usage of the continuation bit, we show the inner loop of the *daxpy* routine from Linpack (Figure 4). Those instructions, which have their continuation bit set, are indicated by {c}.

```
1:
        mov.d    (gr0),S              {c}
        lea      (gr0)gr3,gr0
        mul3.d   T,S,P                {c}
        mov.d    (gr2),S
        add3.d   P,S,S
        mov.d    S,(gr2)              {c}
        lea      (gr2),gr3,gr2
        cmp.l    gr2,gr1
        ble      1b
```

Figure 4. Inner loop of *daxpy* with continuation bit

Synchronization code does not have the continuation bit set; it passes control to the next instruction stream. As a result, it allows the instruction streams which did not yet reach the synchronization point to execute faster at the cost of the synchronizing instruction streams. When two instruction streams executing code which require a different number of cycles to execute before reaching synchronization code, the first stream to reach the synchronization code is required to wait. Although each stream on the CPC executes one cycle per *turn*, each stream on the CPC with continuation bit will execute on average more than one cycle per turn. As long as the streams are executing useful code, the average execution time will remain the same: two cycles + two cycles which is the same as one cycle + one cycle + one cycle + one cycle. Upon reaching the synchronization code, the first instruction stream to reach the synchronization code will execute that code at the rate of one cycle per turn. If the other stream is executing more than one cycle per turn, that stream will reach the synchronization point faster than when it would execute only one cycle per turn.

3. Simulation

In this section we describe the software environment which was used to obtain the results. In the next section we will discuss the results from the simulations.

3.1 Parallel programming model

The parallel programming model used to parallelize the programs is based on the Force model [6]. In the Force model, at runtime, a fixed number of processes execute a single program on a shared memory multiprocessor. The parallel programming primitives include a) *critical section*: only one process is allowed to enter the critical section at a given time, b) *barrier*: processes wait for all other processes to reach the barrier; one process continues to execute the barrier code after which all processes are allowed to continue execution, c) in a *pre-scheduled loop*, loop indices are calculated once and assigned to the processors d) in a *self-scheduled loop*, each processor calculates the next available index of the loop; self-scheduled loops require **atomic** update of the loop index for each iteration.

Pre-scheduled loops can be used if the loops are well balanced. If loops are not well balanced, one processor may complete much faster than other processors and be required to wait until other processors complete their job. In such cases, self-scheduling loops are more efficient, even after taking the added overhead for atomic update of the index variable into account. Both scheduling techniques require absence of dependencies.

3.2 Programming environment

The programming environment for this simulation includes a parallel Fortran compiler, assembler and linker. Simulations are done using the FLATS2*

---

* The FORTRAN compiler is part of the software development environment for the FLATS2

instruction level simulator. In the simulations, a subset of the FLATS2 instruction set was used; while the FLATS2 allows both source and destination operands in an arithmetic instruction, these type of instructions would not be realistic for a highly pipelined machine. A short cycle time would require a RISC like instruction set: load from memory, store to memory, and arithmetic operations on registers.

3.3 Code rescheduling

A special pass of the parallel Fortran compiler does the instruction scheduling and reorganization based on the latencies of the instructions. The latencies used in these simulations (Table 1) are based on the instruction latencies of the Cray 1.

Operation Class	Latency
register move	2
integer alu	4
load	8
store	2
float alu	12
branch	2

Table 1. Operation latencies

The operation latencies for a pipeline with a degree other than 12 are derived from the above table. For example, if the pipeline degree is 3, the latencies are 1, 1, 2, 1, 3, and 1, respectively.

Currently, the instruction reorganizer only considers basic blocks [5]. Techniques such as *trace scheduling* [3] and *software pipelining* [8] can find instruction level parallelism beyond basic blocks. The reorganizer starts with a set

---

computer, a two instruction stream CPC implemented using ECL logic. The FLATS2 instruction set simulator was extended to vary the number of instruction streams.

of instructions which can be scheduled. From this set it selects the instruction with the longest latency and issues the instruction. If the set is empty, no instruction can be issued because of dependencies and a no-op is issued. Finally, a new set of instructions which can be issued is calculated and the process is repeated. If no dependencies between the selected instruction and the previous instruction exist, the continuation bit is set for the previous instruction. Because the latency between the instruction changes from m cycles to 1 cycle, the insertion of the continuation bit influences the calculation of the rest of the schedule. It is possible that by inserting a continuation bit, additional no-ops have to be inserted, increasing the total execution time. To make sure that such a condition does not arise, the compiler has to verify that inserting a continuation bit does not generate worse code. The algorithms to implement this efficiently are outside the scope of this paper.

3.4 Programs

To evaluate the effects of the introduction of the continuation bit, we selected five programs, each with different characteristics. The **Linpack** benchmark consists of the *dgefa* and *dgesl* routines (double floating point), of which dgefa takes over 90% of the execution time for matrices with orders larger than 100. The routine is highly parallel and executes well on vector processors and superpipelined processors (with the inner loop unrolled). **FEM-ICCG** implements the finite element method using the incomplete Cholesky conjugate gradient method. **FFT** implements a fast Fourier transform with a data size of 8192 complex points. The **quicksort** and **mergesort** programs both sort an array of 10000 integer numbers. They include very few floating point operations. These programs are not well suited for execution on superpipelined or vector processors because of the small degree of instruction level parallelism.

4. Evaluation

In this section we show the results from the simulations. It should be noted that effects of cache misses and page faults are ignored. All speedups are given relative to a base machine with a pipeline degree of one. The programs executing on the base machine and superpipelined machines with a pipeline degree of $n > 1$ were all serial versions of the programs presented. The programs for both CPC and CPC with continuation bit were parallelized version using the Force primitives. Sometimes the only difference was the inclusion of synchronization code (the CPC with a pipeline degree one actually executes slower than the superpipelined version with the same degree of pipelining); other times the program was slightly different. The parallel version of mergesort, for example, does the merging of the arrays by two processors, one merging from the top, the other merging from the bottom; the serial version merges from bottom to top. In each case, the version most suited for the architecture simulated was selected.

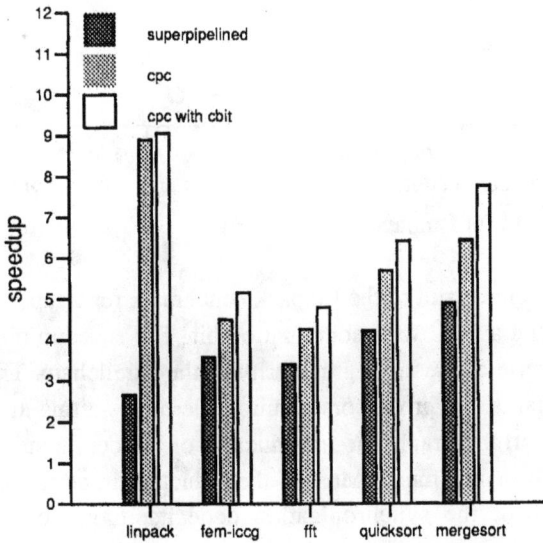

Figure 5. Speedup for a pipeline degree of 12

Figure 5 shows an overview of all programs executed on processors with a pipeline degree of 12. It can be seen from the simulation of the superpipelined processor, that the quicksort and mergesort programs have more instruction level parallelism than the other programs. This is because the quicksort and mergesort programs are integer operation intensive while the other programs are floating point operation intensive. Integer operations have a smaller latency than the floating point operations.

It should be noted that the comparison of speedups is only valid for the execution of the same program. Although mergesort seems to execute better than quicksort, the actual performance is less than quicksort.

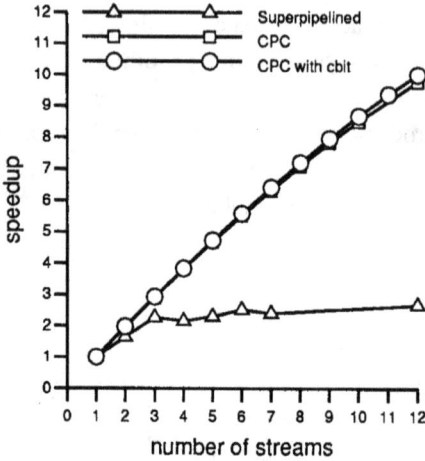

Figure 6a. Speedup for Linpack degfa

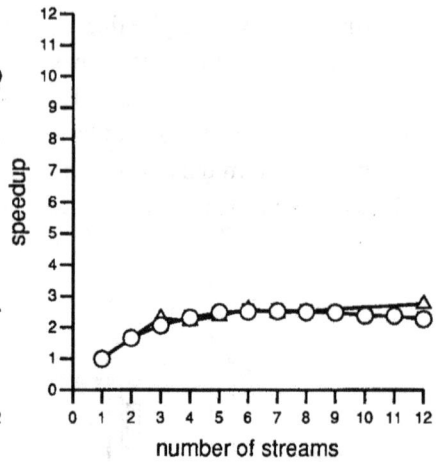

Figure 6b. Speedup for Linpack dgesl

Figure 6. shows the result of the Linpack benchmark for a superpipelined and a CPC processor and a CPC with continuation bit. The speedup of *dgefa* for the CPC is high because of the large granularity of the parallelism. The execution is well balanced, that is, the processors require little time waiting at the barrier. As can been seen from the graph, the introduction of the continuation bit does not increase the performance much. Most of the reduction in performance is caused by the execution of the synchronization code itself, not by waiting at the synchronization point.

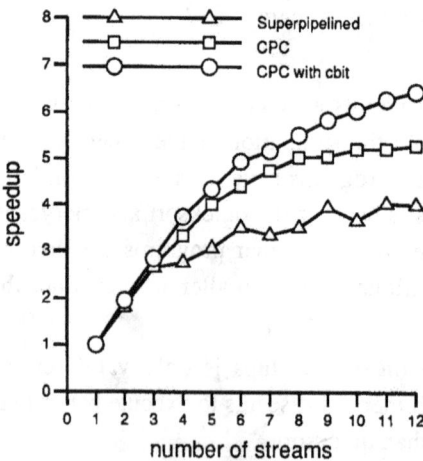

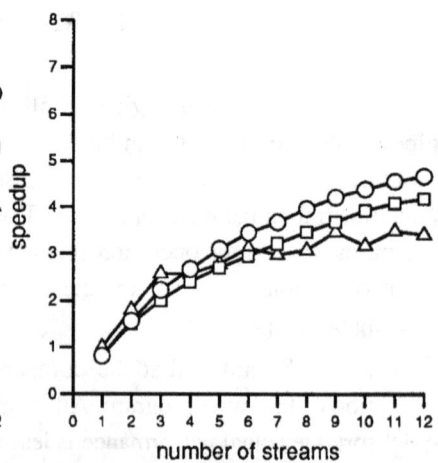

Figure 7. FEM-ICCG - Speedup for MATGEN and SOLV

Figure 7. FEM-ICCG - Speedup for MATGEN and SOLV

Figures 7 to 9 show the results for FEM-ICCG, quicksort and mergesort, respectively. Each of the programs shows a performance increase for a CPC with the continuation bit over the CPC without the continuation bit.

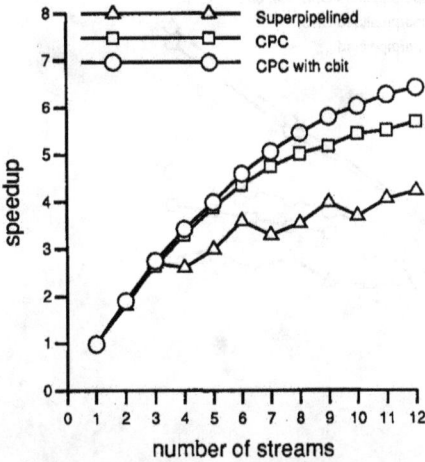

Figure 8. Speedup for Quicksort   Figure 9. Speedup for Mergesort

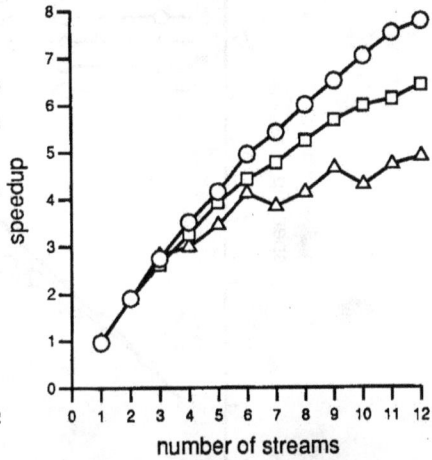

Table 2 shows that for the programs examined, the speedup due to the introduction of the continuation bit is related to the amount of available instruction level parallelism. To evaluate the effect of the continuation bit on a superpipelined CPC, we simulated a superpipelined CPC with a superpipeline degree of three and pipeline degree $n = 3 * m$.

Program	Superpipelined speedup for a pipeline degree of 12	Additional speedup due to continuation bit
Linpack	2.669	+0.156
FEM-ICCG	3.582	+0.653
FFT	3.408	+0.539
Quicksort	4.224	+0.716
Mergesort	4.900	+1.354

Figure 10 shows the results for the FFT. In the case of the superpipelined CPC, the pipeline absorbs most of the instruction level parallelism. Very little parallelism remains to be exploited by the continuation bit.

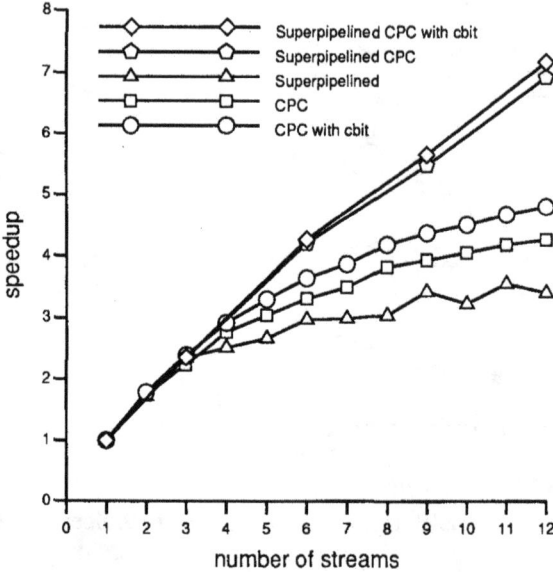

Figure 10. Speedup for FFT

5. Concluding remarks

In this paper we examined the introduction of the continuation bit in the CPC. We found that the continuation bit is better able to exploit the available instruction level parallelism. If the CPC is superpipelined, very little instruction level parallelism remains to be exploited by the continuation bit.

In this paper we did not address the cost of the introduction of the continuation bit. Neither did we consider the effects of the instruction fetch latency. If the cycle time becomes small, the value of the continuation bit may not be available because of the longer instruction fetch latency.

References

[1]   R. Alverson, D. Callahen, D. Cummings, B. Koblenz, A. Porterfield, and B. Smith, "The Tera Computer System", *Proceedings of the 1990 Conference on Supercomputing,* 1990, pp. 1-6.

[2]   T.E. Anderson, "The Performance of Spin Lock Alternatives for Shared-Memory Multiprocessors", *IEEE Transactions on Parallel and Distributed Systems*, Vol. 1, No. 1, January 1990, pp. 6-16.

[3]   J.R. Ellis, "Bulldog: A Compiler for VLIW Architectures", The MIT Press, 1986.

[4]   M.J. Flynn, "Some Computer Organizations and Their Effectiveness", *IEEE Transactions on Computers*, Vol. 21, September 1972, pp. 948-960.

[5]   J. Hennessy and T.R. Gross, "Postpass Code Optimization of Pipeline Constraints", *ACM Transactions on Programming Languages and Systems*, Vol. 5, No. 3, July 1983, pp. 422-448.

[6]   H.F. Jordan, "The Force". In *The Characteristics of Parallel Algorithms*, Leah H. Jamieson, Dennis B. Gannon and R.J. Douglass Ed., The MIT Press, 1987, pp. 395-436.

[7]   N.P. Jouppi, "The Nonuniform Distribution of Instruction-Level and Machine Parallelism and Its Effect on Performance", *IEEE Transactions on Computers*, Vol. 38, No. 12, December 1989.

[8]   M. Lam, "Software Pipelining: An Effective Scheduling Technique for VLIW Machines", *ACM Sigplan '88 Conference on Programming Language Design and Implementation*, Atlanta, Georgia, June 22-24 1988, pp. 318-328.

[9]   M. Sato, S. Ichikawa, and E. Goto, "Multiple Instruction Streams in a Highly Pipelined Processor", *Proceedings of the Second IEEE Symposium on Parallel and Distributed Processing*, Dallas, Texas, December 9-13 1990, pp. 182-189.

[10] K. Shimizu, E. Goto, and S. Ichikawa, "CPC (Cyclic Pipeline Computer) - An Architecture Suited for Josephson and Pipelined Machines", *IEEE Transactions on Computers*, June 1989, pp. 825-832.

[11] M.R. Thistle and B.J. Smith, "A Processor Architecture for Horizon", *Proceedings of Supercomputing '88*, 1988, pp. 35-41.

Reprinted from *Int. J. High Speed Computing*, 3(2), 135 – 156 (1991).
© 1991 World Scientific.

Effects of Multiple Instruction Stream Execution on Cache Performance

Paul Spee, Wong Weng Fai and Eiichi Goto

Abstract

In recent years, there has been a trend towards multiple instruction stream computer architectures. The Cyclic Pipeline Computer (CPC) is an early example of a statically scheduled multiple instruction stream computer. It shares its pipeline among multiple instruction streams in a time-shared manner. The advantages of such machines are that they are capable of hiding latencies, in particular memory access latencies. However, if these instruction streams share a common cache, the cache behavior is adversely affected because the memory access pattern is not characterized by one working set, but by a combination of working sets. In this paper, we will examine the effects of multiple instruction stream execution on the cache miss ratio. While a direct mapped cache might be sufficient for a single instruction stream, our results indicate that this is not true for multiple instruction stream execution. We also found that the set mapping function plays an important role in getting adequate hashing in multiple instruction stream execution.

1. Introduction

In recent years, there has been a trend towards multiple instruction stream computer architectures, sometimes referred to as multi-stream or multi-threaded architectures. In such computers, several instruction streams may share the pipeline in a time-shared manner. Examples of such machines are the HEP [13, 7], CPC [11,12], the Horizon [14], and the Tera computer [3]. The SPARCLE processor [2] provides very fast context switching between instruction streams, but at any given moment only one instruction stream is executing. The advantages of multiple instruction stream processors are that they are capable of hiding latencies, in particular memory access latencies, from the executing programs, especially when the execution pipeline is fairly deep. In traditional processors with a low degree of pipelining, the problem of memory access latency has been overcome fairly successfully by the use of *caching*. In caching, fast memory is used as a cache to hold recent memory accesses in the hope that they will be used again in the near future. A cache operates on the principles of *spatial locality* (if a location is accessed, then the nearby ones are also likely to be accessed) and *temporal locality* (if a location is accessed, then there is a fairly good chance that it will be accessed again). If multiple instruction streams access a common cache, the above principles may not be valid.

Because of the presence of multiple instruction streams, performance of the cache is likely to be degraded. In this paper, we investigate the influence of multiple instruction stream execution of the cache miss ratio. As an example of a multiple instruction stream architecture we use the CPC which we will describe in more detail in Section 2. In that section we will also describe the relation between the CPC and cache. In Section 3 we will present the experimental environment. In Section 4 we will discuss the results of the experiments and we will give our conclusions in Section 5.

2. Multiple instruction stream execution

In this section we will describe the Cyclic Pipeline Computer as an example of a multi-threaded architecture. We will also discuss the use of a cache in a CPC.

2.1. Cyclic Pipeline Computer

The *Cyclic Pipeline Computer* (CPC) was initially proposed as an architecture for Josephson devices [12]. Due to the inherent latching nature of the Josephson devices, it is possible to build very deep pipelines with no pipeline latching overhead. However, research has indicated that superpipelined processors[1] on average achieve a speedup of only two to four times because of control and data dependencies between instructions [9].

The CPC is a shared resource MIMD computer [4] in which both the functional units and the memory are pipelined and shared among multiple instruction streams. Only the hardware which is considered to be part of the *context* of a particular instruction stream, such as the program counter, status registers, and other registers, is duplicated. Figure 1 shows the pipeline diagrams of pipelined, superpipelined, cyclic pipelined, and cyclic superpipelined computers.

---

[1] Superpipelined processors have a basic cycle time which is shorter than the latency of the execution unit. This means in effect that multiple instructions can be in execution at a given time.

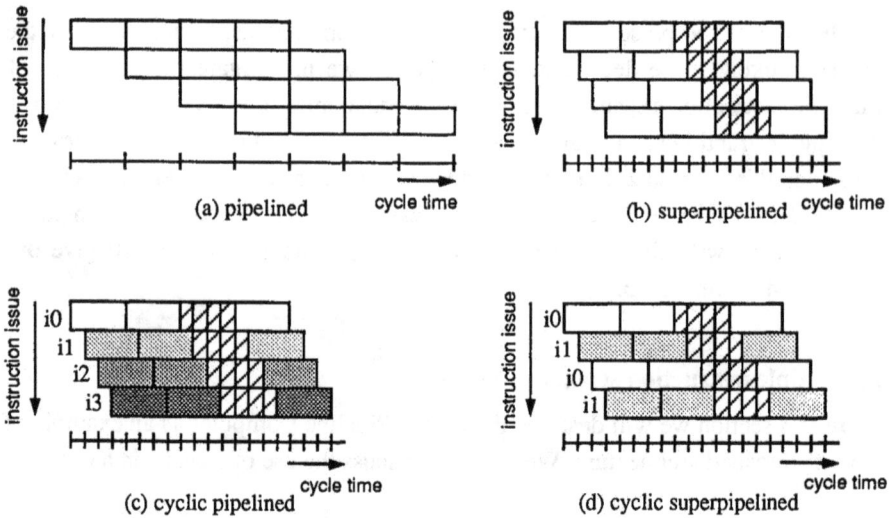

Figure 1. Pipeline diagrams

Unlike some other multiple instruction stream architectures, such as the HEP, the CPC does not have additional hardware to switch instruction streams during execution. Instead, a fixed number of streams are given fixed "time slots" in the pipeline. The tradeoff is between simplified hardware and minimal scheduling overhead against a possibly lower pipeline efficiency. Research has indicated that a CPC can obtain a better performance than a superpipelined processor with the same pipeline structure [11].

2.2. Cache

Cache behavior is often characterized by the *miss ratio* – the percentage of memory references whose results are not available from the cache. Three parameters are often considered when evaluating the miss ratio of a cache. They are *cache size*, *line* or *block size*, and the degree of *associativity*.

In a usual operation of a cache, a cache miss would necessitate the stalling of the pipeline in order that the required operand be fetched from memory. The amount of time the pipeline is to be stalled is directly proportional to the memory latency. In our simulation, memory latency is not considered. In the case where the entire pipeline is stalled, it is clear that the extra overhead introduced by stalling is just the total number of cache misses multiplied by the memory latency per cache miss (which may be a constant number or an average). In the case where individual streams are stalled upon cache misses, the question of performance is a complicated one that depends on the architecture of the multiple instruction stream computer in question. Factors such as the scheduling of the streams for execution, number of streams, structure of the pipeline etc. will interact with the cache miss ratio to determine the actual degradation in performance. Our aim in this paper is to address the issue of the effects of multiple instruction stream execution on the cache and, hopefully, our results will be applicable to a wide variety of multiple instruction stream architectures. Therefore, the specific performance of the CPC is not addressed.

While the effects of the cache parameters on standard cache behavior have been well studied [6], there has been little or no study on the matter with respect to multiple instruction stream execution. The most relevant studies are those on cache behavior in a multiprogramming environment [1]. Such behavior is characterized by operating processes switching contexts after executing for a certain unit of time. The multiple instruction stream execution model, in particular the CPC, however, has a much finer granularity of execution than multiprogramming since an instruction is fetched from a different instruction stream in each cycle. This paper examines the relationship between the three cache parameters and the miss ratio in the context of the CPC.

3. Simulation

In this section we describe the software environment which was used to obtain the results. In the next section we will discuss the results from the simulations.

3.1. Parallel programming model and environment

The parallel programming model used to parallelize the programs is based on the Force model [8]. In the Force model, at runtime, a fixed number of processes execute a single program on a shared memory multiprocessor. The parallel programming primitives include a) *critical section*: only one process is allowed to enter the critical section at a given time, b) *barrier*: processes wait for all other processes to reach the barrier; one process continues to execute the barrier code after which all processes are allowed to continue execution, c) *pre-scheduled loop*, in which loop indices are calculated once and assigned to the processors, and d) *self-scheduled loop*, in which each processor calculates the next available index of the loop; self-scheduled loops require **atomic** update of the loop index for each iteration.

Pre-scheduled loops can be used if the loops are well balanced. If loops are not well balanced, one processor may complete much faster than other processors and be required to wait until other processors complete their job. In such cases, self-scheduling loops are more efficient, even after taking the added overhead for atomic update of the index variable into account. Both scheduling techniques require absence of dependencies between loop iterations.

The programming environment for this simulation includes a parallel FORTRAN compiler, assembler and linker. Simulations are done using the FLATS2[2] instruction level simulator. In the simulations, a RISC-like subset of the FLATS2 instruction set was used: load from memory, store to memory, and arithmetic operations on registers.

3.2. Experimental setup

To evaluate the effect of multiple instruction stream execution on cache performance we selected two programs, each with different characteristics.

The **Linpack** benchmark consists of the *dgefa* and *dgesl* routines (double floating point), of which dgefa takes over 90% of the execution time for matrices with orders larger than 100. The routine is highly parallel and executes well on vector processors and superpipelined processors (with the inner loop unrolled). The program was parallelized using a pre-scheduled DO-loop.

The **Quicksort** program sorts an array of 20,000 integer numbers. It includes very few floating point operations and is not well suited for execution on superpipelined or vector processors because of the small degree of instruction level parallelism. Quicksort is parallelized by maintaining a stack of subarrays to be sorted. The streams pick the next subarray to be sorted. The stack is protected by a critical section.

We varied the following parameters in our experiments: the number of instruction streams p (one to eight streams), the associativity n of the cache (direct mapped and associativities 2, 4, and 8) and the size s of the cache (32 to 512 sets). The line size was kept constant at 32 bytes.

---

[2]   The FORTRAN compiler is part of the software development environment for the FLATS2 computer, a two instruction stream CPC implemented using ECL logic. The FLATS2 instruction set simulator was extended to vary the number of instruction streams.

4. Discussion

In this section we will describe the results of our experiments.

Linpack				
	1 stream	2 streams	4 streams	8 streams
Direct mapped	0.02592	0.02593 0%	0.04639 79%	0.07248 180%
Associativity 2	0.02510	0.02511 0%	0.04288 71%	0.05415 116%
Associativity 4	0.02519	0.02517 0%	0.02552 1%	0.03795 51%
Associativity 8	0.02528	0.02526 0%	0.02524 0%	0.02626 4%

Quicksort				
	1 stream	2 streams	4 streams	8 streams
Direct mapped	0.00799	0.01647 106%	0.04521 466%	0.07081 786%
Associativity 2	0.00698	0.00893 27%	0.01785 156%	0.03963 468%
Associativity 4	0.00700	0.00872 25%	0.00994 42%	0.02649 278%
Associativity 8	0.00700	0.00869 24%	0.00984 40%	0.01108 58%

Table 1. Miss ratios for cache size 512

4.1. Cache miss ratio

As expected and as clearly can be seen from Figures 2 to 5, the cache's performance became worse as the number of instruction streams increased. What was not expected was the very irregular behavior of the cache miss ratio as a function of the cache size. This turned out to be related to the set mapping function and will be discussed in more detail in Section 4.2. Table 1 shows the cache miss ratio for caches with a cache size of 512 sets.

4.2. Set mapping function

To our initial surprise, in multiple instruction stream execution, the set

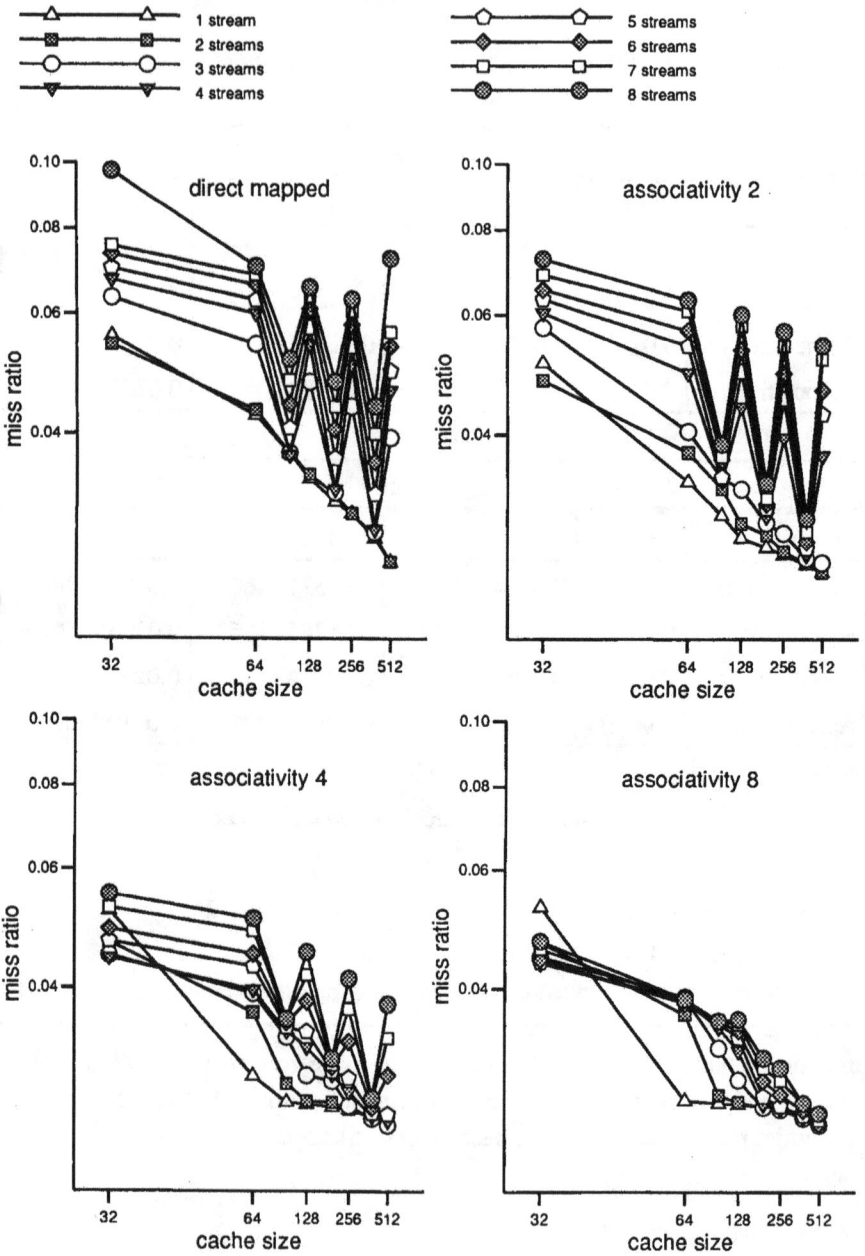

Figure 2. Miss ratio for Linpack

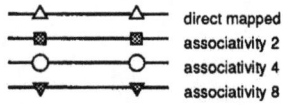

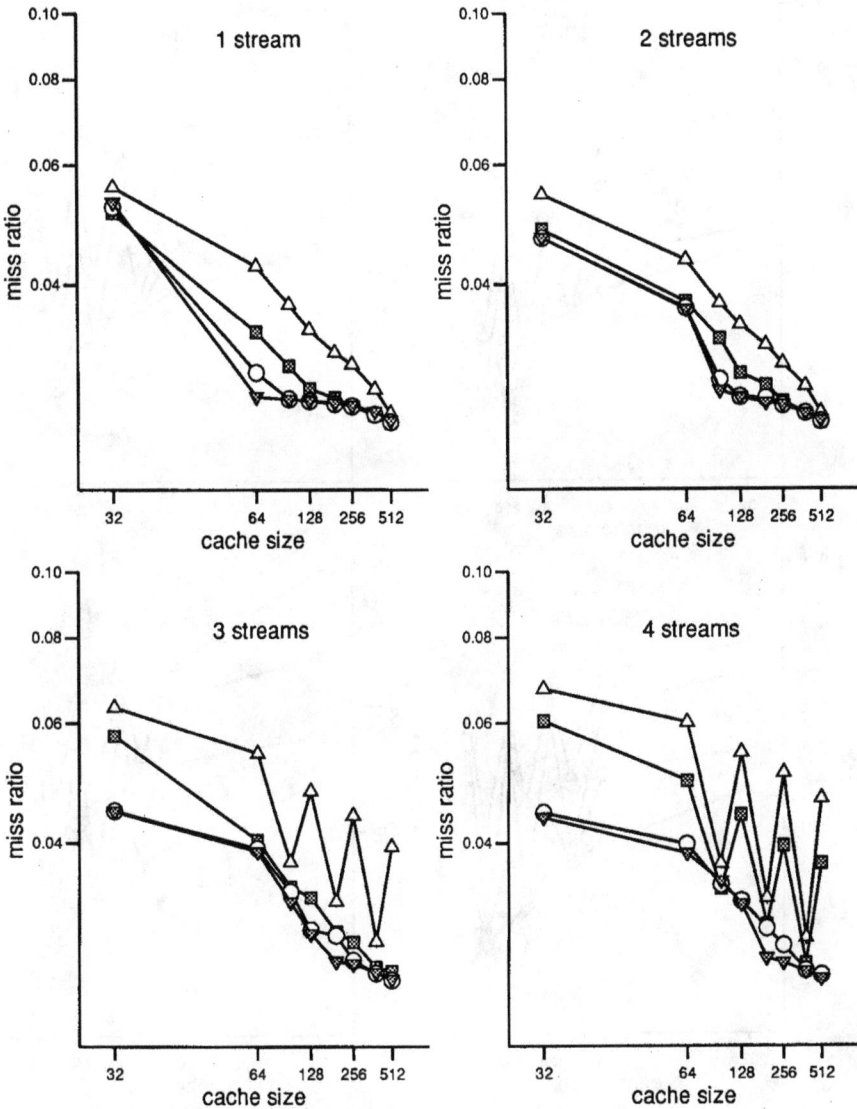

Figure 3a. Miss ratio for Linpack

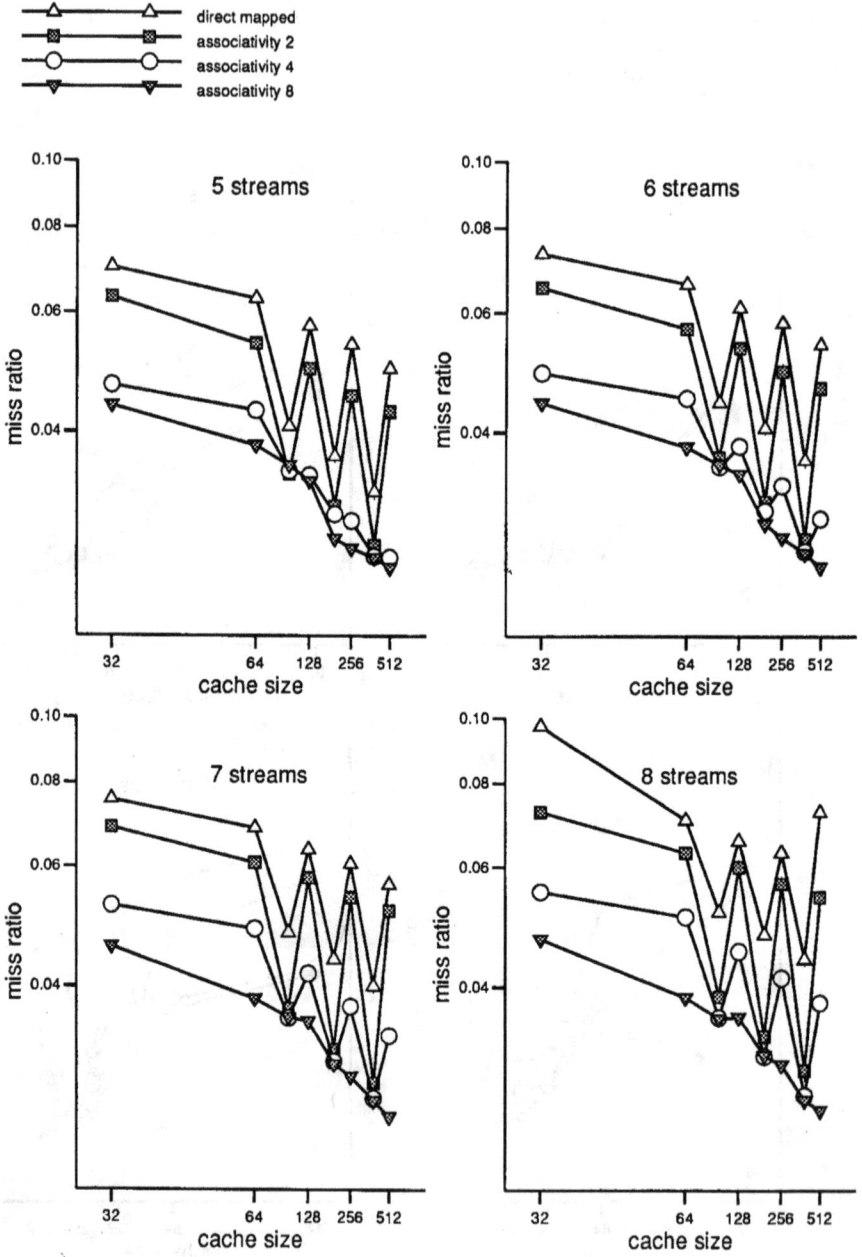

Figure 3b. Miss ratio for Linpack

mapping function plays a much more significant role than in single stream execution. Among the first results that we got were graphs of the nature shown in Figure 2. While the graphs validated the hypothesis that the miss ratio would increase as the number of instruction streams increased, fairly consistently it showed significant jumps in the miss ratio at particular cache sizes. Also, there was a sharp contrast between data for single stream execution compared with those for multiple instruction stream execution. In particular, it became significantly worse as the number of streams was increased.

The set mapping function used in our simulations is $f(x) = x$ mod $size$. For cache sizes (number of sets) which are a power of two, this would be equivalent to $f(x) = x$ AND $(size\text{-}1)$. In other words, the lower bits of x are used to select the set. As can been seen from Figures 3 and 5, the caches with a cache size that is a power of two have a much worse cache miss ratio than the caches with a cache size that is not a power of two. If the accesses are to the stack associated with the streams, the accesses may be mapped on the same set, causing that set to *thrash*.

This result may be generalized. In a fine grain, p instruction stream shared-memory execution model, there is a high probability that either there concurrently exist $p+1$ mutually exclusive *clusters* of accesses (one for each stream's local memory access and one for the global memory to which all streams access) or only one cluster of accesses (when a critical region is being occupied and all other streams are spinning on a lock). By carefully selecting the set mapping function and/or modifying the memory allocation algorithm with the set mapping function in mind, we can achieve fairly uniform mapping.

To verify the effect of the set mapping function on the cache miss ratio, we modified the set mapping function. The criteria for the set mapping function we require are that it must be simple and achieve fairly uniform distribution, and must also be a many-to-1 mapping. Simplicity comes from the fact that it needs to be performed on every memory access and it must use the lowest possible overheads. Thus, the division method recommended in [10] is quite unacceptable. Based on the second criterion, our experiments show that the usual bit extraction algorithm is not good enough. The last criterion is necessary to ensure correctness – an address must never be mapped to more than one location. To be exact, a single address must map uniquely to a *set*, within which it may occupy any line location. The method that we eventually used is a modification of the folding method. The 32-bit address is broken up into the following portions:

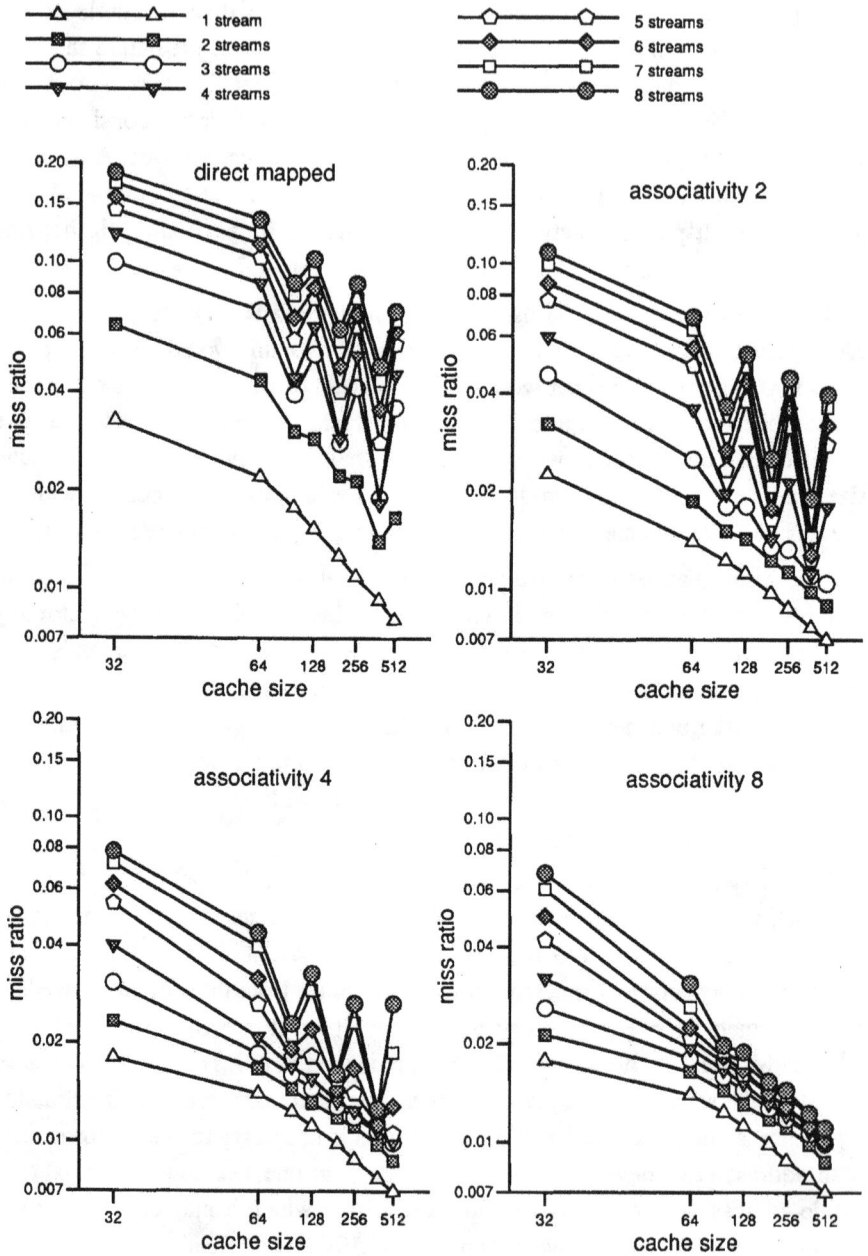

Figure 4. Miss ratio for Quicksort

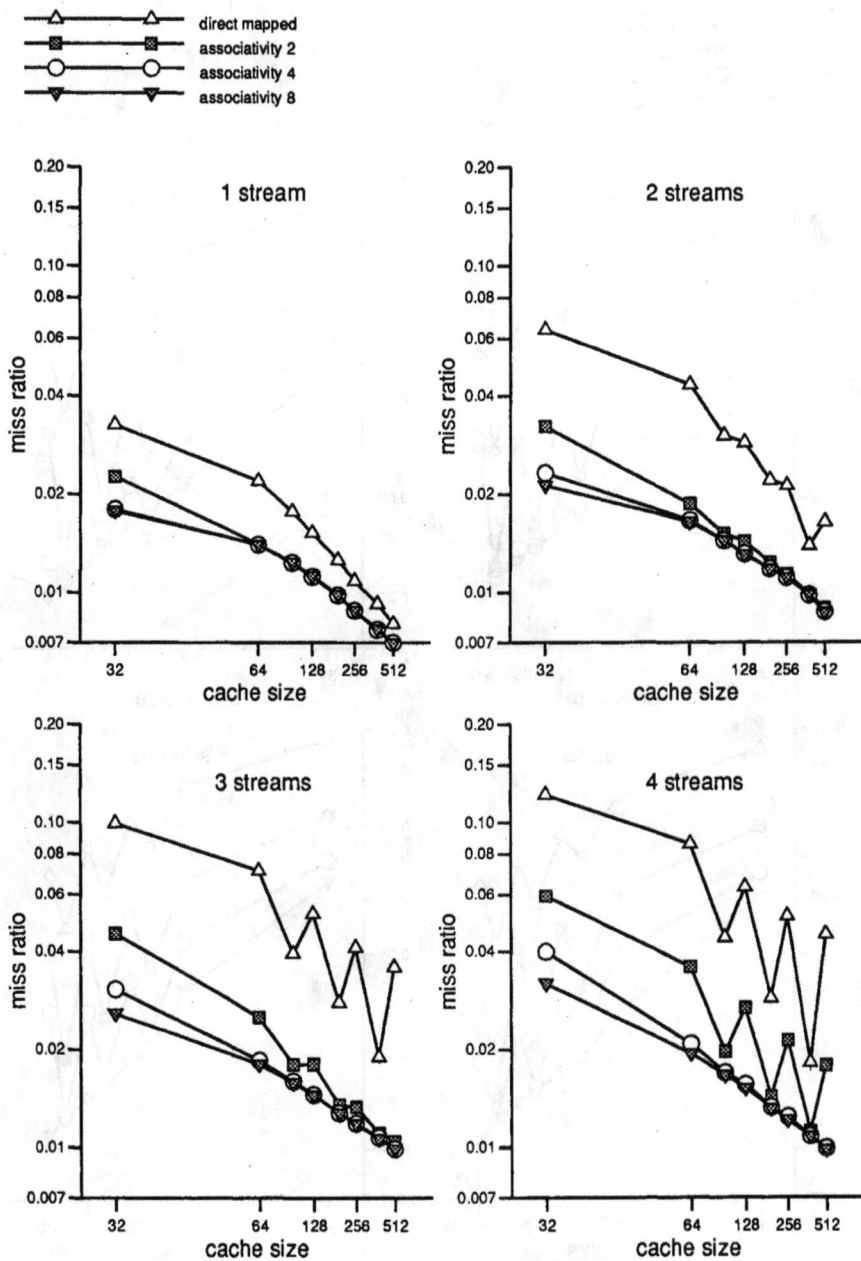

Figure 5a. Miss ratio for Quicksort

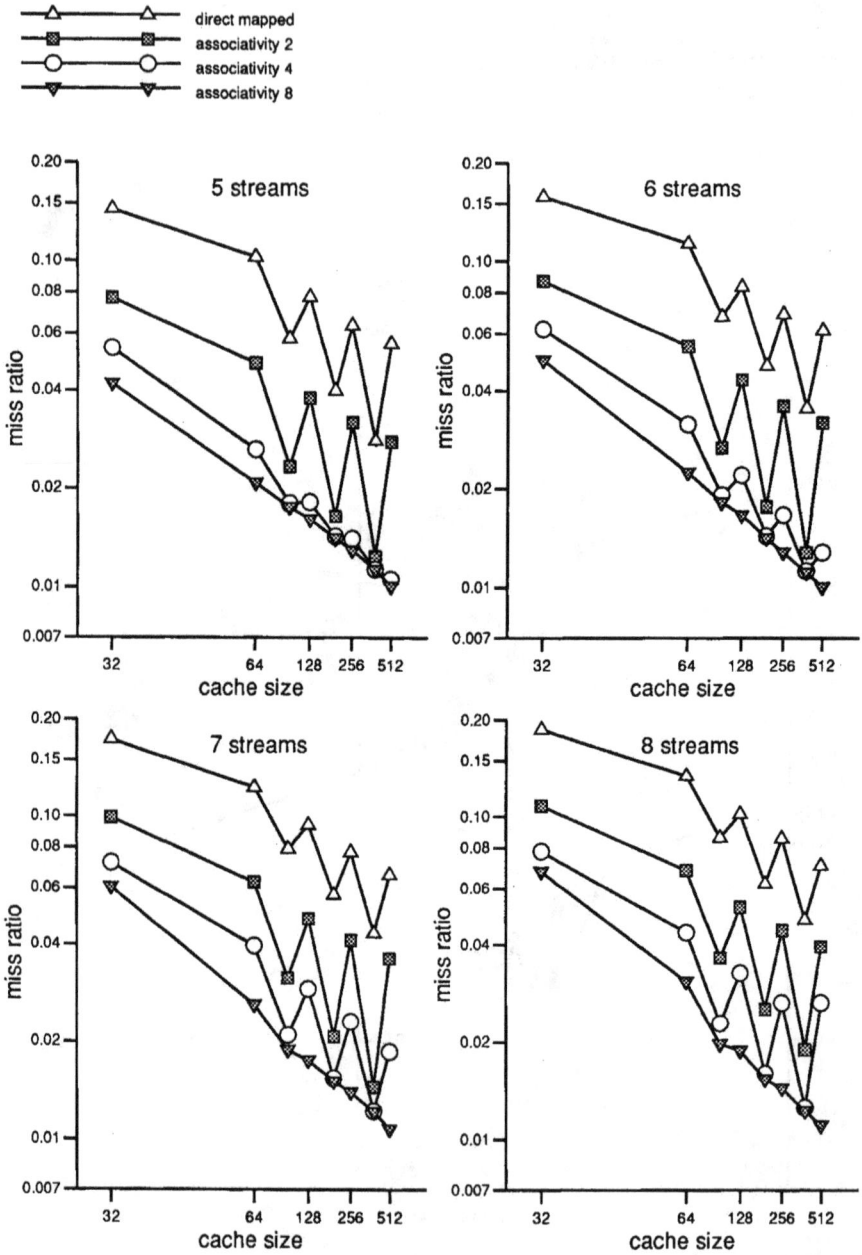

Figure 5b. Miss ratio for Quicksort

31			0
tag	index	displacement	

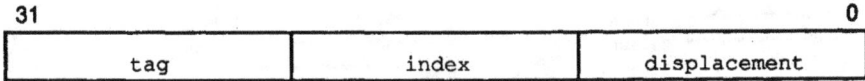

Figure 6. Memory address

In the standard bit extraction algorithm, the index portion is simply used as the cache set address. The problem is that due to the size of the cache, the index portion is usually quite small. Typically, it is about 8 bits. Also, the displacement field is not big either since it is limited by considerations like memory bandwidth and the typical span of spatial locality. Thus, the tag field is the largest of the three. In normal single stream execution, this is not too much of a concern since there tends to be a decrease in variation with respect to time as one moves from the lower order bits to the higher order ones. However, in the case of fine grain, multiple instruction stream execution, this no longer holds. A large enough local memory has to be allocated for each stream. Furthermore, because of the fine interleaving of the streams' execution, if one examines the overall address trace of the pipeline, there will be a number of high order bits which will vary considerably with respect to time. Such a variation does not exist in the single stream processor. Thus, to better even out the hashing, we hashed by taking the *exclusive or* of the tag field with the index field. Because the tag field is much longer than the index field, we can achieve the best results only if we select the portion of the tag field which distinguishes the local memory of each stream.

The effect of the modified set mapping function is shown in Figures 7 and 8. We find that the new set mapping function results in a much better distribution of the memory accesses over the cache sets. The importance of set mapping function was also suggested by Agarwal in relation to multiprogramming environments [1].

4.3. Associativity

Current trends in cache design favor direct mapped caches over associative caches. In an n-way associative cache, n lines are made available to each set. A line brought into the cache may occupy any of the n line locations to which it hashes to. This entails additional effort in the read process as all n lines' tags must be compared simultaneously with the read access's tag after hashing. Therefore, it

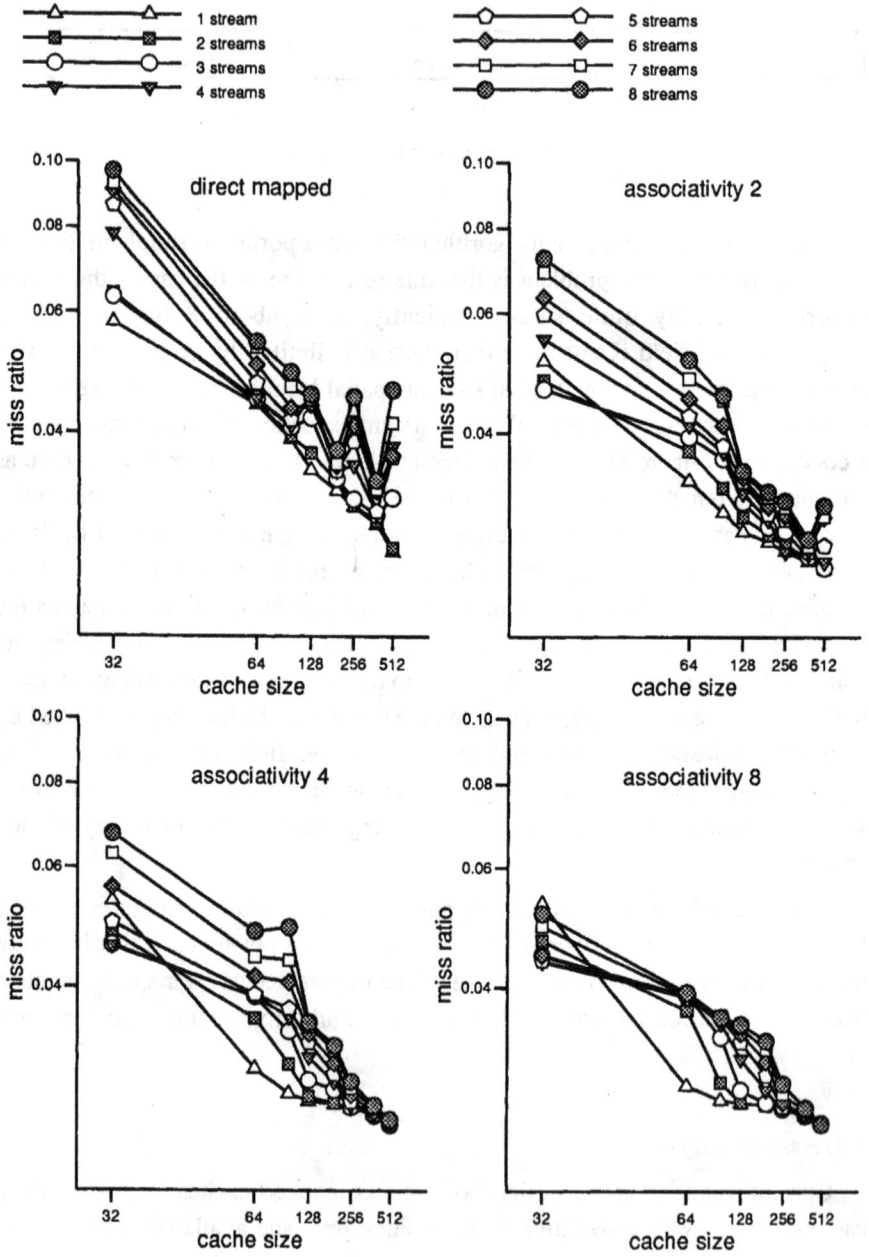

Figure 7. Miss ratio for Linpack (modified hashing)

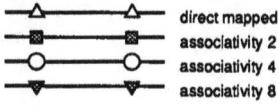

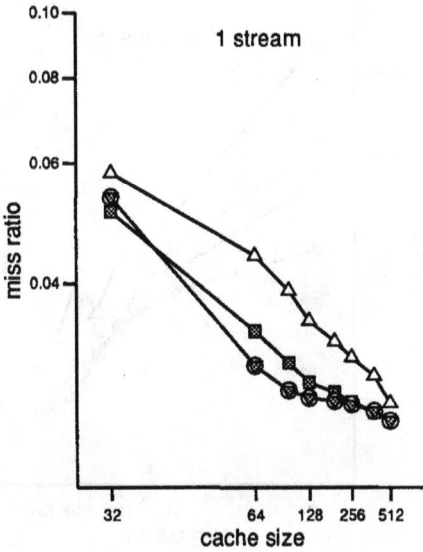

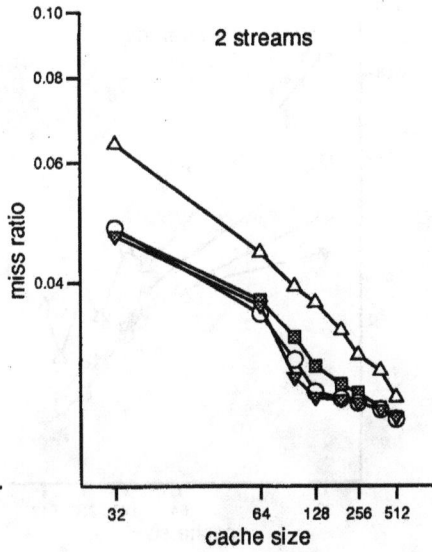

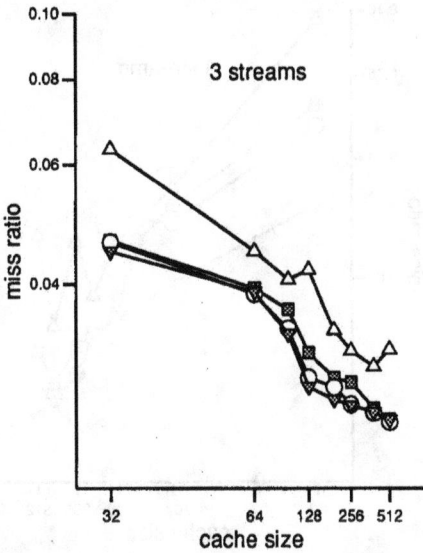

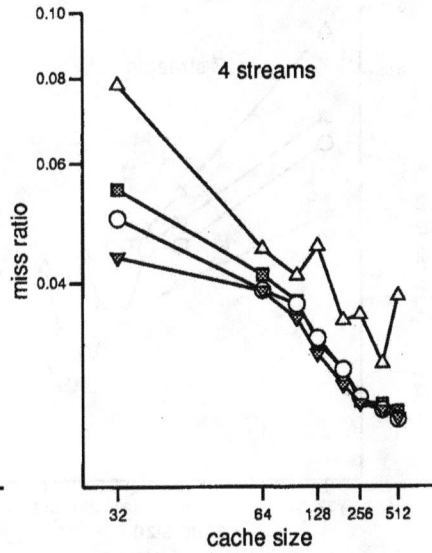

Figure 8a. Miss ratio for Linpack (modified hashing)

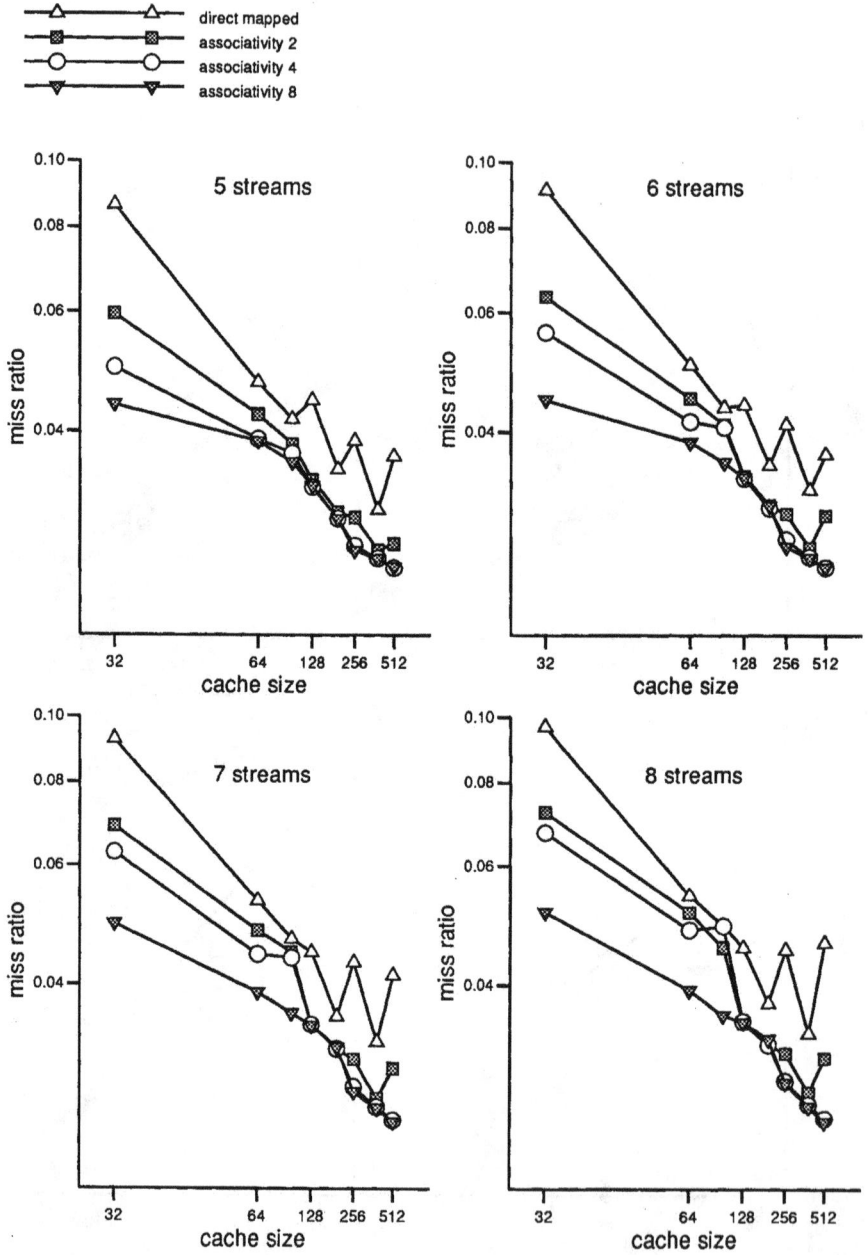

Figure 8b. Miss ratio for Linpack (modified hashing)

is argued that the overhead incurred per access does not justify the relatively small improvement in performance [5].

As our data show, even improving the hashing function does not even out the memory accesses. We argue that in the case of multiple instruction stream execution, associativity is much more relevant than in the case of a traditional single stream processor. The experimental result for a single stream corresponds closely to those published in the literature, i.e. there is a reasonably significant improvement when a set associative cache is used rather than a direct mapped cache. Furthermore, this improvement diminishes as cache sizes are increased. In the case of multiple instruction stream execution, although increasing cache sizes will also result in a reduction of the relative benefits of associativity, there remains a significant gap between the miss ratios because the number of streams are increased even when fairly large caches are used.

4.4. Cache size

One of our assumptions was that increasing the cache size by two should be sufficient to offset the adverse effect of increasing the number of streams by two. Indeed, we expected that because the streams were cooperating in solving one problem, the possibility existed that they accessed the same memory locations, thus, actually reducing the miss ratio.

In Table 2 we show the miss ratios for four cases where the ratio of the cache size s and the number of streams p were held constant. When doubling the number of streams, we also doubled the cache size. We found that because of the thrashing of the cache as described in the previous section, the miss ratio on average became worse. However, with the modified set mapping function, our expectation was confirmed.

5. Conclusion

In this paper, we have examined the effects of multiple instruction stream execution on a cache. We came to the following conclusions:

1. Cache performance degrades when the number of streams are increased.

2. There is an important interaction between how local

memory is allocated and how the cache performs its
hashing. The *bit selection* set mapping function is not
sufficient to avoid interference.

3. Associativity is more important as a means of improving
performance in multiple instruction stream execution than
in conventional single stream execution.

Linpack				
streams/size	1/64	2/128	4/256	8/512
Direct mapped	0.04259	0.03486	0.05061	0.07248
Associativity 2	0.03408	0.02960	0.03959	0.05415
Associativity 4	0.02974	0.02733	0.02823	0.03795
Associativity 8	0.02742	0.02730	0.02663	0.02626

Quicksort				
streams/size	1/64	2/128	4/256	8/512
Direct mapped	0.02197	0.02881	0.05138	0.07081
Associativity 2	0.01404	0.01432	0.02132	0.03963
Associativity 4	0.01399	0.01313	0.01239	0.02649
Associativity 8	0.01400	0.01307	0.01211	0.01108

Linpack (modified hashing)				
streams/size	1/64	2/128	4/256	8/512
Direct mapped	0.04395	0.03737	0.03585	0.04620
Associativity 2	0.03402	0.03009	0.02672	0.03129
Associativity 4	0.03028	0.02758	0.02674	0.02551
Associativity 8	0.02863	0.02706	0.02655	0.02522

Table 2. Miss ratio with *s/p* held constant

As technology improves, making it possible to design deeper pipelines, inescapable limitations, in particular instruction level parallelism, will make fine grain, multiple instruction stream execution attractive. The cache, being a proven cost-effective means of overcoming the memory bandwidth limitation, will also play an important role in such architectures. Our studies, by revealing the interactions between the two, will be useful in the future design of fast, deeply pipelined, multiple instruction stream computers.

References

[1]   A. Agarwal, J.L. Hennessy, and M. Horowitz, "Cache Performance of Operating System and Multiprogramming Workloads", *ACM Transactions on Computer Systems*, Vol. 6, No. 4, 11 1988, pp. 393-431.

[2]   A. Agarwal, B.H. Lim, D. Krantz, and J. Kubiatowicz, "APRIL: A Processor Architecture for Multiprocessing", *Proceedings of the 17th Annual International Symposium on Computer Architecture,* June 1990.

[3]   R. Alverson, D. Callahen, D. Cummings, B. Koblenz, A. Porterfield, and B. Smith, "The Tera Computer System", *Proceedings of the 1990 Conference on Supercomputing*, 1990, pp. 1-6.

[4]   M.J. Flynn, "Some Computer Organizations and Their Effectiveness", *IEEE Transactions on Computers*, Vol. 21, September 1972, pp. 948-960.

[5]   M.D. Hill, "A Case for Direct-Mapped Caches", *IEEE Computer*, Vol. 21, No. 12, December 1988, pp. 25-40.

[6]   M.D. Hill and A.J. Smith, "Evaluating Associativity in CPU Caches", *IEEE Transactions on Computers*, Vol. 38, No. 12, December 1989, pp. 1612-1630.

[7]   H.F. Jordan, "HEP Architecture, Programming and Performance". In *Parallel MIMD Computation: HEP Supercomputer and Its Applications,* J.S. Kowalik Ed., MIT Press, 1985, Ch. 1.1, pp. 1-40.

[8]   H.F. Jordan, "The Force". In *The Characteristics of Parallel Algorithms*, Leah H. Jamieson, Dennis B. Gannon and R.J. Douglass Ed., The MIT Press, 1987, pp. 395-436.

[9]   N.P. Jouppi, "The Nonuniform Distribution of Instruction-Level and Machine Parallelism and Its Effect on Performance", *IEEE Transactions on Computers*, Vol. 38, No. 12, December 1989.

[10] V.Y. Lum, P.S.T. Yuen, and M. Dodd, "Key-to-Address Transform Techniques: A Fundamental Performance Study on Large Existing Formatted Files", *Communications of the ACM*, Vol. 14, No. 4, April 1971, pp. 228-239.

[11] M. Sato, S. Ichikawa, and E. Goto, "Multiple Instruction Streams in a Highly Pipelined Processor", *Proceedings of the Second IEEE Symposium on Parallel and Distributed Processing*, Dallas, Texas, December 9-13 1990, pp. 182-189.

[12] K. Shimizu, E. Goto, and S. Ichikawa, "CPC (Cyclic Pipeline Computer) - An Architecture Suited for Josephson and Pipelined Machines", *IEEE Transactions on Computers*, Vol. 38, No. 6, June 1989, pp. 825-832.

[13] B.J. Smith, "A pipelined, Shared Resource MIMD Computer", *Proceedings of the 1978 International Conference on Parallel Processing*, 1978, pp. 6-8.

[14] M.R. Thistle and B.J. Smith, "A Processor Architecture for Horizon", *Proceedings of Supercomputing '88*, 1988, pp. 35-41.

Shared Memory Multiprocessor CPC

Paul Spee, Wong Weng Fai, and Eiichi Goto

Abstract

The Cyclic Pipeline Computer offers the advantage of better utilization of a deep instruction execution pipeline. In return, the program will have to be transformed into a parallel program to take advantage of the multiple instruction streams that exist in the Cyclic Pipeline Computer. A natural extension to the idea is to consider a multiprocessor system where each processor node is a Cyclic Pipeline Computer. In this paper, we will study such an extension. In particular, we wish to ascertain the effectiveness of the multiprocessor approach.

1. Introduction

The Cyclic Pipeline Computer (CPC) is a computer architecture in which multiple instruction streams share the pipeline hardware in a time-multiplexed manner. In our earlier papers[4,5,6,7], we have demonstrated the advantages of such an approach, particularly in a deeply pipelined processor envisioned in our Quantum Magneto Flux Parametron project. We have built the prototype computer using ECL technology called the FLATS2, developed the system software for it and tested it. The results, as reported elsewhere, show that the Cyclic Pipeline Computer is superior to superpipelined processors of similar hardware requirements. As further work, we have also extended the basic Cyclic Pipeline Computer with the introduction of the continuation bit and we have also studied the effects of multiple instruction streams on cache behavior.

The Cyclic Pipeline Computer while maximizing the overall utility of the pipeline, reduces the throughput per stream. For example, if there are p streams sharing a pipeline, then the throughput per stream would be $1/p$ that of the throughput for one stream running in the same pipeline under ideal situations. The truth of the matter is that dependencies between the instructions of an instruction stream would mean that if only a single stream is running, the pipeline is almost always under-utilized, i.e. there would be less than one result per pipeline clock in the steady state. In the Cyclic Pipeline Computer, better utilization is achieved because after an instruction from a stream is issued, there will be $p-1$ instructions from different instruction streams (and hence no possibility of dependency exist) issued before the subsequent instruction from the same stream will be issued. If p is chosen carefully, then even in the worst case where in each instruction stream, every instruction depends on its immediate predecessor, the pipeline would be still delivering one result per pipeline clock. However, for a given instruction stream, there is result only every $p-1$ pipeline clock cycle.

If one wish to devote the entire pipeline to solving a single problem, then parallel programming is necessary. Using a parallel programming model, one will be able to recode the solution in terms of parallel tasks cooperating to solve the problem. The cost, in terms of overheads introduced, are

1. the need for the parallel tasks to occasionally synchronize and
2. the inherently sequential portions of the code (which are present in all parallel programs) will only be running at $1/p$ the maximum throughput.

Our work on the continuation bit have examined the latter problem. As for programming, a parallel FORTRAN compiler using the Force model [1] has been implemented.

Since using the Cyclic Pipeline Computer would require parallel programming, a natural extension of the Cyclic Pipeline Computer would be to go to a multiprocessor system in which the individual processors are Cyclic Pipeline Computers. This paper seeks to examine such a possibility. In particular, we want to answer the following question :

> *Given a fixed number of streams, what would be the performance gain of spreading these streams across more physical processor ?*

We shall first describe the multiprocessing model that we used, followed by the simulation environment and experimental setup we used to obtain the results, followed by the results and a discussion.

2. The Shared Memory Multiprocessor Cyclic Pipeline Computer

In general, multiprocessing systems may be categorized as shared memory or distributed memory systems. A shared bus multiprocessor is a type of shared memory multiprocessor in which all processors access a single global memory via a common bus. Such systems were among the earliest successful commercial multiprocessing systems designed. One frequent criticism of such systems is that the number of processors in such systems cannot be increased beyond the tens because the bus would simply be overloaded with traffic and thus becomes the central bottleneck. However, these processors have still remained viable in the market because of their good cost-performance and relative ease of programming when compared to distributed memory machines. The bus bottleneck is subdued by having a high speed bus, local memory (or cache) and more powerful processors. We are of the opinion that these types of systems' performance will gain further if the concept of the Cyclic Pipeline Computer were to be applied to them. The aim of this paper is thus to ascertain this hypothesis. Due to the explosive combination of variables, we have to made a number of assumptions.

The multiprocessing model that is assumed in the experiments for this paper is shown in Figure 1. A number of Cyclic Pipeline Computers are connected via a common bus to a monolithic memory system. Each processor has a private cache. However, no particular cache coherency protocol is assumed. Instead, we assume a general write-invalidate protocol while modelling the cache coherency overhead as just an additional time added to each memory write. For our experiments, we assumed a fixed overhead for such a purpose. Because this is not a study on the caches' behaviors, we minimized the number of cache parameters to be varied. The 3 important cache parameters are fixed as follows :

Cache Parameters	Values assumed
Associativity	1. Direct-mapped
	2. 4 way set associate
Line Size	32 byte
Cache Size	2 Kbyte

Table 1. Cache Parameters assumed in simulations.

Our study on the cache behavior of a single Cyclic Pipeline Computer revealed the importance of the hashing function and set associativity [7]. It was based on this previous study that we chose the above factors.

3. Experimental Setup

3.1 Simulator

The experiments reported in this paper are software simulations done on a modifed version of the FLATS2 software simulator. The FLATS2 is a two instruction stream ECL prototype of the Cyclic Pipeline Computer. In its design and development phase, a software simulator was developed to aid the process of developing the testing software for it. We first introduced cache simulation into the simulator. This was done as part of our earlier work. The FLATS2 was built on the assumption of a pipelined memory that works at the same pipeline pitch as the main instruction processing pipeline. Thus, no cache was provided for initially. With the cache simulator, we were able to distinguish easily which forms of memory accesses. Thus, for our current work, it was a matter of changing the way we penalizing memory accesses. The cache simulator is capable of simulating any combination of set associativity, line or cache sizes.

3.2 Compiler

As part of FLATS2's development, an optimizing, parallel FORTRAN compiler based on the Force model was implemented [3]. To program using Force, the user have to insert special annotations into his/her FORTRAN programs. The Force synchronization constructs implemented include critical sections and barriers. Any data in declared as COMMON in plain FORTRAN is assumed to reside in a global memory visible to all tasks. All other data are assumed to be allocated on a private stack and thus invisible to others. In the model, there are a number of parallel tasks that are constantly running. What the actual number of tasks are is not made known to the programmer. In our case, this is simply the number of streams. Except for a barrier, in which only one task will enter and execute, all tasks execute the same code. Parallel execution results from the tasks executing the FORTRAN DO loop with different loop indexes. There are two ways in which the loop indexes are shared among the tasks. In static scheduling, the indexes are shared equally among the tasks. In dynamic scheduling, a task will grab a new index as soon as there finish their current work.

The compiler is an optimizing compiler because it will attempt to reorder the machine instructions so as to minimize the total execution time. To do this, it has to have information regarding the number of pipeline stages and the pipeline latency for each instruction. Thus, it is the compiler which enforces the pipeline latency since in the simulator no consideration is given to this. Also, the FLATS2 instruction set is a CISC instruction set. To ease the restart of the instruction in simulator and to have a better comparison with superpipelined processors, the compiler can be made to generate a RISC subset of the instruction set. Furthermore, the compiler is capable of taking the cache into consideration by assuming the best case scenario for memory access latencies.

3.3 Simulation Parameters

As discussed earlier, we had to fix a number of the variables involved in the experiments. First, we fixed the three crucial cache parameters based on our previous experience. Since the principle investigation is the relationship between the number of streams per processor and the number of physical processors, we fixed the total number of streams while running different combinations of stream number versus physical processor number. We were also interested in examining the competitiveness of the multiprocessor Cyclic Pipeline Computer. Therefore, we have also pitched it against multiprocessors with superpipelined processor nodes. We did so by using the number of streams as the superpipeline degree of the superpipelined multiprocessors.

4. Results and Discussion

We have ran the simulator on the Linpack program which is a program to solve a system of linear equations. The matrix size is 200 by 200. The result in terms of number of instructions executed is then used to compute the relative speedup of each of the execution. The resulting graph is shown in Figure 2.

Overall, the speedup obtained is not unlike those that we have obtained previously. However, the interesting comparison will be within the same number of streams. We observe that there is only a marginal difference between distributing the same number of streams among the different number of physical processors. One can see that locating all the streams on the same physical processor is marginally better than distributing them among more physical processor. This is, however, to be expected. If the streams are all located on the same processor, than there is actually no real global access as there is no distinct global memory and local memory module. Since the memory module within a single CPC processor group is fully pipelined, this will mean that the best speed achieveable.

On the other hand, the degradation observed when we move from a single processor to multiple processor is also not too significant. This may be explained by the nature of the Linpack program in that it is a program which parallelize very well. As such most of the individual streams memory accesses are localized within the local memory. Thus, being a well parallelized program, it scales well from a single processor to multiple processors.

We should point out an important caveat in the above. The processor with 8 streams running on it is assumed to be 8 times faster than each of the 8 processors running a single stream each. This subtle assumption is present in all our previous studies too. The whole purpose of increasing the number of streams is that we can increase the number of stages in the pipeline. The purpose of increasing the number of stages is to increase the rate at which instructions can be issue to the pipeline. To achieve this the pipeline's cycle time (inversely proportional to its speed) must be increased. As the CPC was originally envisioned for the QFP or Josephson junction technology implementation, we do not consider increasing the pipeline speed a problem. However, should we hit the limit and yet desire more speed, this study gives a good indication of what we can do : use multiprocessing techniques. Programs which performs well on the CPC will scale well in a multiprocessor CPC.

5. Conclusion

In this paper, we have examined the possibility of extending the Cyclic Pipeline Computer concept to multiprocessor configurations. Our results shows that keeping the number of streams a constant, moving to a multiprocessor system will mean marginal degradation in performance. However, this would mean a decrease in the pipeline cycle time required to obtain the same level of performance. Therefore, it may be possible to trade off cycle time for processors while keeping performance fairly constant. On the other hand it should be possible to increase performance almost linearly (depending on the nature of the programs) by going to a multiprocessor configuration. But obviously there is a limit. The limit comes when the overhead for global memory access becomes too high due to the increased number of processors and insufficient bus bandwidth (something that is not considered in this study) or when there is insufficient work to keep the number of streams busy.

Although we have examined only a shared memory, in particular, a shared bus variant, multiprocessor configuration, this does not imply that the advantages of the Cyclic Pipeline Computer cannot be brought to the distributed memory multiprocessors. Time is currently the limiting factor as a new programming concept, involving message passing, will have to be supported in the compiler. We do hope that we will be able to perform such an investigation later.

Acknowledgements

The authors would like to express their sincere thanks to Dr. M. Sato who wrote the simulator and compiler which we modified for this work.

References

[1] H.F. Jordan, "The Force". In *Characteristics of Parallel Algorithms*, L. H. Jamieson, D.B. Gannon and R.J. Douglass ed., MIT Press, 1987, pp. 395-436.
[2] S. Ichikawa, "A Study on the Cyclic Pipeline Computer : FLATS2", *Ph.D.*

Dissertation, The University of Tokyo, 1990.

[3] M. Sato, "Exploiting parallelism in Cyclic Pipeline Computer with an Optimizing Compiler", *Ph.D. Dissertation,* The University of Tokyo, 1990.

[4] M. Sato, S. Ichikawa, and E. Goto, "Multiple Instruction Streams in a Highly Pipelined Processor", Proceedings of the Second IEEE Symposium on Parallel and Distributed Processing, Dallas, Texas, December 9-13 1990, pp. 182-189.

[5] K. Shimizu, E. Goto, and S. Ichikawa, "CPC (Cyclic Pipeline Computer) - An Architecture Suited for Josephson and Pipelined Machines", *IEEE Transactions on Computers,* June 1989, pp. 825-832.

[6] P. Spee, W.F. Wong, M. Sato, and E. Goto, "Evaluation of the Continuation Bit in the Cyclic Pipeline Computer", *Goto Quantum Magneto-Flux Logic Project Final Report*, 1991, pp. 252-261.

[7] P. Spee, W.F. Wong, and E. Goto, "Effects of Multiple Instruction Stream Execution on Cache Performance", *Goto Quantum Magneto-Flux Logic Project Final Report*, 1991, pp. 262-278.

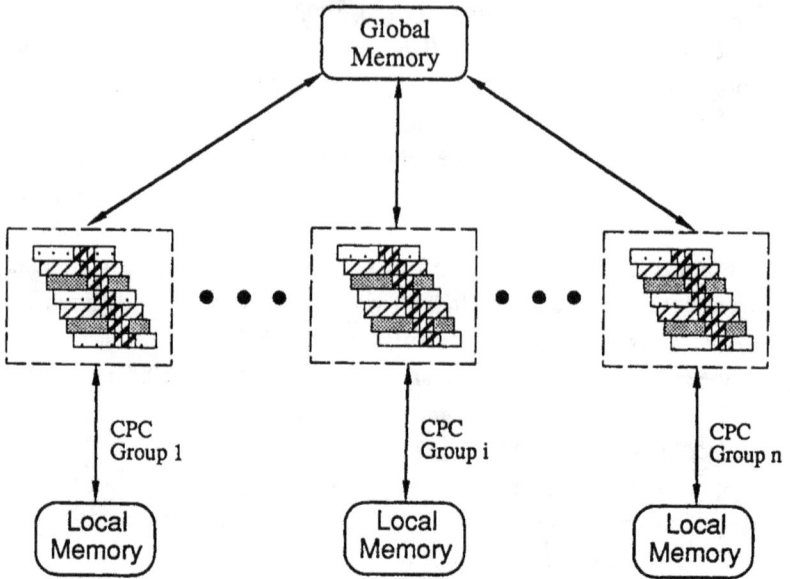

Figure 1. Shared Memory Multiprocessor CPC

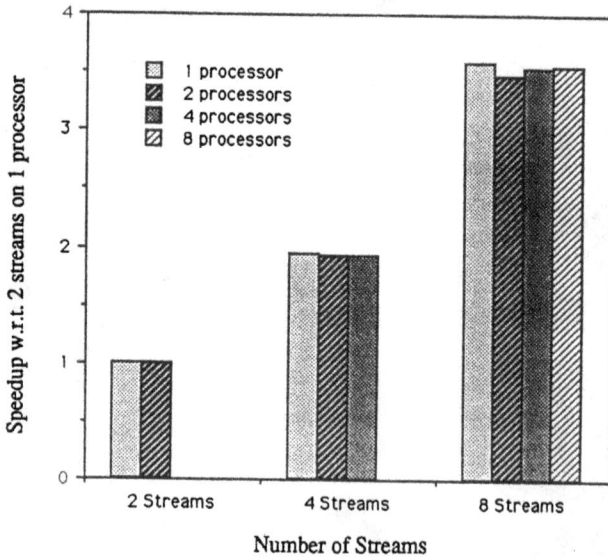

Figure 2. Performance of MultiCPC on Linpack

Reprinted with permission from *Trans. IEICE Japan*, D-1, 329 – 338 (1991).

Evaluation of FLATS2 Instruction Set Architecture

Shuichi Ichikawa and Eiichi Goto

Abstract

This paper describes the instruction set architecture of a Cyclic Pipeline Computer FLATS2, which is implemented with conventional silicon technology. FLATS2 provides range-checking addressing modes (BL addressing modes) and combined arithmetic instructions, which are effective in a wide variety of array processing. In BL addressing modes, any effective address is compared against the base and limit addresses specified in the instruction, then a conditional branch is executed according to the result of range check. This scheme is applicable to loop optimization and other purposes. Combined arithmetic instructions achieve high arithmetic performance, cooperating with BL addressing modes of FLATS2. Some evaluation results of FLATS2 architecture are also presented.

1. Introduction

Josephson logic devices have been researched and developed for future computer systems [1]. The prominent merits of Josephson devices are short switching time and low power dissipation. Adding to these, some Josephson devices have latch functionality with primitive logic operations. For example, Quantum Flux Parametron (QFP) is a basic Josephson logic device invented by Eiichi Goto [2], which has latching functionality and is expected to operate at 10 GHz or higher [3, 4]. Such a latching logic device requires a clock signal to perform logic operation. Therefore, the logic implemented with such latching logic devices is naturally pipelined.

The computer implemented with latching logic devices is thus expected to be pipelined into many pipeline stages, each of which is logically shallow and consequently works at very high frequency. However, it is well known that the performance of a pipeline which is split into many stages is seriously degraded by the resource competition between instructions in the pipeline (*hazards* [5]). Though many techniques have been researched and practiced to avoid hazards, it gets increasingly difficult to avoid performance degradation posed by hazards in highly pipelined computer, such as the computer implemented with latching logic devices.

To resolve the problem, Shimizu, Goto, and Ichikawa [6] proposed *Cyclic Pipeline Architecture (CPA)*, in which the pipeline is timeshared by several instruction streams (virtual processors). Instructions of different instruction streams do no interfere each other, because each stream uses its own resources. Though CPA was originally invented as an architecture suited for Josephson computers, CPA is also effective in existing silicon technology, especially in deeply pipelined computers. To prove the efficiency of CPA, and to obtain the experience to build future Josephson computers, a Cyclic Pipeline Computer named FLATS2 was designed and implemented with existing silicon devices (ECL, TTL, and CMOS SRAM).

This report describes the architectural overview of FLATS2 instruction set, and also presents the evaluation result of FLATS2 instruction set architecture. The evaluation using two virtual processors is out of the scope of this report.

2. Overview of FLATS2 Architecture

In this section, the outline of FLATS2 architecture is described. For more detailed information about FLATS2, please refer to "FLATS2 Architecture Handbook" [7].

2.1 Specifications of FLATS2 hardware

FLATS2 is a cyclic pipeline computer with two virtual processors, which is implemented with silicon devices. Table 2-1 shows the basic specification of FLATS2 implementation. Machine cycle is the cycle time of primitive machine clock, by which the pipeline proceeds one stage. In FLATS2, memory cycle is equivalent to machine cycle time. The transfer rate of memory is thus 117 MB/s for instruction and data, respectively. FLATS2 consists of 26 logic boards, each of which contains from 200 to 400 chips on it. These boards are connected each other by a backplane board and front flat cables, mounted to a rack chassis (about 57 cm × 62 cm × 37 cm) which is air-cooled by 14 fans. This rack chassis is packed into a cubic box with power supplies. Figure 2-1 shows FLATS2 package and logic boards connected by front flat cables.

Machine Cycle	65 ns
Word Length	32 bit (data) + 1 bit (tag)
Real Memory	5.5 M Byte (currently)
Logic Devices	ECL 10K, 10KH, 100K, FAST
Logic Board	465(W) × 323(H)
	Multi-layered, Mutil-Wired
	total 26 boards
Package	960(W) × 1200(H) × 1075(D)

Table 2-1. Basic Specifications of FLATS2

Each word of FLATS2 has one bit address tag for each 32 bit data. This address tag represents that the contents of corresponding data part is an address. The word which has its address tag cleared stands for a numeric data (non address).

2.2 Processor Model

Figure 2-2 illustrates the processor model from the viewpoint of FLATS2 instruction set architecture. IPU stands for Instruction Processing Unit, which controls program sequence and fetches to decode instructions. GVU stands for GV Unit, which performs integer and address calculation on general registers (GV registers). IPU and GVU are tightly connected each other by internal control and data paths to act as a self-contained subprocessor in FLATS2, which has a load/store architecture for GV registers. SPU stands for Sum and Product Unit, which contains registers (SP registers), ALU and multiplier for both integer and floating-point arithmetic. SPU acts as a co-processor or an integrated accelerator of IPU/GVU subprocessor.

2.3 BL Addressing Modes

One of the most distinguishing characters of FLATS2 instruction set architecture is "BL addressing modes." Figure 2-3 illustrates the framework of BL addressing scheme. In any address calculation in FLATS2, the effective address is compared against a given pair of "Base" and "Limit" addresses (BL pair). A BL pair stands for a memory area, which is between base and limit addresses including both ends.

If the effective address is included in the area designated by the given BL pair, the memory access succeeds to fetch the operand. The operand is thus used for the operation, and then the branch is taken to the target address specified in the instruction.

If the effective address is out of the range specified by the given BL pair, the memory access immediately fails. Consequently neither the operation on operands nor the branch to the specified target is performed (that is, the program control is passed to the next address).

All operations related to BL addressing are performed in one instruction cycle by FLATS2 pipeline. After all, one FLATS2 instruction specifies all of the following operations in one instruction cycle.

(1) Address calculations
(2) Comparison of effective address against BL pair (BL check)
(3) Branch on the condition of BL check
(4) Operand fetch (if BL check succeeds)
(5) Operation on operands

This parallelism in each instruction enables the effective processing on various array processing programs, as seen later in this report.

2.4 Instruction Format

Figure 2-4 shows 4 basic formats of FLATS2 instruction set. These four formats have the same length (two word) and the identical format in the first word GVop field is the opcode for GVU, md field selects the operands, and r1/r2/r3 fields designate GV registers which are used in the instruction.

I format is mainly used for GVU operations without address calculations. The second word of I format is a full word immediate, which can be used as an operand of arithmetics. J format is used for various branch instructions, including 4 way conditional branch, compare and branch, and arithmetic with compare and branch instructions. The second word of J format is split into four 8 bit immediates, which is used as offsets to branch targets or as a short immediate for arithmetic with branch instructions.

When address calculations are necessary, K or M format is used. These formats include the field for BL addressing modes; j0, d1 and d2 fields. The field j0 specifies 8 bit offset to the branch target for BL addressing. The displacements for effective address calculations are specified by d1 and d2 fields. The fields of the second word are mostly common between K and M formats. The only difference is t field in K format and SPop field in M format.

K format is used in address calculation instructions and load/store instructions.

Therefore, t field is necessary to specify the target register of the operation. On the other hand, M format is adopted in general arithmetic instructions which is performed by SP unit. SPop field thus specifies the operation of SPU.

If the immediates are required longer than 8 bits in the second word of instruction format, the corresponding long format are available (IL, JL, KL, ML formats). In long formats, two more words follow after the first two instruction words. The L bit in K or M format designates two more words follow. In IL and JL formats, GVop field specifies the format.

2.5 Combined Arithmetic Instructions

SPU contains two arithmetic pipelines; ALU and multiplier. However, usual arithmetic instruction uses only one of them at a time. For example, an add instruction only uses ALU (S unit), leaving multiplier (P unit) idle. To utilize more than one arithmetic unit in one instruction, some combined instructions are defined in FLATS2. These instructions are called "combined arithmetic instructions," because they combine two or more arithmetic operations in one instruction.

The most typical example of combined arithmetic is "rip (real inner product)" instruction. The following is the specification of rip instruction.

Notation	`rip.f  <opr1>, <opr2>`
	`rip.d  <opr1>, <opr2>`
Operation	$S \leftarrow P + S$
	$P \leftarrow R \times U$
	$U \leftarrow <opr1>$
	$R \leftarrow <opr2>$

Apparently, rip instruction overlaps one addition, one multiplication, and two load operations in a single instruction (single instruction cycle). These combined instructions play very important roles in the optimization of various numerical computations, as described in later chapter.

3. Programming on FLATS2 Architecture

3.1 Array Processing by BL addressing

In many array processing programs, the array elements are accessed orderly with a fixed stride in a loop structure. After accessing the last element, the processor escapes from the loop. In FLATS2, the branch-on-range-check facility of BL addressing can be utilized for such array processing. Figure 3-1 illustrates the policy to apply BL addressing to array processing. In the figure, BL pair points to the base and the limit addresses of the array. The elements of the array is accessed one after another, modifying the effective address each time. After accessing the last element, the effective address goes out of the range, consequently a memory access error occurs to change the control flow hereafter.

3.2 Program Example

Lets see a simple example written in FORTRAN (Program 3-1). This piece of code takes the sum of array elements.

```
        sum = 0.0
        do 100 i = 1,10
           sum = sum + array(i)
100     continue
```

Program 3-1. Summation of Array Elements

Here, let sum be a real (32 bit floating-point) variable, and array be a real array of 10 elements. This program can be converted into the FLATS2 instruction sequence shown in Code 3-1.

```
        mov.f    #0f0.0, S
        lea      @_array, vr2
        lea      @_array+36, vr3
        movw     vr2, vr0
L100:   add3.f.j vr2:<4(vr0),S,S,L100
        mov.f    S, @_sum
```

Code 3-1. Summation of Array Elements

The first mov.f initializes S register to zero. The second lea instruction loads the effective address of the first element (array(1)) to vr2, which is used as a base register at L100. The next lea similarly loads the address of the last element (array(10)) to vr3. Vr3 is used as the limit register at L100, because vr3 is the binary pair of the base register (vr2). The movw instruction initializes the pointer register (vr0), which is used in L100.

The body of do statement at L100 is integrated into a single instruction (add3.f.j). This instruction is an M format instruction, which performs the following operations in each instruction cycle.

(1) It first calculates an effective address to fetch memory operand. The effective address is the content of vr0 in this addressing mode.
(2) The effective address is checked against the range specified by the BL pair (vr2 and vr3 here). If the address is out of the range, the instruction is aborted, consequently proceeding to the next instruction.
(3) The operand (array element) is fetched and added to S register.
(4) The specified displacement is added to vr0 as the side-effect of the addressing mode. That is, vr0 is incremented by 4.
(5) Branch is taken to the specified target (L100). Here, the same instruction is executed again.

After executing L100 ten times, vr0 goes out of the range. Consequently, the next mov.f instruction is executed to store the accumulated result to the variable sum.

3.3 Combined Instruction

In the previous example (Program 3-1), only one arithmetic operation (addition) was performed in the innermost loop. That is, only one floating-point operation is performed each instruction cycle. However, by using combined arithmetic instruction of FLATS2, more arithmetic operations can be performed in the innermost loop each cycle. For example, Figure 3-2 shows the program and code sequence to calculate a dot product. In this program, two arithmetic operations are performed in the innermost loop by utilizing *rip* instruction, which is mentioned in the section 2.5.

4. Evaluation

4.1 Some Benchmark Results

Table 4-1 shows the results of some simple benchmark tests evaluated by a single virtual processor of FLATS2. The results of other processors are also presented for contrast.

Architecture CPU + FPU	Clock *MHz*	Average *MIPS*	Dhrystone *KD/s*	Whetston e *MW/s*	Linpack *MFLOPS*
68020 + 68881	20	3	4.3	1.2	0.12
FLATS2 (1 proc.)	15	3.6	6.0	3.1	2.5
SPARC + Weitek	16.7	10	19.	3.9	1.1
R2000 + R2010	16.7	12	25.	9.0	1.8

Table 4-1. Some Benchmark Results

In the table, *MIPS* stands for "Mega Instructions Per Second," *KD/s* stands for "Kilo Dhrystones per Second," *MW/s* stands for "Mega Whetstones per Second," and *MFLOPS* stands for "Mega FLoating Operations Per Second."

The column "Clock" shows the primitive machine clock frequency of each processor. However, the clock value cannot be directly comparable, because the definition of "Clock" is not common among the processors. Average "*MIPS*" is similar. The complexity of instructions of each processor is different, and the result is affected by instruction mixes, therefore *MIPS* rating can be only a rough figure. Instead, some benchmark programs are used in the following sections.

Needless to say, the evaluation result also reflects the quality of C compiler and related library functions, together with the bare hardware performance. For FLATS2, GNU C compiler (*gcc*, version 1.37) was retargeted with some additional features to be adapted for FLATS2 architecture. This modified compiler was used for the evaluation. For other processors, vendor's standard C compilers were used for evaluation.

4.2 Dhrystone

Dhrystone benchmark [8] is a benchmark program to measure integer operation performance. Here, Dhrystone benchmark version 2.1 of C language was used for evaluation. The measured performance of each processor is almost proportional to its average MIPS rate.

4.3 Whetstone

Whetstone is a benchmark program to evaluate the floating-point arithmetic performance, in particular the performance of some elementary functions such as logarithm, exponential, and trigonometrical functions. Whetstone program was originally written in Algol 60, but here we use a C language version. In measuring Whetstone performance on FLATS2, elementary functions were handcoded and optimized by using BL addressing modes and combined arithmetic instructions. As shown in Table 4-1, the Whetstone performance of FLATS2 is rather good compared to its *MIPS* rate, and considering this performance is achieved by only a half of its hardware potential.

In case the elementary functions are compiled by C compiler with neither loop optimization by BL addressing nor combined arithmetic instructions, the measured Whetstone performance gets worse about 12%. This portion (12%) of performance is regarded to be the performance improvement obtained by BL addressing and combined arithmetic instructions.

However, even if this portion is lost, the Whetstone performance of FLATS2 is still good compared to other processors, considering its MIPS rate. One of the reasons guessed to be that FLATS2 instructions can naturally overlap arithmetic operations and memory accesses by using two memory operands in one instruction. This architecture can reduce the load/store overhead of memory operands. Another more likely reason is that FLATS2 can finish a floating-point operation in one instruction cycle. By overlapping the long latency time of a floating-point operation to the execution time of other virtual processor, each virtual processor can use the result of the previous floating-point arithmetic instruction just after one instruction cycle. This characteristic will improve the ratio floating-point arithmetic performance to MIPS rate.

4.4 Linpack

The name "Linpack" stands for "LINear equation systems PACKage." Here, the C version and FORTRAN version of Linpack benchmark is used to evaluate FLATS2 performance.

The most primitive routines in Linpack are called BLAS (Basic Linear Algebraic Subprograms), each of which performs a simple array processing procedure with a small loop structure. As shown before, small loops can be implemented effectively by using FLATS2 instruction set. Figure 4-1 lists the number of instruction cycles which is necessary to perform one iteration of the innermost loop in each BLAS routine optimized by hand-coding, together with the arithmetic density (the number of floating-point operations per instruction cycle) in the innermost loop of each BLAS routine.

As shown in Figure 4-1, most of BLAS routines achieve the arithmetic density as high as equal or more than 1 FLOP/cycle. Only *ddot* has its arithmetic density as high as 2, because a combined arithmetic instruction utilize ALU and multiplier in parallel in the innermost loop of *ddot*. In Linpack benchmark, 69% of the total execution time elapses in the innermost loop of *daxpy*, where the arithmetic density is as high as 1, consequently achieving 2.5 MFLOPS by a 3.6 MIPS FLATS2 virtual processor.

4.5 Livermore

Livermore Loop is a benchmark test developed in Lawrence Livermore National Laboratory to evaluate the performance of supercomputers. This benchmark consist of 24 small program pieces (Livermore kernels) taken from scientific calculation programs frequently used in physics. Here, the first 14 loops (original Livermore kernels) are examined and optimized by hand-coding for FLATS2 architecture to evaluate the numerical performance of FLATS2.

Figure 4-2 illustrates the arithmetic density of the innermost loops of 14 kernels. In the figure, *FLOP* stands for "floating-point operations," and H.M. stands for "Harmonic Mean." Note that arithmetic density (FLOP/cycle) is directly convertible to arithmetic performance (FLOPS) by multiplied by instruction cycle time. In the current FLATS2 implementation, the arithmetic density 1.0 corresponds to 3.8 MFLOPS.

In the Figure 4-2, FLATS2 architecture is evaluated at the following three stages.

(1) basic

The case with basic instructions of FLATS2. That is, each instruction uses maximally two memory operands, one for read and the other for write operand. No combined arithmetic instruction is used, thus only one floating-point operation is performed at most in on instruction.

(2) +rip

In addition to the basic case, *rip* (Real Inner Product) instruction is adopted. Also, the addressing modes to read two memory operands (Read-Read addressing modes) are allowed to support *rip* instruction. This combination enables to overlap two load operations to two floating-point operations (one addition and one multiplication).

(3) +all

The case with all possible combine arithmetic instructions which can be implemented by additional microcoding without modifying the current FLATS2 hardware. The +all case is regarded to represent the maximum performance of the current FLATS2 data path.

As seen from Figure 4-2, the performance of Livermore kernels are improved as much as 16% by adding *rip* instruction and Read-Read addressing modes. Adding all other possible combined instructions (+all), the performance is improved further more (17%), compared to the case of +rip. However, no generally applicable combined arithmetic was found in Livermore kernels besides *rip*, therefore no such ad hoc instructions have been implemented in the current FLATS. In that sense, the +rip case represents the performance of the current FLATS2 implementation. The following evaluation is done under this condition.

The previous evaluation of Figure 4-2 represents the peak performance of the innermost loop. Actually the overhead of initial and terminal procedure burdens the loop to degrade the measured performance from the expected peak performance. To evaluate this overhead, the arithmetic density was measured on various iteration count (n). Figure 4-3 illustrates the variations of the measured arithmetic density of 14 Livermore kernels. The bars "$n = \infty$" stand for the peak arithmetic density of Figure 4-2 (+rip). These bars are regarded as the upper limit of expected performance to be achieved.

As seem from Figure 4-3, the performance decreases gradually in proportion as the iteration count decreases. However, the degree of performance degradation is small, which means that the overhead of loop preparation is small. Consequently, the harmonic mean of the arithmetic density of 14 original Livermore kernels is 0.58 ($n = \infty$), 0.54 ($n = 64$), and 0.46 ($n = 16$), respectively. Converting this arithmetic density to arithmetic performance, a single FLATS2 virtual processor achieves 2.1 MFLOPS ($n = 64$). This is very good compared to its MIPS rate.

5. Conclusion

The architectural overview of FLATS2 processor was presented. The instruction set architecture of FLATS2 was also presented with examples of programming. Several benchmark programs are examined and evaluated on a single FLATS2 virtual processor. The evaluation results proved that the combination of BL addressing and combined arithmetic instructions of FLATS2 architecture effectively performs a wide variety of array processing programs.

Acknowledgements

The authors would like to express the highest gratitude to the members of Goto Project of JRDC for their support to FLATS2 project.

References

[1] A. Barone and G.Paterno, *Physics and Applications of the Josephson Effect*, John Wiley and Sons, New York, 1982.

[2] K. F. Loe and E. Goto, "Analysis of Flux Input and Output Josephson Pair Device," *IEEE Trans. Magn,.*vol. MAG-21, no. 2, pp. 884-887, Mar. 1985.

[3] E. Goto and K. F. Loe, *DC Flux Parametron*, World Scientific, Singapore, 1986.

[4] Y. Harada, H. Nakane, N. Miyamoto, U. Kawabe, E. Goto, and T. Soma, "Basic Operations of the Quantum Flux Parametron," *IEEE Trans. Magn.*, vol. MAG-23, no. 5, pp. 3801-3807, Sept. 1987.

[5] C. V. Ramamoorthy and H. F. Li, "Pipeline Architecture," *Computing Survey*, vol. 9, no. 1, pp. 61-102, Mar. 1977.

[6] K. Shimizu, E. Goto, and S. Ichikawa, "CPC(Cyclic Pipeline Computer)—An Architecture Suited for Josephson and Pipelined Machines," *IEEE Trans. Comput.*, vol. C-38, no. 6, pp. 825-832, Jun. 1989.

[7] S. Ichikawa, "FLATS2 Architecture Handbook," Research Development Corporation of Japan, 1990. (In Japanese)

[8] R. P. Weicker, "Dhrystone: A Synthetic Systems Programming Benchmark," CACM, vol. 27, no. 10, pp. 1013-1030, Oct. 1984.

Fig. 2-1 FLATS2

M bus

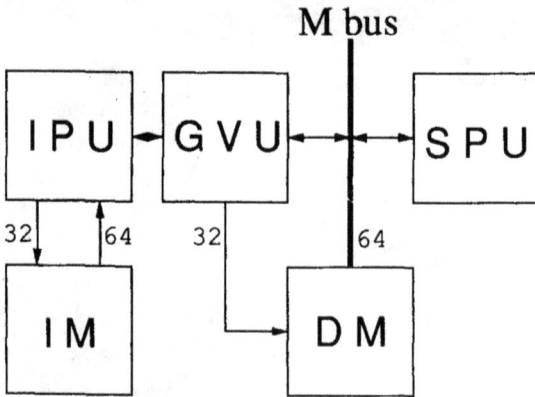

```
IPU : Instruction Processing Unit,
GVU : Gloval/Variable register Unit,
SPU : Sum and Product Unit,
IM  : Instruction Memory,
DM  : Data Memory.
```

Fig.2-2 Block Diagram of FLATS2 CPU

array

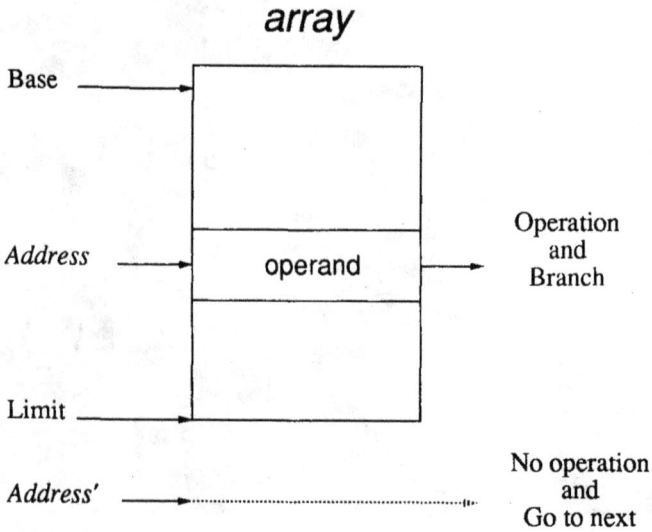

Fig. 2-3 BL Addressing

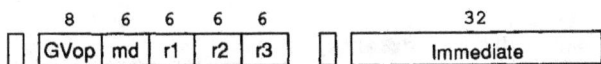

I format

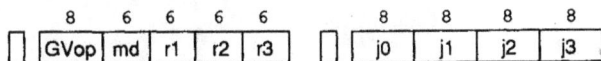

J format

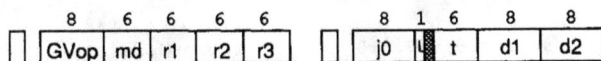

K format

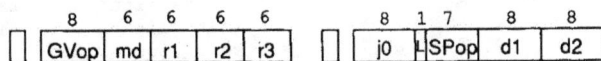

M format

Fig. 2-4 Instruction Format

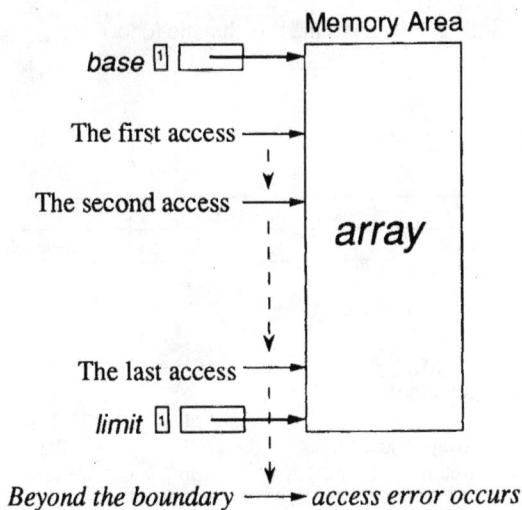

Fig. 3-1 Array Processing

```
       do 30 i = 1,n
          dtemp = dtemp + dx(i)*dy(i)
30     continue
       ddot = dtemp
       return
```

Program 3-2. Double Dot Product (ddot)

```
        asl3.l   vr6,#3,vr0              ; vr8 = dx ; vr10 = dy
        addr     vr0,#-8,vr0             ; vr0 = (n-1)*8
        lea      dseg:(vr8)vr0,vr9       ; vr9  = &dx[n-1]
        lea      dseg:(vr10)vr0,vr11     ; vr11 = &dy[n-1]
        mov.d    #0d0, S                 ; initializing S register
        mov.d    (vr9),P                 ; initializing P register (1)
        mul.d    (vr11),P                ; initializing P register (2)
        mov.d    vr8@<8, R               ; initializing R register
        mov.d    vr10@<8, U              ; initializing U register
L11:    rip.d.j  vr8@<8, vr10@<8, L11    ; self loop of "rip"
        add.d    P, S                    ; terminating the loop
L1:     movw     fp,sp                   ; restore stack pointer
        ret                              ; return to caller
```

Code 3-2. Double Dot Product (ddot)

Fig. 3-2 Combined Arithmetic (ddot)

Linpack routines (BLAS)			
name	note	cycle/loop	FLOP/cycle
dasum	$\sum |x_i|$	2	1
daxpy	$\vec{y} = \vec{y} + a\vec{x}$	2	1
dcopy	$\vec{y} = \vec{x}$	1	1
ddot	$\sum x_i y_i$	1	2
drot	Rotation	6	1
dscal	$\vec{x} = a\vec{x}$	1	1
dswap	Swap $\vec{x}$ and $\vec{y}$	3	2/3
idamax	Return i of max $|x_i|$	3 to 5	2/3 to 2/5

Fig. 4-1 BLAS Rontines

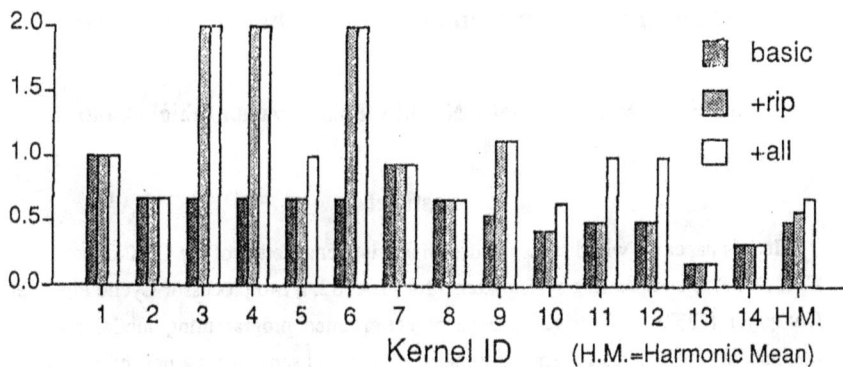

Fig. 4-2 Peak Arithmetic Density

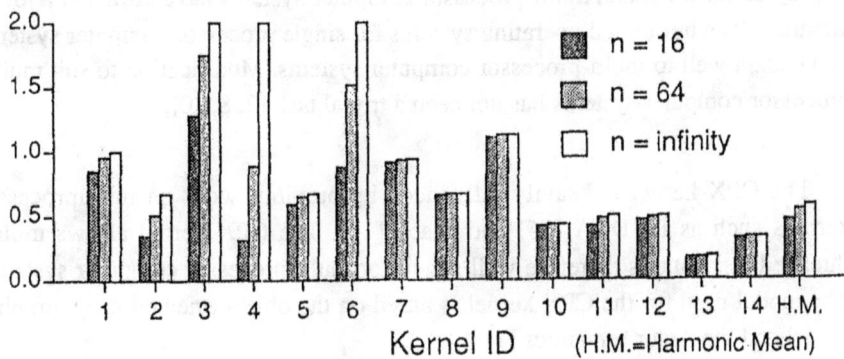

Fig. 4-3 Measured Arithmetic Density

The Design and Implementation of the CPX Kernel

Paul Spee, Mitsuhisa Sato, Norihiro Fukazawa, and Eiichi Goto

Abstract

In this paper we will discuss the design and implementation of the CPX kernel. The CPX kernel is an operating system kernel for FLATS2, a two processor Cyclic Pipeline Computer (CPC). It is based on the object-oriented programming model and its components are defined in terms of objects. The kernel separates the unit of execution from the environment, allowing multiple threads of control to execute in a single virtual space.

1. Introduction

In this paper we will discuss the design and implementation of the CPX kernel for FLATS2 [7, 11], a Cyclic Pipeline Computer which implements a two processor pipelined MIMD computer. A short discussion of the CPC can be found in [12]. In recent years, multi-processor computer systems have attracted a lot of attention. The traditional operating systems for single processor computer systems don't adapt well to multi-processor computer systems. Modification to suit multi-processor computer systems has not been a trivial task [2, 8, 10].

The CPX kernel is heavily influenced by previous work on multiprocessor kernels such as HYDRA [15] and Mach [16]. The CPX kernel allows multithreaded tasks and is therefore well suited for multi-processor computer systems. The model used for the CPX kernel is based on the object oriented programming model and the Actor semantics [1].

In Section 2, we will describe the programming model on which the CPX kernel is based and the functionality provided by the CPX kernel. In Section 3, we will discuss some of the implementation issues. In Section 4, we will evaluate the CPX kernel and mention the effect on the design. The initial evaluation of the CPX kernel had an inherent effect on the design. Feedback provided by the initial evaluation adjusted the design to provide a better implementation.

2. Kernel functionality

2.1 Object oriented programming model

The CPX kernel uses the object oriented programming model. In the object oriented programming model, an object encapsulates data and provides a collection of *methods* (procedures) that can operate on that data[1]. Operations on the data can be performed by sending a message to that object. On receiving the message, the object will select the proper method to perform the request. Objects are represented by *ports*. A port is a *communication channel* (to designate the source or destination of a message) which allows for multiple *clients* (senders) and a single receiver (the object).

Message passing can be either *synchronously* or *asynchronously*. In synchronous message passing, the message is directly passed from the sender to the receiver. The sender is delayed until the receiver executes a receive, or vice versa, the receiver delays until the sender sends a message. The synchronization is implicit. In asynchronous message passing, the messages are buffered. The sender may continue execution without having to wait for the receiver to receive the message. In general, asynchronous message passing supports a higher degree of concurrency. The advantage of the object oriented approach is the increased possibility for parallelism; each object can be executed in parallel.

2.2 Object oriented kernel

The function of an operating system kernel is to hide the hardware from the rest of the operating system, that is, to virtualize the hardware.

The programming model of the CPX kernel is the object server model. A port can represent a type object (super class). Sending a *new* message to this type object, will create a new object of the requested type. The created object is represented by a port.

To perform operations on the object, messages can be sent to the port

---

[1] A third characteristic of object oriented programming is inheritance. New object types can be defined by using existing object types, e.g. they are said to inherit the properties of the existing object type(s).

representing the object. To facilitate implementation of several object types by one task[2] or the management of several objects by one object server, we introduce the concept of port group. A port group is a group of several ports and the port group descriptor behaves like an ordinary port descriptor.

A port group is only allowed in a receive statement; sending to a port group would imply sending a message to multiple ports. A *multicast* as in V [3] is not allowed. The use of port grouping is similar to the use of the *select* statement is Ada [6].

The CPX kernel implements virtual instructions, which can be seen as an extension of the processor instruction set, and *operations* on kernel defined objects.

Figure 1 shows how a class object and instance objects can be implemented. In a multiprocessor computer with a large number of processors, each of the instance objects can be assigned to a single processor. A multiprocessor computer with a small number of processors can implement the object server model. Assigning a processor to each instance object would cause a large overhead because of context switching.

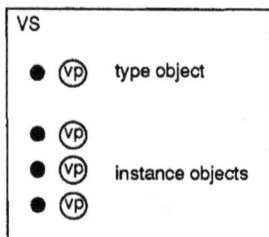

Figure 1a. Active objects

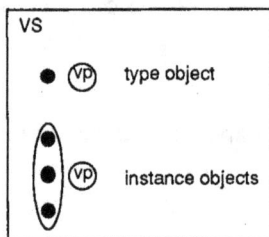

Figure 1b. Object server

---

[2]A task should be considered a program in execution. We don't want to make any assumptions about its structure.

The CPX kernel follows the Actor semantics in that it is not 1.   :ary to implement a request to an object as a *remote procedure call*. It is possible to refrain from specifying an acknowledge port. In such a case, the sender will continue execution; no acknowledge will be sent. It is also possible to specify an acknowledge port, but continue execution until much later. In such a case, we call the acknowledge port a *continuation*. All this increases parallelism.

A. Virtual instructions

Ports are required to implement objects. Therefore, all operations on ports are implemented as virtual instructions. These include the creation and deletion of a port; and the sending and receiving of messages. A special case is the remote procedure call; `port_rpc()` which could be implemented with `port_send()` and `port_receive()`, but in addition to that, it would also require the creation and deletion of an acknowledge port (one kernel entry against four kernel entries).

Messages

Messages can be either *typed* messages or *untyped* messages. Typed messages are structured messages consisting of a number of typed arguments. They are required when we want to

- send a *port capability*[3], or
- send a *memory range*[4] as *copy on write*, or
- send a message between computers with different architectures and we what to do type conversion involving endian or floating point representation, or
- interpret the messages based on their type.

However, typed message have a very poor signal/noise ratio. For each

---

[3] A port capability represents both the reference to the port and the right to perform an operation on that port.

[4] A memory range specifies the start and end of a range of bytes.

argument we require 12 bytes to describe the argument: its type, size and offset into the message structure. Untyped messages, on the other hand, are much shorter and therefore much more efficient. Each message has to be copied once from the user space into a kernel buffer and once from the kernel buffer into the user space.

Another disadvantage of typed messages is that the kernel has to scan the argument list to find arguments it has handle in a special manner.

Send and receive

Messages can be sent and received in either *blocking* or *nonblocking* mode. When a message is received in blocking mode, the process is suspended until a message is available; an optional *timeout* parameter can be specified.

B. Kernel objects

The kernel defines the virtual machine (VM). The virtual machine consists of the virtual processor (VP), the virtual space (VS) and the virtual cache (VC). Each is implemented as a kernel object. The kernel defines the *operations* on the kernel defined objects.

Virtual processor

The virtual processor is the virtualization of the real processor. Its functions are:

- isolate hardware details, such as interrupts, from the rest of the operating system,

- implement multi-programming, by providing a (fixed) number of virtual processors, which are scheduled using pre-emptive scheduling.

The virtual processor will hide details of the hardware implementation. Such details also include the number of physical processors the CPC consists of (FLATS2 implements a two processor MIMD). Low level scheduling is done on a *self-service* basis: each processor will schedule a virtual processor from the pool of virtual processors.

Virtual space

The virtual space hides the details of the virtual memory implementation. The FLATS2 has a single virtual space, a fact which is hidden from the user by the virtual space implementation.

The virtual space not only provides the address space for the virtual processors, but represents the complete environment in which virtual processors execute. When a virtual processor creates a port, the ownership of the port is assigned to the virtual space in which the virtual processor is executing.

It is possible for more than one virtual processor to execute in the same virtual space. In this respect, it is similar to a kernel which provides multi-threaded tasks such as Mach [13]. It provides a large advantage over single threaded tasks such as a UNIX *process*. A context switch between two virtual processors executing in the same virtual space causes less overhead than a switch between two different tasks.

```
{
        new_vp = pick_virtual_processor();
        if (new_vp != old_vp)
        {
                if (new_vp->vs != old_vp->vs)
                {
                        switch context of
                        virtual space;
                }

                switch context of
                virtual processor;
        }
}
```

Figure 2. Context switching

Port capabilities are associated with the virtual space. One way for a virtual space to obtain the send capabilities for a port is by receiving a message containing the port capability. Another way is to explicitly assign the send capability to the virtual space by the vs_port operation. It can be used to assign default port capabilities to a virtual space. The receive capability is associated with port ownership. Because the port ownership cannot be transferred, the receive capability cannot be transferred. Therefore, only the virtual space in which a port was created, has the receive capability for that port.

Virtual memory regions can be allocate within the address space of the virtual space. Only allocated memory regions can be accessed. The CPX kernel follows the Mach [14] approach by defining a *memory object* as a repository for data. A memory object can be mapped on the virtual space by the `vs_allocate` operation.

Virtual cache

Modern computer systems implement cache memories as high speed buffers between the processor and the main memory. The access time to the cache memory is much less than the access time to main memory. The virtual memory of FLATS2 is much larger than the physical memory. The memory manager has therefore to decide which pages of virtual memory to keep in physical memory. Page replacement is based on the Least Recently Used (LRU) algorithm.

The virtual cache represents the usage of the physical memory. With each virtual cache, there is an associated memory object. The virtual cache represents the pages in physical memory, which contain data associated with that object. Its function is similar to the function of a real cache.

3. Implementation

In this section we will discuss some of the implementation aspects of the CPX kernel.

Messages

A message consists of a message header, an optimal message format, and the message body, containing the data (see Figure 3). The message header specifies the number of arguments in a typed message; if the number of arguments is zero, the message is considered to be an untyped message. Furthermore, the message header includes the total message size and a port descriptor. The usage of the port descriptor is different for the send and receive request. In the send request, the port descriptor specifies the acknowledge port. The acknowledge port used to be part of the message body, but that required the message to be typed, although the other data could be untyped. Now the kernel can easily verify the acknowledge port.

In a typed message, each argument requires a *type specification*. A type specification consists of the argument type, the argument size and the offset into the message body where the argument data can be found. The argument type can be either a standard type such as INTEGER, FLOAT, etc., or a user defined type.

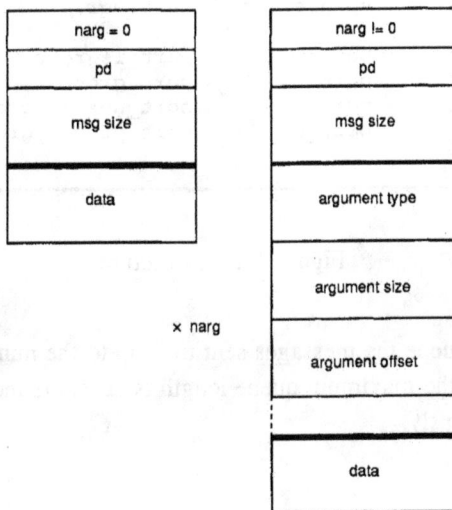

narg = 0
pd
msg size
data

narg != 0
pd
msg size
argument type
argument size
argument offset
data

× narg

Figure 3. Message structure

Ports

A port is represented by a port descriptor. If a virtual space has a port descriptor, it automatically represents the send capability for that port. If the port is owned by the virtual space (port_owner), it also represents the receive capability for that port. The implementation of the port descriptor is very similar to the implementation of the file descriptor in BSD UNIX [9]. The file descriptor is used to index the file descriptor table (kept in the *user structure*) to locate a file structure. The CPX kernel uses the port descriptor to index the port descriptor table which is part of the virtual space structure (see Figure 6).

```
struct port
{
        port_t          port_link;
        int             port_refcnt;
        boolean         port_deleted;
        vspace_t        port_owner;
        object_t        port_object;
        otype_t         port_otype;
        u_long          port_client;

        msg_queue_t     port_mqueue;
        u_short         port_mlength;
        u_short         port_mcount;
        vp_queue_t      port_wqs;
        vp_queue_t      port_wqr;

        boolean         port_isgroup;
        port_t          port_group;
        port_t          port_nextin_group;
        port_t          port_previn_group;
};
```

Figure 4. Port structure

The port will queue the messages sent to it up to the number as specified by port_mlength. If the maximum queue length is zero, the messages are sent and received synchronously.

Kernel objects

All requests related to ports are implemented as system call traps. Currently, all requests to kernel defined objects are implemented by message passing. A library contains code to convert the arguments into a message, send the message to the object, and receive the acknowledgement.

Virtual processor

The Hydra operating system [15] implements *policy/mechanism* separation. Policies are by definition implemented by user-level software that is external from the kernel. Mechanisms are provided by the kernel to implement these policies. The CPX kernel follows this approach. The virtual processor is scheduled using a simple priority-driven scheduling algorithm. Virtual processors at the same priority level are treated in a round-robin fashion. A virtual processor is assigned a time slice and may be rescheduled at the end of the time slice. When a virtual processor is scheduled, its priority is checked. If the priority of the virtual processor or the priority of its virtual space (the priority of its virtual space serves as an upper bound for the virtual processor) has been changed, the virtual processor will be moved to another priority queue. Although the low level scheduler (which implements the mechanism)

implements a very simple algorithm (priority based round-robin scheduling), the high level scheduler (which implements the policy) can implement a much more complex scheduling algorithm. The time a virtual processor executes is accounted to the virtual space in which the virtual processor executes. This allows the high level scheduler to give each task (virtual space + virtual processor(s)) its fair share of resources (cpu time) independent of the number of virtual processors executing.

```
struct     vproc
{
           vp_link_t    vp_link;
           lock_t       vp_lock;

           vp_status    vp_status;
           boolean      vp_kernel_running;
           boolean      vp_will_suspend;
           vp_queue_t   vp_current_queue;
           int          vp_prio;

           port_t       vp_port;
           vspace_t     vp_vs;

           time_t       vp_timer;
           int          vp_id;

           MACHINE      vp_mach;
};
```

Figure 5. Virtual processor structure

Virtual space

The function of the virtual space is twofold. It handles the allocation and deallocation of regions of virtual memory. Normally, each virtual space contains a text region, a data region and for each virtual processor a stack region and gv register frame region.

```
struct vspace
{
        vs_link_t               vs_link;
        lock_t                  vs_lock;

        port_t                  vs_port;
        port_t                  vs_pd[N_PDESCR];
        int                     vs_idx;
        int                     vs_cnt;

        int                     vs_prio;
        int                     vs_cpu;

        struct region_list      vs_dregion_list;
        struct region_list      vs_iregion_list;
        struct region_list      vs_gregion_list;

        vmap_t                  vs_dmap;
        vmap_t                  vs_imap;
        vmap_t                  vs_gmap;
};
```

Figure 6. Virtual space structure

When a memory object is mapped into the virtual space with vs_allocate_with_pager (vs_object, address, size, anywhere, memory_object, offset), a new virtual cache is created to cache the physical pages of the memory object and a new region structure is added to the region list of the virtual space to describe the allocated region.

The region structures (see Figure 7) in the virtual space's region list describe the allocated regions in the virtual space. Only one region can be allocated in a certain address range of the virtual space, e.g. regions can not overlap (but memory regions can be shared).

```
struct region
{
        reg_link_t  reg_link;
        v_addr_t    reg_start;
        v_addr_t    reg_end;
        port_t      reg_cache;
        offset_t    reg_offset;
        region_t    reg_shared;
        port_t      reg_prot;
};
```

Figure 7. Region structure

Virtual cache

The virtual cache contains those pages of the memory object which are in physical memory. Each physical page has an associated core map structure (which use is similar to that of BSD UNIX), which describes the physical page. A physical page can belong to only one cache (it cannot contain the data of two different memory objects). Physical pages are linked into a list (cache_pagelist). The cache_memobj field refers to the memory object which is cached by the virtual cache. Other fields are for *copy-on-write* and *shared* regions.

```
struct cache
{
        cache_t     cache_link;
        lock_t      cache_lock;

        int         cache_refcnt;
        port_t      cache_memobj;
        port_t      cache_shadowobj;
        port_t      cache_copyobj;
        port_t      cache_pagelist;
};
```

Figure 8. Virtual cache structure

The core map structure (see Figure 9) describes the physical page. It gives the the physical address, the offset into the memory object and the cache to which it belongs. It also contains a queue (cmap_ioqueue) to queue virtual processors which are waiting for io (pagein/pageout) on the physical page.

250

```
struct cmap
{
        cmap_link_t          cmap_link;
        lock_t               cmap_lock;

        port_t               cmap_cache;
        offset_t             cmap_offset;
        p_addr_t             cmap_addr;
        boolean              cmap_free;
        boolean              cmap_valid;
        boolean              cmap_kernel;
        boolean              cmap_modified;
        boolean              cmap_copy;

        boolean              cmap_iolock;
        struct vp_queue      cmap_ioqueue;
};
```

Figure 9. Core map structure

Page fault handling

A page fault can occur when a virtual address does not have a valid mapping or when the memory access violates the protection bits. Here we will describe how a page fault is handled for an invalid virtual address.

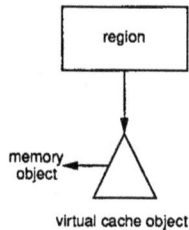

Figure 10a. A region

When a page fault occurs, the kernel searches the *region list* for the region which includes the faulted virtual address. Once the region is found, the virtual cache for the region is known (*reg_cache*) and the offset into the memory object can be easily calculated: *virtual address* - reg_start + reg_offset. Now, a request will be send to the virtual cache object to cache a page from the memory object at the specified virtual address. If the virtual cache cannot locate the page in memory, it will send a message to the memory object with the request to send the data from specified offset and place it in the cache.

Copy on write

The CPX kernel allows regions to be copied *copy on write*. To implement this, two additional virtual cache objects are required. The *copy cache object* contains the original pages after the virtual cache object modifies its pages. The *shadow cache object* contains the pages in the new region, which are different from the original cache object. A shadow cache object is always backed up by a default memory object.

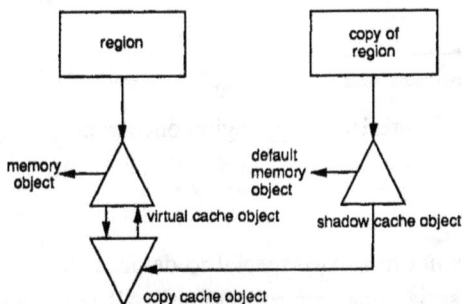

Figure 10b. Copy region

When a page in the virtual cache is modified, the original page is copied to the copy cache object, to make it available to the shadow cache object. Why it is not copied directly to the shadow cache object, we will make clear later. When, on a page fault, the shadow cache object does not have the page, it will send a request to the copy cache object. If the copy cache object does not contain the page, it means the page is still unmodified and the copy cache object will forward the request to the virtual cache.

When the original region is again copied copy-on-write, a new copy cache object is inserted between the virtual cache and the copy cache object (see Figure 10c). If we would not use a copy cache object each time a page is modified, an unmodified copy of the page would have to be copied to *all* shadow cache objects whose region is a copy of the original region. Now, we only have to copy the original page to the copy cache object, where it will be available to all shadow cache objects.

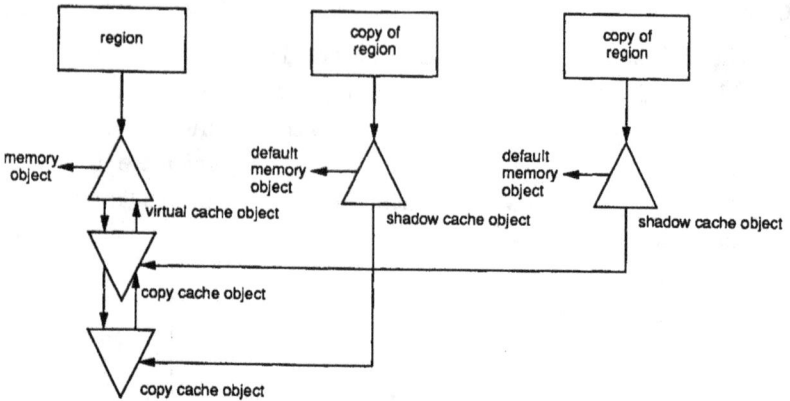

Figure 10c. Copy region once more

IODEV

The FLATS2 does not have any special io devices such as disk controllers, ethernet controllers, serial line controllers, etc. All communication with the outside world has to be done through some special memory called IODEV which is shared with the service processor (SVP), a DEC PDP-11[5]. The IODEV memory consists of 256 short words (16-bit) which are divide into two sections of 128 short words. One section is used for communication from FLATS2 to the SVP and the other half is used for communication from the SVP to FLATS2. Because all processors can access the IODEV memory, we have to make sure access is restricted and data is protected from accidental modification. Of course, it is possible to protect the region with a lock or semaphore, but it is much easier to consider the IODEV memory an object and modification is done by sending a request (message) to the object. In this way we can assure consistency because only the object can change its internal state.

---

[5]The SVP can access the FLATS2 memory directly (DMA).

```
struct iodev
{
        short int   iodev_nmi;
        short int   iodev_int;
        long  int   iodev_port;
        short int   iodev_major;
        short int   iodev_minor;
        short int   iodev_request;
        short int   iodev_size;
        short int   iodev_data[128-8];
};
```

Figure 11. Iodev structure

The message to the IODEV object has the same structure as the iodev structure above. (This is a software protocol and recognized by the SVP.) When a request is received and the IODEV is empty, the IODEV object will copy the message to IODEV. The field iodev_port contains the acknowledge port, to which it should send the acknowledgement of this request.

```
{
        /* receive request */
        while(1)
        {
                receive message;
                copy message to iodev;
        }

        /* handle interrupt */
        read acknowledge from IODEV;
        send acknowledge to acknowledge port;
}
```

Figure 12. IODEV object

The acknowledgement from the SVP is serviced asynchronously. When the SVP sends an acknowledgement, it will interrupt the FLATS2. The IODEV object will read the acknowledgement and forward it to the object specified by the acknowledge port.

4. Evaluation

The CPX kernel was evaluated using instruction set simulators. Two types of simulators were used; one instruction set simulator included the CPX kernel code, enabling the kernel to be executed at real time. The second simulator was executing in real mode, the CPX kernel was compiled into native FLATS2 code and executed on top of the simulator.

The CPX kernel provides all the building blocks to build a complete system, but it is not an operating system by itself. Although the kernel does not have any concept of task or process, it will try to maintain consistency. Each virtual processor is required to have a stack region and a gv region (local register frames) to be able to execute. When a virtual space is deleted, all virtual processors executing in that virtual space are deleted (e.g. its port capability is deleted), All regions allocated are deleted, and all port capabilities are deleted. Deleting a port capability means decrementing the reference count of the port. If the port reference count reaches zero, the port and the corresponding object are deleted.

4.1 Xinu

Xinu [4, 5] is a small UNIX like operating system. We implemented Xinu on top of the CPX kernel to evaluate how well an operating system can be implemented on top of the kernel. Table 1 lists the original Xinu layering compared with the new layering using the CPX kernel in Table 2.

user programs
file system
intermachine network communication
device manager and device drivers
real-time clock manager
interprocess communication
process coordination
process manager
memory manager
hardware

Table 1. XINU layering

user programs
file system
intermachine network communication
device manager and device drivers
real-time clock manager
process coordination (policies)
CPX kernel (VP + VP + VC)
hardware

Table 2. XINU + CPX layering

Using the Xinu operating system, we first concentrated on evaluating the message passing. All requests to the kernel such as vs_create, vp_create, vs_allocate, vp_suspend, are implemented by sending messages to the kernel object using port_send and port_receive. Only typed messages were supported.

description	prog 1	prog 2
smallest number of arguments	1	1
largest number of arguments	5	5
average number of arguments	3	1.5
smallest message size	28	28
largest message size	88	88
average message size	69	36

Table 3. Typed message statistics

As can be seen from Table 3, the overhead to send a message is rather large. To send an argument message (most often a word) we require 24 additional bytes, making the amount of useful information less than 15% of the total message (overhead becomes less as number of arguments increases).

Often, the only reason to use typed messages is the fact that we require the specification of an acknowledge port. We moved the acknowledge port to the header and at the same type reduced the header size to eight bytes. Sending a two argument message (acknowledge port and integer) would have required 44 bytes (12 byte header + 2 * 12 byte format descriptor + 2 * 4 data bytes) using a typed message. Now it requires 12 bytes (8 bytes header + 4 data bytes) using an untyped message.

5. Summary

Nothing is more important for a multiprocessor operating system than good support for concurrency. The CPX kernel supports concurrency by

- allowing multiple virtual processors to execute in a single virtual space (multi-threading),
- supporting asynchronous message passing,
- allowing continuation (in contrast to rpc).

Not only does the CPX kernel support concurrency, the CPX kernel can be executed concurrently. Some multi-processor operating systems allow only one specific processor to execute the kernel (master-slave setup). Other multi-processor operating systems allow only one processor to execute the kernel at any time. The CPX kernel does not make any assumption on when it is executed and where it is executed.

References

[1] G. Agha, "An Overview of Actor Languages", *ACM SIGPLAN Notices*, Vol. 21, No. 10, October 1986, pp. 58-67.

[2] M.J. Bach and S.J. Buroff, "Multiprocessor UNIX Operating System", *AT&T Bell Laboratories Technical Journal*, Vol. 63, No. 8, 1984.

[3] D.R. Cheriton, "The V Distributed System", *Communications of the ACM*, Vol. 31, No. 3, March 1988, pp. 314-333.

[4] D. Comer, "Operating System Design: the Xinu Approach", Prentice-Hall , 1984.

[5] D. Comer, "Operating System Design: Internetworking with Xinu", Prentice-Hall , 1987.

[6] Department of Defense, *Ada Reference Manual*.

[7] S. Ichikawa "A Study on the Cyclic Pipeline Computer: FLATS2", *Master's thesis*, Tokyo University, 1987.

[8] M.D. Janssen, J.K. Annot, and A.J. van der Goor, "Adapting UNIX for a Multiprocessor Environment", *Communications of the ACM*, Vol. 29, No. 9, September 1986, pp. 895-901.

[9] S.J. Leffler, M.K. McKusick, M.J. Karels, and J.S. Quaterman, "4.3 BSD UNIX Operating System", Addison-Wesley , 1989.

[10] C.H. Russell and P.J. Waterman, "Variations on UNIX for Parallel-Processing Computers", *Communications of the ACM*, Vol. 30, No. 12, December 1987, pp. 1048-1055.

[11] K. Shimizu, E. Goto, and S. Ichikawa, "CPC (Cyclic Pipeline Computer) - An Architecture Suited for Josephson and Pipelined Machines", *IEEE Transactions on Computers*, June 1989, pp. 825-832.

[12] P. Spee, M. Sato, N. Fukazawa, and E. Goto, "CPX - An Operating System Kernel for the CPC", *Proceedings of the 6th Riken Symposium on Josephson Electronics,* Wako-shi, March 23rd 1989, pp. 15-25.

[13] A. Tevanian, Jr., R.F. Rashid, D.B. Golub, D.L. Black, E. Cooper, and M.W. Young, "Mach Threads and the Unix Kernel: The Battle for Control", Tech. Rept. CMU-CS-87-149, Carnegie Mellon University, 1987.

[14] A. Tevanian, *Architecture-Independent Virtual Memory Management for Parallel and Distributed Environments: The Mach Approach*, Ph.D. dissertation, Carnegie Mellon University, 1987.

[15] W.A. Wulf, R. Levin, and S.P. Harbison, "HYDRA/C.mmp - An Experimental Computer System", McGraw-Hill , 1981.

[16] M. Young, A. Tevanian, R.F. Rashid, D. Golub, J. Eppinger, J. Chew, W. Bolosky, D. Black, and R. Baron, "The Duality of Memory and Communication in the Implementation of A Multiprocessor Operating System", *Proceedings of the Eleventh ACM Symposium on Operating Systems Principles,* November 8-11 1987, pp. 63-76.

FLATS2 FORTRAN Compiler

Mitsuhisa Sato and Eiichi Goto

Abstract

In this paper, we describe the overview and some algorithms of the FLATS2 FORTRAN compiler. It implements several optimization algorithms with Static Single Assignment(SSA) form. For register allocation, we present a global register allocation algorithm, which allocates registers locally using the approximation of the global register allocation to select good instructions to reference variables.

1. Introduction

FLATS2 is an experimental cyclic pipeline computer[8][15]. The FLATS2 FORTRAN compiler[12], which is an optimizing FORTRAN compiler for FLATS2, implements most of the optimization techniques including common subexpression elimination, constant folding, code motion, strength reduction and global register allocation.

While these optimization would be essential in a commercial compiler, they are also essential to evaluate the machine. Without highly optimized code,the speedup found by machine-specific features might be highly suspect, since the speed-up found by machine-specific features might be strongly biased by the code that otherwise would have been optimized away.

For a loop of array computation, the FLATS2 FORTRAN compiler automatically generates the code using the BL addressing[13] when it finds the code to which BL addressing can be applied. With the optimizing compiler, the BL addressing reduces the execution time of scientific workloads.

For simulation study of highly pipelined machines[14], the FLATS2 FORTRAN compiler can also generate the optimized code using the subset of FLATS2 instruction set for the Load/Store architecture. The additional code scheduling phase in the code generator handles interlocks due to the data dependency to generate optimized code for different pipeline configurations.

In Section 2, we describe the overview of the compiler. To facilitate optimizations, the compiler converts the internal code into Static Single Assignment (SSA) form[3] to perform machine independent optimizations efficiently and simpler. Section 3 presents several redundancy algorithms on SSA form. In Section 4, an extensive peep hole optimization called *code reconstruction* is described. In Section 5, we present a global register allocation algorithm, which allocates registers locally using the approximation of the global register allocation by the priority coloring algorithm. The optimization for the BL addressing and its evaluation results are described in [13].

2. Overview

Figure 1 shows the organization of FLATS2 FORTRAN compiler.

The front-end does the lexical analysis, parsing, and symbol table maintenance. Like many retargetable compilers, it compiles source code into an intermediate code, which is similar to the PCC intermediate code[9]. The front end of the FLATS2 compiler is similar to UNIX FORTRAN 77 compiler, except that it produces special code for BL checking in a DO loop. The BL optimization requires special handling for loop variables. Constant folding and associative-low simplifications are also done during this pass.

The next phase expands the intermediate code into register transfer language (RTL) code[4], a representation roughly equivalent to assemble code. For a non-optimizing compilation, assembly code is generated directly during this phase instead of RTL code.

Any RTL code is machine specific, but the form of RTL code is machine-independent. Most optimization is done in RTL code. The RTL code representation allows the optimizer to optimize machine-specific code in a machine-independent way. For example, a machine-independent algorithm can identify machine-specific common subexpressions in RTL code. After several optimizations, it is easy to translate RTL code into machine assembly code.

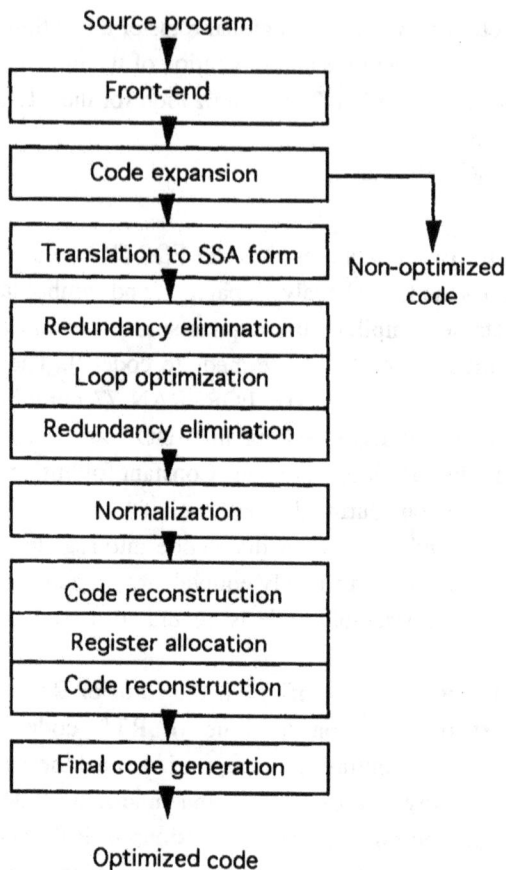

Fig.1. Organization of FLATS2 FORTRAN compiler

The code expansion process is similar to the code generation of PCC. A set of templates is given to describe the effect of the target machine instructions. The code expansion is done by matching the tree of codes and its context with the templates. If a template is found to match the tree and context, the associated instruction is generated. The tree is then rewritten, as specified by the template, to represent the effect of the generated instruction. If no template match is found, the matching routine is called recursively for a subgoal of the computation by default rewriting rules. The templates of the FLATS2 instruction set includes an orthogonal·subset with simple addressing modes. Code quality is achieved through optimization, so the templates for code expansion need not describe the full set of instructions. This makes the code expansion phase simpler, and reduces the number of templates.

The compiler also leaves register allocation to the optimizer. Registers are chosen from an infinite set, and register assignment is performed by the register allocation phase. The front-end and the code expansion phase allocate user-specified local variables and compiler-generated temporaries to pseudo registers. References to global variables in the source program is converted to reference to the labeled memory cell. In RTL code, we consider a pseudo register to be a variable. In FORTRAN, there are no explicit pointer variables to local variables. Only subroutine call statement must take care of aliasing and side effects on local variables passed to other subroutines. Thus, all variables can be thought to be unaliased in the subsequent optimizations. For non-optimized compilation, register allocation is done locally in each statement, since actual instructions are generated at this phase.

The low level representation upon which optimizations are performed consists a double-linked list of machine instructions. Each instruction entry in the list contains the RTL code associated with the machine instruction as well as additional information required by the optimizer and the assembly code generator.

After code expansion, the instructions in the list are partitioned into basic blocks. These comprise the basic unit for which local data flow information is calculated. The control flow graph is built with a node for each basic block and an edge for each transfer of control.

A *join node* is a node that has two or more inedges. A *backedge* of the flow graph is any edge whose destination is an ancestor of its source in the tree defined by depth-first search rooted at the program entry node. (In a reducible graph, the set of backedges does not depend on the arbitrary choices made during depth-first search.) With backedges ignored, the graph becomes a DAG and may be topologically sorted. A *loop header* is any node that is the destination of a backedge. Given a loop header reached by backedges from nodes, the corresponding *loop body* consists of all nodes such that there is a path from the loop header that traverses no backedges. An edge from a node in the loop body to a node not in the loop body is an *exit edge* of the loop. The destination of an exit edges is an *exit node* of the loop.

In optimizing compilers, the choice of data structure directly influence the power and efficiency of practical program optimization. To facilitate optimization, the FLATS2 FORTRAN compiler changes RTL code into static single assignment (SSA) form. There is only one assignment for each variable in static single assignment form. This transformation introduces many new pseudo register variables for each separate variable in the original program, at least one pseudo registers variable for every assignment. The phase single assignment is used for programs that assign to each variable only once when running. Dynamically, a program with loops may assign to the same variable many times, even if only one assignment appears in the program text. To attain SSA form, a new type of assignment statement is added at join nodes of the program so that there is a dominating assignment. These pseudo-assignment will be of the form X $= \phi(Y,Z)$, which means that if control enters along one inedge, X is assigned the value of Y, and if control enters along another inedge, X is assigned the value of Z.

After a program has been transformed into static single assignment form, lexically identical expressions always have the same value, no matter where they occur. A trivial assignment in SSA form can be thought as an assertion that the two variables represent the same value. These properties make several redundancy elimination algorithms such as common subexpression elimination, copy propagation and constant propagation more simple. Loop optimization performs transformation that preserves the consistency of this representation. Without SSA form, data flow information might have to be recomputed each time code motion occurs. After the redundancy elimination phase cleans up redundancies generated by the loop optimization, the *normalization phase* removes ϕ-functions in join nodes.

The *reconstruction phase* replaces sequences of RTL codes with equivalent singletons. The code expansion phase may emit "worst case" code, which is subsequently improved by this phase. It makes the code expansion simpler even for the complicated instruction set of FLATS2. This phase enables a clean separation of the code selection from the machine-independent optimization and register allocation.

The *register allocation phase* maps an unlimited number of pseudo register variables onto a finite set of registers provided by the hardware, introducing spill codes where needed. Our register allocation algorithm can allocate variables in a small number of floating-point registers in FLATS2 as well as the general purpose registers. While the registers are allocated globally, the local register allocation of our algorithm can select the good instruction to reference the variable in memory or registers. After the register allocation, the reconstruction phase is executed again to combine spill codes with other instructions. The *final code generation phase* translates optimized RTL code into assembly code.

3. Redundancy Elimination

The SSA form makes conventional optimizations simpler than the conventional representation of code. The redundancy elimination includes the following optimizations:

1. Constant propagation and constant folding.
2. Global common subexpression elimination.
3. Copy propagation.
4. Loop-invariant code motion.

The induction variable elimination algorithm of the compiler is described in [13].

3.1 Elimination of Trivial Assignments and Common Subexpression

Assignment statements that have trivial right-hand side (a single variable or a constant) have a special meaning in SSA form. Assignment statements whose right-hand side is a variable can be thought of as assertion that the two variables represent the same value. A trivial assignment statement, $X=c$ with a constant c, means that the value of X is c at any use. Given a trivial assignment $X=Y$, we replace every occurrence of one variable (including those in ϕ-function) with the other. This simple process works as copy propagation, while the standard copy propagation needs the data-flow computation for copy assignments.

Thanks to SSA form, identical computations in the text produce the same value. It makes the global common subexpression elimination more simple. The matching computations are really equivalent in SSA form. If statement $s1$ appears on every path from the entry to statement $s2$ in the flow graph, $s1$ *dominates* $s2$. If there are two statements $X=E$ and $Y=E$ where E is a common expression, we replace $Y=E$ with $Y=X$ when statement $X=E$ dominates $Y=E$ in the flow graph.

The initial list of trivial assignments to be removed includes any statements that appear originally in the program. There may also be several computations that happen to have identical right-hand sides initially. Renaming of operands in expressions may make the right-hand side become identical with the right-hand side of another computation. Elimination of common subexpression creates a trivial assignment to be removed, which is added to the worklist of trivial assignments. Removal of trivial assignment and elimination of common expression feed each other until the worklist are empty.

Renaming of the operands of ϕ-functions may create a trivial assignment as follows:

- X=ϕ(Y,Y) is replaced by X=Y
- X=ϕ(X,Y) is replaced by X=Y.

In both cases, the new assignment is added to the worklist of trivial assignments.

To facilitate these replacements for trivial assignments, we maintain a list of uses of each variable in the program. After the replacement, the use list of the replaced variable is concatenated to the use list of the other variable. A *definition statement* *DEF(X)* of a variable X is an assignment statement where X is defined. By the definition of SSA form, X is defined by exactly one statement. A *use list* *USE(X)* is a set of statements where X is used as operand. The algorithm is sketched in Figure 2. Common subexpressions are searched in each use list, when removal of trivial assignments changes the use list. The details of eliminating common expressions are as follows:

```
W = ∅
/* collect initial trivial assignment */
for each variable X do
        eliminate common subexpressions in USE(X)
        if DEF(X) is a trivial assignment then W = W + DEF(X)
        end
while W is not empty do begin
        take a statement X = Y from W;
        for each statement S in USE(X) do
                replace X with Y;
                USE(Y) = USE(Y) + USE(X);
                USE(X) = ∅;
                delete DEF(X);
                eliminate common subexpressions in USE(Y);
                for each statement S in USE(Y) do begin
                        do constant folding on S if possible
                        if S is a trivial assignment then
                        put S into W
                end
        end
end
```

Fig. 2. Redundancy elimination

1. Find statements which have identical computations in right-hand side within the use list, say $V_i = E$ where E is a common expression and i runs from 1 to n.
2. Replace each of the statement by a trivial assignment of the form $V_j = V_i$ if the assignment of V_i dominates the assignment of V_j.
3. Put these trivial assignments on the worklist W for removal.

The ϕ-functions distinguish values of variables transmitted on distinct incoming control flow edges. It enables a *global value numbering* algorithm to track redundant computations access flow graph paths. The redundancy elimination by Rosen[11] eliminates global redundancies involved in a loop using the global value numbering approach. Our algorithm is rather conservative one and eliminates such redundancies in loop invariant code motion of the separate phase explained in the next subsection.

3.2 Loop Invariant Code Motion

Code motion is an important transformation which decreases the execution time. This transformation takes an expression that gives the same result at every iteration of a loop and places the expression in the landing pad.

A *loop invariant statement* is a statement whose operands are either constant or have all their reaching definitions outside the loop. Our algorithm starts with assuming that all variables are invariant. Since each variable has exactly one definition in SSA form, we can find loop variant variables by marking all variables defined in the loop as "variant". The variable without mark is the loop invariant variable. Once we find the statement whose operands are loop invariant, the statement is moved into the landing pad and the variable defined by the statement is unmarked.

When loops are nested, loop-invariant code motion is performed from the inner loop. Since the algorithm does not use data-flow information such as use-def chains, it is not necessary to maintain data-flow information for each loop. The SSA form nicely summarizes the conditions relevant to code motion. An advanced constant propagation algorithm is proposed to delete branches to code proven unexecutable at compile-time[17]. Without SSA form, data-flow information may have to be recomputed each code motion occurs.

Loop invariant information computed in this phase is also used for the loop induction variable elimination.

3.3 Alias Analysis in Loop

If an expression includes a memory reference, we need alias analysis to determine whether the expression is invariant in the loop. For example, in the following loop

```
    DO 10 I = 1,N
10   S = A(J) + B(I)
```

A(J) is a loop-invariant memory reference. The value can be referenced instead in the register loaded from the memory reference in the landing pad. In RTL code, reference to a global variable is represented as reference to the memory cell. If the global variable has no alias in the loop, it can be assigned to a register in the landing pad to reference its value in the register within the loop.

Although the presence of pointers usually makes data-flow analysis more complex, the SSA form enables us to track the effect of pointer assignments across the flow graph. If p receives the value pointing to a memory area, the SSA form makes sure that p points to the memory area at every use of p. The ϕ-function implies that the variable may have both values of operands transmitted on distinct inedges. The algorithm computes the set $REF(p)$ of memory area to which the pointer p may point. We use the recursive function $FINDREF(p)$ of Figure 3, which computes $REF(p)$ for each pointer p. Before each call of $FINDREF(p)$, all pointers are unmarked "visited" to terminate recursive calls:

An indirect assignment by p may modify the memory area of $REF(p)$ The set of modified memory area in the loop is the union of the memory area modified by all statements. If p is a loop-invariant variable and the memory area of $REF(p)$ is not modified in the loop, then the memory reference by p gives the same value at every iterations. As the code motion of loop-invariant variables, the memory reference to the memory area which is not modified in the loop can be moved in the landing pad. It sometimes enables other expressions to move in the landing pad. Since unlike variables in SSA form, the memory area can be modified by more than one assignments in the loop, the data-flow computation is needed to move an assignment to memory.

function *FINDREF(p)*
begin
       if p is "visited" **then return** $\emptyset$ /* empty set */
         mark p "visited";

if *DEF(p)* is a form $p = A \pm c$ where *A* is a label of memory

and *c* is an integer offset **then**

return { *A* };

if *DEF(p)* is a form $p = q \pm c$ where *q* is a pointer

and *c* is an integer offset **then**

return *FINDREF(q)*

if *DEF(p)* is a form $p = \phi(q,r)$ **then**

return *FINDREF(q)* +*FINDREF(r)*

else

the pointer *p* is meaningless;

end

Fig. 3. Alias computation

If no alias is found for a global variable within the loop, it can be assigned to a register. The reference to the global variable is replaced with a compiler-generated variable, and codes are inserted to load its value into the register in the landing pad and update the global variable at each exit node. This transformation reduces expensive memory access for the global variable in the loop. Since reference to an array element with constant index is represented as reference to the memory cell as same as the global variable, above transformation can be applied for such memory reference.

Alias analysis across procedure calls requires interprocedural information; interprocedural analysis is not performed in our compiler. If the loop contains calls, we assume that they could modify any memory area.

3.4 Normalization of SSA form

After optimization on SSA form, the normalization phase eliminates ϕ-functions. Every computation of the form $X=\phi(Y,Z)$ is replaced by an assignment $X=Y$ on one of the entering branches, and by $X=Z$ on the other. Each assignment is placed at the end of the code.

Many variables can be merged together by using their *live range* information. If two variables have disjoint live ranges, then they can be merged into one variable. If each live range for the variables in $X=\phi(Y,Z)$ is disjoint to each other, this variables is replaced with one variable so that no additional statement is placed. An induction variable in the loop is often the case. The live range information is also used for coalescing the source and target in statement to recognize the simple increments of variables.

4. Code Reconstruction

The FLATS2 instruction set is too complicated to emit optimal code by simple pattern matching in the code expansion phase. This phase replaces sequences of instructions with equivalent "larger" instructions to achieves code quality. Because most instructions are executed in the same time in FLATS2, larger instructions are executed faster than the sequence of simpler instructions. Since final instructions are reconstructed from simpler instructions, we call this phase *code reconstruction* . This phase is called before and after the register allocation phase.

4.1 Combining Instructions

The code reconstruction phase seeks a pair of instructions in RTL code that can be replaced with singletons. It symbolically simulates these instructions to learn their combined effect and searches for an instruction with this combined effect by machine-dependent routines, called *instruction recognizer*. If it finds one, it replaces the original instructions with the singleton. The code reconstruction phase computes the combined effect of two instructions by substituting the values assigned to cells in the first for occurrences of those cells in the second. For example, consider the following instructions;

```
r[1] = m[r[0]]
r[2] = r[2] + r[1]
```

where r[1] is dead at the second. Their combined effect is computed by replacing the r[1] in the second instructions with the value assigned to r[1] in the first, and then concatenating the two effect. This yields

```
r[2] = r[2] + m[r[0]]
```

If r[1] is live after the second instruction, its replacement cannot be performed. A conventional peep hole optimizer correct only those sequences that match a few hand-written, machine-specific patterns. The code reconstruction phase combines all related pairs in machine-independent manner.

For autoincrement addressing modes, we treat a simple increment instruction specially. For example, the following codes can be combined into an autoincrement addressing mode.

```
r[2] = r[2] + m[r[1]]
r[1] = r[1] + C
```

yields

```
r[2] = r[2] + m[r[1]];     r[1] = r[1] + C
```

where these assignments are done in parallel * Such a simple increment is recognized in the normalization phase of SSA form by live range information.

Some FLATS2 instructions can perform operation directly on memory operands, and store the result in memory in some operands combinations. The code expansion phase emits code using only one memory operand to simplify code expansion process. The reconstruction phase combines a store operation with other instructions. It also combines an increment with memory addressing in other instructions to make use of autoincrement addressing mode of the BL addressing. Even though the available operand combinations of the BL addressing modes are non-orthogonal because of a fixed length of the FLATS2 instruction, the case analysis is done in machine-independent manner.

Davidson and Fraser's YC compiler [4] uses a similar approach on peephole optimization by using the table which is automatically generated by the machine description. We used a function instead, which is given by a compiler writer, to recognize the instruction. This phase is retargeted by supplying a machine-dependent instruction recognizer. As well as adjacent instructions in text, the code reconstruction phase moves an instruction as needed to increase the chance of combination using a machine instruction dependency graph.

4.2 Instruction Reorganization

Since a related pair of instructions may be separated by other instructions, instruction reorganization increases the chance of combination for such a pair. The reorganization problem has been discussed by many researchers [7][16], related to compile-time pipeline scheduling and compacting of microcode. Like peephole optimization, microcode optimization improves the code by compacting the vertical microoperations into horizontal microinstructions where these

---

* In RTL code, the code for autoincrement addressing is expressed as m[r[1]] = r[1] + C].

operations do not overlap in resource utilization. The peephole optimization, however, often deals with vertical aspects of instruction ordering, involving data dependencies between instructions. It works as a part of the compiler like pipeline scheduling. Possible combinations of peephole optimization is not dynamic, while pipeline reorganization concerns interlocks whose effect is dynamic since the context of a particular instruction determines whether or not that instruction is legal in its current position.

Clearly, instructions in a program cannot be reordered arbitrarily. Certain instruction must remain ahead of other instructions in the resulting code sequence for the overall effect of the program to remain unchanged. To express the constraint to rearrange instructions without compromising correctness, we construct for each basic block a directed acyclic graph (DAG) whose nodes are the instructions in the block and whose edges represent serialization dependencies between instructions. An edge from instruction *i* to instruction *j* indicates that *i* must be executed before *j* to preserve correctness. The DAG takes into account all serialization constraints, including register dependencies, memory dependencies, control transfer instructions such as calls and branches. If the variable which is live at the end of the block, we allocate a special node as the successor to represent the liveness of the variable. An example code sequence and its dependency DAG are shown in Figure 4.

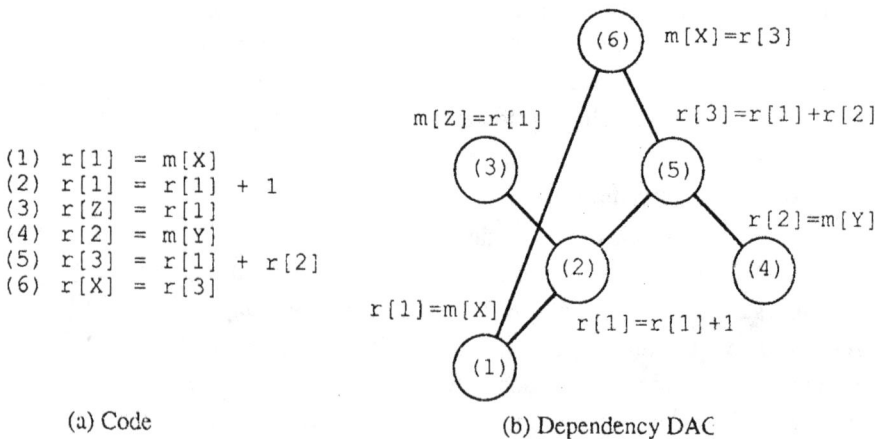

(a) Code

```
(1)  r[1] = m[X]
(2)  r[1] = r[1] + 1
(3)  r[Z] = r[1]
(4)  r[2] = m[Y]
(5)  r[3] = r[1] + r[2]
(6)  r[X] = r[3]
```

(b) Dependency DAC

Fig. 4. Dependency DAG

We serialize definition vs. definitions on any particular resource such as a register to simplify selecting an order without dead lock. Our DAG is the same as that used for the reorganization for pipeline scheduling proposed by Gibbsons[6].

As long as the instructions in the basic block are reordered in some topological sort order of the dependency DAG, the overall effect of the block is the same as its execution in the original order. The algorithm reorders the instructions to find a related pair of instructions to be combined with dependency DAG:

1. An instruction is a candidate for reordering if all its immediate predecessors in the DAG have been reordered.
2. Among the candidates, select an instruction. (We can select the instruction which is executed first in the original order.)
3. Combine the selected instruction with its successor in the DAG if possible. Since the definition is dead after all its uses, the definition have to be used by only one successor. If the instruction is combined to the other instruction, delete it from the DAG. Otherwise, reorder the instruction.
4. Repeat Step 1-3 until all instructions are reordered.

5. Local Register Allocation with Global Approximation

Register allocation can be viewed as the process of mapping an infinite number of variables into the finite set of registers provided by a hardware. An elegant formalization of this problem is the graph-coloring approach first used by Chaitin[1]. The global register allocation is successful in the machine where the instruction set is regular and a large number of registers are available. FLATS2 has a few floating-point registers and their usages are restricted. Our register allocation algorithm allocates these registers locally in each basic block using the approximation given by the proceeding global register allocation. The local register allocation can select the instruction to reduce spill code for the registers. Then it inserts spill codes to keep consistency between basic blocks. It can allocate a large register set as well.

5.1 Register Allocation on FLATS2

FLATS2 has 64 general purpose registers (GV registers), which consists of 32 global registers and 32 local frame registers. Four registers of the local frame registers hold a return address and procedure status informations. The register allocator uses 15 of the 32 global registers. Integer and address variables are allocated to GV registers.

Because the local frame registers are saved/restored by the CALL/RETURN instructions, a variable whose live range includes procedure calls should be assigned to a local frame register. Such variables belong to a different class of registers. The coloring algorithm can easily extend to the case of multiple register classes. The interference graph will only give interferences between variables of the overlapped classes.

The FLATS2 register set has the following problems on register allocation:

1. A BL pair must be allocated in an even/odd GV registers pair. The conventional global register allocator does not take into account allocating overlapping registers of different sizes.
2. Some instructions operate only on registers. A pointer used in addressing mode must also be in a register. To ensure that it is always possible to load the temporary to a register, the allocator needs to reserve registers for this purpose[10].
3. For the floating-point registers, there are several restrictions on their combination of operands. The register usage is also constrained due to hardware restriction. For example, the target of the multiplication instruction must be P register or Q register in the floating-point register set, or memory. The floating point registers are divided to different classes according to their restrictions. As a result, each register class contains one or two registers. If the class contains only one register, the variable allocated by global register allocation must be spilled out frequently at each time other instruction uses other variables in the same class.
4. The floating-point instructions can operate on memory operands directly. Since most floating-point instructions are executed in one cycle even with memory operands, variables can sometimes reside in memory. Because memory operands depend on the operand combination of each instruction, the global register allocation can not take code selection into account.

While the global register allocation can make good use of a large registers set, it often fails for a small registers set. If only one registers is available and two variables need the register, the conflict between these register should then be resolved locally. The local register allocation can select "better" instructions to reference the variable efficiently on register or memory.

5.2 Register Allocation Algorithm

The allocator operates on RTL code, which is machine-dependent, rather than a machine independent intermediate representation. We refer to both user-defined and compiler-generated temporaries as "variables" in this section, because RTL code makes no distinction two, which are represented by pseudo-register variables.

The global register allocation can be thought as an approximation of register allocation. The FLATS2 FORTRAN compiler uses a graph-coloring algorithm called *priority-based coloring*, developed by Chow[2]. Each variable is assigned a priority that is the estimated additional cost if the variable resides in memory rather than in a register. The global register allocation is performed before registers are allocated actually by the local register allocation. For each variables, the global register allocation returns the register assigned globally at each basic block.

The local allocation phase assigns a register for each variable, and computes the following information used to keep consistency between basic blocks in the subsequent phase:

available_expected[n] --- a set of variables whose values the local allocation phase expects to be available in the registers assigned in the global allocation phase at the beginning of block n.

available_gen[n] --- a set of variables which reach at the end of block n and whose values are available in the registers assigned in the global allocation phase at the end of the block.

available_through[n] --- a set of variables whose values are available in the register assigned in the global allocation phase at the beginning of block n, and which do not reach the end of the block or whose values still reside in the register at the end of the block.

modified_gen[n] --- a set of defined variables in block n which reach the end of the block and whose home locations are not updated with the modified value.

Actually, since these are subsets of variables, we can use a bit vector representation for these sets, and the amount of space used will not be prohibitive.

For each use of v in instructions, the local allocation finds the location of v. If v is found in a memory cell and the instruction can perform direct operation on the memory operand, it replaces the use of v with the memory operand. Otherwise, it finds the register r for v to reference the variable in register. If a variable is not allocated to registers in the global allocation phase, we must choose an appropriate register for the variable. We may choose the least frequently used register or the least recently used register as a candidate[5]. The register assigned in the global allocation phase may be used if any. Although we may not follow the approximation by the global register allocation, the globally optimal solutions sometimes belong to the local optimal solutions.

5.3 Inserting Spill Code

Once the local register allocation is done for each basic block, we insert load/store codes to keep consistency between basic blocks. A *live range* of a variable is an isolated and contiguous group of nodes in the flow graph in which the variable is defined or referenced. We define an *available range* of the variable as a subset of the live range in which the value of variable resides in the register. The following sets of variables are computed to find the available range for each node:

available_in[n] --- a set of variables whose value is available in the register assigned in the global allocation phase at the beginning of block n.

available_out[n] --- a set of variables whose value is available in the register assigned in the global allocation phase at the end of block n.

These sets can be computed by the following data flow equation, which is similar to that for available expression computation:

$$available\_out[n] =$$
$$(available\_in[n] \cap available\_through[n] \cap live\_out[n]) \cup available\_gen[n]$$

$$available\_in[n] = \prod_{m \text{ a predecessor of } n} available\_out[m] \quad \text{for } n \text{ is not an entry node}$$

$$available\_in[n] = \varnothing \quad \text{for } n \text{ is an entry node}$$

The live variable information, *live_out[n]*, is used to remove the variable in *available_through[n]* which does not reach the end of the block.

If the value of the variable is changed in the intervening code where it resides in register, the home location of the variable must be updated with the register contents at the end of the code segments unless it is dead on exit. The live range of the variable may be split into several available ranges. Figure 5(a) shows a region of code in which variable X and Y are to be allocated in the register. Figure 5(b) and (c) show possible allocation result and its available ranges with spill codes.

If the local allocation expects the variable to be loaded at the entry of the available range, the load instruction is needed to load the value into the register. If the modified variable in register is live at the exit of the available range, the value must be spilled into the home location. If the available range of the variable covers the whole live range and the variable is used locally in the procedure, no spill code is needed because the variable is dead at every exit.

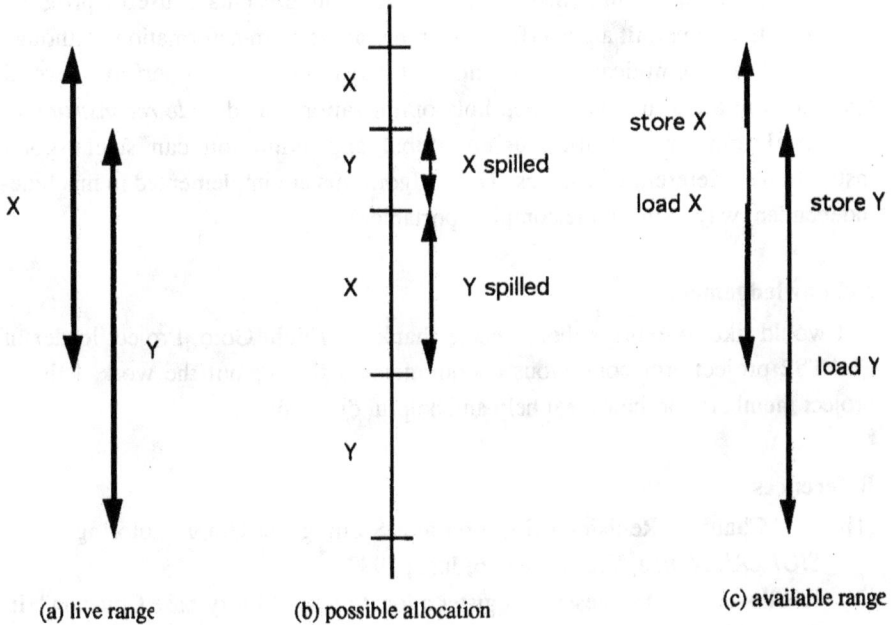

(a) live range   (b) possible allocation   (c) available range

Fig. 5. Example of register allocation

The local allocation phase can compute local information only in the basic block. If the value in the register is changed in some block, its value may be spill out at the exit of the available range to which the node belongs. The following set is computed to know where the value in the register should be store into the home location:

modified_out[n] --- a set of variables whose values are available in the registers assigned in the global allocation phase at end of block n and its values are different from the values in the home locations.

The set *modified_out[n]* is computed by propagating *modified_gen[n]* along with the path of the available range.

6. Summary

The overview and some algorithms of FLATS2 FOTRAN compiler has been presented. To evaluate an experimental cyclic pipeline computer, FLATS2 with quality code, the compiler implements redundancy elimination algorithms with static single assignment (SSA) form. SSA form presents a useful program representation to permit a powerful and simple program transformation. Although FLATS2 has a complicated instruction set and register set to perform several operations in a instruction, a peep hole optimization called *code reconstruction* and local register allocation using global approximation can select good instructions to reference variables. These algorithms are implemented in machine-independent way to make the compiler portable.

Acknowledgements

I would like to express their sincere thanks to Eiichi Goto, Project leader of FLATS2 project for continuous encouragement throughout the work. I thank project members for their great help and helpful discussions.

References

[1] G.J. Chaitin, "Register Allocation and Spilling via Graph Coloring, *ACM SIGPLAN Notice*, Vol. 17, No. 6, June, 1982.

[2] F. Chow and J. Hennessy, "Register allocation by Priority-base Coloring", In *Proceedings of the ACM SIGPLAN '84 Symposium on Computer Construction*, 1984, pp 222-232.

[3] R. Cytron, J. Ferrante, B.K. Rosen, M.N. Wegman and F.K. Zadeck, "An Efficient Method of Computing Static Single Assignment Form", In *Proceedings of 15th POPL*, 1989, pp25-35.

[4] J.W Davidson and C.W. Fraser, "Code Selection through Object Code Optimization", *Trans. on Prog. Lang. and Sys.*, Vol. 6, No. 4, Oct., 1984, pp505-526.

[5] R.A. Freiburghouse, "Register Allocation Via Usage Counts", *CACM*, Vol.

17, No. 11, November, 1974, pp 638-642.

[6] P.B. Gibbons and S.S. Muchnick, "Efficient Instruction Scheduling for a Pipelined Architecture", In *Proceedings of the SIGPLAN 1986 Conference on Compiler Construction*, 1986, pp11-16.

[7] J.L. Hennessy and T.R. Cross, "Postpass Code Optimization of Pipeline Constraints", *ACM Trans. on Prog. Lang. and Sys.*, Vol. 5, No. 3, July 1983, pp422-448.

[8] Shuichi Ichikawa, "A Study on A Cyclic Pipeline Computer: FLATS2", Ph. D. dissertation, The University of Tokyo, 1990.

[9] S. C. Johnson, "A Tour Through the Portable C Compiler", Unix technical document, 1981.

[10] J.R. Larus and P.N Hilfinger, "Register Allocation in the SPUR Lisp Compiler", In *Proceedings of the ACM SIGPLAN '86 Symposium on Computer Construction*, 1986, pp 255-263.

[11] B.K. Rosen, M.N. Wegman and F.K Zadeck, "Global Value Numbers and Redundant Computation", In *Proceedings of 15th POPL*, 1988, pp 12-27.

[12] Mitsuhisa Sato, "Exploiting parallelism in Cyclic pipeline Computer with an Optimizing Compiler", Ph. D. dissertation, The University of Tokyo, 1990.

[13] Mitsuhisa Sato, Shuichi Ichikawa and Eiichi Goto, "Loop optimization with BL addressing", QMFL project report, JRDC, 1991.

[14] Mitsuhisa Sato, Shuichi Ichikawa and Eiichi Goto, "Multiple Instruction Streams in a Highly Pipelined Processor", In *Proceedings of 2nd IEEE Symposium on Parallel and Distributed Processing*, pp 182-189, Dec. 1990.

[15] K. Shimizu, E. Goto and S. Ichikawa, "CPC(Cyclic Pipeline Computer) - An Architecture Suited for Josephson Pipelined-Memory Machines", *IEEE Transactions on Computers*, Vol. 38, No. 6, June, 1989,

[16] M. Tokoro, E. Tamura and T. Takizuka, "Optimization of Microprograms", *IEEE Trans. on Computers*, C-30, No. 7, July 1981, pp491-504.

[17] M.N. Wegman and F.K. Zadeck, "Constant Propagation with Conditional Branches", In *Proceedings of 12th POPL*, 1984, pp 291-299.

Reprinted with permission from *Cryogenics*, 31(9), 786 – 790 (1991).

A New Approach for High-Efficiency Pulse-Tube Refrigerator

Junpei Yuyama, Masahiko Kasuya, Masayuki Nakatsu, Qiquan Geng,

and Eiichi Goto

Abstract

This paper describes a new approach for a high-efficiency pulse-tube refrigerator. A piston is mounted on the hot end of the pulse tube. This new model serves to study the work flow going through the pulse tube without heat exchange. Refrigeration power is found to increase as the work flow reaching the hot-end piston increases. On the contrary, the heat flow released into a room-temperature environment decreases as the work flow increases. This suggests that the work flow becomes more important as the refrigeration power increases.

1. Introduction

Pulse-tube refrigerators have attracted much interest because they have the potential for high reliability. There are no moving components in the low-temperature regions. Their refrigeration mechanisms were previously explained in terms of surface heat pumping [1] where the heat exchange between the gases in the pulse tubes and walls is essential. In the original model (basic pulse-tube refrigerator), the hot end of the pulse tube was closed and cooled with water. Later, the minimum temperature achievable by a pulse-tube refrigerator was drastically reduced by adding an orifice and a large reservoir at the hot end [2], [3]. This model was called the orifice pulse-tube refrigerator. Radebaugh et al. [3] pointed out the importance of enthalpy flow in the pulse tube. Some researchers discussed heat flow and work flow in the pulse tube in terms of thermoacoustic theory [4], [5].

A new model of the pulse-tube refrigerator is constructed [6]. This model, which has a piston on the hot end of the pulse tube, serves to study whether heat exchange between the gases and walls is necessary for pulse-tube refrigeration. From a point of view that the heat exchange is not essential, the pulse tube can be regarded as a gas column through which the expansion work generated at low temperature is carried up to the room-temperature section of the system. Thus, the work flow in the pulse tube is essential in this case. On the other hand, in the basic pulse-tube refrigerator, the expansion work is completely converted into heat in the pulse tube, and cooling-water carries the heat away through the hot-end heat exchanger. In the orifice pulse-tube refrigerator, some expansion work is converted into heat in the pulse tube, and the remaining work reaches the orifice. Viscosity of the gas passing through the orifice changes the remaining work into heat. Both of these processes involve some heat-exchange. To determine the role of heat exchange in the pulse tube, it is important to study the work flow reaching the hot end of the pulse tube. The work flow can be measured with a piston mounted on the hot end.

This model also serves to study the effect of the phase difference between pressure oscillation and gas motion. In orifice pulse-tube refrigerators, phase differences can be changed by adjusting the orifice openings. However, it is impossible to control phase and flow rate independently because flow rates through the orifices also change when the orifice openings are adjusted. There is another approach in which the orifice and reservoir of an orifice pulse-tube refrigerator are replaced with a moving plug [7]. The phase difference cannot be controlled independently even in this approach because the motion of the moving plug is controlled only by the friction of the plug seal. Conversely, a piston mounted on the hot end of the pulse tube can control the phase difference and flow rate independently.

This model is a new approach for a high-efficiency pulse-tube refrigerator because it does not need any irreversible processes contrary to the basic and orifice pulse-tube refrigerators.

This paper describes an experimental study with an expansion piston mounted on the hot end of the pulse tube. The phase difference is electrically controlled using electromagnetic valves and position sensors. The flow rate is independently determined by the piston stroke. The effect of the hot-end piston on the performance of the pulse-tube refrigerator is described and enthalpy flow in the pulse tube is discussed.

2. Enthalpy Flow in the Pulse Tube

Enthalpy flow in regenerators and pulse tubes consists of work and heat flows [4], [5]. The work flow does not involve entropy flow, but the heat flow does. Average enthalpy flow $<H_T>$ in regenerators is given by

$$<H_T> = \frac{1}{\tau} \int_0^\tau H_T \, dt \tag{1}$$

where τ is the cycle period. In ideal regenerators, since temperature oscillation is infinitely small, $<H_r>$ will vanish:

$$
\begin{aligned}
<H_r> &= \frac{1}{\tau} \int_0^\tau H_r \, dt \\
&= \frac{1}{\tau} \int_0^\tau C_p T m_r dt \\
&= \frac{C_p T}{\tau} \int_0^\tau m_r dt \\
&= 0,
\end{aligned}
\tag{2}
$$

where C_p is the specific heat of the working gas and m_r is mass flow rate. Thus, the work and heat flows have the same magnitude and opposite directions in ideal regenerators (Fig. 1(a)). In this section, an ideal regenerator is assumed for clear discussion.

Enthalpy flow throughout our pulse-tube refrigerator is also schematically shown in Fig. 1(a). Enthalpy flow $<H_{com}>$ ($=<W_{com}>$) produced by the compressor is removed at room temperature as heat flow $<Q_{com}>$. Refrigeration power $<Q_c>$ is generated by the expansion of working gas at the cold end of the pulse tube. If there is no heat exchange between the gases in the pulse tube and the tube wall, only work flow $<W_{pt}>$ ($=<Q_c>$) will exist in the pulse tube. The work flow $<W_{pt}>$ reaches the piston mounted on the hot end of the pulse tube. Enthalpy flow in Fig. 1(a) is quite similar to that in a Stirling refrigerator except that the expansion piston is located on the room temperature side instead of on the low temperature side. On the other hand, for basic pulse-tube refrigerators, enthalpy flow $<H_{pt}>$ in the pulse tube consists of work flow $<W_{pt}>$ and heat flow $<Q_{pt}>$ (Fig. 1(c)). The entire work flow changes into heat flow in the pulse tube through irreversible processes such as heat exchange with the the tube wall and heat conduction within the gas. Orifice pulse-tube refrigerators might work without any heat exchange between the gas and tube wall. Work flow in the pulse tube, however, must dissipate while the gas goes through the orifice, and heat generated at the orifice must be removed (Fig. 1(d)). This process must produce some irreversible entropy.

Phase difference between pressure oscillation and piston motion is now discussed. When averaged over one cycle, the work flow $<W_e>$ reaching the hot-end piston is

$$<W_e> = \frac{1}{\tau} \int A_S P \, dX$$

$$= \frac{A_S}{\tau} \int_0^\tau P(t) \frac{dX}{dt} \, dt$$

$$= \frac{A_S P_1 X_1 \omega}{\tau} \int_0^\tau \sin(\omega t + \phi) \cos \omega t \, dt$$

$$= (\frac{A_S P_1 X_1 \omega}{\tau}) (\frac{\tau}{2}) \sin\phi$$

$$= \frac{A_S P_1 X_1 \omega}{2} \sin\phi, \tag{3}$$

where pressure oscillation is $P(t)=P_1\sin(\omega t+\phi)$, piston motion is $X(t)=X_1\sin\omega t$, and A_S is the area of the piston. When the pressure oscillation leads the piston motion by $\pi/2$ ($\phi=\pi/2$), the maximum value is expected in $<W_e>$, suggesting that the maximum value of the refrigeration power $<Q_c>$ ($=<W_{pt}>$ $=<W_e>$) is expected for $\phi=\pi/2$ in the idealized (adiabatic) scheme of our refrigerator (Fig. 1(a)).

3. Experimental Arrangement and Procedure

A schematic diagram of the experimental arrangement of our pulse-tube refrigerator is shown in Fig. 2. The pulse tube is made of type 304 stainless steel, and the dimensions are 280 mm in length, 25 mm in I.D., and 0.5 mm in wall thickness. The regenerator housing is also made of type 304 stainless steel and the dimensions are 300 mm in length, 34.95 mm in I.D., and 0.5 mm in wall thickness. About 700 stainless steel screens of 80 mesh are placed in the high-temperature side of the regenerator, and about 1,800 stainless steel screens of 250 mesh are placed in the low-temperature side.

A crank-driven piston is fitted into a 22.2 mm I.D. cylinder, which is mounted on the hot end of the pulse tube. The crank is driven by an induction motor (61K100RGK-AKF; ORIENTAL MOTOR). The motor brakes the piston motion caused by pressure oscillation. The cylinder wall is cooled with water to protect the piston seals from damage due to heating-up.

A commercial compressor unit (C-30; ULVAC Cryogenics) and two electromagnetic valves (J263A240LT; ASCO) are employed to generate pressure oscillation. A rotating vane is attached to the motor shaft, and two optical sensors are used to detect the vane passing over them. Signals from the optical sensors indicate the piston position. Since the signals are also used to trigger the electromagnetic valves, the piston motion and valve opening/closing are synchronized. The relative angle between the crank assembly and the vane can be adjusted so that the phase difference between pressure oscillation and piston motion can be changed.

Pressure oscillation in the pulse tube is measured with a strain-gauge type pressure transducer (PHS-20KA; Kyowa) . Work flow $<W_e>$ reaching the piston is obtained from data sets on pressure oscillation and piston position. The cold end of the pulse tube is made of copper and is connected to the cold end of the regenerator by a copper tube. A platinum resistance thermometer (PTF-7; Teijin Engineering) and a germanium resistance thermometer (GR-200A; LakeShore Cryotronics) are attached to the cold end of the pulse tube, and a manganin-wire heater is wound around the copper tube. The apparatus is inserted into a vacuum enclosure where a vacuum of 10^{-2} Pa is maintained.

4. Results and Discussion

Minimum temperatures T_{min} are plotted against work flow $<W_e>$ in Fig. 3. Open circles denote T_{min}'s for $\phi \approx \pi/2$ where the maximum value is expected in $<W_e>$, and $\phi \approx 3\pi/2$ where the minimum (negative) value is expected in $<W_e>$ with 30 mm strokes. The solid circles denote similar data points with 10 mm strokes. The solid square denotes T_{min} without any piston motion ($<W_e>=0$) where our pulse-tube refrigerator corresponds to a basic pulse-tube refrigerator. These data points seem to lie on a straight line with a negative slope, showing that it is possible to make T_{min} lower as we raise $<W_e>$ by increasing the piston stroke and/or adjusting the phase difference with given values of pressure and frequency. This tendency is confirmed in Fig. 4. Operating conditions of solid circles are a maximum pressure range of 0.86-1.01 MPa, a minimum pressure range of 0.21-0.29 MPa, and a period range of 0.62-0.74 s. All the data points seem to lie close to the straight line taken from Fig. 3. The open circle in Fig. 4 denotes the lowest temperature (70 K) achieved in this work. The work flow reaching the piston is 30.1 W with a maximum pressure of 18.2 MPa and a minimum pressure of 11.2 MPa, and the cycle period is 0.74 s. This result suggests that the hot-end piston model is more suitable for low frequency operation than orifice pulse-tube refrigerators.

In the idealized scheme of our pulse-tube refrigerator (Fig. 1(a)), refrigeration power $<Q_c>$ is equal to the work flow $<W_e>$ because $<Q_{pt}>$ is zero, which gives

$$<Q_c> \quad =<H_{pt}> \qquad =<W_{pt}> \qquad = <W_e>. \tag{4}$$

When total loss, corresponding to an equivalent heat in-flow $<Q_{loss}>$, is included, Eq. (4) becomes

$$<Q_c> + <Q_{loss}> \qquad =<H_{pt}> \qquad =<W_{pt}> \qquad =<W_e>, \tag{5}$$

which means that

$$<Q_c> < <W_e>. \tag{6}$$

On the contrary, Fig. 5 shows that the refrigeration power extends beyond $<W_e>$, indicated by the arrows, in a higher temperature range. Therefore, we conclude that part of the enthalpy flow $<H_{pt}>$ is released into the room-temperature environment as heat flow $<Q_h>$ (Fig. 1(b)):

$$<Q_c> + <Q_{loss}> \qquad =<H_{pt}> \qquad = <W_e> + <Q_h>. \tag{7}$$

Figure 6 shows the energy balance between enthalpy flow in the pulse tube ($<H_{pt}> = <W_e> + <Q_h>$) and effective heat input ($<Q_c> + <Q_{loss}>$). Letting the minimum temperature be T_1 for $<W_e>=W_{e1}$, we get

$$Q_{loss}(T_1) \quad = W_{e1} + Q_h(W_{e1}) \tag{8}$$

because $<Q_c>$ vanishes at the minimum temperature. If the minimum temperature rises to T_2 because of the work flow $<W_e>$ decreasing from W_{e1} to

W_{e2} ($W_{e1} > W_{e2}$), a similar equation can be obtained:

$$Q_{loss}(T_2) = W_{e2} + Q_h(W_{e2}). \tag{9}$$

On the other hand, if the temperature is kept at T_2 by applying a constant heat flow Q_c, we get

$$Q_{loss}(T_2) + Q_c = W_{e1} + Q_h(W_{e1}). \tag{10}$$

From Eqs. (9) and (10), we get

$$Q_c + W_{e2} + Q_h(W_{e2}) = W_{e1} + Q_h(W_{e1}), \tag{11}$$

which leads to

$$Q_h(W_{e1}) - Q_h(W_{e2}) = Q_c - (W_{e1} - W_{e2}) \tag{12}$$

The dotted lines in Fig. 7 correspond to the slope of the straight line in Fig. 3 and show the rise of the minimum temperature caused by the decrease in work flow $<W_e>$. The curve slopes (solid lines) fitted to the experimental points of the refrigeration power measurements are smaller than the slopes of the dotted lines. This result denotes

$$Q_c < (W_{e1} - W_{e2}), \tag{13}$$

as schematically shown in Fig. 7. Finally, Eqs. (12) and (13) lead to

$$Q_h(W_{e1}) < Q_h(W_{e2}). \tag{14}$$

Equation (14) suggests that the increase in work flow $<W_e>$ makes heat flow $<Q_h>$ smaller although it makes total enthalpy flow $<H_{pt}>$ larger.

5. Conclusions

1. A piston mounted on the hot end of the pulse tube can further reduce the minimum temperature as compared to the basic pulse-tube refrigerator.
2. The minimum temperature lowers further as work flow reaching the hot-end piston rises by increasing the piston stroke and/or by adjusting the phase difference between pressure oscillation and piston motion.
3. Refrigeration power exceeds the work flow in a higher-temperature range, suggesting that part of the enthalpy flow in the pulse tube is released into the room-temperature environment before reaching the hot-end piston.
4. The increase in work flow reaching the hot-end piston reduces heat flow in the pulse tube although it makes total enthalpy flow larger, suggesting that the work flow becomes more important as the total enthalpy flow (refrigeration power) increases.
5. The hot-end piston model is more suitable for low frequency operation than orifice pulse-tube refrigerators. This model reached 70 K with a low frequency of 1.3 Hz.

Acknowledgements

The authors would like to thank Dr. Hiroyuki Yamakawa and Dr. Taiichiro Ohtsuka of ULVAC Japan Ltd for their valuable discussions.

References

[1] W. E. Gifford, and R. C. Longsworth, "Surface heat pumping," *Adv Cryog Eng*, vol. 11, pp. 171-179, 1966.

[2] E. I. Mikulin, A. A. Tarasov, and M. P. Shkrebyonock, "Low-temperature expansion pulse tube," *Adv Cryog Eng*, vol. 29, pp. 629-637, 1984.

[3] R. Radebaugh, J. Zimmerman, D. R. Smith, and B. Louie, "A comparison of three types of pulse tube refrigerators: new methods for reaching 60 K," *Adv Cryog Eng*, vol. 31, pp. 779-789, 1986.

[4] A. Tominaga, "Thermoacoustic theory and its application to refrigerators," *Proc 3rd Japanese-Sino Joint Seminar on Small Refrigerators and Related Topics*, pp. 141-146, 1989.

[5] G. W. Swift, "Thermoacoustic engines," *J Acoust Soc Am.*, vol. 84, no. 4, pp. 1145-1180, 1988.

[6] Masahiko Kasuya, Masayuki Nakatsu, Qiquan Geng, Junpei Yuyama, and Eiichi Goto, "Heat and work flows in the pulse tube" to be published in

Cryogenics

[7] Y. Matsubara, and A. Miyake, "Alternative methods of the orifice pulse tube refrigerator," *Proc 5th Intern Cryocooler Conf*, pp. 127-135, 1988.

[8] R. C. Longthworth, "An experimental investigation of pulse tube refrigeration heat pumping rates.," *Adv Cryog Eng*, vol. 12, pp. 608-618, 1967.

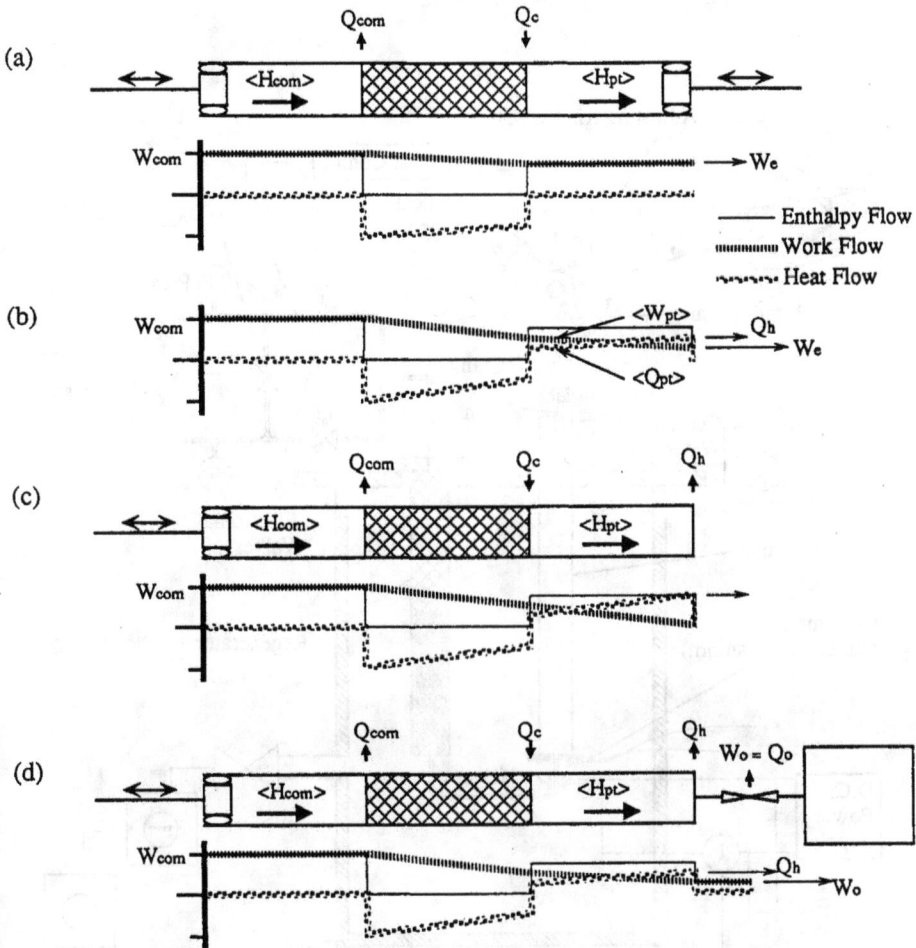

Fig. 1 Schematic diagrams showing configurations of pulse-tube refrigerators and their enthalpy flow;
(a): Ideal enthalpy flow in the pulse-tube refrigerator with a hot-end piston.
(b): Actual enthalpy flow in it. (c): Enthalpy flow in the basic pulse-tube refrigerator.
(d): Enthalpy flow in the orifice pulse-tube refrigerator.

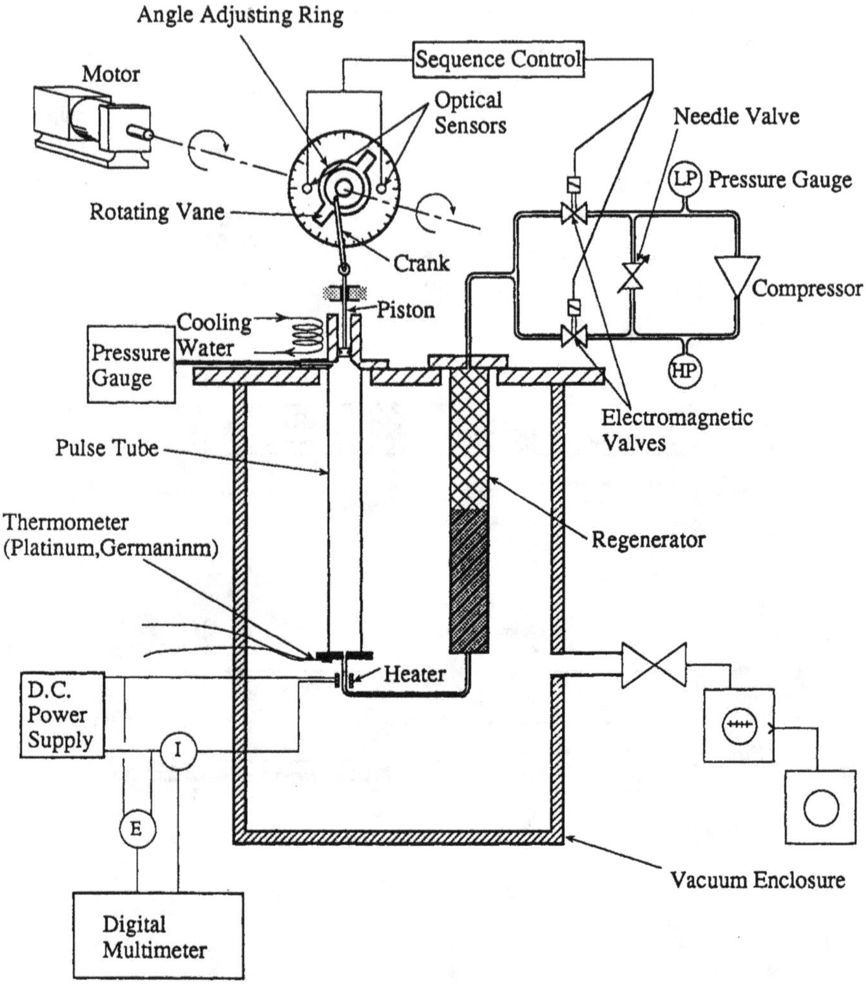

Fig. 2 Schematic diagram of the experimental arrangement of the pulse-tube refrigerator .

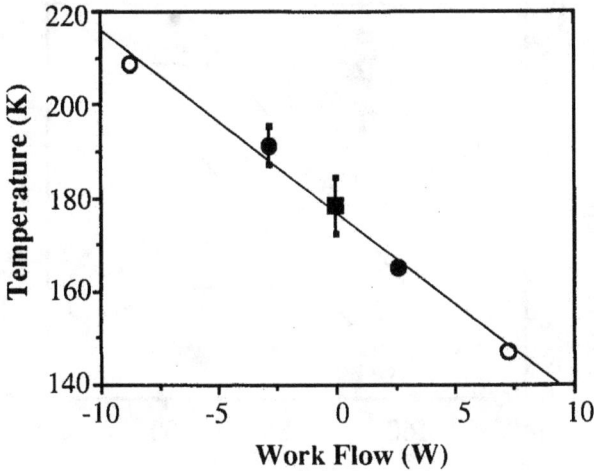

Fig. 3 Minimum-temperature change when the phase difference and piston stroke are changed. Open circles: 30 mm strokes; Solid circles: 10 mm strokes; Solid square: no piston motion.

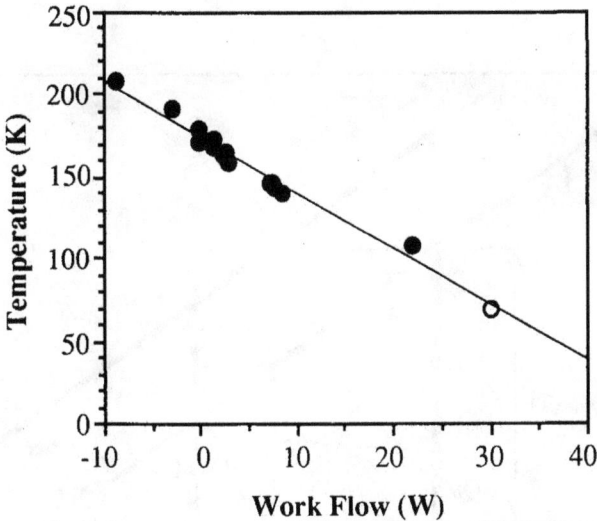

Fig. 4 Minimum temperature as a function of work flow reaching the hot-end piston. Maximum pressures are 0.86-1.01 MPa, minimum pressures are 0.21-0.29 MPa, and cycle periods are 0.62-0.74 s for the solid circles. The open circle denotes the lowest temperature (70 K) achieved in this work with a work flow of 30.1 W (maximum pressure: 1.82 MPa, minimum pressure: 1.12 MPa) and a cycle period of 0.74 s.

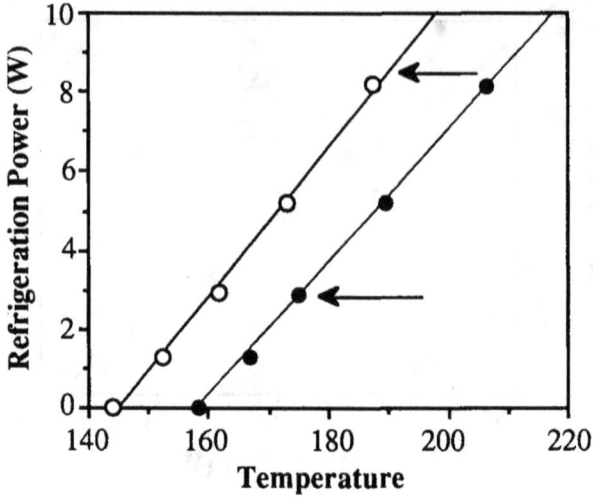

Fig. 5 Temperature dependence of refrigeration power. Solid circles: 10 mm strokes; Open circles: 30 mm strokes. Arrows indicate work flow reaching the hot-end piston.

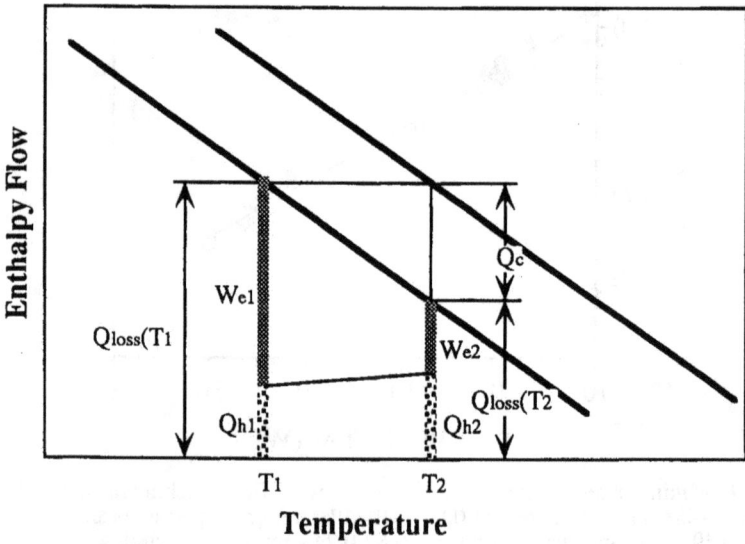

Fig. 6 Enthalpy-flow balance in the pulse tube.

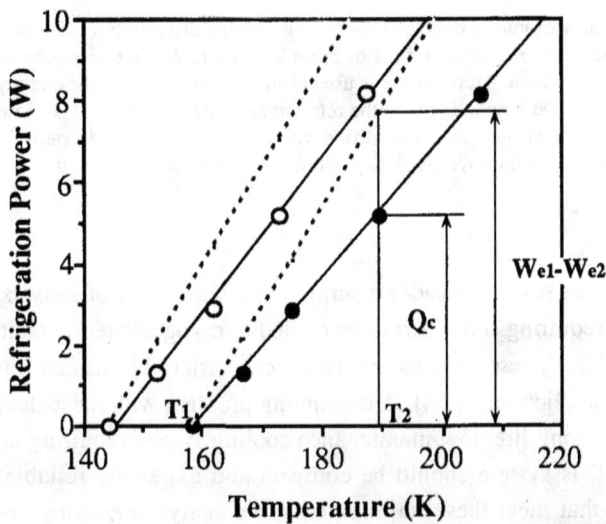

Fig. 7   Minimum-temperature change caused by the change of work flow reaching the hot-end piston and a comparison with refrigeration power.

Entropy Production Analysis of Refrigerators

Qiquan Geng, Junpei Yuyama, and Eiichi Goto

Abstract

This paper examines how the entropy is generated in a refrigeration system and looks at what the parameter dependences of those losses are, why the refrigeration power per unit mass flow rate in a refrigerator is usually small, how to reduce the entropy production in refrigerator and how to increase the refrigeration power per unit mass flow rate. Based on the theoretical analysis, a modified version pulse-tube refrigerator is suggested. Additional ways to improve efficiency of refrigerators are also proposed.

1. Introduction

Over the past several decades a surprisingly wide array of sensors, instruments and devices requiring some part to be cooled to cryogenic temperatures have been developed [1,2]. These devices are used for a variety of military, civil, scientific and medical applications [3,4]. A continuing problem with these devices has been the need for a long-life, low-maintenance cooling system requiring no special skill to operate. This system should be compact and extremely reliable. To develop cryocoolers that meet these requirements, we analyzed entropy production in a typical refrigeration system. In this paper, the results are given, and some potential applications are suggested.

2. Entropy Analysis

2.1 Basic equation

The energy conservation law of the working fluid (helium gas) in refrigerators in the absence of an external field [5] is:

$$\frac{\partial}{\partial t}\left(\rho\varepsilon+\frac{1}{2}\rho v^2\right)+\nabla\cdot\left[\rho\vec{v}\left(\frac{1}{2}v^2+\varepsilon+\frac{p}{\rho}\right)+\vec{Q'}\right]=0$$

(2.1.1)

where the dissipative contribution $\vec{Q'}$ to the energy flux density is given by:

$$Q'_i=q_i+\tau_{i\alpha}v_\alpha$$

(2.1.2)

where

$$\vec{q} = -\kappa \nabla T \qquad (2.1.3)$$

and

$$\tau_{i\alpha} = -\eta \left(\frac{\partial v_i}{\partial r_\alpha} + \frac{\partial v_\alpha}{\partial r_i} - \frac{2}{3} \delta_{i\alpha} \nabla \cdot \vec{v} \right) - \zeta \delta_{i\alpha} \nabla \cdot \vec{v} \qquad (2.1.4)$$

Here ζ is the bulk viscosity, κ the thermal conductivity and η the viscosity.

The law of momentum conservation follows the Navier-Stokes equation is:

$$\frac{\partial \rho v_i}{\partial t} + \frac{\partial}{\partial r_\alpha}(P_{i\alpha} + \tau_{i\alpha}) = 0 \qquad (2.1.5)$$

where $P_{i\alpha}$ is the Euler stress tensor:

$$P_{i\alpha} = p\delta_{i\alpha} + \rho v_i v_\alpha \qquad (2.1.6)$$

The mass and entropy conservation, as well as the Navier-Stokes equation for a classical fluid are:

$$\frac{\partial \rho}{\partial t} + \nabla \cdot \rho \vec{v} = 0 \qquad (2.1.7)$$

$$\frac{\partial \rho s}{\partial t} + \nabla \cdot \left(\rho s \vec{v} + \frac{\vec{q}}{T} \right) = \frac{\Sigma}{T} \qquad (2.1.8)$$

$$\rho \frac{Dv_i}{Dt} = -\frac{\partial p}{\partial r_i} - \frac{\partial \tau_{i\alpha}}{\partial r_\alpha}$$

$$(2.1.9)$$

where s is the entropy per unit mass and Σ/T is the entropy production

$$\Sigma = -\frac{\vec{q} \cdot \nabla T}{T} - \tau_{i\alpha} \frac{\partial v_i}{\partial r_\alpha}$$

$$(2.1.10)$$

Expanding Eq.(2.1.1) leads to:

$$\rho T \frac{\partial s}{\partial t} + \rho \frac{\partial}{\partial t}\left(\frac{v^2}{2}\right) + \rho \vec{v} \cdot \nabla\left(\frac{v^2}{2}\right) + \rho T \vec{v} \cdot \nabla s +$$

$$\vec{v} \cdot \nabla p + \nabla \cdot \vec{q} \, \frac{\partial}{\partial r_i}(\tau_{i\alpha}v_\alpha) = 0$$

$$(2.1.11)$$

where Eq.(2.1.7) and the thermodynamical expression

$$\varepsilon = Ts - pV = Ts - p/\rho = h - p/\rho$$
$$d\varepsilon = Tds - pdV$$
$$dh = Tds + dp/\rho + \mu dn$$

$$(2.1.12)$$

has been used. Substituting Eq.(2.1.6) into Eq.(2.1.5), we obtain:

$$\rho \frac{\partial v_i}{\partial t} + \frac{\partial p}{\partial r_i} + \rho v_\alpha \frac{\partial v_i}{\partial r_\alpha} + \frac{\partial \tau_{i\alpha}}{\partial r_\alpha} = 0$$

$$(2.1.13)$$

If we multiply this equation by Σv_i we get:

$$\rho\frac{\partial}{\partial t}\left(\frac{v^2}{2}\right) + \rho\vec{v}\cdot\ \nabla\left(\frac{v^2}{2}\right) - \tau_{i\alpha}\frac{\partial v_i}{\partial r_\alpha} +$$

$$\vec{v}\cdot\ \nabla p + \frac{\partial}{\partial r_i}(\tau_{i\alpha}v_\alpha) = 0 \tag{2.1.14}$$

Substituting Eq.(2.1.14) into Eq.(2.1.11) and applying the Maxwell equations, we obtain:

$$\rho T\frac{\partial T}{\partial t}\left(\frac{\partial s}{\partial T}\right)_p + \rho T\frac{\partial p}{\partial t}\left(\frac{\partial s}{\partial p}\right)_T + \rho T\vec{v}\cdot\ \nabla T\left(\frac{\partial s}{\partial T}\right)_p$$

$$\rho T\vec{v}\cdot\ \nabla p\left(\frac{\partial s}{\partial p}\right)_T + \nabla\cdot\ \vec{q} + \tau_{i\alpha}\frac{\partial v_i}{\partial r_\alpha} =$$

$$\rho C_p\frac{\partial T}{\partial t} + \frac{T}{\rho}\frac{\partial p}{\partial t}\left(\frac{\partial \rho}{\partial T}\right)_p + \rho C_p\vec{v}\cdot\ \nabla T$$

$$\frac{T}{\rho}\left(\frac{\partial \rho}{\partial T}\right)_p \vec{v}\cdot\ \nabla p + \nabla\cdot\ \vec{q} + \tau_{i\alpha}\frac{\partial v_i}{\partial r_\alpha} = 0 \tag{2.1.15}$$

By assuming that the working fluid follows the ideal gas law, we end up with the basic equation for pipe flow:

$$\rho C_p\frac{\partial T}{\partial t} = \frac{\partial p}{\partial t} - \rho C_p\vec{v}\cdot\ \nabla T + \kappa\Delta T + \vec{v}\cdot\ \nabla p - \tau_{i\alpha}\frac{\partial v_i}{\partial r_\alpha} \tag{2.1.16}$$

2.2 Assumptions in refrigerator design:

Even with Eq.(2.1.16), the analytical solution of refrigerators is still very difficult to obtain. Therefore, some assumptions were made. These included: (1) the working fluid is to be an ideal gas; (2) the velocity of fluid in a pipe can be expressed as $\vec{v} = [0,0,v_z(r)]$ and occurs in a laminar flow (Poiseuille flow); (3) neglecting pressure dependence in the expression of gas heat capacity, i.e., using the average value of pressure p_0 instead of p when estimating gas heat capacity; (4) the temperature variation on r is small $T \approx T_w$; (5) temperature variation along the wall is linear, i.e., dT/dz = constant; (6) $\partial T/\partial t \ll T/\tau$.

Based on these assumptions, in a steady state, we have:

$$\frac{\partial p}{\partial r_i} = -\frac{\partial \tau_{ij}}{\partial r_j}$$

(2.2.1)

$$\nabla \cdot \vec{v} = 0$$

(2.2.2)

It can be shown after some mathematical manipulation that

$$\vec{v} \cdot \nabla p - \tau_{i\alpha} \frac{\partial v_i}{\partial r_\alpha} = -\frac{16\eta U_0^2}{\pi a^2}\left(1 \cdot \frac{2r^2}{a^2}\right)$$

(2.2.3)

where U_0 is the volume flow rate in the refrigerator. Comparison with pressure oscillation term $\partial p/\partial t$ and shuttle term $-\rho C_p \vec{v} \cdot \nabla T$., the term on the right side of Eq.(2.2.3) is very small. Therefore, we have:

$$\rho C_p \frac{\partial T}{\partial t} = \frac{\partial p}{\partial t} - \rho C_p \vec{v} \cdot \nabla T + \kappa \Delta T$$

(2.2.4)

2.3 Pressure oscillation loss

Now, let us look at the temperature variation in the refrigerator due to pressure oscillation. If we define $c_g = \rho C_p$, we can rewrite the basic equation as:

$$c_g \frac{\partial T}{\partial t} = \kappa \Delta T + \frac{\partial p}{\partial t}$$

(2.3.1)

$$p = p_0 + p_1 e^{j\omega t}$$
$$T = T_0 + (T_1 + T_2(r))e^{j(\omega t + \alpha)}$$

(2.3.2)

Substituting Eqs.(2.3.2) into Eq.(2.3.1), we obtain:

$$T_1 + T_2(r) = \frac{\kappa}{j\omega c_g}\Delta T_2(r) + \frac{p_1}{c_g}e^{-j\alpha}$$

(2.3.3)

This leads to:

$$T_1 = \frac{p_1}{c_g}e^{-j\alpha}$$

(2.3.4)

$$T_2(r) = \frac{\kappa}{j\omega c_g}\Delta T_2(r)$$

(2.3.5)

In cylindrical coordinates, Eq.(2.3.5) becomes

$$r^2\frac{\partial^2 T_2}{\partial r^2} + r\frac{\partial T_2}{\partial r} + r^2\frac{\omega c_g}{j\kappa}T_2 = 0$$

(2.3.6)

If we define:

$$r' = \sqrt{\frac{\omega c_g}{j\kappa}}r = \sqrt{\frac{\delta}{j}}\,r$$

(2.3.7)

we obtain a standard Bessel equation. Its solution is:

$$T_2 = \xi J_0(r') = \xi J_0\left(\sqrt{\frac{\delta}{j}}\,r\right)$$

(2.3.8)

Applying the boundary condition at the wall of the tube

$$2\pi a W c_w \frac{\partial T}{\partial t}(r=a) = -2\pi a\kappa\nabla_r T(r=a)$$

(2.3.9)

and expanding J_0 and J_1 to the term, up to 6th, we obtain:

$$\xi = \cfrac{T_1}{\cfrac{\kappa}{j\omega Wc_w}\sqrt{\cfrac{\delta}{j}}\, J_1\left(\sqrt{\cfrac{\delta}{j}}\, a\right) - J_0\left(\sqrt{\cfrac{\delta}{j}}\, a\right)}$$

$$= \cfrac{-\cfrac{p_1}{c_g}e^{-j\alpha}}{\left[(1+2\beta) - \cfrac{\delta^2 a^4}{192}(3+2\beta)\right] - \cfrac{\delta a^2}{4j}(1+\beta)} \tag{2.3.10}$$

where W is the wall thickness of the tube, and

$$\beta = \frac{ac_g}{4Wc_w} \tag{2.3.11}$$

This leads to:

$$\nabla_r T = \nabla_r T_2\, e^{j(\omega t + \alpha)}$$

$$= -\xi\sqrt{\frac{\delta}{j}}\, J_1\left(\sqrt{\frac{\delta}{j}}\, r\right) e^{j(\omega t + \alpha)} \tag{2.3.12}$$

and

$$|\nabla_r T|^2 = \xi\tilde{\xi}\left|\sqrt{\frac{\delta}{j}}\, J_1\left(\sqrt{\frac{\delta}{j}}\, r\right)\right|^2$$

$$= \frac{|T_1|^2\delta^2 r^2}{4}\cdot\cfrac{1 + \cfrac{\delta^2 r^4}{192} + \cfrac{\delta^4 r^8}{192^2}}{\left[(1+2\beta) - \cfrac{\delta^2 a^4}{192}(3+2\beta)\right]^2 + \cfrac{\delta^2 a^4}{16}(1+\beta)^2} \tag{2.3.13}$$

Thus, the pressure oscillation loss in refrigerators is:

$$\frac{\partial G_{\dot{p}}}{\partial z} = \text{Re} \int_0^a 2\pi r \frac{\kappa|\nabla T|^2}{|T|^2} \, dr =$$

$$\frac{\pi p_1^2 \omega^2 a^4}{8\kappa|T|^2} \frac{1 + \frac{\delta^2 a^4}{192} + \frac{\delta^4 a^8}{192^2}}{\left[(1+2\beta) - \frac{\delta^2 a^4}{192}(3+2\beta)\right]^2 + \frac{\delta^2 a^4}{16}(1+\beta)^2}$$

(2.3.14)

2.4 Shuttle loss

Shuttle loss in the refrigerator is determined by following equations:

$$c_g \frac{\partial T}{\partial t} = -c_g \vec{v} \cdot \nabla T + \kappa \Delta T$$

(2.4.1)

and

$$p = p_0 + p_1 e^{j\omega t}$$
$$T = T_0 + (T_1(r) + T_2(r))e^{j(\omega t + \alpha)}$$
$$T_1(r) = T_1^0 + T_1'(1 - r^2/a^2)$$
$$v_z = \frac{2U_0}{\pi a^2}(1 - r^2/a^2)e^{j(\omega t + \phi)}$$

(2.4.2)

Substituting Eq.(2.4.2) into Eq.(2.4.1) and conducting similar mathematical procedures as in section 2.3, we obtain the shuttle loss in our system:

$$\frac{\partial G_{\dot{s}}}{\partial z} = \frac{\kappa U_0^2 T_{zz}^2 \delta^2 (1+2\beta)^2}{2\pi B_2 |T|^2 \omega^2} B'(\beta, \delta)$$

(2.4.3)

where

$$T_{zz} = \frac{dT}{dz}$$

(2.4.4)

$$B_2 = \left[(1+2\beta) - \frac{\delta^2 a4}{192}(3+2\beta)\right]^2 + \frac{\delta^2 a4}{16}(1+\beta)^2$$

(2.4.5)

and

$$B'(\beta,\delta) = \left[\left(\frac{1+\beta}{1+2\beta}\right)^2 - \frac{2}{3}\left(\frac{1+\beta}{1+2\beta}\right) + \frac{1}{8}\right] + \frac{\delta^2 a4}{482}\left[\left(\frac{3+2\beta}{1+2\beta}\right)^2 - \left(\frac{3+2\beta}{1+2\beta}\right) + \frac{1}{3}\right]$$

(2.4.6)

2.5 Cross term

It is very interesting to examine the expression of the cross term of temperature oscillation due to pressure oscillation and shuttle flow. The result is:

$$\frac{\partial G_{ps}}{\partial z} = \frac{p_1 U_0 T_{zz}\delta a^2(1+2\beta)}{B_2|T|^2}\{A_1+jA_2\}e^{j(\pi/2+\phi)}$$

(2.5.1)

with

$$A_1 = \frac{1}{4}\left(\frac{1+\beta}{1+2\beta} - \frac{1}{3}\right) + \frac{\delta^2 a4}{12\times384}\left(\frac{3+2\beta}{1+2\beta}\right)$$

(2.5.2)

$$A_2 = \frac{\delta^3 a6}{6\times192^2}\left(2-3\frac{3+2\beta}{1+2\beta}\right)$$

(2.5.3)

Depending on the phase angle between the flow velocity and pressure, this could be either a positive or negative contribution to the entropy production:

$$\left(\frac{\partial G_{ps}}{\partial z}\right)_{tot} = \pm\frac{p_1 U_0 T_{zz}\delta a^2(1+2\beta)}{B_2|T|^2}\times\{-2A_1\}$$

(2.5.4)

for $\phi = \pi/2$, $3\pi/2$, and

$$\left(\frac{\partial G_{p's}}{\partial z}\right)_{tot} = \pm\frac{p_1 U_0 T_{zz}\delta a^2(1+2\beta)}{B_2|T|^2}\times\{-2A_2\}$$

(2.5.5)

for $\phi = 0$, π.

Numerical estimation shows that under certain conditions, Eq.(2.5.4) could contribute the same order of magnitude as Eq.(2.3.14) and Eq.(2.4.3). This indicates a way to reduce the entropy production in refrigerator systems.

2.6 Viscosity loss

In refrigerator systems, the viscosity loss is represented by $\dfrac{\tau_{i\alpha}}{T}\dfrac{\partial v_i}{\partial r_\alpha}$ in Eq.(2.1.10). In steady-state conditions, $\tau_{\alpha\beta}$ can be expressed as:

$$\tau_{\alpha\beta} = -\eta\left(\frac{\partial v_\alpha}{\partial r_\beta} + \frac{\partial v_\beta}{\partial r_\alpha}\right)$$

(2.6.1)

After some mathematical manipulation, we obtain:

$$\frac{\partial G_\eta}{\partial z} = \frac{8\eta U_0^2}{\pi|T|a^4}$$

(2.6.2)

2.7 Conduction loss

The conduction loss along the z direction can be easily derived:

$$\frac{\partial G_z}{\partial z} = \frac{\pi a^2 T_{zz}^2 \kappa}{|T|^2}\left(\frac{2W}{a}\times\frac{\kappa_w}{\kappa}+1\right)$$

(2.7.1)

where the first term on the right is the heat conduction loss along the wall and the second term is the loss among the gas.

2.8 Discussion

We now have all the formulae representing losses in a refrigerator system. From these formulae we found that all the losses have a different temperature, size, dimension and material dependence. When designing a system, all these factors should be optimized and the mass flow rate should be determined by considering not only the cooling power, but also the cooling power per unit mass as well as the refrigerator sequences.

The most important factor is that the Reynolds number should be kept small. For this purpose, a multitube structure refrigerator is proposed. Through our calculations we found that those fine tubes will not greatly contribute to loss provided the specific heat and thermal conductivity of the construction material is not large and the wall is thin.

3. Application

3.1 Pulse-tube refrigerator design

In refrigerators using a gas as the working substance, the gas expands in the low-temperature part to produce refrigeration power. Work done by the gas is conveyed up through a piston or displacer from the low-temperature part to the room-temperature part, and is then released into the room-temperature environment. If expansion work can be transferred through a gas column, a refrigerator can work without moving components in the low-temperature part. The pulse tube in pulse-tube refrigerators can be regarded as belonging to this category.

Based on the analysis in section 2, a new model of the pulse-tube refrigerator has been proposed [6,7]. This model has an expansion piston at room temperature. The advantage compared with the usual orifice pulse-tube refrigerator is that there is no need for an irreversible element such as an orifice or a throttle valve. In the new model, the expansion work generated at the cold end of the pulse tube is conveyed through the pulse tube, and is then recovered by the room temperature piston. This type of pulse tube has been tested experimentally. The results are given in Refs. [8,9].

3.2 High-efficiency heat exchanger or regenerator design

Based on the formulae given in section 2, we can easily derive the entropy production in a heat exchanger or a regenerator system. The main losses are:

(1) Shuttle heat transfer loss

$$G_s = \frac{11}{48\pi} \frac{\mu^2 C_P^2 M^2}{\kappa_1 z} \left(\frac{\delta T}{T}\right)^2$$

$$= \frac{11}{48\pi} \frac{\lambda^2 a^2 C_P^2 M^2}{\kappa_1 z} \left(\frac{\delta T}{T}\right)^2 = B_1 \lambda^2 a^2 \tag{3.2.1}$$

where M is the molar mass of helium gas and

$$B_1 = \frac{11}{48\pi} \frac{C_P^2 M^2}{\kappa_1 z} \left(\frac{\delta T}{T}\right)^2$$

(2) Viscosity loss

$$G_\eta = \frac{8\eta U^2 z}{\pi T a^4} = \frac{8\eta V^2 \mu^2 z}{\pi T a^4} = \frac{A_1 \lambda^2}{a^2} \tag{3.2.2}$$

where

$$\mu = \lambda a$$

$$\lambda = \frac{\pi \eta N_r}{2M}$$

$$A = \frac{8\eta V^2 \lambda z}{\pi T} = A_1 \lambda$$

$$\kappa_1 = C_1 \kappa_{He}$$

$$\kappa_2 = C_2 \kappa_{He}$$

with the parameters: V the volume flow rate per mole, κ_1 the effective thermal conductivity of cross section of the heat exchanger, κ_2 the thermal conductivity of the wall.

(3) Conduction loss

$$G_z = \frac{\pi a^2 \kappa_2}{z} \left(\frac{dT}{T}\right)^2 = B_2 a^2 \tag{3.2.3}$$

where

$$B_2 = \frac{\pi \kappa_2}{z} \left(\frac{dT}{T}\right)^2$$

By combining these three losses, we can obtain the total loss per unit molar flow:

$$g = \frac{1}{\mu_{tot}} [(G_\eta + G_s + G_z)N]$$
$$= \frac{(G_\eta + G_s + G_z)}{\lambda a}$$
$$= \frac{A_1 \lambda}{a^3} + B_1 \lambda a + \frac{B_2 a}{\lambda} \qquad (3.2.4)$$

where

$$N = \frac{\mu_{tot}}{\mu}$$

Optimizing Eq.(3.2.4) leads to:

$$\lambda_{op}^2 = \frac{24\pi^2 \kappa_1 \kappa_2}{11\, C_\beta^2 M^2} = \frac{\pi^2 \eta^2 N_r^2}{4\, M^2} \qquad (3.2.5)$$

$$N_r(op) = 4.195(C_1 C_2)^{.5} \qquad (3.2.6)$$

$$a_{op} = \left(\frac{A_1}{B_1}\right)^{.25} = 1.0005 \times 10^{-4} T^{1.0735}$$
$$\times z^{.5} p^{-.5} (\delta T)^{-.5} (.01 C_1)^{.25} \qquad (3.2.7)$$

$$N_{op} = 3.824 \times 10^7 T^{-1.72} \dot{M}$$
$$\times z^{-.5} p^{.5} (\delta T)^{.5} (C_1)^{-.75} (C_2)^{-.5} \qquad (3.2.8)$$

A regenerator based on the above considerations has been used in experiments [8,9]. Details of these experiments can be found in Refs. [8,9].

4. Summary

In this report, we performed a thermodynamic analysis of the entropy production in a refrigerator system. Our results show that in a refrigerator, different types of losses exist, having a different temperature, pressure ratio, size, and mass flow rate, as well as material dependence. This indicates that an optimal condition should exist. On the basis of this analysis and the present available technology, a new model of the pulse-tube refrigerator is proposed. The optimal condition for designing a regenerator or heat exchanger is given.

Acknowledgements

The authors would like to express their grateful thanks to Dr. T. Ohtsuka of ULVAC Japan Ltd. for his valuable discussion.

References

[1] A. Barone, and G. Paterno, *Physics and Applications of the Josephson Effect*, John Willy & Sons, Inc., 1982.

[2] K. D. Timmerhaus, *Int. J. Refrig.*, **12**, 246, 1989.

[3] G. Walker, *Miniature Refrigerators for Cryogenic Sensors and Cold Electronics*, Oxford University Press, Monographs on Cryogenics, Oxford UK, 1989.

[4] J.L. Smith, G.Y. Robinson and Y. Iwasa, *Office Naval Research Contract No. N0001483K0327*, Washington, DC, USA, 1984.

[5] H. Schlichting, *Boundary-Layer Theory*, 7th(English) edn. (Translated by J. Kestin), McGRAW-HILL Book Company, New York, 1979.

[6] E. Goto, Q. Geng and J. Yuyama, *Japanese Patent 02-170787*, in application.

[7] J. Yuyama, M. Kasuya, Q. Geng and E. Goto, *Japanese Patent*, in application.

[8] M. Kasuya, M. Nakatsu, Q. Geng, J. Yuyama and E. Goto, *8th RIKEN Symposium on Josephson Electronics*, 41, 1991.

[9] M. Kasuya, M. Nakatsu, Q. Geng, J. Yuyama and E. Goto, to be published in *Cryogenics*, 1991.

Reprinted with permission from *J. Mechanical Engineering Soc. Japan*,
A-57(537), 1191 – 1194 (1991).

Reduction of the Maximum Principal Stress
by Multilayering of Electrodeposited Bellows

Kazunori Chihara, Masahiko Kasuya, Junpei Yuyama,

and Eiichi Goto

Abstract

The maximum principal stress in an electrodeposited multilayer bellows (EDM bellows) is studied by the finite element method. The EDM bellows is made of two kinds of materials which have different Young's modulus , by an electrodeposition method. It is found that the maximum principal stress in the EDM bellows is smaller than that in a single layer bellows. This behavior is similar to that expected for a formed multilayer bellows.

1. Introduction

A refrigerator with a bellows expansion engine is very reliable because no seal component is needed.[1] [2] [3] However, there remains a problem of the lifetime of the refrigerator due to fatigue failure of the bellows itself. To extend the lifetime, the maximum stress in a cycle, which is induced by deflection or internal pressure , should be as small as possible . The maximum stress can be smaller than that in a single layer bellows by multilayering the bellows wall. Ohtsubo et. al. have shown this reduction of stress in the formed multilayer bellows.[4] The formed multilayer bellows, however, is limited in miniaturization size. This is an obstacle in making a small refrigerator. The electrodeposited single layer bellows with 1.5 mm outer diameter is manufactured commercially. In this paper, the stress analysis results of the EDM bellows by the finite element method (FEM) is shown. The analysis is done in two steps. First, the maximum principal stress in the EDM bellows is studied as a function of Young's modulus and sum of the thickness of the hard layers. Second, the maximum principal stress in three types of bellows with various total thicknesses are compared.

2. FEM Analysis

The MARC program is used for FEM analysis.[5] The geometry of the bellows is 80 mm in outer diameter, 50 mm in inner diameter, 60 mm in length and 12 convolutions.

A single layer bellows is assumed to be made of nickel, which is widely used for electrodeposited bellows. The values for Young's modulus and Poisson's ratio used are extrapolated values at 0 K[6] and they are 234 GPa and 0.29, respectively. Half of one pitch is analyzed because of the symmetry of the bellows[†] and divided into 396 elements with 1333 nodes. The load and boundary conditions are 2.53×10^5 Pa (= 2.50 atm) of internal pressure and 4.5 mm of axial deflection. These values are determined by the operating conditions of the refrigerator (1 W at 4.2 K).

The EDM bellows analyzed has three layers. (Fig. 1) The outer and inner layers are assumed to be hard layers, and the center layer is assumed to be a soft layer. The geometry is the same as that for the single layer bellows. Young's modulus for the hard layers is the same as that in the single layer bellows. Young's modulus for the soft layer is varied from 1/10 to 1/100,000 of that of nickel at 0 K. Poisson's ratio is 0.29. The sum of the thickness of the two hard layers is also varied. In the analysis of the EDM bellows, it is assumed that no separation and/or slip occurs at the boundary between the hard and soft layers.

The formed bellows has two layers and a gap between the two layers. The thickness of each layer is half that of the single layer bellows. The Young's modulus and Poisson's ratio of each layer are the same as those in the single layer bellows. The gap is modeled by using gap elements in the MARC program.

Two boundary conditions (pressure and deflection) are applied in three ways (Fig.2) ;

     1) axial deflection is only applied

          r-direction: free at A and B

          z-direction: fixed at A

                          +4.5 / (convolutions $\times$ 2) = 0.1875 mm at B

          internal pressure: 0 Pa

     2) internal pressure is only applied

          r-direction: free at A and B

          z-direction: fixed at A and B

          internal pressure: 2.53×10^5 Pa (= 2.5 atm)

     3) both internal pressure and deflection are applied

          r-direction: free at A and B

          z-direction: fixed at A

                          +4.5 / (convolutions $\times$ 2) = 0.1875 mm at B

[†] The difference of the maximum principal stress between the half pitch model and the 6 convolutions model is 2 %.

internal pressure: 2.53×10^5 Pa (= 2.5 atm).

3. Results and Discussions

3.1 EDM Bellows

The maximum principal stress for the EDM bellows is shown in Fig. 3 as a function of the ratio of the Young's modulus of the hard layers to that of the soft layer, where the total thickness and sum of the thickness of the hard layers are 700 μm and 300 μm. The vertical axis is an absolute value of the maximum principal stress. $\text{Log}(E_{hard}/E_{soft}) = 0$ corresponds to the single layer bellows. When only axial deflection is applied as the boundary condition, which is represented with white squares in Fig.3, rapid reduction of maximum principal stress occurs around the ratio of a Young's modulus of 100-1000.

The origin of this behavior can be explained as follows; when the bellows is deformed by δ, δ is the sum of the displacement of bending deformation (δ_{bend}) and shearing deformation (δ_{shear}) with the minimum strain energy or potential energy. In the case of the single layer bellows, δ_{shear} is negligibly small compared with δ_{bend}, i.e. $\delta = \delta_{bend}$. On the other hand, in the case of the EDM bellows, as the Young's modulus of the soft layer decreases, δ_{shear} increases. Therefore, δ_{bend} of the EDM bellows is smaller than that of the single layer bellows for the same deflection. The maximum stress is proportional to δ_{bend}. Thus, the reduction of the maximum principal stress of the EDM bellows occurs.

This behavior is analyzed by a simple electrodeposited beam model. Deformations δ_{shear} and δ_{bend} for a beam are;

$$\delta_{shear} = \frac{\kappa F L}{G_{eff} A}$$

$$= \frac{\kappa F L}{G_{eff} b \, t_{total}} \, , \tag{1}$$

$$\delta_{bend} = \frac{L^3 F}{12 E_{eff} I}$$

$$= \frac{L^3 F}{E_{eff} b \, t_{total}^3} \, , \tag{2}$$

where

κ : section modulus (=3/2)

F   : external force

L   : length of the beam*

b   : width of the beam (= 1 mm : unit length)

t_{total} : thickness of the beam

A   : cross section (= b t_{total})

I   : moment of inertia of area.

E_{eff} and G_{eff} are an effective Young's modulus and stiffness of multilayer electrodeposited beam;

$$E_{eff} = \frac{E_{soft}\int_{-t_1}^{t_1} y^2\, dy + E_{hard}\left\{\int_{t_1}^{t_2} y^2\, dy + \int_{-t_2}^{-t_1} y^2\, dy\right\}}{\int_{-t_2}^{t_2} y^2\, dy},$$

$$= E_{soft}\left(\frac{t_1}{t_2}\right)^3 + E_{hard}\left\{1 - \left(\frac{t_1}{t_2}\right)^3\right\} \qquad (3)$$

$$G_{eff} = \frac{2\,t_1 + 2\,(t_2 - t_1)}{2\dfrac{t_2 - t_1}{G_{hard}} + 2\dfrac{t_1}{G_{soft}}}$$

$$= \frac{t_2}{\dfrac{t_2 - t_1}{G_{hard}} + \dfrac{t_1}{G_{soft}}}, \qquad (4)$$

where

$t_1 = t_{soft}/2$

$t_2 = t_{total}/2$

E_{hard} : Young's modulus of hard layer

E_{soft} : Young's modulus of soft layer

$G_{hard} = \dfrac{E_{hard}}{2(1 + \nu_{hard})}$: stiffness of hard layer

---

* The length of the beam (L) is assumed to be (outer diameter - inner diameter) / 2.

$$G_{soft} = \frac{E_{soft}}{2(1 + v_{soft})} \qquad : \text{stiffness of soft layer}$$

$v_{hard}, v_{soft} \qquad$: Poisson's ratio (assumed to be $v_{hard} = v_{soft} = v$).

From Eq. 1 ~ Eq. 4 , $\delta_{shear} / \delta_{bend}$ is calculated;

$$\frac{\delta_{shear}}{\delta_{bend}} = \kappa \frac{t_{total}^2}{L^2} \frac{1}{2(1 + v)} \left\{ \alpha \beta (1 - \beta^3) + \frac{\beta^3 (1 - \beta)}{\alpha} + 2\beta^4 - \beta^3 - \beta + 1 \right\},$$

$$(5)$$

where

$$\alpha \equiv \frac{E_{hard}}{E_{soft}} ,$$

$$\beta \equiv \frac{t_1}{t_2} = \frac{t_{soft}}{t_{total}} .$$

$\delta_{shear} / \delta_{bend}$ with respect to α (ratio of Young's modulus) is shown in Fig. 5. δ_{shear} is the same order of δ_{bend} around $E_{hard} / E_{soft} \approx 1000$.

When only pressure is applied as the Young's modulus of the soft layer decreases, the effective Young's modulus and stiffness of the EDM bellows also decreases. Therefore, displacement due to bending of the EDM bellows increases, and thus the maximum principal stress increases as the Young's modulus of the soft layer decreases.

When both conditions (pressure and external deflection) are applied at the same time, there is an optimum ratio of Young's modulus ($E_{hard} / E_{soft} \approx 100$) in which the maximum principal stress is at minimum value.

The maximum principal stress with respect to the sum of the thickness of the hard layers of the EDM bellows is shown in Fig. 6, where the total thickness is 700 μm and ratio of Young's modulus is 100. Figure.6 shows that the optimum sum of the thickness of the hard layer is 200 μm.

3.2 Comparison

The maximum principal stress with respect to the total thicknesses of three types of bellows (the single layer bellows, EDM bellows with $E_{hard} / E_{soft} = 100$ and 200 μm sum of the thickness of the hard layers, and the formed multilayer bellows) is shown in Fig. 7 ~ Fig. 9. The white circle, black circle and white square indicate the maximum principal stress of the single layer bellows, the EDM bellows and the formed multilayer bellows, respectively.

Figure.7 shows that the maximum principal stress due to pressure decreases as the total thickness increases. On the contrary, the maximum principal stress due to external deflection increases (Fig. 8). There is a total thickness in which the maximum principal stress has minimum value when both the pressure and external deflection are applied.

This thickness of the EDM bellows is larger than that of the single layer bellows, because the maximum principal stress due to pressure of the EDM bellows is larger and that due to external deflection is smaller than that of the single layer bellows.

However, figure.9 shows that the minimum value of the maximum principal stress of the EDM bellows (309 MPa at $t_{total} = 700$ μm) is smaller than that of the single layer bellows (342 MPa at $t_{total} = 400$ μm).

4. Summary

1. The maximum principal stress of three kind of bellows (single layer, EDM, formed bellows) is analyzed by the finite element method.

2. The maximum principal stress of the bellows can be reduced by multilayering hard and soft layers by the electrodeposition method, which behavior is similar to the formed multilayer bellows. Since a bellows with smaller and thinner thickness can be made by the electrodeposited method rather than by the formed method, the EDM bellows is useful.

References

[1] H. M. Long and F. E. Simon, *Appl, Sci. Res.*, Vol. 4 , pp. 237-242, 1954

[2] J. L. Smith, Jr, *Adv. Cryog. Eng.*, Vol. 12, pp. 595-661, 1967

[3] H. Nakashima, K. Ishibashi and H. Misawa, *Cryogenic Engineering*, Vol. 22, No.3, pp. 59-63, 1987 (in Japanese)

[4] H. Ohtsubo, K. Kobayashi, Y. Tashiro and T. Ohmori, *Nihon Zosen Gakkai Ronbunsyu,* No. 158, pp. 665-669, 1985 (in Japanese)

[5] MARC General Purpose Finite Element Program, Nippon MARC Co., Ltd.

[6] R. P. Reed and A. F. Clark, *Materials at Low Temperatures*, American Society for Metals, pp. 9, 1983

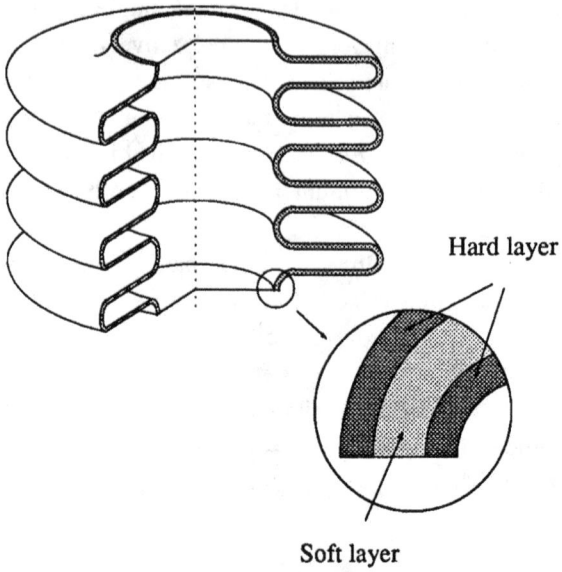

Fig. 1 EDM bellows

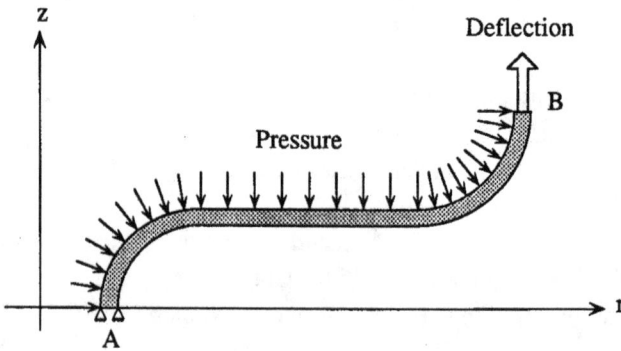

Fig. 2 Model for the finite element method

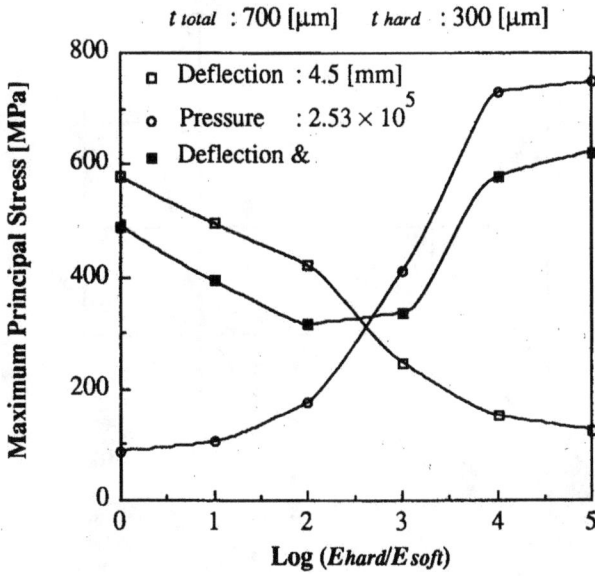

Fig. 3 Ratio of Young's modulus vs. maximum principal stress

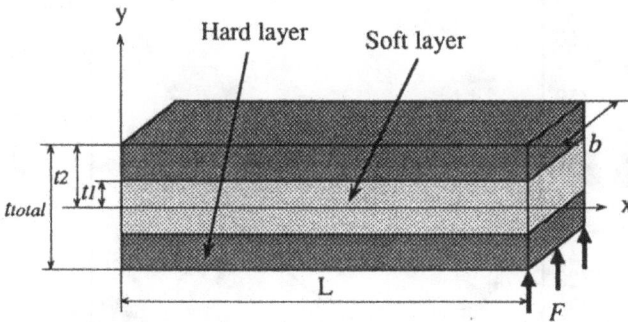

Fig. 4 Electrodeposited multilayer beam model

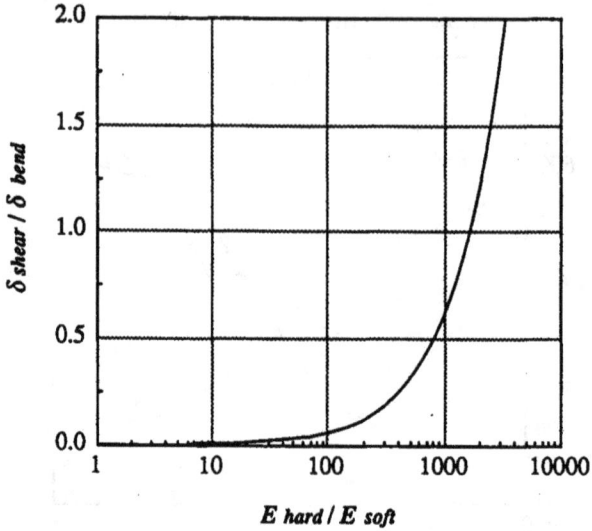

Fig. 5 Ratio of Young's modulus vs. $\delta_{shear} / \delta_{bend}$

t_{total} : 700 [μm]   , Log(E_{hard}/E_{soft}) : 2
Deflection : 4.5 [mm]   ,   Pressure : 2.53×10^5 [Pa]

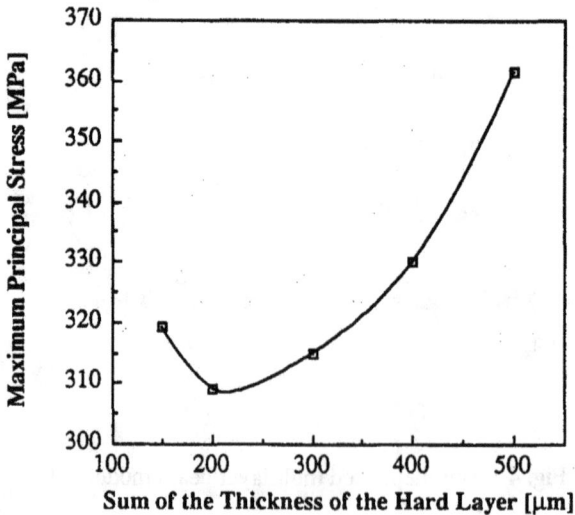

Fig. 6 Sum of the thickness of the hard layers vs. maximum principal stress

$t\,hard$: 200 [μm] , Log($E\,hard/E\,soft$) : 2
Deflection : ----- , Pressure : 2.53×10^{5}

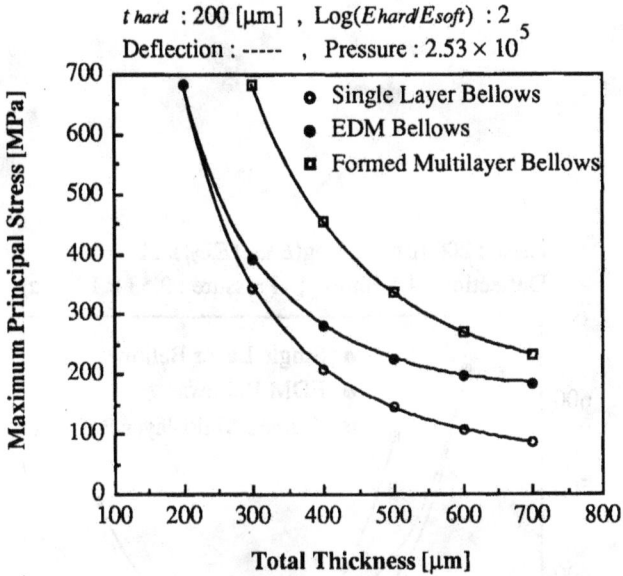

Fig.7 Total thickness vs. maximum principal stress
(internal pressure)

$t\,hard$: 200 [μm] , Log($E\,hard/E\,soft$) : 2
Deflection : 4.5 [mm] , Pressure : -----

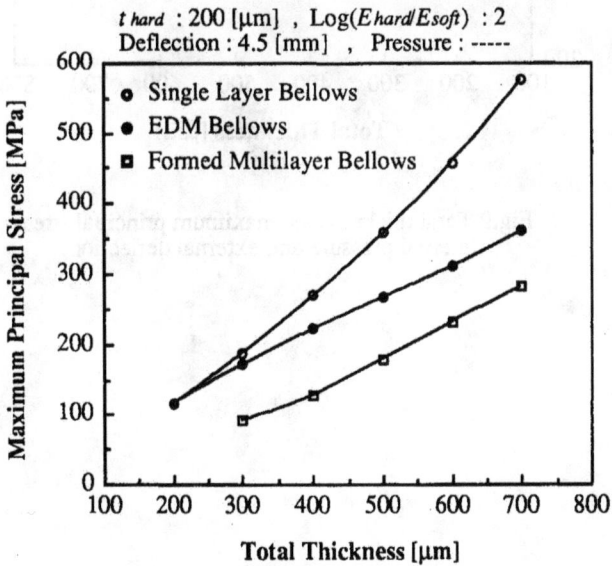

Fig.8 Total thickness vs. maximum principal stress
(external deflection)

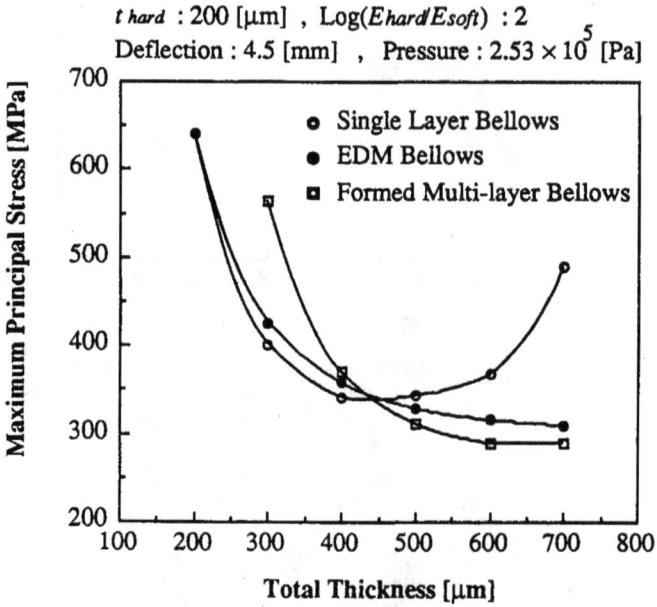

Fig.9 Total thickness vs. maximum principal stress
(internal pressure and external deflection)

Fatigue Strength of Electrodeposited Nickel Films

Masahiko Kasuya, Kazunori Chihara, Junpei Yuyama, and Eiichi Goto

Abstract

To improve the working life of bellows-expander refrigerators, information is needed on the fatigue limit of electrodeposited bellows. To this end, the fatigue strength of electrodeposited nickel films, widely used in manufacturing electrodeposited bellows, is studied. Nickel films are electrodeposited from nickel sulfamate solutions onto aluminum pipes up to 30 μm thick. The pipes are then dissolved, leaving thin-walled hollow nickel cylinders. This shape helps avoid the deteriorative effect of serrations at the edge of specimens.

A staircase-method fatigue test is carried out with a step value of 20 MPa. The fatigue limit of the nickel electrodeposited films is estimated to be 150.5 ± 22.3 MPa. The specimen is examined for thickness inhomogeneity. Standard deviation from the average thickness is evaluated to be 2.0 μm, which means that the cross-sectional area and stress values are evaluated within a margin of error of $\pm 7\%$. The effect of surface roughness on fatigue strength is also examined using two groups of different surface roughness with values of 0.49 ± 0.17 and 0.20 ± 0.09 μm. The difference in surface roughness is found to have no substantial effect on the present results.

1. Introduction

A bellows expander contributes to an increase in reliability of cryogenic refrigerators because it completely seals the working gas (usually helium gas) and prevents impurities from entering low-temperature regions. In a bellows expander, the bellows expands and contracts periodically, and the pressure inside (or outside) the bellows oscillates with a pressure difference across the bellows wall. The bellows wall thus experiences a periodic strain caused by the pressure oscillation and periodic deflection. It is therefore difficult to realize a long-life bellows expander because the periodic strain results in fatigue failure.

The authors proposed a new type of electrodeposited bellows, which is formed by alternate depositions of soft and hard layers, to decrease the stress in the bellows wall caused by the periodic strain. A theoretical stress analysis on this model was carried out using the finite element method (FEM) [1].

In order to estimate the working life of bellows expanders on the basis of the FEM analysis, the fatigue strength of constructing materials is needed. A fatigue test of electrodeposited Ni films, a suitable material for the hard layer, was carried out. Since electrodeposited Ni films are widely used in bellows manufacturing, even apart from the present electrodeposited multilayer bellows, the fatigue strength data is useful in various applications.

For the present purpose, the thickness of test specimens ranges from several μm to several tens of μm. To investigate mechanical properties of such thin specimens, it is important to avoid edge effects and to apply a uniform stress [2][3]. With flat foil specimens, it is possible that a crack will propagate from a serration at the edge, resulting in an apparent fatigue strength substantially smaller than the actual one. Thin cylindrical specimens of Ni electrodeposits were prepared to avoid edge effects. This paper describes the specimen preparation, test procedures and test results. Details have been previously described [4].

2. Testing Procedures

2.1 Preparing Specimen

The test specimen substrates are aluminum alloy pipes 9 mm in O.D. and 70 mm long. The outer 0.1 mm was peeled off to improve surface smoothness and to remove impurities. Thus, the outer diameter became 8.8 mm. The conditioning treatments were as follows:

(1) alkaline solution dip --- NaOH		5	g/l
(2) water rinse			
(3) acid dip ---------------- HNO_3		50	%
(4) water rinse			
(5) alkaline zincate dip ---- NaOH		525	g/l
	ZnO	100	g/l
	Rochelle salt	10	g/l
	$FeCl_3$	10	g/l
(6) water rinse			
(7) copper strike ---CuCN		30	g/l
	NaCN	38	g/l
	Na_2CO_3	30	g/l
	Rochelle salt	40	g/l

       temperature: 40 °C

       current density: 2-3 A/dm^2

       duration: 5-10 s

(8) water rinse

Nickel films were deposited from a nickel sulfamate solution:

Ni(SO3NH2)2	450	g/l
NiCl2 6H2O	5	g/l
H3BO3	30	g/l
sodium lauryl sulfate	4	g/l
1,3,6-naphthalenetrisulfonic trisodium (NTS)	4	g/l

The current density was 2 A/dm^2 with a pH of 4.0 ± 0.5 and a temperature of 40 ± 2 °C. Two aluminum alloy substrate pipes were immersed into the solution, and a current of 1.2 A was applied for 45 min to get a Ni electrodeposit about 30 μm thick. The pipes covered with Ni electrodeposits were then cut into small pieces 50 mm long. After dissolving the aluminum alloy substrates in a 10% NaOH solution, thin cylindrical specimens of Ni electrodeposits were obtained. The dimensions of these specimens were 8.8 mm in I.D., 50 mm long, and 30 μm thick.

2.2 Attaching the Specimen to the Fatigue Testing Machine

A thin cylindrical Ni electrodeposit specimen was slipped onto the central projection of an attachment with the axis of the specimen coinciding with the axis of the attachment. The specimen was then fixed with Stycast 1266 (Fig.1). After Stycast 1266 was cured, the attachment was bolted on the upper flange of the testing machine. The other attachment was bolted on the lower flange, and the specimen was also fixed to this attachment with Stycast 1266. It is thereby possible to align the axes of the testing machine and the specimen, and to avoid failure of the thin specimen due to bending or shearing. Since the surface of Stycast 1266 rises slightly along the periphery of the specimen because of surface tension, stress concentration can be reduced (Fig.2).

2.3 Fatigue Testing

A fatigue testing machine (Shimadzu EHF-F01) was used with a control system (Shimadzu 4880). Only tensile load was applied so as to avoid buckling of the thin cylindrical specimens. While minimum load was fixed at 5 kg (tensile), the loading amplitude was varied by changing the maximum load. The cycle frequency was 30 Hz.

3. Results and Discussion

The cross-sectional areas of the specimens are needed to convert the output of the load cell into stress values. To estimate the cross-sectional areas, thickness measurements were carried out. Outer diameters of the substrate pipes were measured with a digital micrometer before deposition, and outer diameters of the specimens were measured after deposition. The differences between the two values correspond to the thicknesses of the specimens. Six specimens (A-F) were prepared in the same process as the specimens for the fatigue test. These six specimens were used to estimate thickness dispersion within a specimen. After being molded with a resin, specimens A-C were cut along the plane including the axis, and thickness measurements were carried out at six points for each specimen. Specimens D-F were cut along three planes perpendicular to the axis, and thickness measurements were carried out at three points for each cross section (nine points for each specimen). Figure 3 shows the thickness deviations from the average thickness of each specimen. The standard deviation is estimated to be 2.0 μm. Since the average thickness values of specimens A-F are 31.0, 32.3, 39.6, 30.1, 27.6, and 30.1 μm respectively, the cross-sectional area and the stress is evaluated within a margin of error of ±7%.

The staircase method was used to evaluate the fatigue limit, which was assumed to be equal to the fatigue strength at 10^7 cycles. The test was carried out according to the "Standard Method of Statistical Fatigue Testing" recommended by the Japan Society of Mechanical Engineers (JSME).[5] The first ten failure data points are fitted to a straight line in the S-N diagram to give a standard deviation of 23.7 MPa. The step value in the staircase method is then set to be 20 MPa. Figure 4 shows the results of the staircase method with 12 specimens. The fatigue limit of stress amplitude is estimated to be 150.5 ± 22.3 MPa with 95% reliability. All the data points of the fatigue test are plotted in Fig.5, where the straight line is fitted with the 20 failure data points. This curve fitting gives a standard deviation of 25.8 MPa, which is close to 23.7 MPa, derived from the first ten failure data points. The ratio of the step value to the standard deviation is 0.78, which is within the range (0.5-2.0) recommended by the JSME standard.[5]

Finally, the relation between surface roughness and fatigue strength is investigated. The solid squares in Fig.5 stand for the failure data for the specimen group with smoother surfaces. A comparison between two groups with different surface roughnesses is given in Fig.6. Surface roughness (R_a) was measured with a stylus surface profiling instrument (Taylor-Hobson; Surtronics3) with a cut-off length of 0.8 mm. Average values of surface roughness are 0.49 ± 0.17 μm for one group (denoted by crosses and open circles in Fig.5) and 0.20 ± 0.09 μm for the improved-surface group (denoted by solid squares). The S-N diagram (Fig.5) indicates that there is no substantial difference in fatigue strength between the two groups, which suggests that dispersion of fatigue strength does not arise from the variation in surface roughness in the present work.

4. Conclusion

Thin (30 μm) cylindrical specimens of Ni electrodeposits were prepared using a sulfamate nickel solution. A fatigue test was carried out employing a staircase method. The fatigue limit (or fatigue strength at 10^7 cycles) of the stress amplitude is estimated to be 150.5 ± 22.3 MPa.

Acknowledgement

The authors would like to gratefully acknowledge Dr. Toshio Ogata of the National Research Institute for Metals for his valuable discussions. They also thank to Mr. Shohei Natori and Mr. Fujio Takano of Seiko I Techno Research for their specimen preparation.

References

[1] Kazunori Chihara, Masahiko Kasuya, Junpei Yuyama, and Eiichi Goto, "Reduction of the Maximum Principal Stress by Multilayering of Electrodeposited Bellows," *Tran. Jpn. Soc. Mech. Eng.*, vol. 57, no. 537, pp. 1191-1194, 1991.

[2] I. Kim and R. Weil, "Tension Testing of Very Thin Electrodeposits," in W. B. Harding and G. A. DiBari, Eds., *Testing of Metallic and Inorganic Coatings, ASTM STP 947*, Philadelphia: American Society for Testing and Materials, 1987, pp. 11-18.

[3] M. Parente and R. Weil, "Tensile Testing of Electrodeposits," *Plat. and Surf. Fin.*, vol. 71, no. 5, pp. 114-117, 1984.

[4] Masahiko Kasuya, Junpei Yuyama, and Eiichi Goto, submitted to *J. Jpn. Inst. Met.*

[5] *Standard Method of Statistical Fatigue Testing, JSME S 002*, Tokyo: Japan Society of Mechanical Engineers, 1981

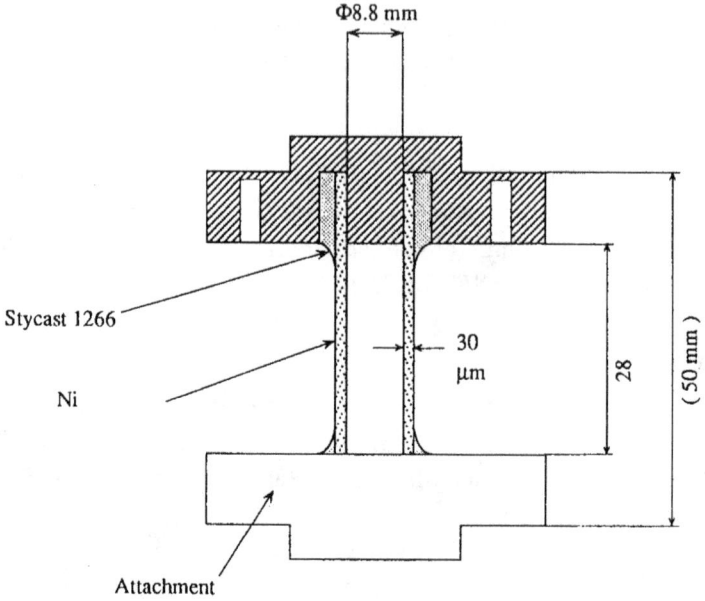

Φ8.8 mm

Stycast 1266

Ni

30 μm

28

(50 mm)

Attachment

Fig.1 Schematic diagram of the Ni specimen and attachments.

Fig.2 Photograph of the specimen mounted on the fatigue testing machine.

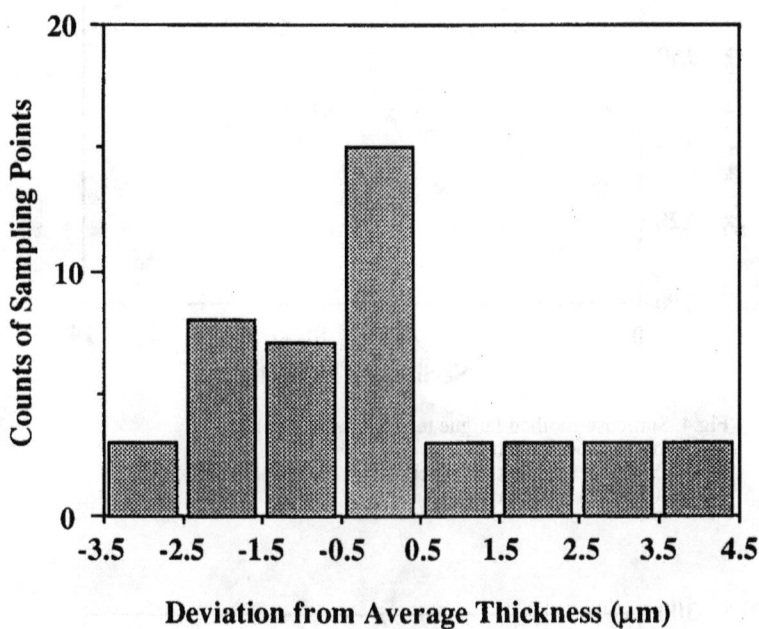

Fig.3 Deviation from the average thickness of each specimen
at each sampling point.
Number of sampling points for each specimen is 6 or 9.
Total number of specimens is 6.

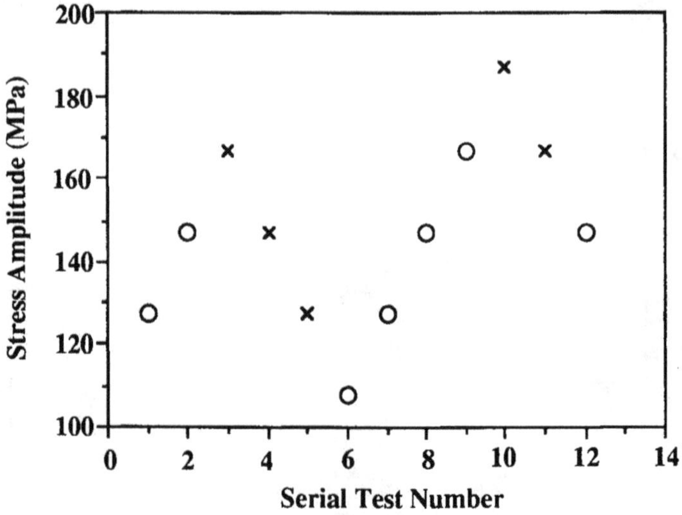

Fig.4 Staircase-mothod fatigue test. Crosses denote
that the specimen fails before 10⁷ cycles.
Circles denote that the specimen survives more than
10⁷ cycles of loading.

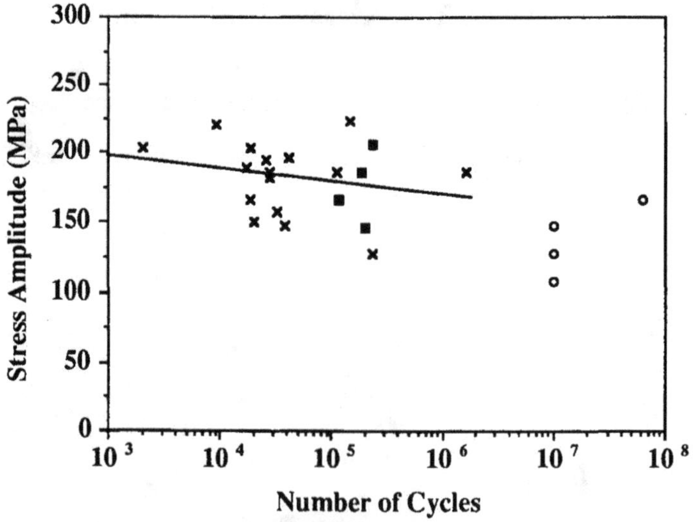

Fig.5 S-N diagram for electrodeposited nickel films. Crosses denote the
number of cycles to failure for less-smooth-surface specimens, and
squres for smoother-surface specimens. Circles indicate the
number of cycles without failure at the end of the test.

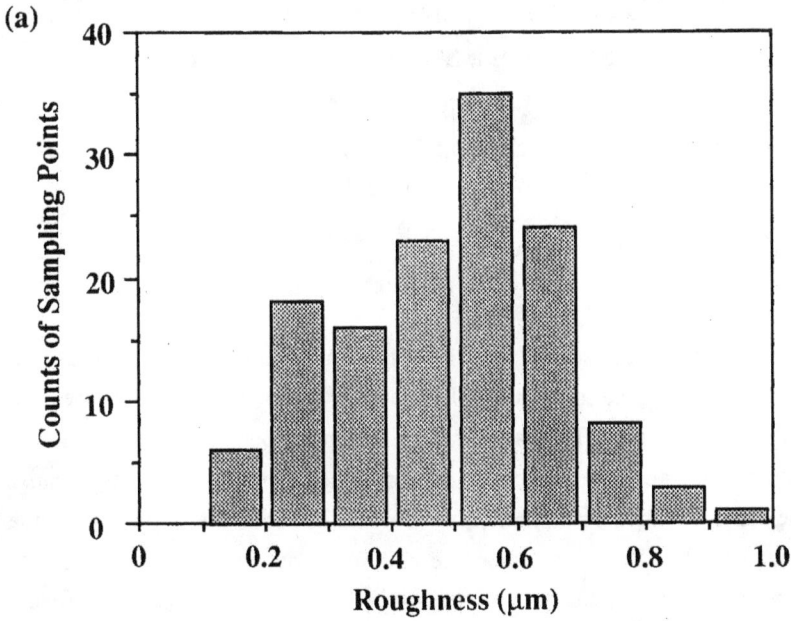

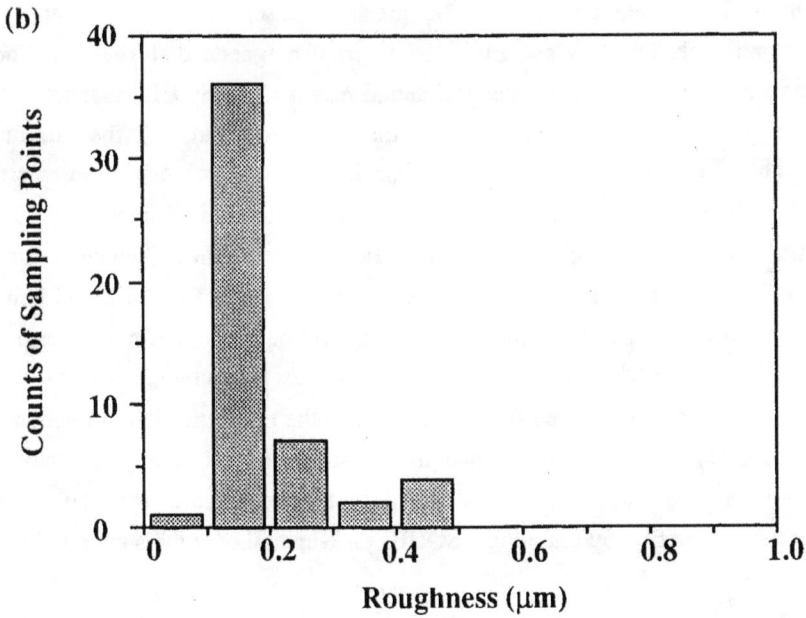

Fig.6 Distribution of specimen surface roughness.
Mandrels for specimens of group (a) are less
smooth than mandrels for group (b).

Detecting Flux Quanta Trapped in Superconducting Films by Scanning a SQUID Pick-up Coil *

Hirofumi Minami, Qiquan Geng, Kazunori Chihara, Junpei Yuyama, and Eiichi Goto

Abstract

The purpose of this study is to detect the flux quanta trapped in a large area superconductor by scanning a SQUID pick-up coil. For this purpose, a new technique is developed. The basic premise is that the perpendicular component of the external magnetic field near the superconductor surface vanishes because of the Meissner effect; the perpendicular component above the trapped flux quanta does not vanish. Therefore when the coil scans over the surface, a change of order of Φ_0 in flux amount through the coil is observed just above the trapped flux quantum. The advantages of this technique are high sensitivity to flux trapped in superconductors and low sensitivity to external magnetic disturbances. These features are confirmed through experimental results. Our SQUID magnetometer system has a spatial resolution better than 100 μm, and that the minimum detectable flux change is less than 0.1 Φ_0. Even in the presence of an external magnetic field (or disturbance) larger than the magnetic field changes arising from trapped flux quanta, trapped-flux-induced field changes can be detected. Using this technique, the experiment, performed with a niobium film in liquid helium and in zero external field, shows that the SQUID output signal has some peaks and valleys with an amplitude of order of Φ_0 over the superconductor and that the field variation due to trapped flux is reduced as the magnetic field, in which the superconductor was cooled through its transition temperature, decreases. In conclusion, we have succeeded to detect flux quanta trapped in the superconducting film by scanning a SQUID pick-up coil over the superconductor.

---

* Revised version to be published in *Cryogenics*.

Sweeping of Trapped Flux in Superconductors Using Laser Beam Scanning*

Qiquan Geng, Hirofumi Minami, Kazunori Chihara,
Junpei Yuyama and Eiichi Goto

Abstract

In 1984, one of the present authors (E. Goto) proposed a micro-heat-flushing (μHF) method for achieving perfect magnetic shielding. In this method, a small area on a superconducting thin film is heated and turned into the normal state. The entire film surface is then swept over by the normal hot spot, which captures the trapped flux and carries it either to an unimportant region or out of the superconductor. Based on this principle, a new technique to remove flux quanta trapped in superconducting film has been developed. It consists of measuring the magnetic field distribution over a superconductor with an rf SQUID and removing the detected trapped flux using laser beam scanning. The trapped flux movement follows the motion of the Ar laser beam exactly. By scanning the laser beam over the trapped flux quanta, the trapped flux is successfully moved to any desired location. We expect to be able to achieve perfect magnetic shielding using this method. Besides this technique is very useful in Josephson junction electronics and other areas which require extremely low magnetic field environments.

---

* Submitted to *Journal of Applied Physics*. Preliminary results appeared in *Jap. J. Appl. Phys. Letters*, 30, L838, 1991.

Technique for Measuring Absolute Intensity of Weak Magnetic Fields by a SQUID Pick-up Coil System[*]

Qiquan Geng, Hirofumi Minami, Kazunori Chihara,
Junpei Yuyama and Eiichi Goto

Abstract

A method to measure the absolute intensity of a weak magnetic field is described. This method uses patterned superconducting strip lines as a spatial modulator of the field and detects the magnetic field distribution over them as a function of applied magnetic fields. The field distribution change measured by an rf SQUID system is proportional to the component of the absolute intensity of the magnetic field at the specimen that is parallel with the pick-up coil axis. The magnetic field intensity can be determined absolutely from about 1 μG by this method. A spatial resolution of the field as good as a few millimeters is obtained. Comparison with other SQUID magnetometers used for same purpose, the advantage of this magnetometer system is very simple and easy to operate. It is possible to reduce the effect of trapped flux by raising the distance between the sample and the pick-up coil. It is also possible to make the whole system more compact using film integration technology for the pick-up coil system. Besides, this magnetometer can be used not only to determine the absolute intensity of uniform magnetic field, but also to detect the field gradient in space or the magnetic impurities in the substrate. The accuracy and the sensitivity of the magnetometer will be greatly enhanced when the pick-up coil is placed close to the sample surface. The narrow strip line patterning sample is recommended to avoid the flux trapping problem in the thin film and to obtain higher spatial resolution. On the other hand, the integrated SQUID pick-up loops (film coil) should be used for increasing the effective pick-up area while reducing the diameter of the pick-up loop. Thus one or two order of magnitude improvement on sensitivity and spatial resolution of this type magnetometer can be expected.

---

[*] Submitted to *The Review of Scientific Instruments*.

www.ingramcontent.com/pod-product-compliance
Lightning Source LLC
Chambersburg PA
CBHW050634190326
41458CB00008B/2267